The Current in Criticism

The Current in Criticism

Essays on the Present and
Future of Literary Theory

Edited by Clayton Koelb and Virgil Lokke

Purdue University Press
West Lafayette, Indiana

Gayatri Chakravorty Spivak, "Imperialism and Sexual
Difference," reproduced with permission from the
Oxford Literary Review, volume 8 (1986), pp. 225–40,
© 1986 *Oxford Literary Review.*

Designed by Greg Corrigan

Printed in the United States of America

Library of Congress Cataloging-in-Publication Data

The Current in criticism.

Includes bibliographies.
  1. Criticism. I. Koelb, Clayton, 1942–
II. Lokke, Virgil Llewellyn, 1915–
PN85.C86   1987   801'.95   87-14549
ISBN O-911198-87-3
ISBN O-911198-92-X (pbk.)

Contents

V

CONTENTS

▼

VI

CONTENTS

▼

VII

Contributors

Jonathan Culler is Class of 1916 Professor of English and Comparative Literature and director of the Society for the Humanities at Cornell University. His *Structuralist Poetics* won the James Russell Lowell Prize of the Modern Language Association for 1975. His other publications include *Flaubert: The Uses of Uncertainty; Ferdinand de Saussure; The Pursuit of Signs: Semiotics, Literature, Deconstruction; On Deconstruction: Theory and Criticism after Structuralism;* and many essays.

Caryl Emerson is professor of Slavic languages and literatures at Princeton University. She is author of *Boris Godunov: Transpositions of a Russian Theme*, editor and translator of *Problems of Dostoevsky's Poetics*, and co-translator of *The Dialogic Imagination: Four Essays by M. M. Bakhtin.* Her many essays include "The Tolstoy Connection in Bakhtin."

Stanley Fish is Arts and Sciences Distinguished Professor of English and Law at Duke University. In 1980, Fish published *Is There a Text in This Class? The Authority of Interpretive Communities.* He is also author of *Surprised by Sin: The Reader in Paradise Lost; Self-Consuming Artifacts: The Experience of Seventeenth-Century Literature; John Skelton's Poetry;* and *The Living Temple: George Herbert and Catechizing.*

René Girard is Andrew B. Hammond Professor of French Language, Literature and Civilization at Stanford University. He is author of *Violence and the Sacred; Deceit, Desire and the Novel; Proust, a Critical Anthology; Des Choses cachées depuis la fondation du monde; To Double Business Bound; Le Bouc émissaire;* and numerous essays.

Joseph F. Graham has degrees in French, English, and comparative literature. His principal research interest has pursued the implications of linguistic theory and cognitive science for the study of literature. He wrote the introduction to and was editor of *Difference in Translation.* He has contributed chapters to the books *Glossary of Transformational Grammar, Translation Spectrum,* and *The Question of*

Textuality and has published articles in journals such as *Yale French Studies, Diacritics,* and *boundary 2.*

Fredric Jameson is William A. Lane Professor of Comparative Literature at Duke University. He earned a B. A. degree from Haverford College and M. A. and Ph.D. degrees in French from Yale University. He has taught at Yale, Harvard University, and the University of California. He is author of several books, including *Sartre: The Origins of a Style; Marxism and Form; The Prison House of Language; Fables of Aggression: Wyndham Lewis, the Modernist as Fascist; The Political Unconscious;* and *The Ideologies of Theory.*

Clayton Koelb, professor of German and comparative literature at the University of Chicago, took degrees in German and comparative literature at Harvard University. Koelb has published many articles and reviews in various scholarly journals and is co-editor of *The Comparative Perspective on Literature: Essays in Theory and Practice.* He is the author of *Thomas Mann's "Goethe and Tolstoy": Notes and Sources; The Incredulous Reader: Literature and the Function of Disbelief;* and *The Invention of Reading: Imagination and Rhetorical Construction.*

Frank Lentricchia is professor of English at Duke University. He has written many books, including *After the New Criticism, Criticism and Social Change,* and *Ariel and the Police.* He is also the author of shorter pieces on Mario Puzo and Don DeLillo, a contributor to *The Cambridge History of American Literature* and *Critical Terms for Literary Study;* and series editor for *The Wisconsin Project on American Writers.*

Virgil Lokke is professor emeritus of English at Purdue University. He is the author of essays on nineteenth-century utopian literature, contemporary literature, and literary theory. He is co-editor of *Frontiers of American Culture* and *Ruined Eden of the Present: Hawthorne, Melville, and Poe.* On Fulbright appointments, he has taught at major universities in Norway and Finland.

Floyd Merrell is professor of Spanish American literature, literary theory and semiotics at Purdue University. He is the author of *Deconstruction Reframed; Semiotic Foundations: Steps toward an Epistemology of Written Texts; Pararealities: The Nature of Our Fictions and How We Know Them;* and *A Semiotic Theory of Texts.*

Gary Saul Morson is professor of Slavic languages and comparative literature at Northwestern University. He is author of *The Boundaries of Genre: Dostoevsky's "Diary of a Writer"* and the *Traditions of Literary Utopia* and *Hidden in Plain View: Narrative and Creative Potentials in "War and Peace."* He is also the editor of two theoretical anthologies—*Literature and History: Theoretical Problems and Russian Case Studies* and *Bakhtin: Essays and Dialogues on His Work.*

Dietrich Schwanitz has been Professor of English Literature at the University of Hamburg, where he also conducts an English theatre workshop, since 1978. Born in 1940, Schwanitz studied history, English, and philosophy at the University of Munster and at the University of Freiburg, where he graduated and received his Ph.D. His publications include *G. B. Shaw: Künstlerische Konstruktion und unordentliche Welt, Die Wirklichkeit der Inszenierung und die Inszenierung der Wirklichkeit, Literaturwissenschaft für Anglisten*, and about 40 articles, many of which reveal his growing interest in systems theory.

Patrocinio Schweickart is an associate professor of English at the University of New Hampshire. She is the co-editor (along with Elizabeth Flynn) of *Gender and Reading: Essays on Readers, Texts, and Contexts*, in which her essay "Reading Ourselves: Toward a Feminist Theory of Reading" appeared. This essay won the 1984 Florence Howe Award for Distinguished Feminist Scholarship. She has published several other articles on theory, feminist criticism, and science fiction.

Gayatri Chakravorty Spivak is Andrew W. Mellon Professor of English at the University of Pittsburgh. She was educated at Presidency College (Calcutta), Girton College of Cambridge University, and Cornell University. She wrote her Ph.D. dissertation with Paul de Man. In 1974, she published an introductory book entitled *Myself Must I Remake: The Life and Work of W. B. Yeats*. Since then, she has translated and introduced Jacques Derrida's *De la Grammatologie*. She is also author of *In Other Worlds: Essays in Cultural Politics.*

Gregory Ulmer is a professor of English at the University of Florida. He received his Ph.D. in comparative literature from Brown University in 1972. He is the author of *Applied Grammatology: Post(e)-Pedagogy from Jacques Derrida to Joseph Beuys.*

Acknowledgments

Among many who contributed to the project that resulted in this volume are those like Prof. Barnet Kottler, of Purdue's Department of English, and Brooke Horvath, a graduate instructor in English. Their initiative was instrumental in conceiving the project. Others, like Prof. Dorothy Leland, of Purdue's Department of Philosophy, and Mark Zamierowski, a graduate student in the Philosophy and Literature Program, gave invaluable assistance in their skillful editing and shaping of key manuscripts. Finally, full tribute must be paid to Janice Becker, editor at Purdue University Press, for her sensitive, careful, and judicious editorial guidance in bringing this volume to completion.

Preface

Not very long ago—as recently as the mid-sixties, in fact—literary criticism seemed to have reached a certain consensus in the United States. Although critics could and did argue about many issues, a few basic things seemed clear: "Modern literary study, unlike that of the nineteenth century, proceeds from the text before it rather than from something that we insist on believing about poetry to begin with. Our responses are more direct to a poem's demands and we seem nearer than Matthew Arnold himself to that disinterestedness which he made a condition of the right critical temper."[1] That was, of course, "before the deluge." With the theoretical revolution that accompanied the reception of structuralism, the post-structuralism of Derrida's deconstructive strategies, the perceived emergence of the "Yale school," and the growing strength of Marxist, feminist, and "reader-response" approaches to literary study, the notion of a secure "text" existing prior to "something we insist on believing about poetry to begin with" came under powerful and constant attack. The consensus that appeared to have been reached in the late fifties and early sixties was definitively shattered.

After nearly two decades of enormous upheaval, with no clear end in sight, the time seems right for at least a tentative assessment of where we are and where we might be going in literary study, of what is current in criticism and of where the critical current might be tending. While it would be premature to attempt now a synthetic overview of a field which is still in such flux, we can freeze the action in a kind of flash photo of many of the principal figures active in the critical arena. That is what the editors of *The Current in Criticism* have chosen to do.

The contributors have been selected as representative of some of the more prominent perspectives in literary theory and criticism. While the majority of the essays tend to focus on theoretical problems, some seek to make their theoretical points by engaging in a discourse that bears the conventional generic markings of literary criticism. What this group of essays seeks to provide, then, is a rather wide spectrum of current thinking, a sampling of some of the arguments, attitudes, and perspectives which participate in the swirl of intense speculative energy that is so characteristic of contemporary literary

XV

theory. Our aim has been to display a range of differences without any deliberate foregrounding of those local preferences and concerns that inhabit in incorrigible ways our own canons, methods, theories, and practice. We set out our own views, in our own voices, later in the volume.

The project of such a collection of essays emerged from an essentially pedagogical motive, and we have made no attempt to obscure or erase that motive from the resulting volume. We began our collaboration not as co-editors but as co-instructors in a course in contemporary theories of literature at Purdue University in 1985. In order to make this course as lively and as "current" as possible, special arrangements were made to secure the participation of a number of distinguished visiting theorists. Purdue University's School of Humanities, Social Science, and Education, through its former dean, Robert Ringel, generously provided funds that allowed us to invite several distinguished speakers to give both a public lecture and a seminar session for the course. We were aware from the outset, though, that the materials supplied by these five scholars could provide a context for extending the range of our endeavor and of our audience beyond the classroom. We therefore offered invitations to additional critics and theorists whose work could serve to broaden the illustrative spectrum of the project. The volume thus represents in a way the seminar we would have offered if funds—and time—had been unlimited. Extensive traces of the continuing threads of the seminar as it contextualized literary theory through the academic term are discernible in the essays of the co-editors, Clayton Koelb and Virgil Lokke, who perhaps never moved very far from their pedagogical role as leaders of the seminar. There is an important pedagogical impulse, too, in a number of the essays contributed by our visitors, some of which, we are happy to say, were partially shaped by the classroom experience. The relation between a theoretical discourse and its audience is not a chaste one—as indeed some of the theoretical discussions themselves make clear—but it can be very fertile.

The essays address a series of specific problems of critical or theoretical practice which are dominant today. Offered at one level of generality is the problem of the taxonomic or classificatory strategies employed by literary theory or criticism. The Introduction encapsulates an attempt by Lokke to address the question of the function of a basic model in the determination of the very questions which are deemed as "proper" to these domains. Related taxonomic questions—such as What kind of "whatever" is literature? and What kinds of literature are there?—become points of focus for the essays by Joseph F. Graham, on "poetry and things"; Koelb, on speech-act problematics; and Dietrich Schwanitz, on systems theory. Such questions are equally relevant to René Girard's concern with exploring "doubling mimeticism" and Fredric Jameson's analysis of the impact of international capitalism on strategies of discourse in Third World literature. Jonathan Culler's concern with an unthematized religious bias that he finds operative within certain prestigious academic forums, Stanley Fish's attention to "anti-foundationalism and theory hope," Patrocinio Schweickart's consideration of relations between the speculations of Habermas and variants of feminist theory, as well as Gregory Ulmer's efforts to chart some of the pedagogical possibilities of grammatology—all pay special attention to the status of critical discourse itself, asking more or less explicitly just what kind of "whatever" criticism or theory is or should be. Both Floyd Merrell's abstract descriptions of the self-reflexive nature of current semiotic speculation and Caryl Emerson and Gary Saul Morson's collaborative delineation of contextualizations in the uses and abuses of Bakhtin reflect issues related to political, ideological, and historical awareness—issues which are explicitly dealt with in Frank Lentricchia's examination of William James and in Gayatri Chakravorty Spivak's treatment of imperialism and feminism. The collection, then, "unifies" itself in its transparent disregard for the conventions of discrete topicalities.

Describing the contents of this volume in such an aggressively abstract way serves only to indicate main tendencies of the essays included and to reveal perhaps that the authoritative and canonical voices here speak amidst a determined heterogeneity. It is a collection rather than a unity, and it is a collection within which the range of contemporary critical threads, Anglo-American and continental, trace their formations and deformations. Here the reader will find current articulations of Marxist, feminist, pragmatist, structuralist, semiotic, and deconstructive positions. Here also are traces of the attempt to formulate identities of a New French Theory and a New German Critique, and even an attempt to find some commonalities of these collectives. Certain sets of paired terms appear and reappear, suggesting perhaps the bounds within which critical discussion is now taking place: framing/unframing, monologic/dialogic, arborescent/rhizomatic, not to mention logocentric/deconstructive. What is most striking about these dyadic oppositions is the interdependence of the opposing notions. We might well be looking at a situation in which (as Lokke suggests in his essay on Jakobson and Bakhtin) an "exclusive either/or" may not be as exclusive as it first appears.

After much discussion and no little gnashing of teeth, the editors have elected to present the essays in the alphabetical order of the authors' surnames. Since the editors believe that "taxonomies are never innocent," and since the editors themselves are no more innocent (or "objective") than anyone else, we have chosen to make our ordering principle thus straightforwardly arbitrary. Such an arrangement is not without its strategic assumptions, though, including especially the assumption that each essay will, as an eddy within the current, generate in passing some hierarchical structure which encloses or excludes some portions or all of the adjacent essays. We do expect the voices in the volume to echo off each other, in spite of or even because of their heterogeneous natures. The essays vary greatly in a number of ways: some are quite brief, others rather lengthy; some are aggressively polemical, others aim toward a more or less descriptive tone. Most are highly sensitive to their own restlessly equivocal status within what is at present a "fallen" and fragmented field of literary studies. This unstable territory seeks constantly to reconstitute itself by making its own boundaries with other equally troubled areas one of the principal subjects of its own discourse. Such intense self-referentiality is the price and the reward of the kind of intellectual endeavor represented by the essays gathered in *The Current in Criticism*. Taken as a whole, the volume can give the reader what we hope will be both a well-rounded and an engaging picture of what some of criticism's most important thinkers "insist on believing about poetry to begin with."

The Current in Criticism is in an important sense the product of a group of Purdue University graduate students and staff members who, over the past decade, informally labelled themselves the Theory Reading Group and set themselves the goal of coming to grips with the intensifying concern with literary theory which has characterized the contemporary moment in the American academic literary scene. Out of this steadily fluctuating yet persisting group came numerous dissertations, much provocative discussion, and a widening familiarity with the challenging texts of important continental and Anglo-American critics and theorists. Under the encouragement of the group to offer a course with all the proprieties of grades, papers and credit, the English Department scheduled a seminar which organized itself around the teaching of five distinguished professors who have made significant contributions to literary theory, both as theoreticians and historians of theory. Professors Culler, Fish, Girard, Jameson, and Spivak each presented public lectures and held seminar sessions with the students. It is this group of public lectures that formed the core around which English 596a, "Contemporary Literary Theory," was developed. These same public lectures framed the possibility of inviting other specialists in literary theory to add their essays to the already assembled group and thus to create *The Current in Criticism*.

From the students and staff of English 596a came the efforts to find alternative ways of reading the variety of speculative texts with which they were confronted. What we sought was a strategy of reading which would place less emphasis upon any comparative evaluation, any ordering and ranking of the texts thematically, and more stress upon an inspection of the texts of the contributors in terms of the taxonomic strategies deployed by each. We sought ways to "describe" the categories each essayist depended upon to generate his/her thematic focus. These attempts proved interesting, provocative, and not-too-surprisingly revelatory of the "bias" which framed the "master" categories by which the essays themselves were being generated, as well as the "bias" of our own superimposed analytic categories. A central issue, then, became the problem of categorization. What relations, if any, seemed to obtain between taxonomies and conclusions, between overt and covert taxonomies, between and among taxonomies themselves, between privileged and suppressed features of given taxonomies? Would it be possible, for example, to determine the ways in which taxonomies themselves determine and are determined by the kinds of problems and the kinds of answers entailed and inscribed in any discursive practice?

One taxonomy which served as an initial structure within which various approaches to literary theory could be differentiated and discussed was the AUTHOR-TEXT-READER + WORLD model. This particular and commonplace structuring device itself, however, soon became the target of close inspection. The "cuts" required by the model seemed all too frequently to be radically incompatible with an understanding and appreciation of the argumentative and rhetorical strategies of the guest professors. Thus a context was created which focused first upon the highly problematic features of what seemed to have become a classificatory cliche. The model also seemed to members of 596a to have had a powerful and determinative force in English studies in the recent past. Within this questioning speculation, the more general problem of the functioning of the categorizing process itself became foregrounded. The essay that follows, then, represents an introduction, although not in the sense that it seeks to describe or summarize the kinds of confrontations and mutual agreements under some appropriate rubric which would characterize this collection of essays. It is an introduction only in that it provides a context within which the essays were initially received and appreciated.

Note

1. Bernard N. Schilling, "Introduction" to *Dryden: A Collection of Critical Essays* (Englewood Cliffs, N. J.: Prentice-Hall, 1963), 1.

Introduction:
Taxonomies Are
Never Innocent

Virgil Lokke

What if there were, lodged within the heart of the law itself, a law of impurity or a principle of contamination?
—Derrida, "The Law of Genre"

Contemporary speculation about those often loosely defined and loosely related areas labelled theory of literature, theory of communication, and theory of discourse has involved the more or less effective displacement of certain models that in past years seemed to offer beginning points, boundaries, and commonalities of focus in talking about our reading and our writing. Modeling operations themselves, as we all well know, have been rendered highly problematic when viewed from either a post-structuralist or a neo-pragmatic perspective. It is from a bias, a perspective more or less congenial to a conflation of these positions, that the following narration proceeds.

Two such traditional models, the literary and the communications models, may well serve as an effective reminder of the terrain, the peculiar geography, of the once presumably conquered and pacified territory through which literary studies and literary theory have just passed, for the taxonomic power of these models seems to have more or less determined the kinds of questions, the kinds of problems, and the terms in which answers could be respectably framed within the discipline. These models are in some senses mirror images of each other, generating within literary studies and communications studies analogous sets of parameters for significant questions and answers in each discipline. The differences between the two represent, from my perspective, rhetorical and ideological naming strategies,

1

useful principally in maintaining territorial boundary markers of academic disciplines. My explorations, however, will focus more intently upon the literary "triangle" rather than the communications triangle, since the discourse which follows was developed to demonstrate the way in which a particular heuristic model has exerted influence upon the determination of problems in literary theory and literary criticism. As a pedagogical tool, this model has served to illustrate *a* range of possible approaches to the study and criticism of literature; as a supertaxonomy, it has served to control, in some hands, *the* scope of available approaches within which reasonable choices could be made.

What follows here is an attempt to foreground some of the problems of the model itself, with its inherent ambiguities, and to note how its degree of specificity and its degree of presumptive inclusiveness vary inversely with respect to each other. In part, then, the following story is a somewhat casual journey through the realm where, in older days, the literary model functioned in our discourse as a source of comforting authority, a comfort once so reassuring that some felt the model sufficiently foundational to permit the energetic pursuit of "empirical" (classify-and-count) studies from its base.

The literary model—which seems to have governed our speculation in patent ways for about, to put it conservatively, fifty or sixty years, and in less obvious ways since pre-Socratic times—is the AUTHOR-TEXT-READER + WORLD model. Using artist, object (of art), audience, and the universe, this model, gracefully articulated in all its static grandeur, occupied "central" prominence in the influential text of M. H. Abrams's *The Mirror and the Lamp* (6–7). Outside the triangulation of the A-T-R lies the World, which, depending upon the momentary idiosyncracies of the discipline, the "interpretive community," or the user of the model, may or may not have relationships with the Author, the Text, or the Reader. As will become clearer momentarily, this supercontext, the World, or Universe, can enter the A-T-R formula only through an apex of the triangle: that is, the Author, Text, or Reader. The Author's, Text's, or Reader's relationship to the World exists only as a function of a prior suppressed or unexpressed taxonomy.

When viewed merely as a diagram, this configuration, the A-T-R + W, can be used to illustrate various kinds of historical examples of past critical and theoretical approaches to literature. Certainly the foregrounding or the privileging of any one of these three-plus-one entities can isolate an identifiable critical or theoretical strategy of past practices. Under the anointing of the author as prime figure, numerous strategies emerge, including most obviously the biographical-autobiographical modes with their rich battery of variants. If the text is taken as central, we derive, among other possibilities, the New Criticism. Reader-response criticism is the product of an intensified focus upon the third term. Should we wish to privilege the fourth term, the World, we have introduced, perhaps for some all too obviously, the politics of a humanism, a theology, a Marxism, a capitalism, some quasi-scientific sociology, or the embedded ideologies of the even vaster enclaves of History or Time.

It is not my intent, however, to show the radically pluralistic possibilities of locating existing literary theories within the diagrammatic configuration of the A-T-R + W, since nearly all the theory of the past has been developed within the confines of this arena. Rather, what I have in mind is to suggest the levelling and tedious similarity of the problems that beset the whole range of "theoretical" strategies which are dependent upon the "literary" model. Like the "communications" model, the "literary" model is a product of the "metaphysics of the same": it implicates the matching of identities as it struggles to explicate the relationships which the model itself has differentiated. It succeeds only in the extent to which the initial distinctions have been rhetorically collapsed.

The implication of my narrative is that the difficult and probably unanswerable questions which confront students of literature are questions generated in part, at least, by the acceptance of the diagram as *model.* There are, it can be hoped, other perspectives which will at least unveil the limitations of the A-T-R + W configuration and challenge the claim to neutrality and universality of the literary/communications type of model, so that our investigations need not be wholly confined to a continuous retracing of the triangular path from post to post. What I wish to suggest is the need to examine the extent to which this particular system of employing initial cuts, distinctions, and definitional strategies is designed to govern the kinds of solutions available and the very problems that we can set for ourselves. More specifically, a correlative purpose is to call specific attention to the kinds of problems or possible answers which are being suppressed by the traditional models we have employed.

The simple, obvious and banal point is that *taxonomies are never innocent.* This is not, of course, to suggest that taxonomies are dispensable; rather, they are indispensable. But what needs to be made as clear as possible is that categories are themselves context-dependent, never neutral, and that their deployment all too frequently conceals their "limitations" as "heuristic" functions. It is "as if" the "as if-ness" of the model is forgotten; the manipulator of the model proceeds "as if"—despite the necessary arbitrariness of the necessary exclusions—one is entitled to make "positive" or "scientific" statements which are no longer merely "heuristic" but "real" descriptions with ontological authority.

Numerous modeling formulations in semantics, linguistics, and information theory employ a similar model which usually appears as Sender, Message, Code, and Receiver (Listener, Hearer, Audience) with or without the term World. Discussion of the context-embedded nature of the model occurs only when the explanatory force of the curtailed model seems to run into solipsism or contradiction, or when it is found to be running short of generative power. Most unusual is the communications model maker or user who carefully explains or even tries to describe the configurations of the context within which the *creator* or user of the model stands.

The model is itself context dependent, and the very obscurity of the environment of the model as a system permits the privileging of a "hidden agenda." Again the "reading" of the "hidden agenda" quite obviously depends upon another contextualization, and that reading upon still another, etc. The presumptive neutrality and authority of the communications triangle, for example, is compromised once we realize the dependence of the model upon a bit of nineteenth-century technology, the telegraph, which embeds the model metaphorically in a relic of an abandoned technology, suggesting further a rather simplistic mechanistic bias, and thereby making it plausible to believe that this model was initially designed to transmit energy rather than meaning. Such a contextualization is, of course, only one of a multitude of "compromising" contexts discernible through a casual inspection from an alternative perspective.

Before proceeding further, I need add that my contention is not that communications models are identical with the predominant literary model, but rather that they perform similar functions and that they commonly exchange roles in an equivocal manner. Unless one has been denied access to the Judeo-Christian tradition from birth, one cannot help noticing that the literary model implicates theological terms whereas the communications model reaches for a quasi-scientific and detached position. We recognize instantly the theological move of placing the author first, an "authorizing" move which gives priority to questions of origins, and of intentions. All too quickly, we discover that this very focusing gesture has necessarily subverted the clear separations between author, text, reader, and the world. Thus the movement in becoming circular connects the world to the author. When we bend the connecting line so that the author has the only significant and direct access to the world, we create a demand for hermeneutic readings. The literary model is radically open to a classical hermeneutic mode, and, as in all classical hermeneutics, the model is dependent upon a mimetic theory of texts; consequently, it seeks adequation as the criterion of truth.

In contrast, the communications model with its stylized rhetoric of detachment and objectivity functions most characteristically in conjunction with a correspondence theory of truth; it seeks equivalence. The presumption of "scientificity" in the communications model is transparent enough. Speech-act theory, for example, which depends upon the segmentalization of the communications triangle of sender, message, and receiver (placing half of the triangle in an equivalence relationship and the other half in a mimetic one), can perhaps be used to illustrate some of the complications of models which play somewhat indecisively between correspondence theories and adequation theories. It illustrates the hybridization and mutual contamination of the categories of equivalence and adequation. In Austin's version, strong features of traditional metaphysical and literary strategies are deployed in the interest of some scientific telos, in pursuit of some ultimate goal of equivalence. In Searle, metaphysical conventions are suppressed to allow for the rhetorical foregrounding of the norms of "objectivity."

If we try to take Austin "seriously" as providing the outlines for Searle's "scientific" and equivalence-dependent speech-act theory, then we can see in *How to Do Things with Words* the move made toward a matching of the "real" with the speech act, where the "real" is the totalizable context. Austin's initial move, however, and perhaps his central concern,[1] is to expose the narrowness and inadequacy of positivist assumptions: "I distinguish five very general classes [of illocutionary speech acts]: but I am far from equally happy about all of them. They are, however, quite enough to play Old Harry with two fetishes which I admit to an inclination to play Old Harry with, viz. (1) the true/false fetish, (2) the value/fact fetish" (151).

What Austin challenges is the model which had installed a noise filter between sender and message and between message and receiver. This filter eliminates as static all sentences which are neither analytic nor synthetic, excluding thereby all sentences which are neither directly nor indirectly falsifiable. Austin's model employs an improved filter at the first juncture (between speaker and message), permitting the passage, as "meaningful," of all utterances which are in some sense verifiable as having properly observed a convention, rule, or practice.[2] This filter excludes all "parasitic," "insincere," "fictional" utterances as being undecidable, problematic, and abnormal because of their being too embarrassingly open to infinite recontextualization. In this model, the second juncture, between message and receiver, is governed by the less stringent approximations of "felicity" conditions. The difference between the two filters and the two junctures leads to the question, Can the "felicitous" pass through the "sincerity" filter? What, in short, is the relation between the two junctures in the model?

Searle, apparently, assumed that Austin had proposed a taxonomy which needed only further refinements before becoming a scientific, even algorithmic, theory. It is as if all that remained to properly constitute a general theory of speech acts was to run up and down the ladder of Austinian abstractions from the constative/performative dyad (readily dispensable) to the illocutionary/perlocutionary pairing and then on down to the terminal pentad of verdictives, exercitives, commissives, behabitives, and expositives, providing for each category a precise and discriminating description. Austin's commission to his disciples was assumed to be an instruction to tidy up, for example, the bagginess of his hurried partitionings. The "scientific" dream of the operation is that speech-act theory would work, that it had its own verification process (a matching of intent and responsive speech act), and consequently that it could totalize the range of speech acts, if only enough bells and whistles, woofers and tweeters could be added to the hi-fi system. Needless to say, this drive for equivalence and ultimate fidelity has remained frustrated.[3]

What literary theorists employing speech-act theory were forced to realize was that they were dealing with another heuristic with rather sharp limitations for their purposes. It offered no program for stabilizing or empiricizing literary texts except, for example, under the strange possibility of translating "parasitic" utterances (under as yet unspecified translation rules) into some "sincere" format before properly identifying their contextualized norm.

Both kinds of models, those of equivalence and those of mimesis, the communications model and the literary model, have demonstrated a contextual and rhetorical dependence upon each other. Proponents of each have used each other through exemplary strategies of persuasive equivocation. The communications model has needed echoic values from the literary model to fend off charges of a myopic positivism, and the literary model has used the communications model to distance itself from any charges of idiosyncracy. Both models, however, share an aspect common to seekers of equivalence or of mimesis in that both are dependent upon re-presentation and a notion of identity. In the quasi-scientific communications model, identity becomes a virtual possibility; in the literary model, where identity is always not quite possible, *mimesis*—always tragic in its implied violence and its defacement of the other—becomes a surrogate for equivalence, an almostness, whose success is dependent upon its destruction of the other. Finally, both models ignore or neglect to include the superimposed position of the model maker, leaving unspecified both the model maker's authorization and the model user's authority. The problem of authorization becomes lost in the gloss of some presumption of a self-evident truth.

Some of the more specific problems of a criticism which places the author at the center of the process involve the question of authorial intention. What, to raise once more the tired question, is the relation between the author's intentions and the "text"? Now this question implicates the problems of the boundaries of each of the key terms in the model, and the traditional response has been to grasp eagerly and confidently for the centering assurances of the age-old notion of unity. Since Baumgarten's *Reflections on Poetry* in 1735— and for that matter, from the beginning of aesthetic speculation— unity, that touchstone of rationalism and idealism, has been the test and the evidence of the intentional goals of aesthetic production. Here we are concerned momentarily with the recapitulation of the presumably initial problem of the author's intentions and the text.

Now we must watch the careful moves of exclusion, mediation, and inclusion. The author as the originator of the text, which was embedded in the author, is now being made manifest through the assistance of the interpreter. In our attributions of intentions to the author, we speak as if he/she owned them. In brief, we can, presumably, identify origins of utterance; we assume in dealing with the text's literal/metaphoric or the conscious/unconscious oppositions that there is a one-to-one relationship between intentions and various kinds of utterance, between "source" and manifestation as text. Both the assumed embedment and the recovery strategies presuppose the notion of an author who has an independent, unitary self, if not always, at least at the moment of textual utterance, and that furthermore, this unitary self—the author—has a clearly proprietary relation to his/her utterances.[4] This is the self, the unique individual entity for which capitalism presumably exists, who owns his unique utterance as he owns the rest of his private property. Such a notion, dependent on "origins," constituted "selves," aggressive "product differentiation," "originality," and "genius," clearly avoids the alternative notions that utterances are in any significant sense societal or communal.

Beyond, however, the immediate and obvious political implications of authorship as ownership—with its need for thematic trademarks, accompanying stylistic branding, and additional signs of the "new and improved" features upon the recognizably "tried and true" versions—there are other problems, specified, for example, in Dominick La Capra's *Rethinking Intellectual History,* which render the author-text relationship extremely problematic. Beyond a blindness to the social and related ideological implications, such assumptions of direct author-text relatedness must ignore the possibility that (a) the author didn't quite know what he was going to write until he wrote it, (b) he wrote in a moment of tension or ambivalence, (c) he was undergoing some kind of physiological urgency or disturbance, (d) his text was simply a fulfillment of certain traditional expectations, (e) the text was a reflection of discursive conventions of the moment, or (f) the text was an indeterminate admixture of all five possible conditions plus one or two possibilities, at least, which have been inadvertently overlooked. Clearly the appeal to the author's intention is, all too commonly, an attempt to foreshorten discourse, an appeal to the authority of the interpreter, an appeal to power under the guise of reasonable and indisputable evidence.

Author-centered criticism sometimes shifts away from direct appeal to authorial intention to something called the author's *life* or to his/her *career.* These strategies, as we well know, tend to find a unity or essence in the author's life in general or in his/her career. The range of possible moves is staggering; however, a few may be listed, such as the one which goes "behind" or "beneath" (depending upon which spatial designate suggests the greater profundity) the "intentions" to find the cause of the intentions, or again the move which sees the source of the text in a combinatory construct of the author's intentions and his/her life in general. Some critics find these moves appealing because they seem to proceed from an elusive innermost essence to a more contextualized term, "life"; thus the strategy is seen as one which puts the interpreter in more confident touch with a marginalized world, marginalized, as it were, by the very strategies initially employed.

All of these strategies involve a positing of at least two entities: text and life of author. Comparing the two, we have presumptive access to a third item—truth. If scientific auras are sought, the comparison becomes implicated in some correspondence theory of truth. If a more classical hermeneutic strategy is involved, the assertions are embedded in a mimetic theory. Sometimes it is completely forgotten that, just as we have two texts to read and compare in the first intentional game (the created "text" of the author's intentions and the author's text as text), once the author's life is introduced we have the text of intention, plus the text of the life, plus the text as text to adjust, contract, skew, and realign in the process of achieving our third interpretation. Immediately the bizarre complexity of these moves—moves generated largely by initial deployment of the A-T-R + W model—becomes clear, and we have to ask ourselves such troubling questions as, How do we constitute the text of a life? and Which biographical features belong to the true canon of the life, and which are excrescent marginalia, at best tangential?

The plurality of life-texts and texts whose proper collation is the object of critical exploration provokes an almost inevitable ranking system of texts and life-texts in which the ranking itself becomes problematic. What is the true text or the true life-text of any given author's work or any given author's life if more than one version should exist? Do we give priority to firstness, middleness, lastness, or perhaps penultimacy? More likely, however, we will play the game of finding the unity of intention—that unified intention which has governed the text—locating it, perhaps, in the unity of consciousness which has presumably generated the text we are using. Then we compare this unity against the comparative unities of other entities such as the various life-texts from which we must again select the most unified of all. Perhaps we should not be too embarrassed to note, even to underline, the banality of our strategies of avoidance, the plethora of prosthetic devices by which we still maintain our power to generate our own texts. Above all, perhaps we should remember that there is not much comfort to be gained by pointing an admonitory finger at our colleagues in the allied disciplines of the so-called human sciences, even if in many cases they either are or pretend to be unaware of the radical precariousness of their own presumably factual utterances about "world history" or "society."

Minimally, we can alert ourselves to the manner in which various texts and "life-texts" are established, circumscribed, identified, and deployed through the convention of using "intentions" as evidence. What takes place is only too clear: the foregrounding of a description of a unity which is matched with another "unity" to reveal an "identity." Each unity, as well as each identity (author, text, life-text, etc.), has been bought at the price of some inescapably "arbitrary" taxonomy—arbitrary only, of course, in the sense that other metaphysical or cultural traditions or practices might have provided other classificatory cuts, but not at all arbitrary insofar as the particular cuts made have close relationships with a given sociocultural configuration.

In telling my story about the literary model, it becomes necessary to mark strongly the shift from a concern with Author to a concern with Text because my own discourse is a constant reminder of the problems of differentiation, especially the difficulty of discussing Author without Texts and without Authors who have presumably become Texts. Since much of what I have said of Authors is equally applicable to Texts, as I shift my focus I admit my bondage to the old model even while I am trying to suggest the need for a new perspective.

As I shift then to a focus upon the term Text, I find a term that is the repository of a host of older notions. This middle term, Text, is the storage vault for notions of objectivity and tangibility, implicated in the idea that the text is in some sense a member of the world of objects. Today it becomes very difficult to stipulate the meaning of Text beyond the recognition that there is no Text without Context. The Text, however, in the traditional employment of the A-T-R + W model, is a designated "outside" of the movement that proceeds across the face of the model. The Text is the manifest; it is the "outside" of what was "inside" the Author. And again, the Text is that which was "outside" in the World before it was "inside" the Author. But now, of course, it finds itself "inside" the Reader. Even a casual inspection of the A-T-R + W model provides an example of the "inside-outside" binary with its characteristic privileging of the "inside" as more spiritual, intense, profound, true, complex, and essential. But, of course, we know that the "outside" also has its privileged domain in other metaphysics.

The interplay and substitutional legerdemain of the "inside" and the "outside" becomes more visible in the fretful marriage of idealism and empiricism—sometimes tipping the balance this way and sometimes that. Here we encounter the inverted hierarchy of a "realism" which privileges the "outside." Richard Rorty in *The Consequences of Pragmatism* details the move wherein the "outside" *really* becomes the "inside" (xv–xvi). Such a "realism" translates "inside" virtues into descriptions of the "outside." Supplementary strategic moves are made by those who, assuming that the "inside-outside" movement includes all possibilities, will never leave well enough alone with the author's text nestled safely within the Reader; rather, they must see the Reader as affecting the World so that readership can in turn reactivate the Author, etc., back and forth. It should be clear by now that the box surrounding the Text must be made to leak in all directions, that is, toward the Author, the Reader, and the World. The utility, the function of the not-so-algorithmic A-T-R + W machine, depends upon the permeability of the boundaries of the key terms.

New Criticism is the most obvious exemplar of text-centered criticism. In its most aggressive formulation, it urged the necessity of a criticism which operated *as if* all significant moves could be made within the textual box. Such an imperative required the generation of a series of frontier guards bearing territorial injunctions—admonitions to the unwary, or pre-game pep talks invoking, under the somewhat spurious guise of traditional logic, the three fearful fallacies (intentional, affective, and pathetic) and thus guaranteeing the development of interpretative or rhetorical strategies for obscuring the imperialist moves of the text. John Fekete, in *The Critical Twilight*, describes the ideological contexts in which this interior politics of reinscription and mystification was nurtured. What I point to here is Fekete's macropolitical description of the politics of the New Criticism. To examine the micropolitics, the local and internal differentiations within the New Critical move toward the reification of the text is a project not undertaken here. Whether or not one should see the New Critical move as an aborted Protestant Revolution, as a Neo-Catholic Renaissance, or as an attempt to find at least marginal acceptance in the "real" world of scientific discourse with equal claims to a transcendence of ideology, is a historical question whose answers are already being sketched by many scholars.

Much of New Criticism's strength of appeal, and perhaps its sole claim to novelty, was its offering of a standard of objectivity to which conflicting disputes could be referred. Idiosyncrasies of reading could be silenced by pointing to the text, to the words in the text, with an indexical intensity and confidence second only to that offered by pointing to the "real apple" in the "real world." New Criticism implicated itself in the possibility of finding almost physical boundaries, contextual insulating fences for words, phrases, or sentences within the solidity of the text, which itself achieved the status of a self-evident fact. At the same time, the results from processing these obligingly self-restricting units were, as we all know, ambivalence, uncertainty, and irony, which were permitted to vibrate for a precious moment before being essentialized, thematized, and restored to their proper stasis.

What I am stressing is the very strong probability that without the presumption of the text as a quasi-empirical control, New Criticism would have been stillborn. An adequate explanation of the need for an empirical foundation in New Criticism requires a broader context than I can offer here. Many tangential factors, such as the structure of university faculties and English departments during the thirties, forties and fifties, are implicated. For example, a quick cataloging of university departments, particularly in the major midwestern universities, reveals that each one had its resident logical empiricist and its resident New Critic. The shared needs of the two are described in *The Consequences of Pragmatism* (xv). The pairings on particular campuses, such as Bergmann and Wellek at the University of Iowa—Bergmann with a philosophy of language out of the Vienna Circle and Wellek with a Neo-Kantian aesthetic out of Roman Ingarden—come immediately into view. Again the collaborative efforts of Wimsatt and Beardsley—a *Thinking Straight* in *Hateful Contraries* which can become *The Verbal Icon*—reflect only in most limited ways the symbiotic, or parasitic, or interactive relationships that obtained in the complex story of the ascendancy and temporary reign of the Neo-Positivists and the New Critics.

The problems of discussing the theoretical foundations of New Criticism are aggravated by the wide differences of opinion among those who either labelled themselves or were labelled as New Critics. In some of these quarters it is difficult to recognize any identifiable theoretical concern except a strategy by which they could, through a newly discovered "close reading," simultaneously denigrate older, "idiosyncratic" effusions about texts and elevate their own sensibility and the sensibility of others. In the classroom and in print, they seemed to offer a renewed and defensible opportunity for the fine honing of discriminatory sensitivities in the intimate engagement with canonical texts. In some of the practicing critics, a strong antitheoretical bias is either implied or made explicit. Despite the differences among the representatives of New Criticism, at least one feature seems widely shared—the search for (or the assumption that the search had already been rewarded) a critical strategy that would reveal an immanence in particular texts and, more broadly, in "literary" texts themselves. Nonliterary texts and literary texts had in some sense to constitute mutually exclusive categories and, for those properly constituted sensitivities, a self-evident difference. As each strategy for the revelation of "literary" immanence sought to assert itself, inescapably such an immanence emerged through various kinds of internal, interdependent relationships within the text itself.

If the relations are seen as external to the text, then of course New Criticism loses its *raison d'être*, and the critic seals off some doors and opens others. Here, the significant "other" might be language, class structure, history, time, myth, evolution, society or "culture." Again, however, to select one is to select many, and the framing process begins anew. An easy example, to borrow once again from La Capra, is to explore the term "culture" (48). He points out that it becomes necessary to decide whether we want to refine the operation by locating the ties to "high" or "low" culture as embedded in a text or in the world or in the world as text. If the point of contact selected is "high" culture, then the problem of canon establishment is central. Here the routes of justification through immanent superiority or through sociological determination are readily available alternatives. We may, if we wish, personify at this juncture History or Time as the invisible hand controlling all moves, thus avoiding an all-too-direct acknowledgment that the critic has access to the eternal verities. It seems, however, evident that the very standards by which judgments have been made are themselves placed in judgment. The possibility seems strong that the selective process itself has much to do with ideological matters, with matters of institutional preservation, with matters of political and economic power, and with particular kinds of functions that canonized texts serve in our educational and political processes. Text-oriented criticism nearly always seeks to demonstrate that the canonized texts must have been selected by hands and eyes that were inexorably attuned to immanence.

The problem becomes interesting when a text-oriented critic seeks to alter or readjust existing textual hierarchies—such as the New Critical move to downgrade romantic poets and elevate the metaphysical poets, or more specifically, to promote Dryden at the expense of Milton—an only partially successful attempt made first by T. S. Eliot and later enshrined in Cleanth Brooks's *The Well Wrought Urn*. Canon revision for the text-focused critic depends upon the demonstration that the earlier "immanence" was a misrecognition and that the later "immanence" is a new truth. John Guillory, a careful analyst of canon formation, cites Eliot as an aggressive strategist of canon revision. Guillory quotes Eliot's contrastive description of Dryden's virtues and Milton's defects: "The great advantage of Dryden over Milton is that while the former is always in control of his ascent, and can rise or fall at will . . . the latter has elected a perch from which he cannot afford to fall, and from which he is in danger of slipping" (Von Hallberg, 339). Guillory's comment on this is that "Eliot's image of flight implies an ironic revision of normative values, because it is not actually the works of the two poets which are being compared but the choices which precede composition, the "perches" from which flight is undertaken" (339).

What Eliot has done is to move completely away from the text of the poem, the poetry itself, to pass judgment—not even in the guise of aesthetic values but in the light of a new system of value, which seems to privilege horizontal over vertical coordinates. What Guillory calls attention to and what needs further inspection is the rhetoric. Eliot strategically moves from the metaphor of "high and low," a Miltonic department, to "narrow and wide," a metaphoric adjustment which permits him to privilege Dryden, echoing in the process the language of Johnson's comparison of Dryden and Pope.

Such juggling of the canonical hierarchies, commonly contained within the academically respectable range of possibilities, represents rather commonplace subject matter for traditional scholarship. Studies in canon formation, particularly those as illuminating as Guillory's, reveal the radical dependence of canonization upon the power of agencies and institutions devoted to the study of "high" art; but at the same time these studies make clear the intense complexity of the circularities and self-referentialities involved, which render the subject opaque to any simple analytic.

Associated problems linked with the Text-World connection include, for example, the problems of the "role of more or less formalized modes of discourse, structures of interpretation and conventions or rules" (La Capra, 56). To what degree, for example, do we regard the relationship between texts and the world as being significantly governed by genres—conventions such as the novel, epic, drama, essay, polemic, panegyric, or lyric? Immediately the whole classificatory system that yields these categories becomes a source of concern. Other genres and subgenres, and sub-subgenres, such as the philosophical essay, the literary essay, the sociological essay, and the historical essay, can yield over at any point of convenience to associated conventions of departmentalization and territorial imperatives which govern our discourses and our exchanges with others. Such lists, then, have only begun their journey through infinite plenitude.

Unless the conventions are observed, how can we tell in advance which discursive practices we can properly ignore?

One kind of literary study has assumed that proper borders can be determined by the principle of "coverage on the part of structures" (La Capra, 56). It would ask, for example, Does this structure adequately cover all examples of lyric poetry, or of tragedy, or of lamentation (the latter in the event we have discovered an improperly obscured genre), or must we expand the structure or exclude a particular text? Is or is not the given text a proper instantiation of the structure? Problems which develop within the blessings of this kind of cutting-up operation include questions such as, Is *Moby-Dick* really a novel? Can we have a long lyric poem? and Is *Leaves of Grass* an American epic? I mention some of these not overly exciting problems only as a reminder that questions like these, and others scarcely differentiable from them, still populate our journals and will, I predict, continue to do so for the foreseeable future. These questions are certainly no less respectable than a host of others that we entertain with high seriousness in the traditionally respectable games that we play—such as, What is the true text? or more modestly, What is the best text of any given work of which more than one version exists? We forget in asking these questions that we must ask simultaneously, Best for what? Too often we ask half-questions, framing them in such a way that their unanswerability is guaranteed. Perhaps we should not be too embarrassed by such frailty. After all, some historians are still operating as if there were a World History into which discrete microhistorical units can be properly nestled.

Questions of a slightly different type are beginning to emerge. These questions station themselves at constituted boundary markers and seek to determine some of the rules of the various articulations which confront us all. These questions confront and foreground classificatory strategies and their functions, textual and contextual. How, for example, do the distinctions between history and literature, fact and fiction, concept and metaphor, *langue* and *parole*, the serious and the ironic, operate in a given text? Or again, how satisfactorily can we describe those quasi-empirical discriminations between textual, stylistic, or strategic discursive practices? In all of these moves, what kind of distinction is being made between theory and practice? Questions such as these seem to require a somewhat different kind of answering service than the ones we have grown all too comfortable with.

As I try to bring the Reader into focus, once again it becomes quickly apparent that boundaries on the term Reader must be made highly porous in order for the term to function within the A-T-R + W model. Various additional adjustments need to be made in the alternate models which shift from Reader to Audience to Interpretive Community, and these adjustments involve considerably more than a simple displacement of the one to the many. Here I shall point merely to the probability that as we contextualize Reader, Audience, and Interpretive Community, we also open different lines of leakage and closure between the terms of the model. For example, when we insert different chips, wheels, or circuit boards to decode the interpretive nets exemplified by the psychoanalytic, hermeneutic (classical), Heideggerian, sociological, or economic taxonomies, so also we reconstitute the reader, audience, or interpretive community.

Pursuing a properly hit-and-run tactic with such a deceptively evanescent target as the literary model shows how little analytic pressure is needed to reveal that in psychoanalytic reader-response theory the Reader becomes the Text and that the Reader's identity themes are what is being read both in Holland's and Bleich's versions of the theory. With Iser, the transparent move is the reinstitution and redecoration of Roman Ingarden's immanent idealism of the Text as reader-response theory. Iser seems constantly forced to reinstitute the Text as Reader, or more simply through some frequently less than careful rhetorical strategies to reestablish the Text as ultimate determinant in cases calling for extreme unction. In Fish's theory, the Reader is reincorporated as Author or as Text, depending upon the exigencies of the situation. The Reader escapes the charge of being located in the idiosyncracies of a specified reader by retreating into the calming indeterminacy of the reader as a strategically inflatable or deflatable "interpretive community" which incorporates the world or all that we need know of it for the interpretive occasion.

One of the insufficiently marked "consequences" of Fish's shift from Reader to "interpretive community" and his insistence that such a move renders his theorizing incapable of having any consequences for textual interpretation, any methodological implications, is that such a move radically undercuts the authority of the entire reader-response project both as theory and as a critical methodology. For example, the Fish-Iser debates clearly illustrated that Iser, along with a host of reader-response enthusiasts, seemed unaware of the extent to which the "success" of his theorizing and of his interpretive textual readings, his methodology and his theorizing, were clearly dependent upon the gross slippage of his key terms. Criticism aimed at Fish flailed helplessly at his fortress term "interpretive community," which was simply a felicitous synonym for "situatedness," and, as such, a recognition of the sociocultural historical embedment of all utterance. As "context" the term becomes unspecifiable (or endlessly specifiable), unbounded, and incompatible with any possible methodological application. The introduction of "situatedness" into reader-response theory reveals in one stroke the insurmountable barriers, the in-built necessity of definitional fudgery of the key terms of the communication triangle in order that the "theory" be translated into a "methodology."

Sociologies of reader-response exist in some abundance. In Lucien Goldmann's *The Hidden God*, the argument both posits and seeks to demonstrate the homogeneity of author and reader. The two, author and reader, Goldmann urges, are really not all that different from each other. On the contrary, Goldmann maintains, as his critic Leenhardt reminds us, "the writer and *his* reader may be considered as equals as long as the social, mental, and ideological distance between the agents of the literary phenomenon is small" (Suleiman and Crosman, 207). In brief, if there is very little difference between Author and Reader, they may, for all practical purposes, be considered as having equal functions. Leenhardt points apologetically to the all too quickly short-circuited tautology and, in the process of making his point, preempts a central burden of my argument when he states that:

> Abstract notions such as "code" and "message" as well as "addresser" and "addressee" are no longer meaningful when applied to literature or any other cultural object, because it is the process of meaning alone, the process of the emergence of meaning, which in every instance gives the cultural object its specific characteristic. (Suleiman and Crosman, 224)

To inspect the various reader-response theories, including the earlier versions of Jauss's *Rezeptionsasthetik*, is to make clear that the distinction between reader-focused interpretations and world-focused interpretations becomes more and more aggressively conflated. On the one hand, the World and its many surrogates—History, Time, etc.—for some is a handy-dandy container for whatever is contained. The World is context and the World is doubly inscribed, first in the model and again in the locus of the model. This double implication renders thoroughly suspect all neatly disjunctive moves. But, of course, the World is also content. It constitutes, for some, an ultimate court of appeals, an ultimate Author, Text, and Reader—a universal pacifier for all things absent, and, on occasion, a universal curse on all things present. It becomes the pressure generating all our ontological redundancies of utterance. The World is the word that permits our articulations, our unit phrases, to function. The World is the necessary but unspecifiable entity in our rhetorical and communications models, and its very necessity as an horizonless horizon dissipates the model as model.

The AUTHOR-TEXT-READER + WORLD model is, in short, a highly unstable explanatory device. Its use has provided us with a facade which obscures some interesting features. It demands a logic which must devote its energy to a constant series of self-cancelling manipulations and must always make cuts in processual operations whose very aggressively self-referential flow must constantly regenerate and mend the very cuts it makes.

One of the burdens of the preceding discussion about the literary and communications models is that these models serve as exemplars of certain traditionally valued problems and that, in one sense, they serve their function admirably. It is not that these models prevent us from finding a "truth"; rather, it is that they offer the promise of giving us a whole arsenal of truths, so many, in fact, that we don't quite know what to do with them all. The burden of this discourse is not that we need a new model to find truth, but rather that these models under inspection are only functional at all within a "representational" or "mimetic" theory and that they create the illusory promise that they can give or generate the very kind of information that the older "scientific" or "idealistic" schemas seemed to offer. One could not say they are wrong models, or that another model would give either empirical or idealistic "information" in firm and stable ways. No model can provide what these models presumed to make available, and these models, whose defects as analytical tools in any strict sense have become so radically transparent, must at best— as tokens of a more positivistic past—coexist with current anti-structuralist speculation and post-structuralist thought. In the light of such thought, the authority and thus the authorizing functions of these older models can be questioned. They must now learn to abide the status of one among many, as structuring devices which still bear the marks of the registration of hierarchical control. As a highly typical example of such models of representation, the literary model has itself lost its presumed isomorphism with "real" Authors, Texts, Readers, and the World.

That any given taxonomic structure loses its unique claim to authority does not mean, however, that the taxonomic structure no longer functions, that it has been abandoned, or that a new taxonomy has effectively replaced it. For taxonomies are usually related or relatable to other taxonomies in some hierarchical positioning which renders them meaningful. The literary model, for example, can be readily embedded in a context provided by the notion of referentiality. It is a particular version of referentiality which operates from the powerful notion of mimesis and provides an epistemic foundation for the A-T-R + W model. Strong support for the model comes also, of course, from the model's isomorphism with the very grammar of our family of languages which, in their positioning of subject-verb-object, project also a commonsense perception of the subject-object relationship of mimesis and of representation—thus seeming to provide a universal grammar for all of experience.

A post-structuralist view of taxonomies would not, it seems, imply that because taxonomies are never innocent they should be abandoned, but rather, would assume their basic indispensability, sharing the notion of Luiz Costa Lima in his essay, "Social Representation and Mimesis," that "We do not look at reality and translate it into a classificatory form. On the contrary, it is the classificatory form which informs us of reality, making some portions of it meaningful. Due to this conversion, things lose their neutral opacity and are no longer just there, they are invested with significance" (450–51). The question Costa Lima poses is, "What in the social world requires those classifications and their precipitate, representations?" Costa Lima's answer is that taxonomies "ensue from the way human interactions take place" (451). Here is not the place to detail Costa Lima's analysis of the function of Irving Goffmann's "frames" and "keying," Alfred Schutz's "types," and Gregory Bateson's notion of "play in the generation of classificatory structures." It is, however, appropriate to explore tentatively the implication of Costa Lima's view of mimesis as the "representation of representation." Such a notion drains *mimesis* of any ontological force and simultaneously eviscerates the force of the notions of equivalence upon which the communications model depends, opening up, as it were, the investigation of the taxonomic conditions of utterance through an unveiling of the lost innocence of modeling itself. All models which retain their embedment in similar theories of representation are equally problematic.

Once the move from representing the "world" to the "representation of representation" is made, an entirely new prospect is unveiled, a prospect in which ontological grounds for differentiating between a representation of the world and the representations are no longer available. We can only, shall we say, differentiate in terms of seriality and not in terms of closeness or fidelity to some presumptively privileged norm. "Firstness," in this case, is no closer to "realness" than is "secondness" or "thirdness"—a referential statement no "closer" than metastatement, or metametastatement. Representation is implicated in the search for "origins." It assumes an initiatory what-so-ever that prompts the mimetic or duplicatory move— an object or a concept which preceded the re-presentation. Characteristically, then, in such modeling there must always be a first, an originating agency which has more "it-ness" than the secondary one. Problems of differentiating the primary from the secondary, or the fictional from the nonfictional representation of the "world," or an author's imagination from a reader's perception, are, from a post-structuralist view, problems only because the model itself creates them as problems. To state the issue in another way: all representation can be considered representation of representation. The laying on of our word *meta* does no more than reinstitute a readily deconstructible hierarchy which was the product of the initial assumption that one can place representations upon some valuational scale of "closeness" to the "real." Once we speak of representation of representation, we have introduced the relative, sociopolitical, historical context, in brief, the environment in its fullness, as the both determinative and yet never fully accessible context of our relativized taxonomic structures.

This determinative yet always incompletely determinable function can be called "practice." Practice then becomes that which ties and binds our previously categorized "subjects" to our "production"; practice is what renders self-reflexive, language-dependent studies always inadequate; practice in this sense is what those projects seeking linkages between the linguistic and the extralinguistic would desire to define and essentialize. Theory is the product of a binary which would permit some controlling function—to become "impractical," to stand outside "practice," outside the contingent, context- and category-embedded flux of being alive.

What seems then to be a most characteristic feature of post-structuralist speculation is its drive toward exploring practice—not in any reconstitutive definitional sense or essentialist sense, but rather to find ways of talking about or at least pointing toward the functions of practice rather than searching for its essence. Such functionally oriented descriptions render the exclusive theory/practice binary irrelevant except as an example of a particular kind of rhetorical practice, which depends upon such binaries for its own proliferation of dyadic configurations.

With the intense focus upon "practice" as function, as the "structuring structures" of everyday life, other kindred terms such as "ceremony," "chora," "desire," "habitus," "political unconscious," and "ritual" have quite independently become points of focus. What has preoccupied post-structuralist interpretative readings of Hegel, Freud, Marx, and other canonized texts, by Lacan, Kristeva, Baudrillard, Bourdieu, Deleuze and Guattari, and many others, is a concern with and a naming of problematic arenas of the prediscursive or extralinguistic functions. These functions are viewed sometimes as generative forces, or again as forcing a recognition of nontranscendent finitude, or as reminders of the otherness which must always escape our taxonomic nets.

No need then to look for a taxonomy of taxonomies, for each taxonomy exists in relation to other taxonomies. A taxonomy is always implicated both covertly and overtly in other taxonomies. Its function is always that of a double agent. It must appear to be stable, definitive, and exclusive of all but the "appropriate" environment; it must also be relative, unspecific, and inclusive. Current speculation in literary theory seeks to cope, overtly and covertly, with such problematic implications.

One of the first texts selected by the Purdue Theory Reading Group for a slow and careful reading was Michel Foucault's *The Order of Things*. Foucault's preface begins with a citation of the memorable taxonomy offered by Borges as quoted from "a certain Chinese encyclopedia." The ensuing discussion of categories in Foucault's text points out that Borges's taxonomy

> destroys the common ground upon which meetings are possible . . . the very site on which propinquity would be possible. The animals "(i) frenzied, (j) innumerable, (k) drawn with a very fine camelhair brush" where could they ever meet, except in the immaterial sound of the voice pronouncing their enumeration, or on the page transcribing it? Where could they be juxtaposed except in the non-place of language? Yet, though language can spread them before us, it can do so only in an unthinkable space. What has been removed, in short, . . . is the table upon which, since the beginning of time, language has intersected space. (xvi–xvii)

Foucault greeted Borges's strange taxonomy with shattering laughter, only, however, to retain an uneasiness:

Perhaps because there arose in its wake a suspicion that there is a worse kind of disorder than that of the *incongruous*, the linking together of things that are inappropriate; I mean the disorder in which fragments of a larger number of possible orders glitter separately in the dimension, without law or geometry, of the *heteroclite*; and that word should be taken in its most literal, etymological sense; in such a state, things are "laid," "placed," "arranged" in sites so very different from one another that it is impossible to find a place of residence for them, to define a *common locus* beneath them all. (xvii–xviii)

The Order of Things is an exploration of ordering processes, their drift, change, and supersessions within specific historical moments of Western culture. As such it notes "ordering codes" and makes "reflections upon order itself," but what Foucault is attempting in his analysis of "the pure experience of order and of its modes of being" is a bit more complex, pressing in upon the quasi-mystical domains of that which is "anterior to words, perceptions, and gestures"—of something which is "more solid, more archaic, less dubious, always more 'true' than the theories that attempt to give these expressions explicit form, exhaustive application, or philosophical foundation." Here it seems that Foucault can be linked with a whole host of post-structuralist theorizers in locating ordering, categorization, and structuring as a process of *practice*. There is, then, no order, no taxonomy, no grid, no table: but there is always already ordering, gridding, tabling which is a thoroughly relational, differential interaction. No need then to tremble at the loss of all order, the sense of all coherence gone, since the ordering process may well have an almost infinite potential.

At the time of this writing, the Theory Reading Group is working its way through Deleuze and Guattari's *Kafka*, wherein we find differences from as well as strong resemblances to Foucault's response to stabilized categories. Deleuze and Guattari's rejection of readings of Kafka which seek to territorialize him within either an Oedipal triangulated taxonomy, or within the hierarchies of some metaphysical-theological configuration, exemplifies perceptions shared with Foucault. What the group finds is a dimension of sameness occupying the plateau of their differences. It is, in short, not an impossible leap from Foucauldian discourse to Deleuze and Guattari's description of a Kafka "machine," of Kafka as experimentation. It is only too easy, perhaps, to find a place in Foucault's *oeuvre* for Deleuze and

Guattari's "Desire is not a form, but a procedure, a process" (Deleuze and Guattari, 8).

One taxonomic problem that confronted the editors of *The Current in Criticism* was that of the arrangement of the procession of authors. Categories of theme, of seniority, of comprehensiveness, of temporality were considered and quickly rejected. In our search for taxonomic innocence, we settled on the presumptive innocence of the alphabet, only to discover that such designed innocence, once contextualized with available alternatives, reflected, only too transparently, another guilt. However, there is ample precedent to be found in Roland Barthes's *The Pleasure of the Text*, wherein the alphabetical design is not quite invisible, perhaps, because it is the most arbitrary (and apparent) of orders. Again the power of the alphabet orders Barthes's *A Lover's Discourse*, wherein a somewhat elaborate justification of such ordering is offered, a justification which, however, seems inappropriate for the essays in *The Current in Criticism*. Even all the hosts of essays on the ordering function of the alphabet, even *S/Z* or *Roland Barthes*, even the graceful and intriguing discourse of Barthes's "Erté ou a la lettre,"[5] cannot, however, save the editors from the responsibility of seeking an escape route or of privileging the beginning or the middle or the end of the alphabet.

Notes

1. In light of J. L. Austin's comments on "excuses" for not doing what he never intended to do anyway, his wit at his own expense, and his impatient apologies for his sloppy categories, Shoshana Felman's reading of Austin in *The Literary Speech Act*, as a very playful speculator indeed, seems at times a more "felicitous" reading than the more "sincere" readings of some of his disciples.

2. In his review of Mary Louise Pratt's *Toward a Speech Act Theory of Literary Discourse*, Joseph Margolies states:

> The interesting failure of speech act theory, then, is this: although language can not but be understood as deployed in terms of speech act contexts, the explanation and analysis of linguistic details may not and need not be systematically connected with whatever regularities may be made out for the

performance of speech acts. It is, in a word, the ubiquity of performing speech acts that cancels out its effectiveness in sorting the linguistic or imaginative aspects of literature . . . there can not be an adequate speech act model for the analysis of literature unless whatever theories provide the most adequate analysis of human society and human history can be rightly subsumed within that model.

3. The troublesome problem is what one means by "conventions," how the term is being used, and the extent to which "conventions" has become the term in which the unexamined indeterminacies of numerous language theorists hide their ambiguities while they scurry around to settle the really important details of their projects. What is meant by governance by convention? Is "convention" a "black box"? An infinitely variable constant? In his essay, "Minimalist Semantics: Davidson and Derrida on Meaning, Use, and Convention," S. Pradhan asks these questions: "These conventions invoke a certain connection between expressions and some of their uses. What sort of connection is it? What special status do they confer on these uses? Why is the connection to these sorts of uses especially revelatory of the semantic nature of expressions? . . . So, we can ask: what sort of tie is it? What makes it special?" (68).

So, we come around to problems about conventions, and habits, and unarticulated rules, and practice, and begin to ask difficult questions about their role in the construction of our explanations.

4. Deleuze and Guattari constantly challenge such a position:

> In what sense is the statement always collective even when it seems to be emitted by a solitary singularity like that of the artist? The answer is that the statement never refers back to a subject. Nor does it refer back to a double—that is, two subjects, one of which would act as the cause or the subject of enunciation and the other as a function of the subject of the statement. There isn't a subject who emits the statement or a subject about which the statement would be emitted. It is true that linguists who make use of this complementarity define it in a more complex way by considering "the marking of the process of enunciation in the enounced statement" (as in terms like *I, you, here, now*). But in whatever way this relationship is conceived, we don't believe this statement can be connected to a subject, doubled or not, divided or not, reflected or not. (83)

5. In *L'obvie et l'obtus*, 95–121.

Works Cited

Abrams, M. H. *The Mirror and the Lamp.* New York: Oxford University Press, 1953.

Austin, J. L. *How to Do Things with Words.* Cambridge: Harvard University Press, 1962.

Barthes, Roland. *A Lover's Discourse.* Translated by Richard Howard. New York: Hill and Wang, 1978.

————. *L'obvie et l'obtus.* Paris: Editions du Seuil, 1982.

Costa Lima, Luiz. "Social Representation and Mimesis." *New Literary History* 16 (1985): 447–66.

Deleuze, Gilles, and Felix Guattari. *Kafka.* Minneapolis: University of Minnesota Press, 1986.

Fekete, John. *The Critical Twilight.* London and Boston: Routledge and Kegan Paul, 1978.

Felman, Shoshana. *The Literary Speech Act.* Translated by Catherine Porter. Ithaca: Cornell University Press, 1983.

Foucault, Michel. *The Order of Things.* New York: Random House, 1970.

La Capra, Dominick. *Rethinking Intellectual History.* Ithaca: Cornell University Press, 1981.

Margolies, Joseph. Review of *Toward a Speech Act Theory of Literary Discourse,* by Mary Louise Pratt. *Journal of Aesthetics and Art Criticism* 36 (Winter 1977): 225–28.

Pradhan, S. "Minimal Semantics: Davidson and Derrida on Meaning, Use, and Convention." *Diacritics* 16 (1986): 66–77.

Rorty, Richard. *The Consequences of Pragmatism.* Minneapolis: University of Minnesota Press, 1982.

Searle, John R. *Speech Acts.* Cambridge: Cambridge University Press, 1969.

Suleiman, Susan R., and Inge Crosman, eds. *The Reader in the Text.* Princeton: Princeton University Press, 1980.

Von Hallberg, Robert, ed. *Canons.* Chicago: University of Chicago Press, 1984.

The Future
of Criticism[1]

Jonathan Culler

In *Hedda Gabler* Eilert Lövborg,
the reformed rake, has published "a big book, dealing with the
march of civilization," which has made quite a stir; but he confides
that "the real book—the book I have put my true self into"—is the
continuation, a book not yet published. "This one," he says, "deals
with the future." "With the future," exclaims George Tesman, a
historian. "But good heavens, we know nothing of the future!" "No,"
admits Lövborg, "but there is a thing or two to be said about it all
the same."[2]

This is very much the situation of those who speak of the future
of criticism. We know nothing of the future but invariably find that
there is a good deal to be said about it all the same, prophesying,
perhaps, that if criticism proceeds on its current course it will bring
about the destruction of literary studies, the decline of civilization, or
at least the end of the English major as we know it. Talk of the future
may be pretentious, may tempt speakers to produce apocalyptic vi-
sions, but it can help one think about the present: what is happening
now in criticism? What are the trends? What are we moving toward?
This is especially important at a time of numerous and varied complaints about literary criticism: fragmentation of the canon; excessive
interest in theory; lack of attention to history, or to canonical texts, or
authors' intentions, or humanistic values, or the common reader.
Thinking about the future of criticism can put talk of crisis in perspective and help one decide where to direct one's efforts by leading
one to imagine what they might produce.

If talk of the future is always talk about the present, what can
we say about literary theory and criticism today that is relevant to its
future?

First, we should note that criticism in America has become
increasingly a university activity. Even such public criticism as we

27

have nowadays is mostly written by university teachers. There is much that could be said about this trend, but for our purposes it means above all that the question of the future of criticism is initially a question about criticism in the university and is tied in with questions about how university structures will adapt to changing social and political circumstances, such as a cultural situation in which the value of acquaintance with literature can no longer be taken for granted, or a political situation where the threat of right-wing dogmatism looms increasingly large. To reflect on the future of criticism is in part to imagine how the organization and orientation of disciplines and teaching within universities can respond to these situations and to ask how university structures are affecting and affected by intellectual activity.

If we think about what has been happening in literary studies recently, for example, we can see that because of the particular characteristics or orientation of certain other disciplines in America—especially psychology and philosophy, but also sociology—many of the most interesting and innovative developments in modern thought have been taken up here not by philosophers but by literary critics and have entered American intellectual life through the field of literary studies. A number of important French thinkers who are not literary critics—Sartre, Lévi-Strauss, Lacan, Althusser, Derrida, Foucault, Lyotard—have been read and discussed in America primarily by students and teachers of literature. This has not been the case in other countries. Only in America, for example, are deconstruction and psychoanalysis particularly associated with literary studies. Though I have listed French thinkers, much the same is true of Germans: Gadamer, Heidegger, Adorno, and Habermas are often discussed here by literary theorists. Perhaps American monolingualism bears some responsibility here. (The idea of reading in other languages is taken more seriously in literary studies than in other fields.) At any rate, when one reflects on the differences in the intellectual scenes in America and in other Western countries, say France, Germany, and Italy, what stands out is not a crisis in American literary studies—literary criticism seems healthier or at least more vigorous here than in France—but rather the parochial character of some other disciplines in America: a philosophy cut off from the continental tradition of Hegel, Husserl, Heidegger, Derrida, for instance.

The fact that all this writing entered American intellectual life through the field of advanced literary studies has two consequences.

First, literature departments have expanded what they teach, usually by including philosophical, psychological, or anthropological writings under the general rubric of "theory," as we call it. In American universities, a course on Freud is most likely to be offered in the French or English departments—certainly not in psychology and until recently not in German either. Nietzsche, Sartre, Gadamer, Heidegger and Derrida are more often discussed by teachers of literature than teachers of philosophy. Saussure is neglected by linguists and appreciated by students and teachers of literature. The writing of such authors falls into a miscellaneous genre whose most convenient designation is simply the nickname "theory," which has come to designate works that succeed in challenging and reorienting thinking in fields other than those to which they ostensibly belong because their analyses of language, or mind, or history offer novel and persuasive accounts of signification.

This expansion of what is taught in advanced literary study is certainly a major source of complaints (that literary study is being corrupted, that literature itself vanishes in a morass of difficult and dubious theoretical writings), but it has made literary studies increasingly, in F. R. Leavis's phrase, "a discipline of thought," though I dare say not exactly in the way he intended.[3] Many of those who teach unorthodox materials in courses offered by literature departments, however, would claim—rightly—that they are working precisely to address the major issues of a liberal education. There is here, in my view, a trend to be encouraged. Literary studies can play a central role if they accept the responsibility of addressing general questions about meaning and textual organization, studying literary and nonliterary texts to develop models of the production of meaning. Instead of worrying about traditional disciplinary boundaries, criticism can work to fill the vacuums created by the orientation of other disciplines within the university.

In addition to expanding the domain of literary studies to include concerns previously remote from it, these new theoretical discourses and perspectives—linguistics, psychoanalysis, feminism, structuralism, deconstruction—have, of course, affected how the discussion of literature itself is carried out. There had been earlier borrowings from other disciplines in American criticism—in the Marxist criticism of the thirties and in psychoanalytic criticism focused on authors, characters, or readers—but these attempts had often seemed reductionist, ignoring complexities of literary language and making the test, in effect, a symptom, whose true meaning lay elsewhere: in the authorial neurosis or social contradiction or philosophical truth it reflected. The versions of European philosophical and psychoanalytical thought that became influential in the 1970s, however, had themselves already undertaken extended reflection on language and meaning and were attractive precisely because they offered richer conceptual frameworks than did the New Criticism for expounding the complexity of literary signification.

Instead of reducing literature to a manifestation of something nonliterary, these various theoretical enterprises—in fields as diverse as anthropology, psychoanalysis, historiography—discovered an essential "literariness" in nonliterary phenomena. They identify the literary not as a marginal phenomenon but as a ubiquitous logic of signification. Literariness is no longer the property of a canon of poems, plays, and novels, but a problematical and inescapable aspect of signification, which can be studied in a variety of discourses.

The field of literary studies has always been capacious. Formerly its scope came especially from the range of *themes* addressed by literary works. Now it has more to do with the ubiquity of aspects of signification that are most evident in literary works but which reappear elsewhere—when one is studying the functioning of philosophical writings, for example, or historical narratives, or psychoanalytical dream-analyses. If there is a unity to literary studies in this new dispensation, it comes not from the canon—women's studies, black studies, and the various theoretical orientations I have mentioned have given us multiple canons and placed on the agenda questions about canon-formation, its mechanisms and costs. The unity, such as it is, comes from attention to mechanisms of signification in texts and textlike situations. Here too lies an agenda for the future—an opening of literary criticism into a general semiotics analyzing signifying mechanisms.

Much of the most powerful work in contemporary criticism has undertaken exploration of the relations between the literary and the nonliterary, or at least moves continually between the two in ways that explore the feasibility of taking one as model for the other. A list might begin with Paul de Man's studies of Rousseau and Nietzsche in *Allegories of Reading.* Focusing on relations between tropological structures and rhetorical force, de Man shows that works traditionally regarded as literary and as expository or philosophical may demand to be analyzed in similar ways. Derrida's readings of Plato, Mallarmé, Kant, and Blanchot pose the problem of the comparability of literary and nonliterary texts. Mary Louise Pratt's *Towards a Speech Act*

Theory of Literary Discourse undertakes to demonstrate that "ordinary language" possesses many of the features of literary discourse and that both literary and nonliterary narratives can be treated by the same models. In *The Sense of an Ending*, Frank Kermode urges the development of a general theory of fictions which would elucidate how fictions generate meaning in discourse of all sorts. Hayden White has advanced this project by studying narrative structures produced by Kenneth Burke's four "master tropes": metaphor, metonymy, synecdoche, and irony. René Girard's account of mimetic desire began, in *Deceit, Desire, and the Novel*, as the study of a fundamental structure of novels—triangular desire, in which what is desired is the image produced by another desire—but from this discovery he went on to argue that such structures are the basis of culture itself. Or again, Edward Said's *Orientalism* moves between the literary and the nonliterary in analyzing the invention of the Orient and Orientals.

It would be no exaggeration to say that contemporary criticism reaches its greatest intensity when focused on theoretically defined problems that take in both literary and nonliterary texts. Those who think of contemporary criticism as a battlefield of conflicting methods miss this shared interest in connecting the literary and the nonliterary.

Developments of this kind lead to an expansion of what is taught in literature departments, whose courses are no longer defined by traditional canons. This proliferation of canons is to many critics the most salient crime or error the academy has committed. For Walter Jackson Bate, our organization of literary studies has helped to bring about the loss of a common culture—for which he blames feminists more than deconstructionists—and William Bennett, Ronald Reagan's secretary of education, has championed the view that to return to "standards" in education would be to return to a canon of the Greeks, the Renaissance, Shakespeare, and those moments of American history calculated to flatter patriotism.[4] Cultural proliferation and specialization are always potential subjects for complaint, especially for those who see education as the transmission of a common heritage (familiarity with a series of cultural monuments) rather than training in habits of critical thinking. But when one thinks about the future of our multilingual, multiracial society, one finds it hard seriously to imagine the establishment of a common culture based on the Greeks or other classics. Such common culture as we have will inevitably be based on the mass media—especially films and television. Schools will not counter this culture effectively by requiring the study of particular historical artifacts, seeking to impose a canon. The struggle against the debilitating effects of mass culture must take place on a different front: by teaching critical thinking, perhaps by analyzing the ideological stakes and structures of mass-media productions and exposing the interests at work in their functioning. Argument about what literary works and what historical knowledge to require will only distract attention from the pressing problem of how to insure that schools encourage intellectual activity by teaching critical thinking, close reading, and the analysis of narrative structures and semiotic mechanisms.

Nostalgia for a narrow canon, the most salient feature of the position Mr. Bennett has been promoting, is difficult to translate into an intellectually defensible program. Any list of books to be taught to everyone is patently unjustifiable: for each book on the list one can think of half a dozen that might be deemed just as valuable. It is said that what used to make people members of the class of British gentlemen was that they had all forgotten the same things. Perhaps George Will's list of the ten books to be required in all high schools is a parodic and belated American attempt to achieve the same effect.

If one asks what is at stake in these proposals, one is struck by the fact that in literary studies a return to the traditional canon would eliminate, above all, courses in women's writing, which are often among the most successful and energetic regions of our literary curricula, courses where literary works are having palpable effects on students' lives. The call for a return to the traditional canon, and especially the classics, which would proscribe all such courses, looks like another attempt in the field of social policy to reassert patriarchal authority.

These repressive inclinations, disguised as plausible proposals to improve an educational system in dire need, make it the more imperative that we work to protect what is frequently called the chaos of contemporary literary studies—at the very least that we not allow the term *chaos* to frighten us into futures less capacious than we might desire. A "normal criticism," elucidating masterpieces within given parameters, is not something we need be nostalgic for. Criticism goes with crisis, itself generates a rhetoric of crisis, insofar as it calls one to rethink the canon and to reflect on the order of a culture's discourses and the relations among them. That is a task that criticism faces in the future.

One source of energy in criticism today, and thus part of the agenda of the future, is the call to history—the demand that criticism and theory become more historically responsible, first by taking account of their own historical character as products of the society to whose culture they contribute, and second by taking some responsibility for the historical plight of their societies and working for change. These calls emerge frequently in arguments that particular critical approaches should be rejected for their failure to be socially progressive.[5] However, it is notoriously difficult to work out the political effects of a theoretical orientation. The evident difficulties of calculating the social effects of well-known theoretical works of the past—Kant's or Freud's, for example—where we have benefit of hindsight, amply indicate the unreliability of advance judgments we might make or the difficulty of developing an a priori test for current approaches or orientations.

What we can do here is to think less about theoretical positions themselves—attempting to assess their degree of conservativism or progressiveness—and reflect instead on institutions and, where we can identify effects of critical approaches, attempt to imagine changes. One example, an area in which I think criticism bears some responsibility for aspects of a dangerous current trend, I would like to approach through the writings of William Empson, one of the great critics of our century.

Empson died in April 1984. His last book is *Using Biography*, a collection of essays on Marvell, Dryden, Fielding, Yeats, T. S. Eliot, and Joyce. There is a certain winning zaniness about Empson's later writings—as he digs into and speculates about his authors' views, purposes, and tones of voice, defending them against a professional academic criticism. Critics' general inclination has been to praise Empson's genius while dismissing these late essays as hopelessly eccentric. I recall loudly voicing this opinion myself when hearing him give a series of lectures on Coleridge and the "Spirits of Electricity" in Cambridge in 1971. I am now inclined to think, however, that what is regarded as eccentric in his writings in fact gives us a valuable perspective on criticism and the academy. The very fact that we are inclined to dismiss his views as eccentric shows how disinclined we are to confront the aspects of academic criticism that he reveals to us.

Most of the biographical essays combat an underlying imperative of contemporary criticism: to interpret works as reflections on or of eternal truths and hence to deny authors their idiosyncratic views. In "Natural Magic and Populism in Marvell's Poetry," seizing upon a sentence by Émile Legouis, Empson writes:

> Excellent, but what can this mean when translated out of High Mandarin except that Marvell was still able to believe in fairies. Modern Eng. Lit. is extremely shy of making this admission

about any serious author, but it was not considered so ludicrous then. From as early as 1590, at least ten of the Cambridge colleges, including Marvell's own, had the *De Occulta Philosophia* of Cornelius Agrippa in their libraries; and this tells you how to call up nymphs in water-meadows.[6]

Empson's main target is the Christianizing interpretations fostered by the critical ideology of the Eng. Lit. establishment, which eliminates fairies and other odd beliefs, drawing quasi-Christian interpretations out of anything that seems spiritual or transcendental. In "The Variants for the Byzantium Poems," he observes that "English and American critics interpret Yeats's poems as implying Christian doctrines whenever that is possible, and when they find it impossible, they treat the passage with a tactful sigh as merely a lapse, because they cannot conceive of a good man, with a good heart, holding any other religious belief. . . . he cannot really believe in Theosophy; at best that would be a kind of play-acting" (163). Working with the drafts and Yeats's statements about the poems, Empson reconstructs a more interesting "science fiction narrative": about a city which is not heaven at all, but "a bustling metropolitan stage, for the ghosts of many periods and many nations arrive there and purge themselves, much as an Edwardian gentleman, after the excesses of the season, would purge himself at Bath or Baden-Baden" (164).

Empson's resistance to the underlying Christianizing aesthetic emerges as an interest in the idiosyncratic beliefs of authors and a willingness to spell out and criticize their religious views. In an article on *The Waste Land* facsimile, Empson takes up the passages of Jew-baiting that Eliot for the most part eliminated and shows their relation to Eliot's religious preoccupations and the private griefs Eliot claimed the poem was about. Rejected by his father—left his inheritance only in trust rather than outright—Eliot rejected his father's and grandfather's Unitarianism and embraced the belief in Christ's divinity and sacrifice. "Unitarians describe themselves as Christians," Empson writes, "but deny that Jesus was God, whereas Eliot was beginning to feel a strong drag towards a return to the worship of the tortured victim. Now if you are hating a purse-proud business man who denies that Jesus is God, into what stereotype does he best fit? He is a Jew of course" (197). "Eliot wanted to grouse about his father and lambasted some imaginary Jews instead." Empson recalls:

What the Unitarians had chiefly revolted against, though they seem to have lost their battle by being too tactful about it, was

the nightmare belief that the Father was given a unique "satisfaction" by the Crucifixion of his Son. It was to this that Eliot
returned with a glum eagerness. . . . Around 1930 I was
sometimes allowed into Eliot's office to find books for review. . . . I was much impressed by the chalk-white face with
the swollen purple lips, and felt confident that he had been
brooding over the Crucifixion all night, or some other holy
torture. (198)

Noting that producers of Eliot's plays "had to coax him into taking
out all those casual hair-raising descriptions of martyrdoms," Empson explains that he "thought it rather fun to have a friend of such a
medieval frame of mind, besides, it was interesting historically. . . .
Not till I got back to England in 1952, and realized how the influence
of Eliot had worked out, did I feel I had been given a direct peep
into the monstruosity of the religion" (199).

Empson wants to make us recognize Eliot's legacy: the failure
to question religious values and the inclination to Christianizing interpretations that imbues the critical ideology of the Eng. Lit. estab-
ljlishment. What he particularly resists is the presumption, fostered
by Eliot's and Northrop Frye's identification of Tradition with
Christianity and the New Critics' association of poetic language with
the paradoxes of religious discourse, that the most powerful and
appropriate interpretation is one which relates elements of the work
to a symbolic order where the oppositions and values are essentially
those of an aestheticized Christian doctrine.

"When I was young," Empson writes, "literary critics often
rejoiced that the hypocrisy of the Victorians had been discredited,
or expressed confidence that the operation would soon be complete.
So far from that, it has returned in a peculiarly stifling form to
take possession of critics of Eng. Lit." (203). Among other things,
there is

a strong drive . . . to recover the children for orthodox or
traditional religious beliefs; well, showing them how these beliefs operated in standard authors of their own tradition is of
course a good way to do it, providing an actual use for the Eng.
Lit. with which the schools have been saddled. The material is
processed with confident firmness to suit this intelligible policy;
and when you understand all that, you may just be able to
understand how they manage to present James Joyce as a man
devoted to the God who was satisfied by the crucifixion. (203)

He calls this "the Kenner smear," after the most energetic and resourceful of the recuperators. "The chief claim of this theory is that

Stephen Dedalus is presented not as the author when young (though the book-title pretends he is) but as a possible fatal alternative, a young man who has taken some wrong turning or slipped over the edge of some vast drop, so that he can never grow into the wise old author (intensely Christian, though in a mystically paradoxical way) who writes the book" (204). Empson marshals internal evidence and biographical materials to oppose the American spiritualizers of Joyce, "the basic purpose" of whose "interpreting," he writes, "(I take it no one would be eager to deny this) has been to prove that Joyce was not really opposed to Christianity. . . . From the evidence of the letters and the Ellmann biography, his critics would be more sensible to blame him for an obsessional hatred of the religion" (213). In any event, "He would regard it as an enormous betrayal that, since his death, everything he wrote has been twisted into propaganda for the worship of the torture-monster" (216).

Readers have found such remarks in rather poor taste, signs of an unfortunate obsession: "The most tedious part of his mind," as Denis Donoghue smugly calls it.[7] No doubt the sharpness of Empson's language comes from the frustration of being dismissed as eccentric and tangential when he is trying to combat precisely the unreflective acceptance of Christianity that makes attacks on it seem odd and tedious behavior. It is the blitheness of critical Christianizing that irritates: "Mr. Wilson," he writes of one critic, "invents his ghastly insertion with easy confidence, because the only Heaven he can conceive is the Christian Heaven, where the God who was 'satisfied' by crucifying his son forces his chosen to gloat as he does eternally in a total realisation of the tortures of the damned" (173).

The consistent direction of Empson's argument might suggest that he panoptically imposes his antireligious views, but he claims to take up those important cases where the Christianizing aestheticism has got out of hand. His desire to do battle with Christianity may seem quaint, but in fact, he sees how thoroughly modern criticism belongs to what the future will doubtless call the Age of Eliot. We critics of the Age of Eliot have been unable to see our method for what it is; we accept Christianity as Tradition and think it bad taste to argue about religious dogma; we regard Eliot's religion as a personal matter which, of course, informed the poetry but otherwise need not concern us. We see the religious commitments of American New Critics as merely anecdotal. Empson, whose years in the East gave him a different perspective, sees the pervasiveness of unacknowledged Christianity in our critical tradition and the way literature has been enlisted in covert aestheticizing religiosity.

In a postscript to Christopher Norris's excellent *William Emp-son and the Philosophy of Literary Criticism*, Empson registered dissent from the view that "anything I had printed for the last quarter century was irrelevant nonsense, to be dismissed briefly with a sigh." "I have not," he maintained,

> been entertaining myself with frippery in my old age; . . . I have continued to try to handle the most important work that came to hand. In 1953, having returned from China, I started teaching in England, so that I had to attend to the climate of opinion in Eng. Lit. Crit., if only because of its effects on the students. This was the peak of the neo-Christian movement . . . perhaps it was already subsiding by the time I was prepared to attack it, but even so I was not making a fuss about nothing.[8]

If religion has subsided in England, it has not in America, though we teachers of literature frequently tend to dismiss it as a quaint survival—all the while explicating it in the classroom as we teach Eliot, Milton, Donne, Coleridge, and even Shelley, Yeats, and Joyce. Students are taught not to question the religious values or principles adduced in literary interpretation. (To argue about religion is immature.) In fact, in literary studies religious discourse has become not just respectable but unquestioned. "For the majority of Eng. Lit. critics, especially in America," Empson writes, "it seems to have become a convention to pretend that one has never heard of the opinions of the Enlightenment" (208). Truly, one finds these days in literature departments people with all manner of views, but seldom anyone who seriously attacks religion. Marx and Freud, who lie behind militant literary theories of today, began powerful critical analyses of religion, but their followers have neglected to pursue this. Critics have abandoned the historic mission of education: to fight superstition and religious dogmatism. Our most famous critics—Northrop Frye, Wayne Booth, Geoffrey Hartman, Hugh Kenner, Harold Bloom—are in their different ways promoters of religion. Recently, there has been a revival of interest in the sacred. Instead of leading the critique of dogmatic mythologies, literary criticism has contributed to the legitimation of religious discourse and religious questions. Hartman, one of the leaders of the attempt to bring together literary and religious studies, has even proposed that literature departments be rechristened "Departments of Mystery Management."

It could be argued that despite its beneficial effects in certain times and places, religion is historically one of the greatest sources of evil in the world, but we think it tactless to mention this. We have no evidence for the existence of God, but don't want to raise the question. Religion is arguably among the most potent repressive forces in America today, but teachers of literature do not raise their voices against it—thinking it irrelevant but all the while honoring the Eliots and Hartmans who promote religious values and attitudes. Religion provides the ideological legitimation for antifeminist politics and other movements of political reaction, yet feminist critics do not attack religion itself, only its patriarchy. Politicians of all stripes now appeal to God without fear of ridicule. Arguments about prayer in the schools never attack religion itself, and priests call, without fear that this will redound against them, for laws to conform to their religion. One wonders how much responsibility for this state of affairs lies with schools and universities, which have abandoned the task of combatting superstition and have failed to foster a critique of religion. If universities *are* at fault, then much blame must fall on teachers of literature, for we, not the scientists, historians, or philosophers, are the ones who have been assigning Milton and Eliot and teaching students not to question their religious values.

Few critics deliberately promote religion; most do the work of legitimation quite unknowingly. I, at any rate, came to see what was happening here only through the sustained "eccentricity" of Empson's collected essays, when reflecting on the nature of the orthodoxy that successfully imposed this label. If criticism does bear some responsibility for the legitimation of religion, America's cultural predicament suggests that the critique of religion and religious values is a task it should seriously take on, and with it the exploration of alternatives, which is the tougher issue: what are the viable forms of humanism in a post-Enlightenment age? Literary works, and the cultural history of the societies from which they arise, provide abundant materials for both a critique of religion and the exploration of alternative values.

Those critics who will not actively challenge religious discourse themselves, for fear of being thought tedious and immature, ought at least to be willing to provoke discussion of religious themes and implied religious values, encouraging students to identify, for instance, the sadism, sexism, and ideological obfuscations of literary works imbued with religion, encouraging them to consider Catholicism or Protestantism or Judaism as interesting ritualistic systems—like Balinese cockfighting—which may have pernicious as well as beneficial social and intellectual consequences. We must also fight to keep alive the critical, demythologizing force of contemporary theory—a force which the Geoffrey Hartmans of the world are busily working to capture and divert to pious ends. "Down with the priests" seems an unlikely motto for the academy today, but Empson helps us to see that we ought to begin by asking ourselves and one another just why it is so very unlikely. This is one of the immediate tasks that face those who entered literary studies or took up literary criticism because of their concern for our culture and its values.

It is not clear exactly how we ought to proceed—doubtless in different ways, as befits the diversity of our critical talents and concerns—but I can offer several remarks to indicate at least something of what I have in mind. First, let me say that in citing Empson's critique of the Christianizing interpretations of authors who held more idiosyncratic or interesting views, I do not wish to deny that some authors have sought to be orthodox Christians. *Paradise Lost*, for example, is a poem that strives to be Christian (Empson argues, of course, that what makes the poem so good is that it makes God look so bad), and one would not wish to separate *The Divine Comedy* from Christianity. I am not suggesting that we err in teaching such works but that we err in treating their religious doctrine too unquestioningly and that we ought to approach it as another questionable informing ideology.

Perhaps an appropriate model might be our treatment of works such as *The Merchant of Venice* and *The Taming of the Shrew*. When we teach these plays today, we do not hesitate to distance ourselves from their overt anti-Semitism and sexism. We make this an issue for debate: are the plays endorsing these attitudes of the day, and how does this affect our response to them? We would, I imagine, frown on a pedagogical approach which treated sexism or anti-Semitism with such respect as we generally give Christian doctrine, or rules as irrelevant arguments about how far they are pernicious. We could do much the same with the religious doctrines of literary works: enforcing a critical distance instead of uncritically explicating. In fact, authors with apologetic aims, such as Dante and Milton, are in some ways easy to teach appropriately, for the details of belief (who will go to hell; what angels are really like) cry out for critical discussion—which can prove quite amusing and engaging. The transcendentalizing critical recuperations of later poets such as Shelley are more pernicious; in cases like this the struggle is harder.

My argument is that our treatment of literature has helped give a legitimacy to religious discourse and has enabled believers or fellow travellers to take religious positions without fear of ridicule. One striking feature of the intellectual situation in America today is the lack of a tradition of antireligious satire or mockery that might keep the sanctimonious in check—or, should we say, keep them honest. We have no American Monty Python, for example, and tend to assume that mockery of religion is in poor taste, or more important, pointless. The English tradition of mockery is much stronger than ours, doubtless because of institutionalized religion in public schools and the existence of a Church of England. Perhaps if Ronald Reagan succeeds in establishing an Official American Christianity, with its school prayer and official "family values," antireligious satire will make an appearance on the American scene. Perhaps we ought to be preparing ourselves for this in the classroom, encouraging not respect but a keen sense of the ridiculous.

I thus propose to add the critique of religion and religious values—resistance to criticism's unknowing legitimization of religious discourse—to the four tasks proposed earlier for the future of criticism:

1) Criticism should, by its capacious, interdisciplinary concerns, work to foster the central role in liberal education that has fallen to literary studies (broadly conceived) by virtue of the narrow orientations of some other disciplines in the university.

2) Criticism, in keeping with the interests of recent theory, should pursue the general analysis of signifying mechanisms in texts of all kinds, reading literary works against nonliterary, and making criticism, in effect, an expanded rhetoric.

3) Criticism must reflect more seriously and resourcefully on the relation of traditional literary study to the mass media, which will inevitably produce a substantial part of our nation's common culture. How do we want to think about these narratives, which is what most of the media's offerings are? While analyzing rhetorical structures and effects, criticism must address the problem of the relations among the various discourses of our culture.

4) Finally, we must resist pressures to return to a narrow canon, which may seem tempting as a way of affirming standards. Criticism, with its current interest in canon-formation, can analyze such proposals: their ideological stakes, their selection of certain areas for marginalization, their possible intellectual costs.

These seem to me important tasks—there is a good deal for criticism to do in the future—and tasks that in many respects continue work currently underway. I offer them with some hesitation, since, as Ibsen's historian in *Hedda Gabler* maintains, "we know nothing of the future"; but these projects, I suggest, are sufficiently interesting and valuable to be pursued even without reliable knowledge of what is to come.

Notes

1. This talk was delivered at Purdue University, the University of Utah, the University of Oklahoma, and the State University of New York at Binghamton. I am grateful to these audiences, whose questions helped to guide my thoughts. I have discussed some matters touched on here in "What Are Things Coming To?" *ADE Bulletin* 80 (spring 1985): 8–10; and in "A Critic Against the Christians," review of *Using Biography*, by William Empson, *TLS*, 23 November 1984, 1327–28.

2. Henrik Ibsen, *Collected Works* (New York: Scribners, 1918), 10:86–87.

3. F. R. Leavis, *The Living Principle: English as a Discipline of Thought* (London: Chatto and Windus, 1975).

4. See W. J. Bate, "The Crisis in English Studies," *Harvard Magazine* 85, no. 1 (1982): 46–53; and William Bennett, *To Reclaim a Legacy: A Report on the Humanities in Higher Education* (Washington: National Endowment for the Humanities, 1984).

5. For references and discussion, see my article, "Some Problems in the 'History' of Contemporary Criticism," *MMLA Bulletin* 17, no. 1 (spring 1984): 3–15.

6. Empson, *Using Biography* (London: Chatto and Windus, 1984), 12. Page references for further quotations from this volume will be given in the text.

7. Denis Donoghue, review of *William Empson: The Man and His Work*, ed. Roma Gill, *TLS*, 7 June 1974, 597.

8. Empson, "Postscript" to *William Empson and the Philosophy of Literary Criticism*, by Christopher Norris (London: Athlone Press, 1978), 205.

Penultimate Words

Caryl Emerson and Gary Saul Morson

*[In modern criticism,] there is no understanding of
evaluative non-predetermination, unexpectedness, as it
were, "surprisingness," absolute innovation, miracle, and
so forth.*
—Mikhail Bakhtin[1]

A few years ago, Bakhtin scholars
were asking themselves which word of Bakhtinian coinage would
become the next "ism." Would polyphonism, heteroglotism, carni-
valism, or dialogism be the theory to confront formalism, structuralism, and post-structuralism? Evidently, dialogism has prevailed, and
articles have already begun to appear synthesizing dialogism with
that ever-present trio, Marxism, Freudianism, and feminism. Nothing desiccates like success.

Dialogism has had different meanings for different scholars, but
for almost all it has remained an "ism"—a reduction of Bakhtin's
vast, complex, subtle, and often contradictory body of thought to a
common denominator. It has often been claimed that Bakhtin repro-
cessed and restated the same idea throughout his life, applying it to
different spheres of culture, and inventing various neologisms for it.
Allegedly, the central idea remained stable and (to use a Bakhtinian
phrase) self-identical.

In his essay on the "chronotope," Bakhtin identified a key
assumption of ancient biographers that defines their work. In their
narratives, a person's basic qualities are given from the outset.
Throughout a lifetime, those qualities may be manifested in numerous intriguing ways, but they never fundamentally change. In this
respect, he argued, ancient biography constitutes the polar opposite
of the novel, a form in which all personal characteristics are seen as
developing in unexpected and unpredictable ways. Ironically, in describing Bakhtin, his admirers have largely adopted the example of
Plutarch, rather than of Jane Austen. This approach facilitates po-
lemics, but impoverishes his thought.[2]

43

This approach seems particularly inappropriate in describing Bakhtin's development, because it clashes with some of his key tenets and concerns. Not only did his thought undergo genuine, surprising, unpredictable change, but the nature of change itself was one of the problems that most occupied his attention. His works evoke a world, not of repetition and restatement, but of innovation and creativity. As he stressed in the Dostoevsky book, *"nothing conclusive has yet taken place in the world, the ultimate word of the world and about the world has not yet been spoken, the world is open and free, everything is still in the future and will always be in the future."*[3]

"Unfinalizability"

If there *is* a core idea in Bakhtin's works, then it is one that challenges the very notion of core ideas in the usual sense. Bakhtin's central concept was "unfinalizability" (*nezavershennost'*), his name for the human tendency to defy all that purports to be fixed and stable. By their very nature, humanness and individuality confer the ability to outgrow all definitions of mankind and the self: so long as people are alive, their essence is not to have a permanent essence. They *surprise* others and themselves, and demonstrate that "everything is still in the future and will always be in the future."

Because Dostoevsky had discovered a way to communicate this sense of human unfinalizability, Bakhtin judged him to be the greatest novelist who ever lived. Dostoevsky's radical formal experiments were all designed with the aim of enabling readers to examine the experience of postponing individual identity. Dostoevsky's characters

> all acutely sense their own inner unfinalizability, their capacity to outgrow, as it were, from within and to render *untrue* any externalization and finalizing definition of them. As long as a person is alive he lives by the fact that he is not yet finalized, that he has not yet uttered his ultimate word. . . . man is not a final and defined quantity upon which firm calculations can be made; man is free, and can therefore violate any regulating norms which might be thrust upon him. . . .
>
> A man never coincides with himself. One cannot apply to him the formula of identity A ≡ A. (*PDP*, 59)

For Bakhtin, the antithesis of freedom is the all-embracing system, the "table of logarithms" at which the underground man sticks out his tongue. Identity is always postponed and always about to be postponed. Not "always already" but "ever about to" is Bakhtin's (anti)formula.

To say that unfinalizability was a core idea for Bakhtin is not to say that all he did was to restate it in different ways in different periods or apply it to different topics. Bakhtin's thought experienced genuine growth. Each time he reconceived unfinalizability he did so in ways that yielded fundamentally new insights, surprising, it would appear, even to himself. His development in no sense resembled the growth of a seed into a plant, because the future growth of a plant is already largely predetermined in the seed. Rather, we might say his ideas evolved as species do: each stage results from a set of compromises; in no sense does it contain the next stage; and it may lead at any time to many different results.[4] In effect, Bakhtin's concept of unfinalizability itself remained unfinalized.

Bakhtin's religious concerns inform his thinking about unfinalizability. Apparently, he hoped to overcome the traditional dichotomy between religious or metaphysical world views that admit creativity and freedom, and positivist and determinist scientific world views that do not. He continually tried to redefine the world and the scientific study of it in a way that incorporated the reality of freedom and genuine innovation. Nature and culture, language and people, art and society all *play*, create, innovate, and evolve unpredictably. Each of Bakhtin's theories—on psychology, discourse, literature, and time—presupposes that unpredictable change, not just change, is an essential characteristic of the object of study.

War on System: The Formalists

My attitude toward Formalism: a different under-standing of specification . . . not "making" but creativity.
—Bakhtin (*E*, 372)

Bakhtin's complex dialogue with the Russian Formalists centered on their militant assertions that literature, language, and culture are all systems. To Bakhtin, the very notion of a system suggested "finalizability," whereas he viewed the world as unfinalizable: as an interaction of systemic and nonsystemic elements, each of which merge and emerge in largely unpredictable patterns. Although culture does indeed contain some ordered elements, it never quite achieves full systematicity; it is closer to those loose composites that general systems theorists call "aggregates." The world clusters and unclusters; local instances of order interact with random elements, some of which cohere, others of which lead to disorder. The constant and active presence of these opposite forces insures that there will always be both unpredictability and predictability, justified expectations and interesting disappointments. "Official" culture acts to establish as much predictability as possible, and so constitutes a "centripetal" force; but random events in everyday life and countervailing forces from "unofficial" culture upset predictability, and exert a fragmenting, "centrifugal" pull in opposite directions.

At their most sophisticated, the Formalists developed a diachronic model of systems. "The history of a system is also a system," declared Jakobson and Tynyanov, who thus greatly expanded the power of Formalist/structuralist theory.[5] For Bakhtin, that increasing power must have posed an increasing threat, because it limited still more the role of what he considered to be real creativity.

The Formalists dismissed creativity as a myth. Like the Hegelian Spirit, the all-powerful Formalist system was the only active principle, the operator that accomplished everything, using individuals simply as tools. The irrepressible and insouciant Osip Brik declared that "If there were no Pushkin, *Eugene Onegin* would have been written all the same. America would have been discovered even without Columbus."[6] For Brik and Shklovsky, literature was the product only of earlier literature, much as for Fish, literary criticism changes only because of the dynamics of the profession of literary criticism.[7]

Jakobson and Tynyanov posited another source of literary change: the interaction of the literary system with other systems. Systems respond to each other. To understand the history of literature or of any other cultural system, one must trace the dynamics of all systems, for culture as a whole is "a system of systems." If this formulation seems more adequate to us than the wholly internalist model of Shklovsky and Brik, it did not to Bakhtin, for it still meant that all change, anywhere in human experience, is systemic. Tolstoy once observed that "if we concede that human life can be governed by reason, the possibility of life is destroyed."[8] Bakhtin, in a similar spirit, saw the Formalist exclusion of fundamentally unsystemic and unpredictable innovation as the beginning of death.

Formalist thinking about literature represented an extension of Saussurean descriptions of language, both of which were attacked by Bakhtin. Language, he insisted, was not a system, either as a whole or in the mind of any speaker. For the collective and for the individual, language is always composed of many different "languages" that constantly compete for ascendancy, a phenomenon Bakhtin called "heteroglossia." Moreover, each of these languages contains random elements. Language, literature, and culture proceed by dialogues among systems and by dialogues between all systems and the unsystemic. These dialogues insure that language will always have enough consistency to be comprehensible and enough inconsistency to produce continual surprises.

Dissolving Oppositions

> *My attitude toward Structuralism: I am against enclosure in a text. Mechanical categories: "opposition," "change in codes" . . . But I hear voices in everything. . . .*
> —Bakhtin (*E*, 372)

Bakhtin detected symmetrical errors in prevailing forms of linguistics and psychology. Modern social thought, he argued, repeatedly presupposes an unbridgeable opposition between the social and the individual, the specific act of behavior and the general social rule. Competing schools merely dispute which antipode is to be resolved into the other. Saussure's opposition of *langue* and *parole* quintessentially incorporates this fundamental opposition of the particular to the system; Freud presumed an analogous opposition but resolved it differently. Bakhtin saw this way of thinking as a prison house locking out all possibility of understanding the relation of self to society. Therefore, it was necessary to rethink that opposition, or, more accurately, to think it away.

Bakhtin believed that his concept of dialogue broke the impasse. In his framework, the fundamental unit of language is not the sentence, not the behavior of a single speaker or writer, but rather the exchange, in which both speaker and listener are simultaneously active. Each utterance must be jointly produced by both speaker and listener, as the listener's actual and potential responses exert a shaping effect on everything about the utterance, from its tone and choice of words to its syntax and content. Add to this combination a "third person," the world, which is not only the subject, locale, and potential judge of the exchange, but also a factor in shaping each utterance from within. Given such a model of language, no one can predict what he or she will say on any occasion, because the utterance is the product of several sources. I do not own or produce my words, we all do. And if *we* produce *my* words, then I do not really know what I will say until I have said it.

Bakhtin further insisted that all human thought is linguistic. Thought is nothing more nor less than "inner speech"; it is entirely verbal. Bakhtin doubted that there could be nonverbal thought. Even if there were such a thing as nonverbal thought, he often contended, it could not have any meaning, significance, or value. "Authenticity and truth inhere not in existence," Bakhtin wrote near the end of his life, "but only in existence that is cognized and uttered" (*E*, 342). What is not uttered, or at least utterable, must, for one reason or another, be dismissed. Bakhtin has been justly criticized for this militant "logos-centrism." For Bakhtin, the world contains and produces everything, and nothing is left for the silent mood, the gesture, unspoken responses to a rock or a sunset, wisdom born of mysticism and solipsism.

Thinking, according to Bakhtin, is a process of holding imagined dialogues with others, whose voices and values have been heard before and then internalized. Consequently, heteroglossia, dialogue, and the competition of centripetal and centrifugal forces are internal as well as external phenomena. Just as real dialogue produces surprising results, so, too, does individual thought—because it is not really *individual* thought at all. The psyche, Bakhtin concluded, is an "extraterritorial part of the organism" and exists on the boundary between self and others. The unpredictable processes of language and society take place within the self.

The converse is also true: as the individual is fundamentally social, society is fundamentally individual. Just as the notion of a self that must be socialized is a contradiction in terms, so is the notion of society apart from the individuals who "implement" it. Freud errs because he imagines that socialization represses the self, when in fact it creates it; the Marxists err in presuming that an abstract *socium* clones individuals who, taken together, mirror its contradictions, when in fact they produce them. One theory privileges the first person of dialogue, the other the second and third; Bakhtin privileges dialogue itself, which is the interaction of all of these. Dialogue has the last word, or, rather, the penultimate one, because it never ends.

Polyphony

Bakhtin sought evidence in literature for his more general theories of human behavior; but literary examples not only provided illustrations for his concepts, they also changed them. In contrast to the Formalists, who predicated their theories on a radical divergence between the literary and the nonliterary, Bakhtin recognized no difference at all. His generalizations based on literary works apply to everything else in the cultural universe. Dialogue is everywhere.

Bakhtin's various theories of literary genres contradict each other because they were produced at different stages of his intellectual evolution. But they all reflect his fundamental concern for the open, the unfinalized. In addition, they all communicate his belief that the novel, and especially the Dostoevskian novel, is the genre that best embodies unfinalizability.

At its best, as exemplified by Dostoevsky, the novel is "polyphonic," Bakhtin argued. In the 1920s, he located genres between the poles of "polyphony" and its antithesis, "monologism," the novel and Menippean satire lying closest to the first pole, catechism and all other forms of "direct, unmediated discourse directed exclusively towards its object" lying closest to the second. One incorporates irregularity, the other regularity. As Bakhtin saw it, *this* opposition, not dynamics and stasis, was the proper one, because dynamics can take a regular form, as in Formalism and Marxism.

Polyphony goes beyond the mere juxtaposition or sequential sounding of contrary voices and ideas. The musical metaphor implies that many voices are heard at the same time, uttering the same word differently. Thus, the same word simultaneously exhibits different values, "pitches," and "rhythms." By repeating this process in the course of a work, the orchestrator—the novelist—can make the unrepeatable particularity of each utterance resonate. Voices join other voices to produce the timbre and intonation of a given communication.

Dostoevsky's invention of polyphony represents for Bakhtin a "Copernican revolution" in literature, because it changed the relation of the author to a literary work, much as the Copernican system changed the relation of the earth to the other planets. The earth became just another planet in the solar system and the author just another participant in the novel's dialogues. This change allowed characters a measure of freedom from the author's all-determining plan; the character achieved the power to surprise the author, to say and do things the author had not guessed before, to demonstrate essential unfinalizability.

Bakhtin's theory anticipates Sartre's distinction between "living" and "telling" in *Nausea*. Readers of a novel know that actions must contribute to the story or they would not be there at all; the fact that something is told guarantees its significance. When Pip gives a pork pie to a convict, readers may be certain that the incident will make a difference, and it does. Tolstoy rejected traditional novelistic plotting because it falsifies life in this way; Bakhtin presumed that Dostoevsky rejected it because it constrained the freedom of characters.[9] When the author plans the ending in advance, significance is guaranteed, but there is a cost: characters must conform to a preset pattern, they can only do what will fit, and each action can lead only in one direction. Monologic narrative cancels the most fundamental aspect of human experience—the *openness* of each action and moment, which can potentiate many patterns but which need not conform to any.

Freedom demands surprise, and surprise is possible only when there is a measure of ignorance. The author must abandon his "surplus" of knowledge about his characters; he must not know in advance how they will think, what they will do, or what the result of any particular thought or action will be. In a polyphonic novel, "the author retains for himself, that is, for his exclusive field of vision, not a single essential definition, not a single trait, not the smallest feature of the hero: he enters it all into the field of vision of the hero himself" (*PDP*, 48). The author does not illuminate the hero, the hero illuminates himself.

Among the many questions raised by Bakhtin's concept of polyphony, the idea of the "self-illuminating hero" is perhaps the one most vulnerable to criticism. Authors *do* create characters, of course, and a character *created* as "self-illuminating" still remains, in all essential respects, a created character. His surprises must still be orchestrated, so how can they be surprises? The self-illuminating hero seems like a contradiction in terms.

In an early essay, "Author and Hero," Bakhtin draws an analogy which may elucidate his concept. He compares the relation of the author to his character to the relation of one person to another whom he sees and to whom he responds. To interact with another, one must "finalize" the other to the extent that one guesses what the other is likely to do next. But ideally and ethically, one should finalize "only for the moment" and keep in mind that the other, as a person like oneself, can upset all possible definitions.[10] If one treats others in this way, one both finalizes and does not finalize, defines and leaves undefined, in effect, views the other as an *open character.* The polyphonic author ostensibly relates to his hero in the same way. Whether these two situations are really analogous is itself an "open" question.

Because a word spoken about oneself always differs from the same word spoken by another, polyphony changes the story in an essential respect. To be described by another is to be finalized; but to describe oneself is to retain the power of rendering false one's own self-characterization. Self-analysis contains a loophole. It implicitly declares at every moment, "That is what I used to be, but no longer am," or (as the underground man repeatedly declares): "I will tell you another thing that would be better, and that is, if I myself believed an iota of what I have just written. I swear to you, gentlemen, that I do not believe one thing, not even one word, of what I have just written. That is, I believe it, perhaps, but at the same time, I feel and suspect that I am lying myself blue in the face."[11]

Only by adopting a polyphonic perspective, only by renouncing authorial "surplus," can a novelist represent "a self that is not identical to itself," a self that can surprise. Here Bakhtin implicitly advanced a theological, as well as a poetic, argument. Substitute "God" for author and "man" for character, and one sees that, in endowing man with free will, God became the first polyphonic creator. He does not command, but engages in dialogue with his creatures: "Christ as truth. I put the question to him," wrote Bakhtin in his last notes.[12]

A polyphonic novelist renounces foreshadowing, narrative irony, and predetermined plot. Bakhtin implied that God renounced predestination and omniscience so that he might *address* (and be addressed by) human beings.

For Bakhtin, polyphony functions as a theory not only of the structure of texts, but also of the creation of texts—which may be why he called the first edition of the Dostoevsky book *Problems of Dostoevsky's Creativity.* (The word *tvorchestvo*, like the English *creation* or *work*, may signify both the product and the process.) Polyphonic works differ from monologic ones because they are produced differently. Bakhtin here tacitly disputes the two most influential received theories of creativity and implicitly suggests an alternative.[13]

On the one hand, polyphony differs from the account of creativity favored in classical poetics and, in Bakhtin's time, by the

Formalists. The Formalists liked to cite Poe's essay on "The Philosophy of Composition," in which creation is described as essentially algorithmic. "It is my design," declared Poe, "to render it manifest that no one point in composition is referrible either to accident or intuition—that the work ['The Raven'] proceeded, step by step, to its completion with the precision and rigid consequence of a mathematical problem."[14]

In some sense, the solution of a mathematical problem already exists before it is sought. Thus, creation is effectively reduced to discovery (Columbus and America). The process of creation becomes nothing but the labored attempt to locate a concealed object; it produces nothing genuinely new. The classical account thus denies "unfinalizability."

The alternative, the romantic theory of creativity, recognizes the possibility of the new, but only as an unexpected gift resulting from a burst of inspiration. Creativity is exceptional; history and life proceed mechanically, prosaically, until they are interrupted by a force from outside. From a Bakhtinian perspective, this account impoverishes the everyday world. Bakhtin viewed creativity as ongoing. He saw a world of ceaseless birth and growth. Just as the dialogues of everyday life are always changing language, and just as speech changes the speaker, so creativity happens everywhere and always, and is always and everywhere about to happen. Therefore it cannot be true that "when composition begins, inspiration is already on the decline," as Shelley stated.[15] The entire process of writing—like the entire process of living—produces the new.

Both of these theories, the "algorithmic" and the "inspirational," are, in Bakhtin's terms, monologic, because they presuppose a preexisting plan that need only be executed. But a polyphonic creator, like Dostoevsky, deliberately creates without such a plan because, as Edouard observes in Gide's *Counterfeiters*, "it is essentially out of the question for a book of this kind to have a plan."[16] More accurately, the plan has to be of a special sort.

The "plan" consists of identifying a set of unfinalizable voices and imagining a series of situations that will provoke these voices to speech and redefinition. Creation, both divine and literary, produces not a finished world but a range of possibilities, of potentials for interesting and unpredictable histories. The plan and the plot emerge as the novel is being written. Thus, authorial intention cannot be located at any single point in the process of composition; neither at the beginning nor the end does the whole book exist in the author's mind. Both intention and unity are matters of process; therefore, to understand polyphony these concepts must be fundamentally reconceived.

Undoubtedly, Bakhtin exaggerated the degree of polyphony in Dostoevsky's novels. Several critics have observed that these works do manifest a plan and appear to have been written with a plan in mind. Perhaps this is why Bakhtin never analyzed any of Dostoevsky's novels as a whole.[17] Most likely, he sensed that polyphony occurred at odd moments, perhaps producing the best passages in Dostoevsky's novels, but was not sustained throughout an entire work. This consideration was almost irrelevant to Bakhtin, however, because his central concern was not to analyze *Notes from Underground* or *The Brothers Karamazov*, but to identify a special process of composition—and of living.

Chronotopes and Anachronism

The concept of the "chronotope," which is in no sense derivable from the concept of unfinalizability, nevertheless specifies and enriches it. "Chronotope," as Bakhtin defines his coinage, is a particular way of understanding and representing the interrelationships of space and time. Bakhtin understood time as historical and space as social; therefore, his neologism might best be translated as "a particular complex of sociohistorical relations." There are as many chronotopes in literature as in life.

Texts embody particular chronotopes. Each narrative genre is composed of those texts embodying a given chronotope. Thus, in each genre, "time, as it were, thickens, takes on flesh, becomes artistically visible [in a particular way]; likewise, space becomes charged and responsive to the movements of time, plot, and history. The intersection of axes and fusion of indicators characterizes the artistic chronotope."[18]

The nature and possibility of action is always conditioned by space and time. According to the chronotope essay, selfhood lies in a person's actual and contemplated actions; space and time, therefore, condition selfhood. "The image of man is always intrinsically chronotopic," and varies from genre to genre.

Some genres, for example, represent time and space "abstractly," as mere background to actions that in principle could happen anywhere and anytime; other genres represent time and space specifically and actively, as shapers of the thought and actions of characters. In one case, time is a mere parameter, in the other it is an operator; and among genres that represent time as an operator, its workings vary. People are different depending on the nature of time.[19]

No one could mistake the country and period described in *Middlemarch, Pride and Prejudice,* or *Fathers and Children,* because these narratives depend on richly detailed and highly specific descriptions of social milieux to explain why each character makes some choices, rejects others, and cannot even conceive of still others. Turgenev's novel could not be transposed from Russia to England, or from the late 1850s to the late 1880s, because in another time or country the plot, including all of the social forces that shape thought and action, would make no sense. But in Greek romances or adventure stories such transpositions could and did occur. In romances, the same catalogue of selves is always available; in true novels, selfhood changes with its milieu and changes its milieu. Actions, thoughts, and personalities possible at one time, and in one genre, are not possible in others. The novelistic chronotope, like human history and individual biography, incorporate *anachronism* and what might be called *anatopism.* These concepts permit and explain the possibility of surprise, of constant unexpected change, of unfinalizability.

Carnival

"The will to destroy is a creative will," proclaimed the Russian anarchist Mikhail Bakunin. Carnival is the name Bakhtin gave to the spirit of creative destruction, to revivifying parody. Realized most perfectly in a specific type of medieval festival, carnival may arise anywhere and anytime real laughter threatens to shatter in a guffaw the centripetal forces and values of prevailing social norms.

In the Dostoevsky book, Bakhtin developed the concept of polyphony and applied it to Dostoevsky; in the book on Rabelais, he developed the concept of "carnivalization" and applied it to Rabelais and the specific institution of carnival. In both books, one may value the concept while rejecting the application, and Bakhtin seemed to realize this. In effect, he used literary and historical themes as illustrations of his concepts, which nevertheless have an interest and perhaps a validity of their own. In our view, however, carnival is Bakhtin's weakest concept.

In *Rabelais and His World* and elsewhere, Bakhtin described the novel as the genre of high literature that most fully expresses the spirit of carnival. Although he traced the origin of the novel to Rabelais, he also berated modern novelists for achieving only "reduced laughter." Thus he implicitly acknowledged that his primary interest lay not in any specific set of texts, but in a world view.

Carnival represents what Bakhtin conceived of as the pure spirit of laughter: pure because "genuine laughter" mocks everything serious, completed, and finished. In medieval carnival, such laughter parodied official life and official feasts, which, Bakhtin observed, consecrated "all that was stable, unchanging, perennial: the existing hierarchy, the existing religious, political, and moral values, norms, and prohibitions. It [the official feast] was the triumph of a truth . . . that was put forward as eternal and indisputable."[20] By contrast, carnival, in its own special language, denied these supposedly eternal truths, asserting that there are no eternal truths. Carnival parodied the official norms of its day only synecdochically: they stood for all norms that might ever claim eternal truth. The spirit of carnival is not reformist, but antinomian: it preaches the "joyous relativity" of all things.

"Carnival was the true feast of time, the feast of becoming, change, and renewal. It was hostile to all that was immortalized and completed" (*R*, 10). Bakhtin's language reveals the links between this concept and his other theories: carnival exalts the open, the incomplete, the "unfinalizable." Even if particular carnivals failed to incarnate this spirit, Carnival, the ideal of Carnival, was ever ready to break through the quiet humdrum rules of daily life and put them to scorn. Carnival is the Platonic ideal of anti-Platonism, of Heraclitianism. The epigraph for chap. 3 of *Rabelais* is drawn from Heraclitus: "Time is a playing boy who moves the draughts. Dominion belongs to the child."

Carnival comprises a specific chronotope or, rather, antichronotope, all its own. In mocking all possible norms, it espouses in utopian fashion the value of people free of all social definitions and ranks. Thus, playful inversion of rank and dress is common in carnival. Carnival peers beyond history to the world of Saturn, that is, of both the Saturnalia and the Golden Age, over which Saturn presides. The chronotope of carnival is the chronotope of utopia. It is the utopia anticipated by Bakunin, rather than Marx, a time not of static perfection, but of eternal joyous change and experiment, of creative destruction for its own sake. A playful millenarian, Bakhtin celebrated pure anarchic, orgiastic, eternal revolution.

The grotesque abounds because Carnival laughter violates all finished wholes. The official and polite image of the body is distorted as carnival focuses on the apertures and orifices: "The body discloses its essence as a principle of growth only in copulation, pregnancy, childbirth, the throes of death, eating, drinking, or defecation. This is the ever unfinished, ever creating body, the link in the chain of genetic development. . . . The individual is shown at the stage when it is recast into a new mold. It is dying and yet unfinished; the body stands on the threshold of the grave and the crib" (R, 26). Carnival represents biological unfinalizability.

Bakhtin imagined that the spirit of carnival is liberating both for individual people in everyday life and for society as a whole. As his own biography illustrates, laughter offers a loophole of hope. "Analysis of a serious face (fear or threat). Analysis of a laughing face," so Bakhtin projected another study during his last years. "Seriousness burdens us with hopeless situations, but laughter lifts us above them and delivers us from them. Laughter does not encumber man, it liberates him" (E, 338–39).

But in the celebration of his concept, Bakhtin clearly overlooked evidence that the social effects of carnival and antinomianism are profoundly dangerous. A reading of Norman Cohn's celebrated study of medieval millenarianism and antinomianism, *The Pursuit of the Millennium: Revolutionary Millenarians and Mystical Anarchists of the Middle Ages*, might serve as a reminder that for those who reject all norms, all is permitted—and practiced: orgiastic murder, pogroms, immolation. What Bakhtin describes as joyous relativity Cohn depicts as promiscuous criminality; carnival is the spirit of the millenarian crusaders and, in our time, of the Reich to Last a Thousand Years.[21]

Even within the Bakhtinian universe, carnival fails to accomplish what Bakhtin claims. By its very nature, a pure spirit of subversion and parody produces nothing new, it only rejects whatever has been or might be produced. Ambrose Bierce defined a conservative as someone enamored of the evils of the past, as distinguished from a liberal, who would replace those evils with new ones. Where carnival avoids pure destruction, it can lead only to a paralyzing cynicism. Its best representation might be the petty, parodying, but ultimately tedious devil who appears to Ivan Karamazov: "'Scolding you, I scold myself,' Ivan laughed again, 'you are myself, myself only with a different face. You say just what I am thinking . . . [you] are incapable of saying anything new!'"[22]

Either from cunning or naivete, Bakhtin typically ignores the dark side of his favorite concepts. In Carnival he sees only the joy of parody, not the danger of irresponsibility and violence. His social theory of the self also ignores the frightening aspects of "extraterritoriality." He forgets what Dostoevsky obsessively recalls: the power of others over our psyche may lead not only to benevolent communion, but also to internalized tyranny. The self may be moved not to an open dialogue, but to defensive self-protection: "You made me do it. You ruined my chances by making me see myself that way." Some of Bakhtin's current admirers also overlook the possibility that "dialogics" may become oppressive. Like the totalitarian state watching over the individual, dialogics may turn joyful relativity into cynicism and shut the open door.

Discourse in the Novel

Three discrete theories of the novel have been described thus far: the genre best realized by polyphony, a genre with a specific chronotope, and the carnivalized genre. More successful than any of these is Bakhtin's "discourse" theory of the novel. Classifying genres by the way in which they represent language, Bakhtin concluded (or presumed) that the novel represents language as it really is (that is, as Bakhtin thinks it really is): as dialogic.

Heteroglossia, always a characteristic of language, is not exploited by all genres. In lyric poetry, Bakhtin contended, "the natural dialogization of the word is not put to artistic use, the word is sufficient unto itself." By convention, the lyric poet speaks a timeless language, and writes as if that language were the only possible one. "In poetic genres, artistic consciousness . . . is fully realized within its own language . . . The language of the poet is *his* language, he is utterly immersed in it, inseparable from it, he makes use of each form, each word, each expression according to its unmediated power to assign meaning (as it were, 'without quotation marks') . . ." Though the poet may endure agonies in creating his work, "language is an obedient organ" in the finished work. The poet demonstrates the ultimate adequacy of poetry and the language in which it is written; there can be no other languages, except inadequate ones. "The language of the poetic genre is a unitary and singular Ptolemaic world outside of which nothing else exists and nothing else is needed. The concept of many worlds of language, all equal in their ability to conceptualize and to be expressive, is organically denied to poetic style" (*DI*, 285–86).

Of course, Bakhtin mischaracterizes lyric poetry and its language. He does so in order to create yet another antipode of the novel. Lyric in "Discourse in the Novel" is the analogue of Greek romance in "Forms of Time and of the Chronotope."

The inferior genre is always "Ptolemaic," the superior one is "Copernican." As in the Copernican universe the earth is just another planet, so in the novel literary language is just one among many. The technique of the novel as a genre is to create a dialogue among the many languages of daily life, with all the value judgments and world views that adhere to each. Prenovelistic genres, such as Menippean satire, may represent diverse languages, but only the novel dialogizes them. The author's speech is not exempt from the genre's fundamental law of dialogization and enjoys no ultimate privilege. He does not speak *the* truth, but only his truth, and implicitly acknowledges the possibility of doubt. His language emerges as just another professional jargon.

Dialogization occurs when forms of speech interact: "voices," "speech zones," "speech genres," "languages of heteroglossia," and their related "ideologies," value systems, and conceptualizations of the world all dispute, parody, stylize, confirm, or deliberately ignore each other within a single utterance, even a single word. Novels create "double-voiced" words and condense the conflicting languages of heteroglossia into "microdialogues." For example:

> It is a truth universally acknowledged, that a single man in possession of a good fortune must be in want of a wife.
> —*Pride and Prejudice*

> He was secretly beginning to feel irritated. Bazarov's complete indifference exasperated his aristocratic nature. *This son of a medico was not only self assured: he actually returned abrupt and reluctant answers, and there was a churlish, almost insolent tone in his voice.*
> —*Fathers and Children*[23]

The novelist's speech in these examples is a "hybrid": the utterance is spoken by the author, but the author adopts words and turns of phrase that are typical of particular characters with particular world views in particular situations. In each case, therefore, we hear, at the minimum, a clash between two voices, between the "accent" that a character would give a specific word, and the "counter-accent" of the author. In some cases, several voices may conflict in a single utterance, which is one reason why novels are often difficult to read aloud.

This definition of the novel excludes works that Bakhtin's other definitions include. From the perspective of discourse, rather than carnivalization, Rabelais is not a novelist, but a "pre-novelist." Novelistic discourse begins in the late eighteenth or early nineteenth centuries. Moreover, not all prose narratives of the nineteenth century are novels either: *Barchester Towers* dialogizes heteroglossia, but *Moby-Dick* resounds in a different way.

Perhaps the essence of novels—noveleness—is concentrated in one type of double-voiced word, the "word with a loophole." This type of discourse takes the dialogicality of the novelistic word to an extreme. The "word with a loophole" exaggerates the openness of discourse in the novel, and so results in pure instability.

In loophole discourse, each statement anticipates a particular series of reactions and answers them in advance; indeed, it also answers responses to those answers in advance, *ad infinitum*. The loophole speaker's goal is to avoid finalization and the self-definition that any commitment would imply. His statements are decoys. They never state anything; they frustrate the listener's habit of characterizing and finalizing the speaker. Their function is to defeat any specific function: they are, in Bakhtin's phrase, *"pure function"*:

> A loophole is the retention for oneself of the possibility for altering the ultimate, final meaning of one's own words. If a word retains such a loophole this must inevitably be reflected in its structure. This potential other meaning, that is, the loophole left open, accompanies the word like a shadow. Judged by its meaning alone, the word with a loophole should be an ultimate word and does present itself as such, but in fact it is only the penultimate word and places after itself only a conditional, not a final period. (*PDP,* 233)

Although Dostoevsky's underground man invites others to challenge his exaggerated self-denigration, he carefully protects himself from the possibility that they will not. He retains a loophole: so you were foolish enough to believe me! "Can you imagine that I am ashamed of it all, and that it was stupider than anything in your life, gentlemen?" (*PDP,* 234). Even when it is not stated so explicitly, the loophole response is latent in each of his statements, which bend under the weight of an infinity of additional responses the speaker is prepared to make to anything the other might say. As a result, "the style of his discourse about himself is alien to the period, alien to finalization, both in its separate aspects and as a whole" (*PDP,* 235).

Of course, such a radical pursuit of unfinalizability constitutes a form of illness (and of lying). Surprisingly, Bakhtin often seems unconcerned with this possibility. For example, in his essay on "The Problem of the Text," he privileges response—*any* response—over the awful desert of silence that (quite possibly) some untruths deserve. "For the word (and consequently for a human being) there is nothing more terrible than a lack of response. Even a word that is known to be false is not absolutely false, and always presupposes an instance that will understand and justify it, even if in the form: 'Anyone *in my position* would have lied, too.'"[24] The political naivete and moral tolerance displayed in such a reaction could strike one as frightening. Bakhtin's position is ethically questionable; but clearly the *necessity for response* is so central to his system that he leaves the less rarefied questions of deception and demagoguery to fend for themselves.

Bakhtin tends to forget that unfinalizability cannot be a primary goal, because, in its pure form, as pure function, it excludes the possibility of the new. Some sort of commitment must be extended to innovation, to definition, or nothing can be created at all. To hold everything in reserve, to keep everything potential, is to reduce potential itself to a mere potential. Absolute unfinalizability merges with total closure. As Borges has argued, an inescapable labyrinth may contain either *no* turns or an infinite number of equally pointless turns. The alternative must contain real possibilities and, to be real, some of these possibilities must at some time be actualized. Although no product may exhaust creativity, creativity demands that at some time something meaningful be produced.

Escape from the Labyrinth

Modern literary theory has offered us two extreme positions, which threaten an endless and pointless oscillation. Recently, we have encountered various theories of pure function, which dissolve in advance whatever might be said. It would be a mistake to call such theorists relativists, because they do not even commit themselves to relativism. Their very style bears an uncommon resemblance to that of their predecessor with a loophole, the man from the underground.

Paul Feyerabend's influential study, *Against Method: Outlines of an Anarchistic Theory of Knowledge*, advocates loophole science. Scientists should acknowledge that logic and consistency enjoy no privilege, he argues. They should recognize that facts are always theory laden, and therefore there can be no facts. They should admit that whatever passes for knowledge at a given time is fundamentally a matter of power. From these tenets, Feyerabend concludes that there is nothing wrong with "the Church, the State, a political party, public discontent or money" dictating scientific conclusions. "Anything goes," including self-contradiction, which properly "dissolves into nothing the detailed determinations of the understanding, formal logic included."[25] Hayden White recently maintained that because there are not historical facts *per se*, historians may and should devise whatever account would best suit their political goals. Stanley Fish, starting from the theory that texts have no intrinsic meaning, has now reached the conclusion that the only possible arbiter of interpretive disputes is power.

Feyeraband, for one, defends his approach as truly humanitarian and libertarian, but in the loopholes of these cunning texts is revealed a deep cynicism. What Raskolnikov said of ethical standards is now said of standards of truth and falsity: if there are no facts, then all is permitted. We have witnessed a rapid move from pure libertarianism (anything goes) to pure theoretical totalitarianism (there is only power) because, as Bakhtin understood, there is really no difference between these positions. As Shigalyov puzzles in *The Possessed*, "I am perplexed by my own data and my conclusion is a direct contradiction of the original idea with which I start. Starting from unlimited freedom, I arrive at unlimited despotism."[26]

Perhaps Bakhtin's increasing popularity reflects the ease with which he may be transformed into yet another extreme relativist. One can easily imagine Bakhtinian epigones endlessly proving that the polyphony of the world makes any statement about it impossible; that everything in culture is always already, or ever about to be, carnivalized; and that all words are equally loophole words. Such a development would be only an extension of current practice, which produces countless readings of the following sort: because all texts are equally self-consuming, self-deconstructing, or self-referential, so, too, is this poem by (fill in the author's name). Or, this poem, too, can be read like that other one, which was famously analyzed by (fill in the critic's name). Nothing is more mechanical than pure anti-mechanism, nothing more hackneyed than the relentless pursuit of the new for its own sake; nothing tires more quickly than the Gospel According to Bakunin. Approached in this way, Bakhtin's works would become just another path to the underground, and Bakhtin himself just a novelistic Virgil leading us through another theoretical inferno.

Loophole theory probably arose as a reaction to its opposite, which might be called semiotic totalism: the idea that we do or can possess an account that will determine and fix the meaning of every-thing. Life is nothing but language, man is a sign, and we have (or are developing) the grammar and syntax of human existence. Thus have structuralists enthused in their more euphoric outbursts. And, of course, versions of Freudianism and Marxism, too, forever wait in the wings for an opportunity to deny the openness of the world. As Sartre observed, such theories repeatedly discover what they already know, and their proponents write as if "the duty of the event is to verify the *a priori* analyses of the situation." In the application of such theories, man "is dissolved in a bath of sulphuric acid," and an essential human quality is lost: innovation, *creativity*.[27]

Bakhtin understood that innovation demands both centripetal and centrifugal forces, that distinctions are essential if anything meaningful is to be said, and that creation is possible only if one both holds convictions and entertains doubts. Both extreme relativism and extreme dogmatism betray unfinalizability. "The polyphonic ap-proach has nothing in common with relativism (or with dogma-tism)," Bakhtin cautions in the Dostoevsky book. "But it should be noted that both relativism and dogmatism equally exclude all argu-mentation, all authentic dialogue, by making it either unnecessary (relativism) or impossible (dogmatism)" (*PDP,* 69).

Notes

1. M. M. Bakhtin, "K metodologii gumanitarnykh nauk," in *Este-tika slovesnogo tvorchestva* (Moscow: Iskusstvo, 1979), 370. Further refer-ences, given in the text, are to *E.* The essay is translated as "Toward a Methodology for the Human Sciences," in Bakhtin, *Speech Genres and Other Late Essays,* ed. Caryl Emerson and Michael Holquist, trans. Vern McGee (Austin: University of Texas Press, 1986).

2. For an example of this approach, see Tzvetan Todorov, *Mikhail Bakhtin: The Dialogical Principle,* trans. Wlad Godzich (Minneapolis: Uni-versity of Minnesota Press, 1984).

3. Bakhtin, *Problems of Dostoevsky's Poetics*, trans. and ed. Emerson (Minneapolis: University of Minnesota Press, 1984), 166. Further references, given in the text, are to *PDP.*

4. As Stephen Jay Gould has argued, evolution tinkers, follows many paths, proceeds unpredictably and in surprising ways.

5. See Jurij Tynyanov and Roman Jakobson, "Problems in the Study of Literature and Language," in *Readings in Russian Poetics: Formalist and Structuralist Views*, ed. Ladislav Matejka and Krystyna Pomorska (Cambridge: MIT Press, 1971), 79–81; and Gary Saul Morson, "Return to Genesis: Russian Formalist Theories of Creativity," in *Russian Formalism: A Retrospective Glance. A Festschrift in Honor of Victor Erlich*, ed. Robert Louis Jackson and Stephen Rudy (New Haven: Yale Center for International and Area Studies, 1985), 173–94.

6. Osip M. Brik, "T. n. 'Formal'nyi metod'" ("The So-called 'Formal Method'"), *LEF* 1 (1923): 213.

7. See Stanley Fish, "Transmuting the Lump: *Paradise Lost*, 1942–1982," in *Literature and History: Theoretical Problems and Russian Case Studies*, ed. Morson (Stanford: Stanford University Press, 1986), 33–56.

8. Leo Tolstoy, *War and Peace*, trans. Ann Dunnigan (New York: Signet, 1968), 1,354 (first epilogue).

9. In our view, Bakhtin was mistaken in his ascription of radical freedom to Dostoevsky's characters, much as he was mistaken in denying it to Tolstoy's characters. See Emerson, "The Tolstoy Connection in Bakhtin," *PMLA* 100, no. 1 (January 1985): 68–80; and Morson, *Hidden in Plain View: Narrative and Creative Potentials in "War and Peace"* (Stanford: Stanford University Press, 1987).

10. The neo-Kantianism of Bakhtin's early essay is obviously apparent in this formulation.

11. Fyodor Dostoevsky, *Notes from Underground*, pt. 1, chap. 11, in *"Notes from Underground" and "The Grand Inquisitor,"* trans. Constance Garnett, rev. Ralph Matlaw (New York: Dutton, 1960), 33.

12. "Iz zapisei," in *E*, 353. For more information on Bakhtin's religious views, see Katerina Clark and Holquist, *Mikhail Bakhtin* (Cambridge: Harvard University Press, 1984).

13. Bakhtin speaks briefly of the creative process in the Dostoevsky book and elsewhere. We write "tacitly" and "implicitly" because we are reconstructing an argument that seems to follow from Bakhtin's ideas, but which he never extensively developed. For more information on the implications of this account of creativity, see Morson, *Hidden in Plain View;* Emerson, "The Inner Word and Outer Speech: Bakhtin, Vygotsky, and the Internalization of Language," *Critical Inquiry* 10, no. 2 (December 1983): 245–64; and Morson and Emerson, *Mikhail Bakhtin: Creation of a Prosaics* (Stanford: Stanford University Press, forthcoming).

14. Edgar Allen Poe, "The Philosophy of Composition," in *Great Short Works of Edgar Allen Poe*, ed. G. R. Thompson (New York: Harper and Row, 1970), 530.

15. Percy Bysshe Shelley, "A Defense of Poetry," in *Critical Theory Since Plato*, ed. Hazard Adams (New York: Harcourt Brace, 1971), 511.

16. From the chapter, "Edouard Explains His Theory of the Novel," in André Gide, *The Counterfeiters*, trans. Dorothy Bussy (New York: Random, 1955), 188. We are following the thread of Bakhtin's thought here, but are aware that it is somewhat illogical and inaccurate. First of all, even if Dostoevsky did create "polyphonically," it does not follow that everyone does. Moreover, Dostoevsky's notebooks would appear to offer strong counterevidence to Bakhtin's description of Dostoevsky's creative methods.

17. For an alternative reading of *Notes from Underground* that is more adequate to the work as a whole, see Jackson, *The Art of Dostoevsky: Deliriums and Nocturnes* (Princeton: Princeton University Press, 1981).

18. *The Dialogic Imagination: Four Essays by M. M. Bakhtin*, ed. Holquist and trans. Emerson and Holquist (Austin: University of Texas Press, 1981), 84–85. Further references, given in the text, are to *DI*.

19. We borrow the terms "parameter" and "operator" in this sense from Ilya Prigogine. See his *From Being to Becoming: Time and Complexity in the Physical Sciences* (San Francisco: Freeman, 1980); and Prigogine and Isabelle Stengers, *Order Out of Chaos: Man's New Dialogue with Nature* (New York: Bantam, 1984).

20. Bakhtin, *Rabelais and His World*, trans. Helene Iswolsky (Bloomington: Indiana University Press, 1984), 9. Further references, given in the text, are to *R*.

21. Norman Cohn, *The Pursuit of the Millennium: Revolutionary Millenarians and Mystic Anarchists of the Middle Ages*, revised and expanded edition (New York: Oxford University Press, 1970).

22. Dostoevsky, *The Brothers Karamazov*, trans. Constance Garnett (New York: Random, 1950), 776.

23. Italics Bakhtin's; passage as cited in *DI*, 317. Bakhtin observes: "The third sentence of this paragraph, while being a part of the author's speech if judged by its formal syntactic markers, is at the same time in its choice of expressions ('this son of a medico') and its emotional and expressive structure the hidden speech of someone else (Pavel Petrovich)."

24. Bakhtin, "Problema teksta v lingvistike, filologii i drugikh gumanitarnykh naukakh," in *E*, 306. Also see Bakhtin, "The Problem of the Text in Linguistics, Philology, and the Human Sciences," in *Speech Genres*, 127.

25. Paul Feyerabend, *Against Method: Outline of an Anarchistic Theory of Knowledge* (London: Verso, 1975), 52 and 27.

26. Dostoevsky, *The Possessed*, trans. Constance Garnett (New York: Random, 1963), 409.

27. Jean-Paul Sartre, *Search for a Method*, trans. Hazel E. Barnes (New York: Random, 1958), 124, 44 and 99.

Anti-Foundationalism, Theory Hope, and the Teaching of Composition

Stanley Fish

In the past twenty years, the literary landscape has been transformed by the emergence of theory. Although it remains true that theory is not seriously taught in the majority of our departments of literature and is a regular part of the curriculum in only a few avant-garde outposts, it is nevertheless the case that much of the energy—and especially the polemical energy—in the literary academy is centered on theory; so much so that even those whose acquaintance with theory is secondhand regularly debate its value and its consequences. Not surprisingly, the question of theory has found its way into discussions of the teaching and practice of writing, and, also not surprisingly, the appearance of theory in the world of composition has provoked the same expressions of hope and fear that attend its appearance in every other discipline.

It is theory hope—the promise that theory seems to offer—that is my subject, but it is a subject that cannot be approached without first posing the basic question of what, exactly, theory is. It is a large question and one that could be pursued on any number of levels, but I would like to begin at the most general level by saying that, in general, theory comes in two forms; although even as I say that I want to qualify it by saying that by some arguments the second form of theory is not properly theory at all. Be that as it may, the two forms of discourse that at least announce themselves as theory are foundationalism and anti-foundationalism. By foundationalism I mean any attempt to ground inquiry and communication in something more firm and stable than mere belief or unexamined practice.

65

The foundationalist strategy is first to identify that ground and then so to order our activities that they become anchored to it and are thereby rendered objective and principled. The ground so identified must have certain (related) characteristics: it must be invariant across contexts and even cultures; it must stand apart from political, partisan, and "subjective" concerns in relation to which it must act as a constraint; and it must provide a reference point or checkpoint against which claims to knowledge and success can be measured and adjudicated. In the long history of what Derrida has called the logocentric tradition of Western metaphysics, candidates for the status or position of "ground" have included God, the material or "brute act" world, rationality in general and logic in particular, a neutral-observation language, the set of eternal values, and the free and independent self. Every foundationalist project assumes the existence and availability of one or more of these grounds, and it is from this assumption that its program of research proceeds in the direction of building and elaborating a model.

As an example of such a model, it is convenient to recall the linguistics of Noam Chomsky, at least in its early or pure form. As Chomsky himself describes it, the goal of his theory is the construction of a "system of rules that in some explicit and well defined way assigns structural descriptions to sentences" and does so in a way that "does not rely on the intelligence" of the assigning agent, of whose beliefs, cultural situation, educational experience, etc., the system remains independent. What it does rely on is a set of formal constraints which have the characteristics I have already cited: abstractness, generality, invariance across contexts. Once these constraints have been discovered and put in place, the resulting machine— Chomsky calls it a "competence grammar"—would be able to divide sentences "into the well-formed and the ill-formed just on the basis of their syntactical structure, without reference to the way things are in the world, or to what speakers, hearers or anyone else believes" (Chomsky, 8 and 4).

In short, the successful foundational project will have provided us with a "method," a recipe with pre-measured ingredients which when ordered and combined according to absolutely explicit instructions—and the possibility of explicitness is another foundationalist assumption—will *produce*, all by itself, the correct result. In linguistics, that result would be the assigning of correct descriptions to sentences; in literary studies, the result would be the assigning of valid interpretation to poems and novels; and in the teaching of composition, the result would be the "discovery of rules that are so fundamental as to be universal," rules that if followed would lead directly to coherence, intelligibility, readability, persuasiveness, etc.

In this last sentence I have quoted from an excellent essay by Patricia Bizzel, who goes on to rehearse some of the assumptions informing the work of foundationalist theorists of composition. They tend, she says, to see in all stages of the composing process "the same basic logical structures"; they tend also "to see differences in language use as superficial matters" because they believe that "the basic structure of language cannot change" and is "isomorphic with the innate mental structures" that enabled one to learn a language in the first place (Bizzel, 215). Students who have difficulty writing are somehow out of sync with their own innate structures, and it is a matter simply of getting them back in touch with the right internalized standards which they can then proceed to apply and actualize in different situations. One need only add to Bizzel's account the assumptions of a fixed and stable world with which both the innate mental structures and the universal forms of language are isomorphic, and a fixed and stable self whose operations are or should be as regular as the formalisms to which it is allied. As Richard Lanham puts it, in a capsule characterization, the foundationalist world picture includes "a positivistic social reality just 'out there' and a self just 'in here', half way between the ears" (Lanham, 21). Robert Scholes offers another characterization in a chapter entitled "Is There a Fish in This Text?": "a complete self confronts a solid world, perceiving it directly and accurately, always capable of capturing it perfectly in a transparent language. Bring 'em back alive; just give us the facts ma'am the way it was; tell it like it is; and that's the way it is" (Scholes, 132). Scholes rehearses this scenario only to ridicule it, to give it the label of a "naive epistemology" and to declare forthrightly what the essays by Bizzel and Lanham certainly imply, that "this . . . epistemology . . . is lying in ruins around us" (Scholes, 133).

What has ruined it, at least in these reports, is anti-foundationalism, a set of notions or way of thinking to which Scholes, Bizzel and Lanham obviously subscribe. Anti-foundationalism teaches that questions of fact, truth, correctness, validity, and clarity can neither be posed nor answered in reference to some extracontextual, ahistorical, nonsituational reality, or rule, or law or value; rather, anti-foundationalism asserts, all of these matters are intelligible and debatable only within the precincts of the contexts or situations or paradigms or communities that give them their local and changeable shape. It is not just that anti-foundationalism replaces the components of the foundationalist world-picture with other components; instead it denies to those components the stability and independence and even the identity that is so necessary if they are to be thought of as grounds or anchors. Entities like the world, language, and the self can still be named; and value judgments having to do with validity, factuality, accuracy, and propriety can still be made; but in every case, these entities and values, along with the procedures by which they are identified and marshalled, will be inextricable from the social and historical circumstances in which they do their work. In short, the very essentials that are in foundationalist discourse opposed to the local, the historical, the contingent, the variable, and the rhetorical, turn out to be irreducibly dependent on, and indeed to be functions of, the local, the historical, the contingent, the variable, and the rhetorical. Foundationalist theory fails, lies in ruins, because it is from the very first implicated in everything it claims to transcend.

Such, at any rate, is the anti-foundationalist argument, which has been made in a variety of ways and in a variety of disciplines: in philosophy by Richard Rorty, Hilary Putnam, W. O. Quine; in anthropology by Clifford Geertz and Victor Turner; in history by Hayden White; in sociology by the entire tradition of the sociology of knowledge and more recently by the ethnomethodologists; in hermeneutics by Heidegger, Gadamer, and Derrida; in the general sciences of man by Foucault; in the history of science by Thomas Kuhn; in the history of art by Michael Fried; in legal theory by Philip Bobbit and Sanford Levinson; in literary theory by Barbara Smith, Walter Michaels, Stephen Knapp, John Fekete, Jonathan Culler, Terry Eagleton, Frank Lentricchia, Jane Tompkins and Stanley Fish, and on and on. Obviously it is not an isolated argument; in fact today one could say that it is the *going* argument. And yet, it would be *too much* to say that the foundationalist argument lies in ruins. It is in fact remarkably resilient and resourceful in the face of attacks against it. The resistance or persistence of foundationalism usually takes the form of a counterattack in which the supposedly disastrous consequences of anti-foundationalism are paraded as a reason for rejecting it. Those consequences are usually said to extend to the loss of everything necessary to rational inquiry and successful communication. As one anti-anti-foundationalist, Israel Scheffler, puts it, without the anchor of determinate facts and an independent rationality, "there are no controls, communication has failed, the common universe of things becomes a delusion and in place of a community of rational men following objective procedures in the pursuit of truth we have a set of isolated monads, within each of whom belief forms without systematic constraints" (Scheffler, 19). This is a dark prophecy, a foundationalist nightmare vision in which a liberated self goes its unconstrained way believing and doing whatever it likes; but it is also a misreading of anti-foundationalism at one of its most crucial points, the insistence on situatedness. A situated self is a self whose every operation is a function of the conventional possibilities built into this or that context. Rather than unmooring the subject, as Scheffler charges, anti-foundationalism reveals the subject to be always and already tethered by the local or community norms and standards that constitute it and enable its rational acts. Such a subject can be many things: certain, confused, in turmoil, at rest, perplexed, sure. But the one thing it cannot be is free to originate its own set of isolated beliefs without systematic constraints. Whatever anti-foundationalism is or isn't, it cannot have the negative consequences feared by those who oppose it.

This brings us finally to the specific subject of this paper, the consequences of anti-foundationalism for those who do not oppose but welcome it and find in it the basis not of a fear but of a hope. As it is usually expressed, that hope follows directly from the demonstration that foundationalist methodology is based on a false picture of the human situation. Since it is not the case, as foundationalists assume, that the "scene" of communication includes a free and independent self facing a similarly independent world to which it can be linked by the rules of a universal language, a methodology based on these assumptions will necessarily fail of its goal. And conversely, if the true picture of the human situation is as anti-foundationalism gives it—a picture of men and women whose acts are socially constituted and who are embedded in a world no more stable than the historical and conventional forms of thought that bring it into being—if this is the correct picture of the human situation, then surely we can extrapolate from this picture a better set of methods for operating in the world we are constantly making and remaking, a better set of rationales and procedures for making judgments, and a better set of solutions to the problems that face us as teachers of writing.

Now, it is not hard to understand why so many have sought a methodological payoff for composition in the arguments of anti-foundationalism. Those arguments, with their talk of change, transformation, contextual variability, selves dissolved in institutional roles, etc., seem perfectly suited to the new emphasis on process over product, the replacement of a standard of correctness by the fluid and dynamic standard of effectiveness, the teaching of strategies rather than of rules and maxims, the ascendancy, in a word, of rhetoric. Indeed it is no longer accurate to call this shift in orientation "new" since, as Maxine Hairston has observed, at least in some quarters "the admonition to 'teach process, not product' is now conventional wisdom" (Hairston, 78). In anti-foundationalism it seems that the new conventional wisdom has found a new paradigm, one that we can presumably tap in order to put our wisdom into operation. This heady prospect is all the more attractive because it gives us a way of explaining what is least perceived to be the failure of our efforts to date. We can now tell ourselves and others that if we have not succeeded it is because we have been laboring under the wrong epistemological assumptions, and now that we have found the right ones, success or at least dramatic improvement should follow.

As a card-carrying anti-foundationalist, I would certainly like to believe that the arguments to which I am committed will have a beneficial effect on the teaching of writing. But I am not convinced, and I would like to rehearse with you the reasons for my skepticism. On one point, I am not a skeptic: there is at some level a natural "match" between anti-foundationalism and a process-oriented or rhetorical approach to composition. Indeed another word for anti-foundationalism *is* rhetoric, and one could say without too much exaggeration that modern anti-foundationalism is old sophism writ analytic. The rehabilitation by anti-foundationalism of the claims of situation, history, politics and convention in opposition to the more commonly successful claims of logic, brute fact empiricism, the natural and the necessary, marks one more chapter in the long history of the quarrel between philosophy and rhetoric, between the external and the temporal, between God's view and point of view. But does the fact that anti-foundationalist arguments and the slogan of writing as process in some sense "go together" mean that the first can serve as a methodological resource for the second or that, conversely, the elaboration of the second depends on a prior understanding of and commitment to the first? Let me break that question down into three smaller questions: first, does anti-foundationalism as a model of epistemology provide us with directions for achieving the epistemological state it describes? Second, is it the case that if we learn the lesson of anti-foundationalism, the lesson that we are always and already situated, we will thereby become more self-consciously situated and inhabit our situatedness in a more effective way? And third (and most practically) will the teaching of anti-foundationalism, to ourselves and to our students, facilitate the teaching of writing? My answer to all three of these questions is no; and moreover, it seems to me that it is an answer dictated by anti-foundationalism itself. It is also an answer implicit in one of Derrida's characteristically enigmatic pronouncements: "This situation has always already been announced" (Derrida, 9). By "this situation" Derrida means the situation in which knowledge is always and already mediated, the situation in which language rather than being the mere medium or instrument with which we interrogate the world is itself the origin of the world, of our modes of interrogation and of ourselves. It is the situation that Derrida comes to announce in *Of Grammatology* and elsewhere; yet he says it "has always already been announced." Derrida's point is that since it has always been announced, it cannot be discovered, at least not in the sense that would give us a purchase on it that we did not have before. That is, the realization that something has always been the case does not make it more the case than it was before you realized that it was; you are still, epistemologically speaking, in the same position you were always in. The fact that we are now able to announce that we are situated, does not make us more situated, and even when we could not announce it, being situated was our situation.

Ah, you say, but now we really *know* it because we know it self-consciously. But to say that is to make self-consciousness something one achieves in a space apart from situations and to make self-conscious knowledge a knowledge more firm and more "true" than the knowledge we have without reflection. This is of course a general assumption of liberal thought—that the only knowledge worth having is knowledge achieved disinterestedly, at a remove from one's implication in a particular situation—but it is an assumption wholly at odds with anti-foundationalism, and it is certainly curious to find it at the heart of an anti-foundationalist argument. That is, it is curious to have an argument that begins by denying the possibility of a knowledge that is independent of our beliefs and practices end by claiming as one of its consequences the achieving of just such an independence. But this is precisely what is claimed when the anti-foundationalist insight is said to provide us with a perspective on what we have been doing such that we are now in a position either to do it better or to do something we haven't been able to do before.

And indeed, any claim in which the notion of situatedness is said to be a lever that allows us to get a purchase on situations is finally a claim to have escaped situatedness, and is therefore nothing more or less than a reinvention of foundationalism by the very form of thought that has supposedly reduced it to ruins.

This is what happens in many of the essays in which anti-foundationalist theory is linked in a causal way to a revolution in the teaching of composition. As an example consider Kenneth Bruffee's influential piece, "Liberal Education and the Social Justification of Belief." Drawing on the arguments of Kuhn, Rorty and myself (a trio now so prominent in the field that it can be thought of as a single personage with the name KuhnRortyFish), Bruffee avails himself of the vocabulary of paradigms, interpretive communities, and the social justification of belief, and finds in it a program for the reform of teaching. We should, he says, introduce our students to "the notion of knowledge communities" and to the idea that knowledge is a function of belief rather than of an unmediated communication with the world or with a self-declaring truth. Once we help students "recognize that they are already members of communities of knowledgeable peers" then we can proceed to build from that knowledge to wider and wider communities (Bruffee, 108). The initial step then is one of "self-awareness," and in order to bring it about we should, according to Bruffee, ask students "to identify" in nonevaluative terms their own beliefs and the beliefs of the local, religious, ethnic, national, supranational and special-interest communities they are already members of:

> Protestant students from Kansas City, Jewish students from Atlanta, Catholic students from Boston, Vietnamese from Michigan, Polish Americans from Toledo, Chicanos, . . . blacks and whites, . . . middle class and poor, rock fans, bridge players, hockey addicts—people from potentially every conceivable community would become aware of what the beliefs of their own communities from the beliefs of other communities, and in what respects the beliefs of most communities are identical . . . And this would help students learn how beliefs affect the way people within a community, and people of different communities, interact with each other. The curriculum would help students make these discoveries in part through self-conscious analysis, and in part through self-conscious efforts to join the several disciplinary communities that constitute the faculty of an institution of liberal education. (Bruffee, 108–9)

The appearance of the word *liberal* in this last sentence is no accident, for what Bruffee has done in this paragraph is redescribe anti-foundationalism so that it becomes a new and fashionable version of democratic liberalism, a political vision that has at its center the goal of disinterestedly viewing contending partisan perspectives which are then either reconciled or subsumed in some higher or more general synthesis, in a larger and larger *consensus*—a word Bruffee uses again and again. Now I have nothing to say against this goal—at least not here—except that it is incompatible with anti-foundationalism because it assumes the possibility of getting a perspective on one's beliefs, a perspective from which those beliefs can be evaluated and compared with the similarly evaluated beliefs of others. That is, what anti-foundationalism teaches (and I apologize for saying this yet again) is the inescapability of situatedness, and if situatedness is inescapable, students could not possibly "identify, in nonevaluative ways their own beliefs," because as situated beings some set of beliefs of which they could not be aware would be enabling any identification they might make; and therefore, the act of identification would from the very first be "evaluative" through and through. One could escape this logic only by saying that while the operations of the mind are always a function of context, in one operation—the identification of its own context and that of others—it is independent. Such an exemption is obviously contradictory and marks a return in Bruffee's discourse of the foundationalism he has supposedly banished. The project of building a larger and larger consensus on the insight of anti-foundationalism can only get started if the first tenet of anti-foundationalism—the situatedness of all knowledge and of all acts of knowing—is forgotten.

It is forgotten, as I have said, in the name of liberalism, and this brings up a point that deserves a paper of its own: anti-foundationalism has always been thought of as a position on the left, and one whose consequences will be favorable to the left-wing goals of reform and revolution. The reasoning is understandable: since the lesson of anti-foundationalism is that the world and its facts are not given but made, does it not follow that those who have learned the lesson will feel free to make them again? But even to ask the question in this way is to fall into the error I have already identified, the error of thinking that a conviction as to the circumstantiality of everything we know can afford us a perspective on our circumstantial knowledge and enable us to change it. What one must remember is that circumstantiality—another name for situatedness—is not something one can escape by recognizing it, since the act of recognition will itself occur within circumstances that cannot be the object of our self-conscious attention. Thus revolution and reform can take no particular warrant from anti-foundationalism, and to think otherwise is once again to make the mistake of making anti-foundationalism into a foundation.

To put the matter in a nutshell, the knowledge that one is in a situation has no particular payoff for any situation you happen to be in, because the constraints of that situation will not be relaxed by that knowledge. It follows then that teaching our students the lesson of anti-foundationalism, while it will put them in possession of a new philosophical perspective, will not give them a tool for operating in the world they already inhabit. Being told that you are in a situation will help you neither to dwell in it more perfectly nor to *write* within it more successfully. When Bizzel urges that we "teach students that there are such things as discourse conventions," that is, teach anti-foundationalism, she is open to the same criticism that she levels at foundationalist theorists who, she says, "assume that the rules we can formulate to *describe* behavior are the same rules that produce the behavior" (Bizzel, 234). But that is also her assumption insofar as she believes that a description of how we come to know what we know can be turned into a set of directions for knowing. As a searching critique of method, anti-foundationalism cannot itself be made the basis of a method without losing its anti-foundationalist character.

But perhaps the link between anti-foundationalism and composition can be preserved by making it weaker. One might argue that even if anti-foundationalism cannot serve as a lever with which to master situations, it can direct us to a new area of instruction. This is in effect what is urged by Scholes when he says that "what the student needs from the teacher is help in seeing discourse structures themselves in all of their power and fullness" (Scholes, 133) and by Bizzel when she predicts that "the staple activity of . . . writing instruction will be analysis of the conventions of particular discourse communities" (Bizzel, 218). Here the advice is, if all knowledge is situational, then let's teach situations.

The trouble with this advice is that in its strongest sense it cannot be followed and in its weaker sense it cannot help but be followed, even when it hasn't been given. It can't be followed in the strong sense because it would amount to teaching situations as if (1) they were a new kind of object to which we could now turn our attention, and (2) we could achieve a distance from them such that our accounts of them would be a form of "true" knowledge. But of course both these "as ifs" once again reinvent foundationalism by substituting for the discredited notion of determinate facts the finally indistinguishable notion of determinate situations and by rendering unproblematic our relationship to these newly determining entities. The truth is that a situation is not an entity, but a bundle of tacit or unspoken assumptions that is simultaneously organizing the world and changing in response to its own organizing work. A situation is always on the wing, and any attempt to capture it will only succeed in fixing it in a shape it no longer has. Moreover, any attempt to capture it must itself be mounted from within a situation, and therefore the knowledge afforded by such an exercise is not only out of date but disputable. In short, if the teaching of the theory of situations is inefficacious, the teaching of situations themselves is impossible and a contradiction in terms.

In another sense, however, the weak sense, teaching situations is not only possible but inevitable, irrespective of one's "doctrinal" position. For if anti-foundationalism is correct and everything we know is always a function of situations, then everything we teach is always situational knowledge, whether we label it so or not. That is to say, even if a student is being presented with a piece of knowledge—of grammar, of propriety, of whatever—as if it were independent, detached, and transferrable (i.e., "cashable" in any and all situations), it is not thereby *rendered* independent, detached and transferrable. Therefore composition teachers are always teaching situations because they can do nothing else.

Thus, for example, all classical rhetoricians regard metaphor and other figures as departures from ordinary or normative speech, as forms of inappropriateness that are nonetheless useful and even necessary in this or that situation; but while the normative is supposedly the measure of figurative appropriateness and is constantly invoked as the unchanging ground against which departures can be measured and assessed, it in fact never appears in the long catalogues offered us by Quintilian and others. What does appear is example after example of speech that is effective in particular situations; and so many are the situations and so protean and shifting are the figurative possibilities, that one cannot escape the conclusion that situatedness and not correctness is the rhetorician's true subject. Consequently while those who have been taught by and now teach Quintilian may think that they are adhering to a foundationalist model, and may defend such a model against relativistic incursions, they are in fact teaching what Bizzel and Scholes and others now urge them to teach.

Or, for another example, consider the case of E. D. Hirsch, until recently one of the most prominent champions of a pedagogy based on normative notions of correctness, readability and quantifiable effects. As many of you will know, Hirsch has recently recanted and now says along with everyone else that the "formal elements of language cannot be successfully separated from vast domains of underlying cultural information" and that therefore "we cannot do a good job of teaching, reading and writing if we neglect . . . particular cultural vocabularies" (Hirsch, 145). Does this mean that Hirsch wasn't doing a good job earlier or that he was teaching something beside cultural vocabularies before he came to recognize the impossibility of avoiding them? I would venture to guess that he was as good a teacher of composition before he saw the contextual light as he is now. Not only does being converted to anti-foundationalism bring with it no pedagogical payoff; being opposed to anti-foundationalism entails no pedagogical penalty.

Everything I have said so far can be reformulated in terms that might seem paradoxical, but are not: if all knowledge is situational and we are always and already in a situation, then we can never be at any distance from the knowledge we need. Anti-foundationalism cannot give us the knowledge we seek because its lesson is that we already have it. This is explicitly the lesson taught by Polanyi in the name of "tacit knowledge." Tacit knowledge is knowledge already known or dwelt in; it cannot be handed over in the form of rules or maxims and theories; there is, as James Reither observes, "no transition from 'knowing that' to 'knowing how'." And yet, Reither apparently forgets his own observation when he asserts that knowing that knowledge is tacit "provides a theoretical rationale" for certain ways of teaching as opposed to others, for ways of teaching that will help "bring about" a "tacit integration" of otherwise empty maxims. But this is to turn the knowledge that knowledge is tacit into a recipe for achieving it, when of course the lesson of tacit knowledge is that it cannot be achieved by recipe, by the handing over of an explicit maxim, even when the maxim is itself. As an argument that denies the possibility of learning by rule, the theory of tacit knowledge cannot legitimate some set of rules for learning. Neither can it rule out any. According to Reither, once we know that knowledge is tacit, we know that "students cannot learn to write only by being told . . . hundreds upon hundreds of explicit maxims" (Reither, 38–39). But of course this is itself a maxim and one that is contradicted by history: insofar as there has been and continues to be such a pedagogy, many of the students subjected to it have learned how to write; and they have learned how to write in part because the maxims they are given are not explicit at all, in the sense of being detached from a tacitly known practice, but are the precipitation of a practice, whether they are presented as such or not. The notion of tacit or situational knowledge is simply too powerful to be endangered by a method that is ignorant of it; indeed, in the strongest sense a method cannot be ignorant of it, no matter how much it tries. The lesson of tacit knowledge—the lesson that it cannot be the object or the beneficiary of self-consciousness—must be extended to the theory of itself. Knowing that knowledge is tacit cannot put us in more possession of it or enable us to possess it in a heightened way; and *not* knowing that knowledge is tacit cannot deprive us of it. To make the notion of tacit knowledge either into a recipe for learning or into a set of requirements for a "good" pedagogy is to exempt it from its own insight.

The conclusion I am reaching is a conclusion approached by J. Hillis Miller, who then immediately shies away from it. Miller reports that "empirical studies of the relative effectiveness of different theories of teaching writing are not . . . reassuring. They suggest that students will get somewhat better whatever the teacher does, perhaps through sheer praxis. One learns to write by writing" (Miller, 55). Miller, as I have said, shies away from this conclusion, and he does so in the name of a belief "in the reasonableness of things"—a belief that translates into a conviction that there simply must be a connection between theory and practice. Miller's "swerve" is a strong testimony to the need felt by many to believe that what they do can be justified or explained by a set of principles that stands apart from their practice, by a theory. One cannot argue against that need, nor can one dismiss the narrative of self-discovery it often produces, the narrative in which conversion to a theory leads directly to a revolution in practice. But this is a narrative that belongs properly to a foundationalist hero, to someone who has just discovered a truth above the situational and now returns to implement it; it cannot, without contradiction, be the narrative of an anti-foundationalist hero who can only enact his heroism by refusing to take either comfort or method from his creed.

It is a hard move to make or not to make, because it brings so little immediate satisfaction and leaves the would-be theorist with so little to do. After having announced that foundationalist epistemology "lies in ruins" Scholes asks, "what do we do in response to this situation?" and rehearses two alternative courses of action: "either we can assume that our practice has nothing to do with theory, or we can make the opposite assumption and try to use the new developments in . . . post-structuralist theory as the basis of a *new practice* in the teaching of composition" (Scholes, 133). Since this is only page five of a twenty-page essay, we know in advance which alternative Scholes will choose, and by choosing it he gives himself the incalculable advantage of having something to say and something to sell. I have had a lot to say, but I have nothing to sell, except the not-very-helpful news, if it is news, that practice has nothing to do with theory, at least in the sense of being enabled and justified by theory. This leaves me and you only a few worn and familiar bromides: practice makes perfect, you learn to write by writing, you must build on what you already know; but anti-foundationalism tells us that these bromides are enough, tells us that as situated beings our practice *can* make perfect, and that we already know more than we think. Perhaps I should apologize for taking up so much of your time in return for so small a yield; but the smallness of the yield has been my point. It is also the point of anti-foundationalism, which offers you nothing but the assurance that what it is unable to give you—knowledge, goals, purposes, strategies—is what you already have. And come to think of it, that may be an offer you can't refuse.

Bibliography

Bizzel, Patricia. "Cognition, Convention, and Certainty: What We Need to Know about Writing." *Pretext* 3, no. 3 (1982).

Bruffee, Kenneth. "Liberal Education and the Social Justification of Belief." *Liberal Education* 68, no. 2 (1982).

Chomsky, Noam. *Aspects of the Theory of Syntax.* Cambridge: Harvard University Press, 1965.

Derrida, Jacques. *Of Grammatology.* Baltimore: Johns Hopkins University Press, 1976.

Hairston, Maxine. "The Winds of Change: Thomas Kuhn and the Revolution in the Teaching of Writing." *College Composition and Communication* 32, no. 1 (February 1982).

Hirsch, E. D. "Reading, Writing, and Cultural Literacy." In *Composition and Literature*. Edited by W. B. Horner. Chicago: University of Chicago Press, 1983

Lanham, Richard. "One, Two, Three." In *Composition and Literature*.

Miller, J. Hillis. "Composition and Decomposition: Deconstruction and the Teaching of Writing." In *Composition and Literature*.

Reither, James A. "Some Ideas of Michael Polanyi and Some Implications for Teaching Writing." *Pretext* 2 (1981).

Scheffler, Israel. *Science and Subjectivity*. Indianapolis: Bobbs-Merrill, 1967.

Scholes, Robert. *Textual Power: Literary Theory and the Teaching of English*. New Haven: Yale University Press, 1985.

Interview with
Stanley Fish

Stanley Fish's essay "Consequences" is a part of a conversation that began with the publication of "Against Theory" by Steven Knapp and Walter Michaels in the summer 1982 issue of *Critical Inquiry.* Recently the responses to that essay, including Fish's, were reprinted in a volume edited by W. J. T. Mitchell entitled *Against Theory* (Chicago: University of Chicago Press, 1985). When Fish agreed to participate in the critical theory seminar at Purdue University, he granted the directors of the seminar an informal interview about the problems generated by the arguments of his essay. The provocative stance assumed in the essay points to important problems in theory and criticism which continue to invest the total spectrum of theoretical discourse, most centrally those theorists who find it necessary to engage in the highly problematic arena of metatheory.

What follows here is an interview, unplanned, undisciplined, and unfocused. Three of the interviewers were staff members at Purdue: Dorothy Leland of the Philosophy Department; Virgil Lokke of the English Department; and Peter Hühn, a visiting professor from the University of Hamburg, assigned to the Purdue English Department. Brooke Horvath and Mark Zamierowski were graduate students in English and philosophy at Purdue. The text of the interview has been edited in the sense that some wordiness has been reduced, along with some redundancies and ventures into fragments of incoherence, syntactical and otherwise. The edited text does not aim to be a perfect rendition of every utterance, a graphic duplication. This transcript remains, however, a reasonably faithful reproduction of continuous portions of a much longer discussion which Fish generously granted us.

▼

LOKKE: I have a question concerning your rhetorical or definitional strategy, about the kind of definitional strategy which set up an either-or: theory is either this or it's nothing.

FISH: Or everything.

LOKKE: Or everything. Now, when you start thinking about the various definitions of theory, the range of . . .

Fish: Uses of the word . . .

Lokke: It's been a tissue of equivocations from the word *go.* I'm wondering if maybe this is a factor in the definitional strategy you deploy. Does "theory" function like a pivot word in your discourse, like *pharmakon,* almost . . .

Fish: You mean the Derridean thing? No, not actually.

Lokke: Well, that's what I wanted to . . .

Fish: No no no no. Look, it seems to me that although it's quite true that the word *theory* has had many uses, and has been used in many ways, in the context that I'm addressing (the claims and counterclaims, the fears and hopes attached to the notion of theory in literary studies), it's proper to draw the line as I've drawn it. When in *Structuralist Poetics* Culler said that what we need theory for is to move to a level other than the level of interpretation, he was endorsing a vision of theory in which it was very important that the activity *be on a wholly other* plane than the plane which he felt was bankrupt. For him and for many others, the whole idea of theory was to escape from the endless sequence of interpretations and capture something that could be universal in the Chomskian sense.

Lokke: But there is also a thrust in "Consequences" which says, "My definition is a correct definition of theory." Isn't there a problem about what authorizes the correctness of that definition?

Fish: It's correct in that people who engage in theoretical projects have as their goals and therefore as their claims the content of the definition that I offer; it's correct in that sense. It's also correct in the sense that if they didn't have those goals and those claims, they themselves would no longer want to engage in the activity. I think that these essays on the consequences of theory have exactly the feeling of the essays on stylistics in *Is There a Text in This Class?* in which I show what it is that the stylisticians want: they want to escape from interpretation into a formal algorithmic dream. Now, I'm not saying that that's what theory means in science; I'm not saying that that's what theory means in any other discipline (it *is* what theory means in law, but that's another matter). The justification for writing about theory in this way is to be found in the attitudes which have crystalized around it in the *literary* academy, which are, on the one hand, *theory fear* and, on the other hand, *theory hope.* That is, on the one hand those who think that theory will open the floodgates to anarchy, and on the other those who think that theory will take us forward to Utopia or backward to Eden. And I'm saying that both are wrong, and wrong for the same reasons, because they both think in different ways that theory is foundational. The anti-foundationalists who indulge in theory hope finally think theory is as foundational as the foundationalists do; it's just that their foundation has to be built after everything else has been torn down.

LELAND: It seems to me that some of the objections to your view that theory has no consequences for practice are linked not just to your definition of theory but also to your understanding of what counts as a practical consequence. Sometimes what people want to know when they ask about the consequences for practice of a theory is this: is the theoretical position, on the whole, consistent with my critical practice? The legitimacy of this sort of concern about practical consequences is brought out quite nicely in *Is There a Text in This Class?* when you argue that, yes, it is consistent with the anti-foundationalist stance for one to say in critical practice that a certain reading of a text is unacceptable. This is one sort of notion of "consequence" that concerns many of us. One wants to know: if I adopt this theory, what warrants do I have for making the kinds of claims I want to make in the conduct of my critical practice?

FISH: The judgment that a reading of a text is unacceptable is made from within a perspective that cannot be examined because it is the very ground of any examination that might be made. Anti-foundationalism tells us that all perspectives rest on an unstable (because historically constituted) base; but to have learned that lesson is not to have destabilized any perspective in *particular*; and it is in particular perspectives that we assert and judge. Let's say *I* think that what I'm doing when I produce a reading of Herbert or Bacon or somebody is proceeding on a specific set of assumptions, but in fact, from someone else's point of view, I'm not proceeding within *those* assumptions at all. "So what?" The dispute between us would be about the correct *account* of my practice, not about the correctness of the practice. It's often assumed that if you do something, and also have a theory and account of what you do, the theory and account must be in some matching relationship to the activity. And I say "no." When you do something, you're doing something, and when you give an account, you give an account (which is also doing something). They're two different games, and they don't have any relationship to one another whatsoever.

LELAND: You're right, they *may* have no relationship whatsoever. On the other hand, I think that some people want to know about the implications of a particular theoretical stance because they want to know if they can "live with it." For example, anti-foundationalism raises questions about the authority of one's claims. It raises these questions because, initially, anti-foundationalism has, or seems to have, for people the kind of "theory fear" you have . . .

FISH: Yes, it seems to lead to relativism or paralysis.

LELAND: But when they begin to explore the implications of that theory, they understand that anti-foundationalism doesn't have that as, let's say, a practical epistemic consequence at all. And when they ask about it in this kind of context, when they ask about the consequences of theory for their mundane literary critical activities, that's the kind of thing they're wanting to explore. They want to know things like, What are the practical ramifications or consequences of conducting critical practice in conformity with anti-foundationalist theory? On your account of these consequences, once they fully understand the theory, once they understand that within any given interpretive community there are criteria for what counts as an acceptable reading and what does not, then they also understand that they can, in good faith, go ahead and tell their students, "Nope, that's an unacceptable reading."

FISH: Absolutely right, that's right. So that the problems that are raised by anti-foundationalism when its arguments are first heard are problems that should be dissolved once it is understood that it does not offer itself as a new method. In the place of the rage for methodology that it has dispossessed, its lesson is neither one of, as I put it today, a brave new world nor of a world where you can do anything you like. It's very hard for people to understand this, I've found. I must say, the "Consequences" essay that we discussed in part today is the least liked essay I've every written. Nobody likes it. I have suspicions about my mother. One of the things that people didn't understand about the essay is that the smallness of its point *is* its point. The determined unwillingness of the essay to claim for itself any more than it will claim for theory: that is its point. I like to think of it as subtle; someone else will think of it as empty. But this kind of argument, to my knowledge, hasn't been made before.

LELAND: Part of the problem I had with the essay concerns the way in which you set up the issues. You want to claim that theory has no consequences, but your arguments pertain to only a limited, although important, notion of theory. So, to make the whole thing work, other (and perhaps more plausible) notions of theory are eliminated. When I read the essay, I thought "Well, okay, here's a whole different notion of what theory is and does that he's going to throw out," and it was never clear to me why, except for the fact that each failed to meet the criteria of what counts as a theory laid out by Hirsch and others. The first part of the essay was very clear. It was clear to me that you were criticizing a specific conception of theory—the Chomsky model—and I could see the grounds upon which you wished to claim that this sort of theory doesn't have the methodological consequences it purports to have. But then, when you began to get into other notions of theory . . .

FISH: Which other notions?

LELAND: Well, the notions of theory you referred to when you talked about what some people would like to call theory . . .

FISH: Yes, generalizations from empirical data or beliefs of a certain sort. Again, I'm always willing to say, as I do again and again, that if you want to call generalization "theory," fine, but in calling generalization "theory," you will have in effect cut the ground out from under the strong theory claims (that theory is special) in which theorists themselves have so much of an investment.

LOKKE: That introduces a problem, though. Holding up this strategic limitation, this exclusive focus on only one definition of theory, theory as an algorithmic machine, since it runs counter to much of our experience of or our usage of the term, creates a kind of initial barrier, so that . . .

FISH: Right, I agree with you. The fact that people use theory in all kinds of ways is a fact. But in relation to the point that I'm making, it's important only when I get to the end and show that all of those ways, except for this way, take away the claims of theory to be special. Now, that's what I'm trying to do, too. So in effect all I'm saying is "Look, theory is used in a lot of ways, and used, sometimes, as if it were more or less equivalent to belief or assumptions or generalizations. But once you think of theory in that way, it's lost its magic."

LELAND: Special in what senses?

FISH: Special in the senses that people think it's special!

LELAND: Why? What are some of their reasons for thinking it's special?

FISH: They think it's special for the Culler reasons, they think it's special for political reasons; they think that theory is an adjunct to the achievement of critical self-reflexivity and self-consciousness; they think that theory—and this is from the Frankfurt school—is the way to see clearly the constraints that fetter human thought. There's lots of reasons why they want to put theory in a special position, and it's only because they do that they get so mad at this essay. If I were writing an essay and saying, "You know, there's nothing very special about mustard," no one would get excited. People have an investment in the specialness of theory. That's what this is an attack on.

ZAMIEROWSKI: What's your investment in showing that it's not special?

FISH: My investment is because my entire project in all of the work I do is an antiformalist project. But it seems to me that the people who want to make theory special want to have a new form or not-so-new form of formalism. That's why, in the paper I read last week, all of the moves that seemed to me to be the wrong moves were making anti-foundationalism into a foundation. The danger is that whatever gains anti-foundationalist insights may be thought to have achieved would be undone once theory is simply put in the place of what has been, if you like, deconstructed. In fact, the claims made for theory are very much like the claims that used to be made for literature, before theory deconstructed literature. It used to be said of literature that it was the kind of activity which is to the side of or above other kinds of activity, that to have literary experience was in some way to be operating on a higher level. It was said of the literary experience that it would help us to reform our ways of thinking, to rise above received opinion. All of those claims are now made for theory. So that's my stake in it.

HORVATH: This may be like asking a gambler to explain how he wins, so you may not want to answer this, but Virgil started out mentioning rhetoric. People who have a great desire to justify their practice have two ways to go, at least. They can find a theory that justifies it, or they can decide that there's no relationship and their practice is justified anyway and go about their business.

FISH: Well . . . well, go on.

HORVATH: It would seem that a lot of people who find your theory attractive find it attractive because they've found a theoretical way of dismissing theory.

FISH: Yes, I agree.

HORVATH: And, in the light of contentions I've heard this week, in the space between your talk and this afternoon, people are walking around saying "Well, the only reason Fish is so persuasive is because he manipulates definitions so skillfully." And Walter Davis says your method of argument involves constructing an outlandish example to make binding points. Anyway, in the light of all this I'm wondering if you could speak a little bit about your work's rhetorical dimensions.

FISH: What was the first part of your question?

HORVATH: The first part of my question tied into the notion of people buying your theory, or finding it persuasive, because it justifies them doing what they do already without having to . . .

FISH: That's an unfortunate consequence of an argument like "Consequences." It's a political consequence. This argument is very much disliked by friends of mine like Jonathan Culler and Barbara Smith because they see it as they see the Knapp and Michaels essay, "Against theory," as giving comfort to know-nothing obscurantism which they associate with the "pre-theoretical" era. People, they complain, will hear this as a way of reinforcing the antitheoretical prejudice that already exists so powerfully in the pages of *The New York Review of Books* and elsewhere, from the pens of conservative thinkers like Roger Shattuck and Helen Vendler. Now, I think that this is a possible consequence of an essay like "Consequences." I think it's an unfortunate consequence, and I don't think it's a dismissable consequence because, given the fact that this essay is going to do political work in the world, one has to worry about the kind of work it is doing. I, of course, think that's a misreading of the essay.

HORVATH: Well, that is how I feel it relates to rhetoric. Your work compared to most other theorists, is so incredibly accessible that it's a happy place to jump in, and one immediately finds exactly what one is looking for, chances are. It almost short-circuits the problem for me; it's like instead of waiting out the storm, you can come right back in from the storm after you've stepped outside.

FISH: Now, I wish you wouldn't go to metaphors; I'm sorry, it doesn't ever help. The seventeenth-century Royal Society was right: they should all be eliminated. The kinds of justifications that people will find for their work are the kind of justifications they always find, justifications which are more or less set or demanded by the context of inquiry, so that, for example, if you are making an argument about genre or about an author, or about a style or so forth, you're answerable to—or in relation to—some notions of evidence, and reasonableness, etc., etc., that are already part of the argumentative or disciplinary context into which you have entered; justification is always something that is demanded of you. But the means of justifying are not exclusively theoretical and indeed are rarely theoretical at all; as someone said this afternoon, there are times when it's a good thing to bring in a theory in defense of a position that you're working out in whatever field it is. But that's only one of many possible modes of justification, and in fact it is not, at least in our field, one that has traditionally been very powerful.

HÜHN: I'd like to ask a question about the relation between this essay and some of the later essays in *Is There a Text in This Class?* You developed there the concept of interpretive communities. That would probably count as a theory. You just said that theories may have or may not have consequences, but in that book, you said that the concept of interpretive communities doesn't have any consequences, cannot have any consequences, for practice. How do these two statements work together?

FISH: Well, because the kinds of consequences that people would expect it to have would be methodological. In other words, is it the case that the theory of interpretive communities, once it was understood, would be the basis for some method of literary interpretation? And my answer to that question is no, because it is itself not a method, but an attempt to account for the ways in which methods emerge, become powerful, do their work, are discarded, and so forth. To know that notions of rightness and wrongness, correctness and incorrectness, relevance and irrelevance are all functions of historically constituted communities, is not to be in possession of knowledge that will change the way that you operate in any one of those communities. In other words, there's no relationship between giving an account of the way interpretation is done and doing an interpretation. Once you start to do an interpretation, you're once again back in the game of doing interpretation; giving accounts of interpretations is one activity, doing interpretations is another. It seems to a lot of people that they should be intimately related, and my thesis is that they're not.

HÜHN: But they might have an impact upon an interpretive community in such a way that people, if they accepted this theory, would no longer appeal to the text, nor to the reader, but to the interpretive community explicitly.

FISH: Not at all. Look, when I go back into the classroom to teach Milton, I point to the text. Now, when I'm a theorist, I know (*know*: it's a very interesting word) that the text I'm pointing to is a consequence of just the kind of interpretive act I am then performing. But what relationship has that knowledge to what appears so indisputable to me when I open up my Milton? No relationship whatsoever. The fact that I know, in some theoretical corner of my mind, that the text that is so palpable to me now is so because of a whole succession of historical conventions and interpretivist events doesn't make it any less palpable. Now that may sound bizarre, but if you think about it for a moment, it isn't bizarre. When you pick up Milton, or Fish, or anybody, and start to read, it isn't the case that, as you do it, all of the fancy theoretical accounts of what you're doing are in any way interfering with or affecting what you're doing. That's the same mistake as thinking that, when you're not doing philosophy in a formal sense, everything that you're doing is nevertheless a disguised and probably a debased version of philosophy.

LOKKE: O.K. This poses another question. Now suppose, when you're doing philosophy, you're simply abiding by a series of generic conventions. And when you're doing literary criticism, you're abiding by a series of conventions, and when you're doing theory, you have another set of conventions.

FISH: More or less like philosophy.

LOKKE: More or less like philosophy. Now, one can describe these basically rhetorical conventions, and sometimes they overlap and sometimes they're discrete. In each case, the generation of these conventions is a kind of practice. But the question, then, is: if you have something like the generation of an interpreting machine, like a theory machine, as you generate, as you create that textual, theoretical machine which is going to cut out and define boundaries, you still have descriptive differences between these different conventions, so that you have a clear-cut boundary between one convention with respect to theoretical analytics and other conventions which articulate texts and practices of other kinds. Can any idea then provide a principle of differentiation among these sets of conventions, for example, a difference between the general and the local?

FISH: There's no difference between the general and the local. See, the mistake is to think that theory is general. Theory is just local, it's just a local kind of activity; it's like eating pizza, or going to the bathroom; the mistake always is to think that it has a privileged relationship to other activities. As soon as you get rid of that notion . . .

LOKKE: What I was wondering about concerns the boundary lines that are drawn between these various articulations and the boundary that's being drawn within a special set . . .

FISH: Well, look; the boundaries are being drawn, but they could be challenged. It's an empirical question, as, in fact, all questions are empirical questions. I'm saying something like the following:

when you do philosophy and/or literary theory, there is a certain set of concerns, ways of arguing, stakes that are involved, known and recognized problems, legitimate and illegitimate formulations, and so forth. When you go to do literary criticism, there is also such a set. The question is, What's the relationship between the two? The answer that theory or some theorists want to give is that this first kind of activity has a governing or masterlike relationship to the second. And my entire effort is to deny that. But also to acknowledge the power of that claim as a political fact which has had a lot of consequences. More people are interested in theory than in analyses of seventeenth-century religious lyric poetry because they think that theory is going to help them to do everything, whereas an analysis of seventeenth-century religious poetry, presumably if it helps them at all, would just help them to better understand seventeenth-century religious poetry; they think that theory is a discourse of such a general kind that if you get your theoretical arguments right, you empower or enable yourself when you then descend to the mundane, quotidian business of explicating "Sunday Morning" or some other poem.

HORVATH: Just from personal experience, the one direct consequence theory had on my practice at one time was to make me so incredibly self-conscious that I couldn't DO it. For example, I got off on a tangent a few years ago, reading theories of paragraph development and what makes a paragraph and things like that—of course, they were little machines but . . .

ZAMIEROWSKI: You mean like Christiansen?

HORVATH: Christiansen, and Rogers, and people that—well, I apologize for this. But I did it. And the point is that I read so much of it, that when I was writing completely unrelated essays and things like that, I kept looking at these things that—you know, I was marking off these paragraphs, and starting to doubt my reasons for doing that, and it became a big problem till I finally flushed all that stuff out of my mind, and that seems to be one direct consequence that you have from . . .

FISH: But you don't have to flush it out of your mind if you think of it in itself as a separate area of interest. The only reason it was messing your mind up is because you kept thinking; you would stop what you were doing and say, "Well, why am I doing this? What are the epistemological foundations of my activity, or as the post-structuralists put it, 'What is the status of my discourse?'" and so forth and so on. Anyone who would ask that question now should be taken out and shot immediately.

HORVATH: I just asked the one question.

FISH: It's because you were taught, or felt, somehow, that if you were steeped in the theory of the paragraph, surely when you actually sit down to write one of the little buggers, the theoretical discussion should help you. Instead (as you report), you're paralyzed.

HÜHN: While I agree that this could be the effect, is it not also possible that someone does practical criticism and tries to reflect on this, then tries to modify his own practice by thinking about it—by trying to foreground the principles, solve the principles, some of the premises involved?

FISH: Give me an example.

HÜHN: If you analyze a poem, for instance, you can try and observe yourself, what you do, and then can modify that and make it explicit to yourself, in order to bring yourself forward. Isn't that possible? Not excluded?

FISH: Well, yes and no. I mean, in general, of course, it's not true; that is, you can't interrogate your own practice in order to get some kind of distance on it. The interrogation itself would occur within some assumption of what the practice was. So that the self-consciousness, the distance that you might get on some of your practice would, in fact, be a self-consciousness or distance only within a part of the practice that was, at that time, not being examined, because it would be the unexamined ground, or background, within which everything was occurring. It's always possible to return to the category of beliefs, to put some of your beliefs on the table, but only because the beliefs that are in fact legitimizing the self-conscious ones as beliefs are not on the table. You can't take apart every plank.

HÜHN: But you can take apart any single one—as long as you leave the others unobserved for the time.

LELAND: Some people would argue that some of those planks are so deeply embedded in the way in which one sees the world . . .

FISH: Absolutely right.

LELAND: . . . you could never get at them.

ZAMIEROWSKI: I have a question which relates to Brooke's point that you do seem to get a lot of rhetorical, polemical—and maybe you'd call it "heuristic"—mileage out of setting up binaries. What do you call this? You said this afternoon that you don't like middle positions; that they're not interesting.

FISH: That's right.

ZAMIEROWSKI: And there are three binaries that come readily to my mind: formalism/antiformalism, foundationalism/anti-foundationalism, professionalism/antiprofessionalism.

FISH: That's right.

ZAMIEROWSKI: And my concern is to see how you see those three sets of binaries as a consistent move within your work.

FISH: I think they all line up perfectly. That is, all of these binaries are slightly different but finally not very different ways of asserting the primacy of something that stands apart from history, rhetoric, the marketplace, the world of business, politics, interest, etc. It's against that assertion that I'm continually arguing; it's a kind of search-and-destroy mission in which I find or at least claim to be able to find again and again that people have slipped back into essentialism, foundationalism, antiprofessionalism, and formalism.

ZAMIEROWSKI: But there's another twist to this.

FISH: Especially in the essay called "Anti-foundationalism." I argue then that slipping back is not something one can avoid because one part of the thesis that everyone is situated is that to be situated is not to have a distance on one's convictions. We are all, in some sense, necessarily foundationalists, formalists, and antiprofessionalists. The essay on antiprofessionalism makes the point at the end that antiprofessionalism is necessary to professionalism. In fact, I'd say that antiprofessionalism is professionalism in its purest form. Because what antiprofessionalism IS is the ideology of professionals; that is, the ideology of advancement by merit and not by interest. Professionalism and antiprofessionalism is, in a way, an emblem of the human condition. The human condition is, as I see it, always to be embedded in a context of historical flux and change—and always, at each and every moment, to be firmly persuaded of the ahistoricity, or the essentiality, or the foundationality of one's present beliefs and convictions. That's what I meant last week when I said that I want to make a distinction between living BY anti-foundationalism, and living it OUT. You can't live BY it; you can't take it around and then have it alter what you're going to do. But we're all living it OUT. Which means that we're all simultaneously and irredeemably foundationalists. This is not unlike what Derrida says in *Of Grammatology*:

LOKKE: With Derrida, it's implicit in the nature of language itself that you cannot escape being logocentric any more than . . .

FISH: Any more than you can *make* your logocentrism work.

LOKKE: That's right. And the opposite goal, of total dispersion, of—

FISH: Yes, total dispersion is the dream of one branch of post-structuralism. Some of de Man's followers *court* dispersion.

LOKKE: I'm not sure that makes any sense.

FISH: They want to escape assertion. They hate totalization, hate closure. So they keep trying to make texts leak. They want slippage, and leakage, and sometimes shrinkage.

LELAND: Indeterminacy?

FISH: They want indeterminacy, and I'm here to say that there's no such thing as indeterminacy. There's no such thing as indeterminacy in the sense of that wonderful polysemous vision that Roland Barthes calls up in the first ten pages or so of *S/Z*, where he said: "What we want is a plural text which you can enter from any place" and so forth and so on, where there's no beginning and no end and no middle. All of which is an old theological concept.

LELAND: And it's also a dream of total liberation from any kind of conceptual . . .

FISH: Absolutely. So that the dream—the desire for dispersion—is the desire for escape from the old-fashioned fascistic concept of closure. I like fascistic concepts myself. All my tendencies are totalitarian.

LOKKE: I want to be scattered all over the ocean. (Laughter.) But really, Derrida's point is that you cannot even articulate diffusion or dispersion without being logocentric.

FISH: Absolutely, absolutely.

LOKKE: But this poses another kind of problem in the argument. On the one hand, one needs logocentrism or whatever term you want to use. On the other hand, you need the other. But every time you do an either-or, you're over on one side. Now, if you start an either-or-or-or-or-or, you're over on the other side. But you look at texts in one sense in the either-or aspect, but you've got to inspect them also from the possibility of the or-or-or-or sense.

FISH: Yes and no, depending on what kind of exercises you're performing. What I want to say is that the or-or-or-or exercise is one kind of thing; but when the question is put to you, What do you think happened? that's another kind of thing. The other point is this: you always have an answer of the other kind. I mean, I may have a very highly developed historically contextual notion of why Milton studies have taken the shape they do, and, as I said last week, in that contextual history, I myself as a person who wrote a book in 1967, have a small part. But, if I'm in my class, and someone says to me, "What do *you* think about this line or passage in *Paradise Lost?*" I just tell them, and you always have an answer to that question even though, when you're doing what we might call metacriticism, your obligation is *not* to give an answer to that question. But metacriticism is not what we do all the time, and it is not even something we can do for very long. One of the promises that deconstructionists seem to hold out is that you can keep on doing it forever. But you CAN'T keep on doing it forever, because it's only one move. Now, it's a very powerful move, but being only one move, its power will bear only so many repetitions. How many times can you demonstrate that the very nexus or node which enables a discourse has been suppressed by its rhetoric? I think it's a very powerful thing to demonstrate, but after you've demonstrated it about forty-five times—taken it from Paris to New Haven to Topeka—then you begin to find that your audience is running out on you. And you decide to go to the north-west corner of Montana, and you get there, and they're waving copies of various Parisian journals at you, and you know the game is UP! You've got to find something else to do. Everybody knows about dissemination and the supplement, you just can't RETAIL the stuff anymore. So you have to find new stuff to retail.

HÜHN: I wonder about the interpretive strategies in communities in your position: wouldn't one natural consequence of that position be to analyze how the interpretive community and interpretive strategies are conditions that serve in powerful social situations? Would that be a natural extension of . . .

FISH: Yes, that would be a project that a person could follow; in fact, there are people who are doing this kind of work now. But unfortunately, at least from my perspective, the people who are doing it most vigorously are doing it from a narrow political basis; there is this group called GRIP, a group for research into professionalism in institutions; its members are putting out a series of reports, GRIP reports, in which they are analyzing precisely the conditions of persuasiveness and power and influence in the profession and in all professions, but mostly in the literary profession. Unfortunately, from my point of view, their assumption is that what they are uncovering is a record of horror, betrayal, and hegemonic imposition on innocent people. What they're continually discovering is power relations, and what they're continually saying as they discover them is: "Oh, my God, how awful that there are such things as power relations." Even though they're continually citing Foucault as a source, they ignore the fact that Foucault argues against a view of power as something which is located only in one group within a society. But these people do very interesting work, up to the point in which they turn on their "Oh my God isn't this awful!" machine. They do things, for example, like study how it is that there came to be departments of American studies in American academies. The crucial move turns out to be—I remember this study because I read it a couple of weeks ago—the crucial move turns out to be when the journal, *American Quarterly*, was moved from Minnesota to the University of Pennsylvania because Robert Spiller, and Americanists at the University of Pennsylvania, got some foundation—I don't remember what it was—to support it. This is a wonderful Foucauldian point: that simple bureaucratic change, in effect, set the strategy and the content of American studies for a long time. Other people are doing investigations of the appearance of anthologies and what is in anthologies, and how they work, and where they were adopted and why, and who did them, and whose pupils did them, and so on.

LELAND: This is going back to old stuff, but it relates, in a way, to how disciplines of knowledge get set up. Would you still be willing to accept the dichotomy between persuasion and demonstration? Would you . . .

FISH: Well, it wasn't a dichotomy; what I was saying especially in the last few pages of the book—in fact I do say it in the last paragraph—is that persuasion and demonstration, although they're opposed, are necessarily interrelated in the following way: something that is felt to be a powerful demonstration is felt to be so only as a consequence of an act of persuasion, which has been for so long in force, that it isn't felt as an act of persuasion any more but as one of those pieces of firm foundation from which one can reason or perceive. Although I want to say that everything is persuasion, I also want to say that, as an experienced fact, demonstration is a consequence of extraordinarily successful acts of persuasion. I only separate persuasion and demonstration, finally, to show the impossibility of separating them—to show that every act of persuasion has the goal of becoming the basis finally of some method of demonstration.

LELAND: When I read that material, I guess I thought that you were holding up persuasion and demonstration as two competing models of critical activity. This worried me because I thought, "While a model of persuasion applies when we are talking about establishing the interpretive criteria of the community, when we engage in critical activity within a given interpretive community, we're primarily engaged in demonstration."

FISH: Absolutely; I couldn't agree with you more because—and to say that of course is to show once again how the charge of relativism doesn't really follow—because the strong assertion is ex-

actly as you put it, that within any community demonstration is the
name of the activity that you are performing, so that yesterday, when
I was teaching *Paradise Lost*, I was busily saying "Well, look, this is
what's going on here, and the reason is because you see this and you
see that, and, as we know, if you have this, then it must be the case
that . . . ," and so forth and so on. As you can tell from the way I
talk, there's no one more committed to demonstrative modes of
thinking and reasoning that I am—which seems to some people to
be a paradox and a contradiction. But it doesn't seem so to me.

LELAND: Part of the problem may lie in a confusion over two
different senses of the notion of interpretation—interpretation understood as a shared background of beliefs and practices, and interpretation understood as an individual activity—something I do which
presupposes this background but which isn't, or doesn't belong to,
the background itself.

FISH: That's right.

LELAND: Because it really struck me, and it's been a long
time, when I read "What Makes an Interpretation Acceptable?"—
what struck me was your discussion of an imaginary Eskimo reading
"A Rose for Emily" and your claim that one circumstance that would
establish this reading as acceptable would be the discovery of a letter
in which Faulkner confesses to fantasies about being an Eskimo
changeling. The discovery of the letter would be the discovery of a
relevant fact. It would be accepted as a piece of evidence for the
Eskimo reading, and it would be accepted as such because it conforms to accepted criteria for what counts as evidence for a reading.
The important point is: given the criteria, the acceptability of the
reading is open to demonstration by appealing to appropriate facts.

FISH: Yes, yes, you're absolutely right.

LELAND: But, for me the problem was that you also wanted
to say things like "The interpretation creates the facts." This causes
difficulties if we take "interpretation" to mean some particular reading. The Eskimo reading doesn't create the facts which would make
it acceptable. Rather, these facts are something we can imagine discovering. We can do this because we are members of the appropriate
interpretive community—we're privy to its standards of evidence,
procedures of verification, etc. In an important sense, the "interpretation" of the interpretive community, its framework of intelligibility,
relevance, and relation doesn't create the facts either. Instead, this
framework functions as a prior condition for discovering . . .

FISH: A fact.

LELAND: A fact.

FISH: And seeing a fact, and also for labeling other modes of discovery as aberrant modes, which then could have at some future time their day. It's like—it's a crapshoot, really. In the world of business someone is always saying "Well, I could have been in on the ground floor of Pepsi-Cola in 1917, you know; boy, was I stupid!" He wasn't stupid! It just wasn't possible in 1917 to determine what was the right way to go. The right way to go has, in fact, now simply become obvious because of events that followed. Now that we're all historians of our present activity, the answer has become obvious; the right thing to have done was X, Y, Z, and why did I waste those three and a half years doing A, B, C? I'm now in fact involved in a very hard situation where I'm trying to decide—my wife and I are trying to decide—whether we should move to a new university. And I know that in four or five years it's going to be clear to me what I should have done. But I also know that it's not going to become clear to me now, and I'm just going to have to take some kind of step, and in four or five years I will have constructed a story in which it turns out that it was the right move.

ZAMIEROWSKI: I get a sense that there's a striking similarity between what you are doing in recent work and what Lyotard is doing in *The Postmodern Condition*, beginning with the idea of narrative pragmatics or of disturbing any kinds of metanarrative or some kind of stable formation, as well as the idea of trying to fumble around for some kind of concept of what justice means in the postmodern condition. I was wondering how you see, or if you bother to consider, your own position *vis à vis* either post-structuralists or an investigation into postmodernism, such as Lyotard's.

FISH: Well—not the latter. The whole modernism/postmodernism context of discussion simply mystifies me because I don't have any handle on any of your terms. I've been looking at *Innovation-Renovation*, edited by Ihab Hassan and Sally Hassan, that has Lyotard and a bunch of others debating this issue, and I read it diligently, but with an increasing sense of how distant I am from its concerns, so I'll have to pass on that one. But as for the relationship between the work I do and post-structuralism, I see it as very close, in one sense, and yet, when I go and give talks, orthodox post-structuralists often get fairly upset at what I do. And that's because, I think, many of them have become apostles of dispersion in the way in which you were talking about earlier, Virgil, and they see me, quite rightly, as someone who isn't interested in dispersion but is after all going to go out and happily perform acts of closure, acts of "authoritarian" interpretive stipulation. In general, I find myself very sympathetic to the kind of arguments and perspectives of post-structuralism, as I understand it, which includes the Derrida of *Of Grammatology* and surrounding essays; Foucault, especially in central chapters in *History of Sexuality* and *The Archeology of Knowledge, The Order of Things* and even parts of *Discipline and Punish* (which seems to me a more troubled text); as well as the Roland Barthes of *S/Z* and some of the essays in the *Collected Essays,* "Science of Literature" and "History of Literature," etc. I find all of that very sympathetic; but I also seem . . . I myself make connections—strong connections, maybe stronger than Derrida, Foucault or Barthes would have wanted to—between post-structuralist thinking and Anglo-American thinking of the kind produced by Rorty, by Kuhn, by a group of sociologists called ethnomethodologists and others working in the sociology of knowledge, i.e., people who are doing the things that I spoke of today: studies of laboratory life, which elaborate and uncover the rhetorical and interpretive processes that are continually constituting the object of investigation. For me, post-structuralism and neo-pragmatism go together. What distinguishes me somewhat from many post-structuralists is my writing style. I will say, with all of the immodesty that I can muster, that I'm one of the best writers going. I'm not indulging here in any Philistine dismissal of a style like Derrida's, because I think Derrida's style works, and I think it's absolutely brilliant, and I love to teach it; but as a stylist in the English sense, that is, the sense that has been given to us by Dryden and really not very much changed since then, I think I'm the best stylist in Anglo-American literary studies. And for that, I gain something and I lose something. We've talked about this before. What I gain is accessibility: people feel "I can read this." But what I, of course, lose is everything one might gain if people said, "I can't read it. He's so difficult; he's so DEEP!" I can easily be seen as SHALLOW, because my prose goes so limpidly from sentence to sentence. I work like hell at it, as we all do.

LOKKE: But you lose something else. You create the illusion that there are no barriers to entry.

FISH: Yes, that's true.

LOKKE: And that means that you're going to get the kind of results—you're going to get a certain kind of misunderstanding.

FISH: Well, I get my kind of misunderstanding, Derrida gets his, but the thing about me is that my style is pedagogical. I'm a pedagogue. I'm a teacher. I hate sabbaticals. I don't know what to do. I run around and go out in the street and grab people: "You want to hear about interpretation?" I just HAVE to have someone to teach, to explain things to. And that's exactly what my writing style is geared to. It's always seemed incredible to me that an institution, for some reason, has paid me to realize my heart's desire, which is to lock people into a room so that they can't get out and have no choice but to listen to me! (General laughter.)

Bottom's One-Man Show

René Girard

In *A Midsummer Night's Dream*, two groups of human beings spend the night in the wood. The first consists of four unhappy lovers who tear each other apart, the second of some local craftsmen who prepare a play for the celebration of Theseus's wedding.

Wretched as it is, their stage adaptation of *Pyramus and Thisby* remains beyond the capacities of these illiterate amateurs. But their passion for the theater is intense, especially in the case of Bottom, a born actor with an enormous appetite for impersonation.

At the craftsmen's first meeting—in act 1, scene 2—Quince, the director, distributes the various roles. Bottom gets asked first. He will play the leading man, Pyramus. He wishes it had been "a tyrant," but it is a lover and a lover will do. Bottom feigns indifference, but he is so eager to act, so excited by the prospect, that he will grab any role. Speaking compulsively, he announces that he will "move storms." Eager to stop this ranting, Quince turns to Flute and asks him to play Thisby.

Flute feels awkward at the thought of a woman's role. He tries to excuse himself on the ground that he has "a beard coming." Bottom begs Quince to let him have the role of Thisby. He will not give up playing Pyramus; yet he wants the other role as well, and immediately, even though he knows nothing of the story, he tries to show what he can do with it:

> And I may hide my face, let me play Thisby
> too. I'll speak in a monstrous little voice. "Thisne!
> Thisne! Ah, Pyramus, my love dear! thy Thisby
> dear, and lady dear!"[1]

99

Quince disagrees. He thinks that the hero and the heroine should be played by different actors:

> "No, no, you must play Pyramus; and,
> Flute, you Thisby."

In order to avoid further trouble, Quince hurriedly proceeds to assign two more roles, Thisby's mother and Pyramus's father, with no interference from Bottom this time, but then comes the turn of the lion. The role goes to Snug, who complains that he is "slow of study" and requests "a written score." You may do it "extempore," Quince replies, "for it is nothing but roaring." To Bottom, this reluctance of the prospective lion is an irresistible temptation and, once again, he asks for the role:

> Let me play the lion too. I will roar, that I
> will do any man's heart good to hear me. I will roar,
> that I will make the Duke say, "Let him roar again;
> let him roar again."

The role leaves little room for interpretation, but Quince is so irritated that he challenges Bottom's understanding of it:

> An you should do it too terribly, you
> would fright the Duchess and the ladies, that
> they would shrike; and that were enough to hang
> us all.

> *All.* That would hang us, every mother's son.

The craftsmen hang on every word of their leader and then always mimic him in a chorus. In the face of unanimous opposition, Bottom makes a hasty retreat. He is too much of a mime not to give an audience what it requests:

> I grant you, friends, if you should fright the
> ladies out of their wits, they would have no more
> discretion but to hang us; but I will aggravate my
> voice so that I will roar you as gently as any suck-
> ing dove; I will roar you and 'twere any nightin-
> gale.

As long as Bottom gets his role, whatever the populace wants, the populace will get. But even if the lion, now, sounds like a night-ingale, it must retain some features of the former beast or it would not be identifiable as such. Bottom is turning it, therefore, into a birdlike lion, a warring conflation of opposites, some kind of monster. Too much mimetic adaptability is seen as unfavorable to the creative imagination. It would seem to stifle it, but beyond a certain threshold—which Bottom is crossing—the two tend to merge. With his most remarkable talent for changing anything into anything else, Bottom's handling of his various roles already resembles the process of mythological metamorphosis. Unlike Alberich of *The Ring*, Bottom has no need of magical contraptions such as the *Tarnhelm*. At the slightest signal from his public, he can transform himself, now into a ferocious dragon, now into the sweetest little nightingale.

An exasperated Quince repeats in no uncertain terms that Bottom will play no part but Pyramus. Next, the question arises of how the moon should be represented, and also the dreadful wall, the famous wall that cruelly separates the two lovers. The solution almost goes without saying. Let an actor impersonate the wall, let an actor impersonate the moon.

Bottom would love to be that moon, Bottom would love to be that wall. To play the beloved as well as the lover does not satisfy his appetite for acting; in addition, he wants to be the obstacle that stands between the two. He and his fellows can passionately embrace even those objects that seem to lie beyond the wildest dreams of impersonation, turning them into an infinite number of theatrical parts. All of these Bottom would like to keep for himself, and even the most insignificant ones he can relinquish only with the sense of a huge personal loss.

Try as he may, Quince will not find a role that does not suit Bottom's talent. *Mimesis* is running wild. Even the slightest hint, now—almost any gesture—can trigger new impersonations. The man reminds us of a suggestible subject in the hands of a clever hypnotist. The only difference is that he needs no hypnotist; he is gifted and mixed up enough to play both roles, the hypnotizer and the hypnotized. He enters into all conceivable and inconceivable roles with such passion that he is losing sight of his own personality.

The first scene with the craftsmen, as well as the first scene with the lovers, takes place in the city, whereas the second takes place in the woods. Each group seems to have some business out there, but the real business is the midsummer night madness.

We can see right away that, in the interval between act 1 and act 3, the bumpkins' excitement has not abated but increased. Bottom is the first to speak, as always, and he finds a way to compel the attention of Quince:

> *Bottom.* There are things in this comedy of Pyramus
> and Thisby that will never please. First, Pyramus
> must draw a sword to kill himself; which the ladies
> cannot abide. How answer you that?

Quince was the one, earlier, who conjured up the specter of the frightened ladies *à propos* of the lion. Bottom cleverly extends this concern to the suicide of Pyramus. He mimics the argument of Quince and wraps himself up in the mantle of the *metteur en scène.* The better to manipulate Quince, he surrenders once again to his hysterical penchant for mimicry and shows us that his talent for impersonation is not limited to theatrical roles. He undermines the authority of Quince by turning himself into a second Quince and a contagious example to everybody else. Quince cannot silence him, this time, without silencing himself.

> *Snout.* By'r lakin, a parlous fear.

> *Starveling.* I believe we must leave the killing out, when all
> is done.

> *Bottom.* Not a whit! I have a device to make all well.
> Write me a prologue, and let the prologue seem to
> say we will do no harm with our swords, and that
> Pyramus is not killed indeed; and for the more bet-
> ter assurance, tell them that I Pyramus am not
> Pyramus, but Bottom the weaver. This will put
> them out of fear.

Once again, of course, the only purpose of Bottom is to monopolize the stage. He wants to be the prologue and the epilogue and every-thing in between.

In his desire to prevent any confusion between a simulated death and a real one, Bottom wants the fictional Pyramus—himself—to emphasize his real identity; but he devises his prologue in such a way as to suggest the opposite of what he means.

The prologue should say: "My name is Bottom and I am merely pretending to be a certain Pyramus whose suicide is feigned"; but Bottom names Pyramus first, in the first person, saying in fact: "I Pyramus" as if it were his real identity and wishing, no doubt, that it were. And then, when his real name, Bottom, finally shows up, it is treated as an actor's part in the title page of a printed play; it is followed by a mention of the man's trade. The prologue says: "Bottom the weaver," which is the way the name appears in the listing of roles at the beginning of *A Midsummer Night's Dream.*

We are listening, we feel, to an actor named Pyramus who has to play a fictional weaver named Bottom, a modest role with which he is not very pleased. Inside the play, this belief is wrong but, from the spectators' standpoint, it makes good sense. We are actually watching a play that includes a fictional weaver named Bottom. It is quite possible that the actor might be named Pyramus.

Bottom contaminates us with his own madness; we share in the general dizziness, but so mildly that not even the most timid ladies can be frightened. It feels like a few bubbles of champagne on an empty stomach.

In order to describe what is going on here, the grayish jargon of "identity crises" and "split personalities" will not do. It may be appropriate to the static condition of the contemporary neurotic, patiently rehashing his various "problems" and the interminable "analysis" of the same, until death do them part. It is ridiculously inadequate here. Bottom's crisis is more tempestuous and *critical* than the neurotic's condition but, unlike that of the psychotic, it will leave no traces. It is temporary, and it will have a resolution. It is also collective. Bottom is only the supreme exemplification of what happens to all his companions.

This crisis is an attenuated or partly ritualized version of the mimetic crisis described in *Violence and the Sacred.*[2] All words, images and gesticulations intended by the craftsmen as a preventive against the imaginary panic of the ladies are really worsening symptoms of that crisis. As they exhibit their mimetic symptoms to one another, they also mimic them, bringing them to fever pitch. The entire scene describes a mimetic contagion of lost identity that affects Bottom most spectacularly but not him alone, as we soon shall see.

The "I Pyramus" is only a portent of things to come. It represents a transitional phase on the road to a collective hallucination similar to the climax of a primitive ritual, because all rituals are the more or less ritualized reenactment of the real crisis that precedes.

Shakespeare is aware that the theater is itself a form of ritual, and—like all rituals—it can go wrong, it can revert to the real mimetic crisis in which it originates. This is what happens with the craftsmen, but only to a certain extent. The comedy will not turn into a tragedy.

A few lines down we have another clue to the rapid disintegration of Bottom's normal handling of reality. Our old friend the lion once again serves as a catalyst. We can surmise that, between the two meetings, this lion has haunted the imagination of the mechanicals. Now even the quiet ones, Snout the tinker and Starveling the tailor, begin to evince panic.

> *Snout.* Will not the ladies be afeard of the lion?

> *Starveling.* I fear it, I promise you.

> *Bottom.* Masters, you ought to consider with your-
> [selves], to bring in (God shield us!) a lion
> among ladies, is a most dreadful thing; for there is
> not a more fearful wild-fowl than your lion living;
> and we ought to look to't.

> *Snout.* Therefore another prologue must tell he is
> not a lion.

> *Bottom.* Nay; you must name his name, and half his
> face must be seen through the lion's neck, and he
> himself must speak through, saying thus, or to the
> same defect: "Ladies," or "Fair ladies, I would wish
> you," or "I would request you," or "I would
> entreat you, not to fear, not to tremble: my life
> for yours. If you think I come hither as a lion, it
> were pity of my life. No! I am no such thing; I am
> a man as other men are"; and there indeed let him
> name his name, and tell them plainly he is Snug the
> joiner.

Just as Bottom imitated Quince a little earlier, now Snout imitates Bottom. His turn has come to emulate Bottom and demand still one more reassuring prologue after the style of his hero. But Bottom does not recognize the idea as his own when he hears it from the mouth of someone else. Great artists do not like to be copied. Just as he had been interrupted by Quince, he now keeps interrupting Snout; he has a brighter idea: a speech by the dumb beast himself. As the actor will "name his name" and fasten himself solidly to his real identity, "half his face must be seen through the lion's neck."

The first metamorphosis of the lion was not scary enough. Now we have a second one. A creature half-man, half-beast is uncannier than a combination of beast and beast, uncannier, *a fortiori*, than the honest-to-goodness lion demanded by the original script. The mere invention of this improved monster sends shivers down the spine of the inventors.

This fragment of a human face surrounded by leonine features looks strikingly like the sort of primitive mask that Shakespeare had probably never seen but that his genius invents almost *ex nihilo*. The playwright's sense of timing is excellent. We have reached the moment when the participants in an orgiastic ritual would put on masks quite similar to the one imagined by Bottom: weird compositions of animal and human features. The inspiration is very much the same because the experience is the same. Bottom and his friends are going through the type of crisis after which rituals are patterned.

Bottom's compulsive impersonations resemble the possessive trance as much as the resulting images resemble primitive masks. The craftsmen live in a culture that does not encourage such phenomena. But perhaps the distant past was different. At one time, the midsummer festival may have been a ritual similar to the orgiastic rituals in ancient and primitive cultures.

Turn-of-the-century anthropologists such as Sir James George Frazer thought that they were the first to rediscover that origin, but, two and three centuries ahead of modern research, Shakespeare already thought along similar if not identical lines. The midsummer festival figures only in the title. The play itself contains one single mention of "the rites of May," and that is all. This inconsistent vagueness does not really matter. All these festivals were similar; any one of them can provide the ritual framework in which the experience of Bottom and the craftsmen can be fitted because they were all generated by the type of mythical genesis that Shakespeare describes.

The possessive trance may closely resemble playacting, but it is an error simply to equate the one with the other, as some researchers such as Michel Leiris have been inclined to do. When genuine, the trance represents a degree of involvement so great that the impersonation becomes involuntary and cannot be stopped at will. Correspondingly, it represents a high degree of self-*dispossession*, higher, no doubt, than what normally happens in the Western theater.

It all happens to Bottom. Shakespeare seems to regard the theater as a mild form of the trance, one that must derive from the "real thing" originally and can revert to it on occasion—with highly predisposed individuals such as Bottom, or when the circumstances are favorable.

All our craftsmen tacitly assume that the weaker sex in their audience—which really means the queen of the Amazons and her attendants—will be extremely prone to panic. Their principal reason for thinking so is that they themselves are on the verge of a panic. It is normal for people in that condition to project it outside of themselves. They detect a threat of imminent panic somewhere in the vicinity and devise hasty measures against it. As they try to implement these measures, they make one another believe that the panic has already arrived, which indeed it has, as soon as everybody believes that it has. Their strategy is the one an infinitely clever man would select if he had joined a group of terrorists with the express intention of triggering a mass panic.

The solicitude for the ladies is a facade behind which the craftsmen can unleash their imaginations and produce more and more horrifying monsters. As the craftsmen try to reassure the hypothetical fears of others, they only succeed in scaring themselves out of their wits, and *there is not the slightest difference between their self-induced but nevertheless objectively real panic,* which is a sociological event occurring in the real world, *and the ritual pattern to which that panic necessarily conforms,* because all ritual originates in some event of this type.

A transitional product of Bottom's "seething brain," the humanlike lion belongs to a phase more advanced than the birdlike lion of the previous phase; it corresponds to an intensification of the crisis, a greater loss of "self-identity." But the final and climactic phase is still to come.

In the second phase, we already have full-fledged monsters—creatures no longer "species-specific," as the modern specialists would say (rather redundantly and mimetically, being threatened themselves with undifferentiation). But the craftsmen do not yet quite *believe* in the reality of their own creations.

Give them one more minute and they do. This is the only difference between the ass-headed Bottom and the shenanigans that precede this not-so-mysterious apparition. To all his friends, Bottom has become a real monster. And we are apprised of the fact in a manner so strikingly suited to the force of the hallucination that we are likely to miss the point entirely.

Shakespeare treats Bottom's amazing *translation* both as if it were "the real thing" and also as if it were a prank that Puck is playing on the bumpkins. But Puck is no one but the spirit of the entire midsummer night. And the progress of its spirit can be traced both in an irrational manner by following the evolution of Puck, which pleases the light-hearted and absent-minded spectators, and in the slightly less transparent manner of our analysis, which does not uncover anything that Shakespeare has not intentionally written into his text. The anthropological genius of the playwright displays itself openly from the beginning to the end of this magnificent text.

The apparition walks upon the stage. The imaginary products of Bottom's "seething brain" have been elevated to the status of "real" characters. This shift in the dramatic handling of the theme expresses the climax of the crisis with such power that it makes it invisible to the average spectator. Even the best critics have yet to understand what their author is really up to.

If the spectator has missed the manner in which the monstrous gradually insinuates itself among the near-hysterical craftsmen, he/she will take Puck, Oberon, Titania, and their cortege of fairies at face value, mistaking them for the heroes and heroines of one more subplot that is just as independent of the other two as these two are, or rather seem to be, of one another.

From the simultaneously structural and genetic standpoint of our "neo-mimetic" criticism, the "translation" of Bottom and the intervention of the "fairies" mark the culmination of the dynamic process triggered by the collective decision to perform a play. It is not a magical irruption, a sudden and inexplicable disturbance in a static situation of bucolic peace among people going peacefully about their business of acting, it is the climax of successive structural transformations that are related to one another in such a way that, ultimately, they must be regarded as a *continuous process*. This precedence of continuity over discontinuity is not a return to a pre-structural perspective.

Out of mimetic sympathy with Bottom, mixed with a good deal of exasperation, the craftsmen all cross the threshold of hallucination simultaneously in act 3, scene 1:

> [*Enter* Puck, *and* Bottom *with an ass's head.*]
> *Bottom.* "If I were fair, Thisby, I were only thine."
> *Quince.* O monstrous! O strange! We are haunted.
> Pray, masters, fly, masters! Help!
> [*Exeunt* Quince, Snug, Flute, Snout, *and* Starveling.]
> . . . .
> *Quince.* Bless thee, Bottom, bless thee! Thou art
> translated.

Quince is first to tip over the brink, and he takes everybody with him; or rather, everybody follows him into the abyss of unreason because everybody imitates him. Until then, Quince had seemed the most clear-headed of the lot; the asinine interruptions of Bottom must have undermined his strength. In a sense, he does not lose his mind: he finally sees with his own eyes the ass-headed monster that keeps persecuting him.

Half the face of an ass can be seen through Bottom's neck. The body remains mostly human, being that of a great lover, but it takes more than a mere Thisby to conquer this Pyramus. It takes the queen of the fairies whom, to a large extent, Bottom himself has become. She talks as wittily as a prologue, but he retains a curious predilection for hay, as well as the immobility of a brick wall, another well-known characteristic of the ass.

If we do not see the mimetic process behind the weird metamorphosis of Bottom, we will have to believe that *someone* rather than something is responsible, and we will have to reinvent Puck, or Robin Goodfellow, the hobgoblin of English folkore, or perhaps Oberon, Titania, etc. They can all be metaphors for the entire process because they all are the products of Bottom's "seething brain."

That is why they reproduce the antics of the craftsmen and of the lovers at their own supernatural level. And since Puck is supposed to plant only a cardboard ass-head upon the real head of Bottom, even the ladies and the critics that would be most offended by any degree of mimetic undifferentiation between violence and the sacred do not have to understand anything and therefore fear nothing.

The habitual reading is that the intervention of Puck and the intersection of the three plots depend on no rationally intelligible sequence. Shakespeare is "playing" in haphazard fashion. Puck provides a welcome break with the trivial realism of the craftsmen, a delightful diversion but no more. The important thing, today, is that the play should make no sense at all. The play must be as senseless as the lovers and the craftsmen imagine their experience to be. It must be the child of a capricious and unmotivated imagination. If we tried to make sense out of it, we would spoil the pleasure of the text.

The chaotic and the discontinuous are present at the dramatic level only, for the spectators who watch the play as naively as the craftsmen and the lovers experience it. There is another rationale for the various incidents that Shakespeare has deliberately inscribed into the play, but he has done so in such a fashion that only a certain type of attention will see it.

When Bottom turns into an ass and marries Titania, the panic that had been brewing for a while reaches ebullition. The same generative force produces the entire world of the fairies that earlier had produced the still-half-believed "translations" and conflations of various beings, the monstrous mixture of a lion and of a man, and the metamorphosis of the lion into a nightingale.

If Bottom could choose one theatrical role and stick to it, he would not lose his mind. One single impersonation would have enough stability and permanence to prevent the generation of monsters. The weaver becomes drunk on a kaleidoscope of impersonations that keeps revolving faster and faster.

He resembles these clowns whose act consists in changing suits so fast that they seem to be wearing the same suit all the time, but it is made up of many colors and shapes all jumbled together. Bottom ends up with a very strange costume, indeed. Maybe it is Joseph's "coat of many colors."

Bottom's roles are too different from each other to be arranged into a harmonious "synthesis," Hegelian or otherwise, and yet Bottom assumes them all almost simultaneously and with such passion each time that he commits himself totally to each one simultaneously.

Inside Bottom, as in the uterus of their mother, there are always a Jacob and an Esau fighting for supremacy, and many other twins as well. Bottom cannot fail to be torn apart, literally shredded by all these totalitarian claims upon his undivided attention. His is the *diasparagmos* of the actor, his mimetic passion.

Beyond a certain threshold, the feverish impersonations of Bottom impinge upon one another as the multiple images in a cinematic film and breed a whole host of monsters. Then the swirl becomes so dizzying that another threshold is reached, and Bottom himself becomes the monster, first in the eyes of his fellows, then in his own eyes as well, mimetically.

As new impersonations keep crowding in, the whole system becomes destabilized, then explodes into fragments that tend to reorganize in weird bits and pieces like a mosaic of broken glass. Bottom is "translated" into a sparkling jumble of fragments from his various roles, with a unifying preponderance of the original ass.

▼

What is the relationship between the two subplots? Can the craftsmen have anything in common with the four mixed-up lovers? The first have gathered to perform a play, the others to love and hate one another. Does their Eros have an affinity for the frantic theatrical impersonations of a half-crazed Bottom?

It certainly does. In order to justify this assertion, I must summarize the argument of an earlier essay about the four lovers.[3]

With the help of Theseus, Hermia's father seeks to prevent his daughter from marrying Lysander. The boy and girl flee to the woods. On their heels comes Demetrius in hot pursuit of Hermia, whom he still loves even though she no longer loves him. On his heels comes Helena in hot pursuit of Demetrius, whom she ardently loves even though he has never loved her.

It seems that the first two lovers have a sound enough reason to flee their Athenian homes. Fleeing one's parents and other oppressive political forces is a comic prop so traditional that it is taken at face value. It is never examined, and yet this time the theme is deceptive in the sense that there is a more convincing cause for the troubles of the lovers. The parental figures are no more responsible for getting the frenzy started than the fairies, a little later, for making it worse.

Even in the case of Lysander and Hermia, "true love" needs no parental or supernatural interference to run into trouble. Shakespeare slyly informs us that, until Lysander appeared upon the scene, Hermia was happy enough to marry Demetrius. Her father's choice was her own choice.

This information is unnecessary to the plot, but it is highly suggestive of an instability among the four lovers that cannot be blamed on the older generation or even on the disruptive influence of the midsummer spirit.

Lysander may well be the original troublemaker. It would be wrong, however, to attach too much importance to him personally, or to anyone else for that matter. In this play, individuals as such do not matter. The traditional critics correctly observed their lack of personality and their interchangeability, but they mistakenly regarded it as a weakness of the play, as something unintended that Shakespeare would have remedied if he had been able to.

In reality, Shakespeare is in complete control of his literary effects, but his goal is the opposite of the only one these traditional critics could conceive, which was the creation of stable character differentiations. Shakespeare wants to show the pressure of fads and fashions inside a group of idle young aristocrats. It can become so intense that it extends to matters of the heart.

Shakespeare portrays what happens to adolescents who read too many romances and choose to live in a world of literary imitation. Taking fictional heroes as models predisposes them to real-life experiments with erotic mimicry, and the results can be simultaneously disastrous and comical. They become a "living theater."

Everybody feels compelled to choose what everybody else has already chosen. The two boys are never in love with the same girl for long, but at any given time they are both in love with the same girl—Hermia first, Helena later. Neither one can desire anything that the other one will not immediately desire as well. Even the girls are carried away in the end by the dominant desire—the one fashionable desire—and compelled to yield to the mimetic pressure of uniformity. This is the reason Helena, at the beginning, seems to desire Hermia even more than Demetrius. The reason is that Hermia is already desired by the two boys; she is the star of the entire show, and Helena feels irresistibly attracted by her success.

All characters do their falling in love according to the falling in love in the vicinity. They remind us of these modern consumers who already have everything and never experience a real need, therefore, but who cannot hear that a product is "popular" or see people standing in line to buy something without rushing themselves to join that line. The longer the line, the more valuable the prize seems at the end of it. But the line can dissolve as quickly as it will re-form behind something else. The queue that forms behind Hermia at the beginning will shift to Helena in the middle of the night for no reason whatever.

Let us listen to the first encounter of Helena and Hermia in act 1, scene 1:

> *Hermia.* God speed fair Helena! whither away?

> *Helena.* Call you me fair? That fair again unsay.
> Demetrius loves your fair, O happy fair!
> Your eyes are lodestars, and your tongue's sweet air
> More tuneable than lark to shepherd's ear
> When wheat is green, when hawthorn buds appear.
> Sickness is catching; O, were favor so,
> [Yours would] I catch, fair Hermia, ere I go;
> My ear should catch your voice, my eye your eye,
> My tongue should catch your tongue's sweet melody.
> Were the world mine, Demetrius being bated,
> The rest I'll give to be to you translated.

The homosexual flavor is undeniable. Shakespeare certainly wanted it there. For this, we cannot pin the blame or the merit—whichever term we choose—upon some authorial "unconscious." The only serious critical question is: why did the author do it? I doubt very much that he wanted to demonstrate the cleverness of Jacques Lacan, or even of Sigmund Freud. I also doubt that he wanted to promote an "alternative life-style." Shakespeare must have had a purpose of his own when he wrote these lines.

There is a passage in *Coriolanus* with an even more unmistakable homosexual flavor, but this time the two characters are male. *Vis-à-vis* Coriolanus, his sworn rival, Aufidius expresses sentiments similar to those of Helena for Hermia.

If you compare the two passages, you will see that the only common feature is the mimetic rivalry of two characters, male or female. The gender makes no difference at all. Quite as ardently as Helena, Aufidius desires something his rival possesses in great abundance, military glory. Aufidius wants the many victories of Coriolanus. Helena wants the many lovers of Hermia, her superior erotic glory. In front of Coriolanus, Aufidius feels like a failure. In front of Hermia, Helena feels like a failure.

A few lines after our passage, Helena is alone and, in a soliloquy, vents her bitterness against her rival. She claims that she is just as pretty as Hermia. Should we conclude that her mood has changed, or that she was a hypocrite in the previous scene? The answers are a little more complicated. Helena's worship of Hermia is more than a polite compliment. It is just as genuine as the hatred of a moment later. Aufidius also feels ambivalent towards Coriolanus.

The mimetic model is worshipped as a model and hated as a rival. The duality is inescapable; desire cannot mimic its friends without turning them into irritating obstacles, but the mimetic lover never seems to understand the self-generated process of his/her own frustration and keeps complaining that someone else is interfering with "true love."

To Helena, Hermia is perceived as a paragon of success, the true goddess of everything a normal girl may wish—elegance, wit, glamor, erotic triumphs . . . How can Hermia fail to be more interesting than either of the boys since she dominates both of them, at least for the time being . . .

The homosexual connotations must be acknowledged but must not blind our critical eyes to the context. Helena's fascination for Hermia is part of a larger story, the story of the mimetic rivalry. In an erotic triangle, the obsession can become so acute that the rival of the same sex tends to supersede the object of the other sex.

Demetrius, the object of Helena's desire, rates only half a line in this passage, which is not much compared to the eleven lines dedicated to Hermia. This type of inbalance gets worse and worse as the mimetic crisis intensifies and the obsession for the rival increases.

Here again, the midsummer night is a description of a deepening crisis.

Beyond a certain threshold of intensity, the veritable object becomes the model. If we conclude that Helena has to *be* a homosexual in the same sense that she is a tall, blonde girl, or Hermia short and a brunette, we freeze solid a relationship that should be kept light and airy. We surrender our wits either to the current pedantry of sexuality or to the former puritanism. The two are equally disastrous for the understanding of what Shakespeare is talking about, which we would all understand intuitively if we were dealing with it in a real-life situation.

A Midsummer Night's Dream is much more like a real-life situation than people with their heads full of nihilistic critical theory will ever realize. The final predominance of the model means that the ultimate goal of mimetic desire is that model's "being." This ontological mirage is a must, of course, in a play that is a veritable encyclopedia on the subject, written by the greatest expert ever:

> Were the world mine, Demetrius being bated,
> The rest I'll give to be to you translated.

The last verse sums up and transcends the erotic poem that we quoted before, in the same sense that the metaphysical dimension sums up and transcends the more physical aspects of mimetic desire.

Those who desire mimetically are really trying to exchange their own despised being against the glorious being of their victorious model. Like Bottom, they seek a total metamorphosis, and ultimately their wish will be granted in the same paradoxical fashion.

How can Helena hope to reach her goal? How can she be *translated* to Hermia? Through imitation, of course: the exchange that follows makes it abundantly clear that the only technique of metaphysical desire is *mimesis:*

> O, teach me how you look, and with what art
> You sway the motion of Demetrius' heart.

We must take this language literally. "Teach me how to impersonate you" is what Helena is asking Hermia. We should not regard this effort at impersonation as a mere consequence of some preexisting desire. We should not regard it only as a cause, either. It is really a circular process in which Hermia's choice of Demetrius, before Lysander's arrival upon the scene, is both a cause and a consequence of Helena's own choice.

Helena would like to resemble her model in everything; she wants every feature of her body to be an exact replica of Hermia's. Her ultimate desire is to worship herself rather than Hermia, but the only conceivable method to achieve that goal seems to be to worship the more successful Hermia first and to become a perfect duplicate of the person she really wants to be.

This is what magazines and books about fashionable people are, in our world anyway. They are how-to books. This is a recurrent problem with self-worship. The would-be worshipper always ends up worshipping someone else.

When Helena's hour of success finally arrives, it is too late for her; she can no longer enjoy it. She has been buffeted too much during the midsummer night. She believes she is the victim of some kind of hoax. Her newly found lovers are as sincere as they always were, and yet she is right not to trust either one. Each new combination proves more unstable and short-lived than the previous one.

Everybody ends up equally frustrated. The final outcome is conflict, failure and despair for everybody. No desire is ever fulfilled, and no desire is ever reciprocated, because all desires are one and the same. In order to respond to one another, desires must be differentiated; identical desires will all converge on the same object and can only *cross* one another.

Why is the system of mimetic desire so unstable? Why must the long-suffering Helena finally exchange places with Hermia and become everybody's idol while Hermia now is universally loathed? The reason lies with the universal dependence on *imitation*. The unanimous mimetic convergence seems enormously convincing because it does, indeed, convince everybody. It seems destined to last forever, and yet it is anchored in a pure mimetic effect rather than in anything concrete and objective. It floats half an inch above the ground, and in one instant, the same wind of fashion will topple the idol that it had erected a few instants before.

Ultimately this universal snobbery of imitation constitutes a surrender to pure randomness. The dabbing of the "wrong eyes" with the magical potion is unnecessary as a method of accounting for the fickleness of the lovers, but, like all mythical themes, it half reveals the disquieting truth that it dissimulates. We choose to desire mimetically, but then mimetic desire chooses for us; it deprives us of all power to choose and discriminate. This is what the operation of the love juice suggests quite explicitly. It makes Titania as well as the young people fall in love *at random:*

> *Oberon.* Having once this juice,
> I'll watch Titania when she is asleep,
> And drop the liquor of it in her eyes;
> The next thing then she waking looks upon
> (Be it on lion, bear, or wolf, or bull,
> On meddling monkey, or on busy ape),
> She shall pursue it with the soul of love.

The name of the potion thus introduced in act 2, scene 1—*love-in-idleness*—is a satirical barb at the type of people portrayed in the play. Only youngsters with nothing to do, like the aristocrats of Shakespeare's time, or the entire well-to-do middle class in our day, can waste their time playing such self-destructive games as our four lovers.

The laws and patterns of mimetic desire govern the entire theater of Shakespeare, I believe, if only negatively, in such plays as *As You Like It* that do conform much more consistently than *A Midsummer Night's Dream* to the conventions of traditional romance. Much of the play runs completely counter to these laws, but in a spirit of caricaturally slavish obedience to the mystique of "true love" that really amounts to another form of satire, and therefore another assertion of mimetic desire.

Other plays of Shakespeare illustrate only certain aspects of mimetic desire, fragments of the entire crisis-and-resolution pattern. *A Midsummer Night's Dream* represents the whole dynamic cycle in a speeded-up version that can fit the time frame of a single night.

This is the same fundamental process as in the great tragedies. In their common desire to distinguish themselves from one another, the four lovers engage in a mutual imitation that brings about a warring confusion of everything and ultimately would result in violent murders, were it not for the "supernatural" intervention of Puck and Oberon.

The characters' interpretation of what happens is very much like that of the average spectator, totally blind to the logic of mimetic desire and open, therefore, to suggestions of scapegoating on the one hand and supernatural intervention on the other. The one and the other enable the victims of mimetic desire to not identify mimetic desire as the real culprit and to substitute someone or something else as an explanation.

Their view of the mimetic process is the very reverse of the truth. As all the characters become more and more alike in their undifferentiated frenzy, they perceive an immense difference between themselves and their models. As a result, they themselves feel more and more inferior, or beastly, and they perceive their models as more and more superior and divine. Between these two extremes, emptiness prevails and common humanity is on the way out. Physical violence enters the picture, and the four wander at the edge of the inhuman. Their language reflects the shift. When they speak of themselves they use images of animality and confuse their models with various supernatural figures and even gods.

As the night advances, these images become more insistent. During this last evolution, the four seem to lose control entirely; they feel dizzier and dizzier; their perception becomes blurred. They are moving closer to the trancelike condition of the participants in orgiastic rituals. Shakespeare is obviously writing his own playful reconstitution not so much of the rituals themselves as the type of hysterical mimetic conflicts that must lie behind them.

This is what we already observed in the case of the craftsmen. As the cauldron boils over, the lovers lose their ability to distinguish their overworked metaphors from real beasts and real divinities. Beyond a certain threshold, these metaphors assume a life of their own, but not an "independent" life in the sense of their being well separated from one another. The system is too unstable for that; the substitutions and recombinations are occurring too rapidly.

The youngsters start taking their beasts and their gods seriously at the point when they can no longer tell them apart. Gods and beasts are on the way to forming these weird assemblages that we call mythical monsters. As a result of the dismembering and disorderly *remembering* of normally differentiated creatures, with no regard for the original differentiation, all sorts of fantastic creatures appear.

We already know which ones actually appear. We are back with our old friends, the ass-headed Bottom, Puck, Oberon, Titania and all the fairies. The subplot of the four lovers constitutes a gradual genesis of the mythical metamorphoses that parallels the genesis in the subplot of the craftsmen.

This invasion of the four lovers' speech by animal images corresponds to the excessive preoccupation of Bottom and his companions with the lion and to the early metamorphoses of that terrible beast. In both subplots the images of infrahuman and superhuman creatures prepare the ground for a final metamorphosis that is the same in the two subplots.

After the four lovers wake up and leave the wood, they give Theseus and Hippolyta their own account of what happened during the night. This account is not given on the stage because it would be a repetition of everything that has occurred to both groups during the midsummer night. In other words, the four lovers end up "dreaming" more or less the same "dream" as Bottom and his friends. Even though the two groups are not aware of one another's presence in the woods, they both participate in the genesis of the same mythology, and that is why the fairies are supposed to interfere with both groups.

The craftsmen and the lovers take a not-so-different road to end up in exactly the same place. This comes as no surprise to us. We found, indeed, that the erotic desire of the lovers was no less mimetic than the impersonations of the actors. The tendency for the idolatrous *imitatio* to focus not on one adolescent permanently but on this one now, then on another, then on a third, constitutes the equivalent of Bottom's urge to play all the roles and turn *Pyramus and Thisby* into a one-man show.

In each case, it is the same *hybris*, the same desire to dominate everyone and everything, that ends up destroying the goal it tries to reach because it destroys the very order that makes domination significant. This is the demise of "degree" in Ulysses' speech in *Troilus and Cressida*. This is the essence of tragedy.

What Shakespeare sees better than the Greeks is the reason why *hybristic* pride is self-defeating at the individual level. Mimetic desire is a desire for self-centeredness that cannot be distinguished from mimetic "de-centering," from the desire to "be" the model. A more radical alienation cannot be conceived. It lies at the root of the subject and depends on no sexual, economic or other determinations—unlike all the partial alienations of Marxism, Freudism and other contemporary theories. The four lovers resemble Bottom in their desire for turning the group into a one-man show and their ultimate inability to do so.

We can understand why Shakespeare resorts to the same word to express what the lovers desire and what happens to Bottom in the middle of the rehearsal. The lovers desire to be *translated* to their models. When Bottom turns into the ass-headed monster, Quince says to him: "Bottom, thou art translated."

Translation expresses both the desire for the *being* of someone else, and the paradoxical "success" of that desire, the monstrous metamorphosis. In both subplots the metamorphosis is the reward or, rather, the punishment for this desire.

The two subplots are closely patterned on one another. In both instances, the first scene is a distribution of roles. In principle, each character is supposed to play a single role, but in each case, signs of instability and disintegration immediately appear.

In both instances, as the crisis worsens, we shift from the city of Athens to the wood nearby. This is what the young people in England were supposed to do on midsummer nights. The wilderness is the right place, ritually speaking, for the two escalations of mimetic frenzy and the commingling between human and supernatural beings, the temporary destruction of civilized differentiation.

In both instances we have the same two levels of interpretation that I distinguished *à propos* of the craftsmen: 1) the dramatic level takes the monsters and fairies at face value, regarding them either as a genuine apparition or as a gratuitous product of a purely *individual* imagination, which is what Theseus does in his great speech; 2) a "genetic" level sees these same monsters and fairies as the product of mimetic impersonation gone mad, mimetically affecting all the characters in the two subplots.

Everything is alike in both subplots. Shakespeare makes the whole scheme of mimetic desire obvious to the point of caricature, and then he channels it into a dramatic effect that disguises it, for the benefit of those—the immense majority—who would rather not acknowledge the existence of mimetic desire. As in the case of the actors, the mimetic behavior produces the very mythology that it needs to transfigure its own folly into the mischievousness of Puck.

The author must maintain the illusion that a "true" pairing of the quartet exists. There must be a "right" combination: the myth of "true love" demands it. If it does not have the permanence required, or if it cannot be found at all, we can always pin the blame on the "fairies," or, better still, on the Oedipal father represented by Egeus, or on the power of the state represented by Theseus. These are the only fairies in which a modern critic is allowed to believe, the Freudo-Marxist fairies.

The happy ending of a comedy is one of these conventions that must be respected. The author does not want to offend the possible censors in his audience, or the really pure at heart. Unlike our modern demystificators, even in his most daringly cynical plays, Shakespeare always allows for the possibility of innocence, as if there were no deep resentment in him, or as if it were somehow transcended.

———————▼———————

The characters in the two subplots have no contact at all during the night. They come together only during the play within the play. The craftsmen are on stage and the lovers in the audience. It is traditional as a result to regard the two subplots as unrelated or loosely related. The comical antics of the craftsmen serve as an introduction to the play within the play, but their relevance to the work as a whole remains problematic.

The play is about monsters and has often been regarded as a trifle superficial, an elegant but somewhat empty fantasy, a mosaic of unrelated themes. The current fashion of incoherence and discontinuities has made this view more popular than ever, and yet it is completely false. But the formidable coherence of the play is of a sort that traditional criticism has never suspected.

With the blessing of its author, the play turns into a serious theory of its own mythological aspects, which most spectators and critics have always interpreted and will continue to interpret as a pure fantasy, arbitrarily superimposed on the more realistic aspects of the work. The force of the mythical metamorphosis ultimately stems from the craftsmen's and lovers' excessive taste for "translation," or for a type of "identification" that must be identified with *mimesis*, imitation, both because it is Shakespeare's view, and because it accounts for everything in the play. Shakespeare's own theory is the best theory of the play and of the anthropology behind it.

The proof that I have Shakespeare's blessing when I speak as I do is to be found in the smart reply of Hippolyta to the rather stodgy positivism of Theseus in act 5, scene 1, when he tells her what she should believe regarding the cause of the midsummer night. Like Polonius, Theseus does not say anything that is not true, and yet he understands nothing. Hippolyta understands everything. In my earlier article, I have quoted her in connection with the lovers only; I will quote her here once again more appropriately, in connection with the craftsmen as well:

> But all the story of the night told over,
> And all their minds transfigur'd so together,
> More witnesseth than fancy's images,
> And grows to something of great constancy;
> But howsoever, strange and admirable.

Shakespeare reveals the patterns of mimetic desire and their relationship to mythic creation so powerfully in the subplot of the four lovers that the case for its presence can be made on internal evidence only. No help is needed from the other subplot, the theatrical *mimesis* of Bottom and his friends.

But this help is always available, and a comparison of the points the two subplots have in common is enormously enlightening. Mimetic desire remains controversial, no doubt, but since Plato and the *Poetics* of Aristotle, *mimesis* has been the major concept of dramatic criticism. In the Renaissance, the mimetic interpretation was not simply the preferred interpretation, it was just about the only one.

In *A Midsummer Night's Dream*, the presence of *mimesis* as a Shakespearean theme is unquestionable. I assume, therefore, that my readers will have no difficulty agreeing with me on this point: the subplot of Bottom and his friends entails a perpetual and perfectly explicit reference to *mimesis*.

Mimesis is certainly part of the picture in the case of the craftsmen, but something else is needed to complete that picture. The aesthetic *mimesis* of the philosophers and the critics does not explain why the craftsmen decided to perform *Pyramus and Thisby*. They are not professional actors. They did not embark on their theatrical enterprise for aesthetic reasons primarily, or to make a living, or even out of a sense of obligation to the duke. To celebrate the wedding of Theseus, they might have come up with something better suited to their cultural shortcomings. Why did they choose to do a play?

The obvious answer is: personal ambition, narcissism, desire, mimetic desire. Since all the craftsmen show up every time they are summoned, since not one of them is ever missing, the same desire for impersonation must possess each and every one of them, including the most timid, the ones who stand at the other extreme of Bottom and act out the part of the reluctant actor. The reluctance of the reluctant actor means the same thing, ultimately, as the extreme eagerness of Bottom.

Bottom, we found, could never settle on any role, not even the leading one, the most flattering to his ego. His avidity was finally punished, or rewarded, by his metamorphosis into a monster.

Most people enjoy watching a play, but the more they enjoy it, the more they also enjoy being watched by others and therefore performing as actors. The craving for impersonation corresponds to a perfect fusion of *mimesis* and desire.

The desire for the theater consists not in imitating some specific model but in the undifferentiated avidity of Bottom that inevitably conflicts with the pretentions of Quince and the other actors, just as the desires of the four lovers must necessarily "cross" one another.

In the case of the lovers, the one component that is identified most easily is desire. The critic does not have to demonstrate that desire belongs in the picture. But here again, this is not the whole picture; something more is needed to account for the systematic and almost algebraic aspect of the lovers' antics.

If we have *mimesis* plus desire in the case of the craftsmen, we must have desire plus *mimesis* in the case of the lovers. The second component must be imitation or impersonation. The picture is reversed, but to Shakespeare, obviously, it is fundamentally the same picture.

If *mimesis* is really present in the case of the actors, the case for a *mimesis of desire* that would belong to Shakespeare's own conception of both subplots and of the entire play becomes inescapable. A mimesis of desire can always reverse itself into a desire for mimesis. The two subplots are *perfect* mirrors of one another, and together, they breed the fairies. This triunity is the unity of *A Midsummer Night's Dream*.

Unlike the ancient and modern students of imitation, unlike the Freudian students of desire, Shakespeare is not merely aware that imitation and desire cannot be divorced from each other; he realizes that, far from being the bland ingredient that the modern world sees in it, a source of sheepish gregariousness in society and of a platitudinous "realism" in the arts, *mimesis* (because of its admixture of desire) is an explosive combination. It constitutes the disruptive factor par excellence of human relations, the major reason for the fragility of even and especially the closest friendships and the most tender erotic relationships. The closer the friends, the more likely they are to imitate one another's desires and therefore to turn into enemies. This is Shakespeare's tragic as well as his comic insight par excellence, and it is undistinguishable from the fusion of mimesis and desire that he perpetually portrays.[4]

Notes

1. William Shakespeare, *A Midsummer Night's Dream*, in *The Riverside Shakespeare*, ed. G. Blakemore Evans (Boston: Houghton Mifflin Company, 1974). All subsequent quotations in the text are taken from this same source.

2. René Girard, *Violence and the Sacred* (Baltimore: Johns Hopkins University Press, 1978).

3. "Myth and Ritual in Shakespeare: *A Midsummer Night's Dream,*" in *Textual Strategies,* ed. Josue Harari (Ithaca: Cornell University Press, 1979), 189–212.

4. This essay should lead to a consideration of the play within the play. The theme is too rich, however, and too long for the present essay; it will be instead the subject of a separate essay, the third in a three-part study of *A Midsummer Night's Dream.* The author apologizes for his long delay in treating the fascinating encounter between the two types of mimetic actors.

Of Poetry and Names, Science and Things

Joseph F. Graham

At the end of an article on Proust and proper names, Roland Barthes raises the question that asks ". . . whether it is possible to be a writer (*écrivain*) without believing, somehow (*d'une certaine manière*), in the natural relation of names and essences. . . ."[1] The force of the question in that context is clearly rhetorical, and the answer is surely negative: no, it is not possible to be a writer without believing in that natural relation of names and essences. This means that all writers believe, in some way, and not only as a matter of fact, just happening to believe; rather, they believe by force of necessity. Thus it is impossible to be a writer and not believe, for believing is a necessary condition for writing: you simply cannot write without that belief. Moreover, the sense of the question along with the thrust of the answer in that context is not just biographical or merely psychological, for it is meant as a matter of poetics, specifically concerned with the poetic function of language as defined by Roman Jakobson.

Though Proust is the case in point, Barthes insists that the Proust in question is the writer in Proust and the Proust in the *Recherche du temps perdu*, who is both the writer and the narrator of a story about writing (*l'histoire d'une écriture*). That story tells how the writer came to write the novel and thus how he came to be a writer. It is a story about the very conditions to obtain for that mode of writing. And as such, it is not only a story but also a theory of writing where writing is significantly related to naming. Both in fact and in content the story has for its origin, for its end, and even for its moral, something to do with proper names. Because certain names are as essential in the novel as they were crucial for the novel, Barthes can claim that the entire *Recherche* emerges from a few names. He finally draws this general conclusion from that particular example: ". . . the poetic function, in the widest sense of the term, would thus be defined by a Cratylian consciousness of signs and the writer would be the reciter of that great secular myth according to which language imitates ideas and, contrary to the strictures of linguistic science, signs are motivated" (158). Poetics as the study of the poetic function would then become onomatopoetics, the study of the poetry in names, when duly extended and so construed. As he extrapolates from Proust to poetry, Barthes also shifts from names to words and then to signs in a move that gives his final claim full range over a very wide context.

Names have long been paradigmatic and no less problematic for the study of language in general. There is a philosophical debate about names and naming that extends from the most ancient to the most recent figures in the Western tradition, from Plato and the pre-Socratics to Kripke and current semantics. At issue throughout, despite many differences, has been the very nature of verbal representation, the relation of language to the world, whether it be arbitrary and conventional or natural and somehow motivated. The same debate emerges in modern linguistics with Saussure and the subsequent controversy over the arbitrariness of the linguistic sign. Jakobson in particular has argued against Saussure and all those who would separate linguistics from poetics or otherwise contest the real unity and utility of a general semiotics.

This question of representation in and through language holds special interest for the study of literature, since the literary use of language has generally been characterized as more mimetic or iconic, and in that sense more natural, than ordinary use. In much of modern criticism, the quality of literature, both as fact and as value, is still described as a certain manner, style, or mode of discourse which presents meaning with full intensity and immediacy. The word embodies the object, the image radiates the feeling, and the phrase mimes the experience. The language of literature is said to be metaphorical rather than literal, oblique rather than direct, and opaque rather than transparent. And in this way at least, many literary critics believe the Cratylian myth to be true of literature at its best and so in its essence. They would therefore agree with Barthes in defining the poetic as the onomatopoetic. Not all critics would agree, however, and some would disagree quite sharply, or so it would seem.

There has been a concerted effort in recent years to extend from metaphysics to aesthetics a critique of presence that renders suspect any form of evidence or adequacy. Certain critics also see literature itself as participating directly in that same critical mode of disabusement by always already reversing or somehow deconstructing the dubious values of aesthetic representation inherited from a metaphysical tradition. Paul de Man appears to be just such a critic who dissents from the received opinion about the nature of literature. His comments are pointed, and some even directed against Barthes, or so it would seem.[2] For there may be no direct confrontation or real opposition, after all.

This point needs qualifying for at least two reasons. It is often difficult to understand the exact thrust and full force of critical opposition to the linguistic naturalism that has long dominated our thinking about literature. We still find reason to agree with Barthes in thinking that it is really impossible not to believe in Cratylism for literature, or at least not to believe in some way. Now it could be that we cannot very well think otherwise because our thoughts are determined by some massive prejudice of metaphysics, yet it could just be that we can only think of literature as such, simply because literature is such. There would then be good reason to believe in Cratylism inasmuch as it was true of literature. This question of belief for criticism is not just biographical, either. Some critics may not appear to believe or may appear not to believe, and some may even deny any belief of the sort. Yet it could still remain virtually, if not strictly, impossible to be a literary critic and not believe. All critics would then be true believers in some form of naturalism or realism, even those who might insist upon their own version of the truth as the reverse. Such is my conjecture and indeed my conclusion, by way of anticipation. The long way of argumentation begins again with Barthes.

To recapitulate: Barthes has drawn a lesson for literature from his reading of Proust. He takes the *Recherche* as a story about the writing of literature, a story which serves as an allegory for the origin and nature of literature. He claims that what holds for Proust also holds for any other writer, in the rather special sense he gives that term or title *écrivain*. They all share a common belief about the language of literature, namely the traditional belief that in literature at least there is some natural relation between name and essence or sound and sense. Such a belief is intrinsic to literature because necessary for literature. It would also be sufficient to characterize literature to the extent that onomatopoeia, as the making of names broadly construed, would comprise the very mode of representation specific to literature. An onomatopoetics would thus constitute a complete aesthetics for literature.

The status of a discipline so defined seems rather strange, inasmuch as its subject would really be an error or illusion. Onomatopoetics would be the study of a particular myth and its effects on the language of literature. The myth is admittedly false, yet the effects are presumably real. Barthes is perfectly explicit, if somewhat elliptic, on the first point. The myth is opposed to science, the science of language that is linguistics. According to myth, signs are motivated, natural and mimetic; according to science, they are not. Because it is allied with myth, literature appears regressive or nostalgic. It runs counter to the progress of knowledge, in dogged pursuit of an impossible dream. The belief about language embodied in literature would have to be either false or simply quaint, depending upon how seriously it was meant. It could only be true and progressive if signs were somehow motivated in a way that was denied or ignored by the science of language. Barthes does not consider such an alternative, surely because he already concedes the linguistic truth that verbal signs are not motivated but arbitrary, not natural but conventional, not iconic or mimetic but symbolic. Then he faces the embarrassment of having to admit that literature is based on a mistake, a mistaken belief about language.

One way to avoid some of that embarrassment would be to argue that not all writers, any more than all critics, are so deluded or mistaken as to suppose that language could actually reproduce the world, if only in literature. It would be incumbent upon such a defense to adduce counterexamples showing that a naturalism so naive was not the only belief to hold for literature. Gérard Genette has done just that in his *Mimologiques*, which follows the fortunes of Cratylism from Plato to the present.[3] He tells a different story about literature and draws a very different conclusion. To begin with, he reads the myth of naturalism historically and finds a significant degree of local variation. There is more than one version to the belief in an ideal language, for it can be thought either past and lost, or yet to be attained. Also it can be conceived as something either given or achieved, either common or rare, so that it could be quite ordinary or purely literary. It can even be recognized for what it is, no more than an ideal, and so a product of imagination—an object of desire and the subject of dreams, but nothing actual or real. It can then be seen or at least taken as an illusion that should receive criticism rather than credence. Whereas dreams remain innocent like games, there is a danger in false belief which literature itself should denounce. We can imagine anything without harm as long as we know what we are doing. Literature may encourage such imaginings for pleasure, though not finally endorse them as true. Its lesson would then be negative and essentially critical, hence not all that different from the strictures of a science opposed to any naturalism for language.

In the history of Cratylism, as recounted by Genette, there comes a crucial point which corresponds to an awakening or some manner of enlightenment. That moment coincides with the rise of modern linguistics, and it finally brings a general if gradual recognition of the truth about language. Yet even after the basic fact of convention has been firmly established by science, the myth of naturalism endures, but only in the form of a wistful dream or clever game, for it is no longer taken literally or seriously. Proust plays an important role for Genette in that final stage, precisely because his work exhibits the very lesson to be learned from linguistics and therein marks the triumph of modern science over an ancient superstition about the force of language in literature. So it is that Genette reads Proust against Barthes.[4] The *Recherche* does not so much confirm as deny the need for Cratylism in literature. It is indeed a story of discovery, with progress from ignorance to knowledge, from illusion to insight, and it should be read as an allegory of writing informed by a theory of language. Genette agrees to that extent. The difference of interpretation lies rather in what is said to be the actual substance of that discovery and the conclusion of that theory. The terms are the same in both readings: nature and convention, but their order and their values are reversed.

Genette describes a course of mental development whereby the protagonist eventually matures in his understanding of language. Marcel the child was naive in believing that language had magical powers easily evoked and readily deployed. He was compensating for his own weakness in a fantasy of omnipotence that gave full control over the world with a mere command of language. His experience as an adult is disappointing and disabusing. He finally comes to realize his mistake and to recognize that the relation between sound and sense is not solidarity or affinity but disparity, not resemblance but difference. There is no real accord between the two, only a subtle illusion. He learns that he cannot trust language and that in his search for truth he had better put his confidence in things themselves rather than in words alone. At the end of a chapter on Proust, Genette draws his conclusion from that lesson. The *Recherche* contains both an admission and a rejection of what is felt to be a very strong temptation. It is the temptation of an illusion, the very attractive and seductive illusion of realism which would lead us astray and fool us into false belief. Realism tempts us to believe in the accuracy of names by having us suppose whatever we name to be however we name it. We simply draw the wrong conclusion from a mistaken impression, in thinking that words represent things as they really are. The illusion has two sides or aspects: a semantic illusion which supposes a natural relation of sound to sense, and a referential illusion which supposes the identity of meaning and referent, or sense and object. Both forms of realism are denounced in the *Recherche*, as read by Genette.

The story that takes Proust from naturalism to conventionalism, and from realism to some manner of idealism, combines psychology and morality with epistemology and ontology. As a quest for truth, its significance is deeply personal and yet highly philosophical; as an adventure in learning, the events are cathartic in effect and their consequences both hermeneutic and semiotic. The same plot also serves to characterize the development of science which Genette describes in terms taken directly from Freud. Science requires that we renounce pleasure and accept reality for what it is, however it is, whether we like it or not. Thus science can be chastening, even humiliating, for in this case we are required to sacrifice that most cherished belief in our ability to know the truth about the world. Here we have to accept the bitter fact about ourselves, that believing in realism is just another form of narcissism, and if somewhat more intellectual no less presumptuous in taking desires for reality. Linguistics only became a science by repressing all such hope for an ideal language and by refusing any naturalism whatsoever in its method or object.

Genette makes this last point quite clear. What applies to language in general also applies to science as a particular instance of language. The language used by science is no less conventional than any language mentioned or studied by science, otherwise science would be mysteriously or magically exempt from the very consequences of its own discovery. A rigorously consistent science of language was therefore impossible without the epistemological break that abandoned realism or belief in any natural substance of language. Science accepts as a matter of convention or stipulation the basic yet groundless foundation of all language including its own. The very act of assuming language to be a construct, both arbitrary and abstract, was constitutive because necessary as a condition for language and for science, but not as a truth about either. Conventionalism could only be a prejudice, or what Genette calls a *parti pris*, and so the result of a decision rather than a prior fact of the matter. Science calls for such allegiance in a spirit of sacrifice.

The desire for an ideal language of truth was repressed by science only to return as a fantasm in various guises which still represent a strong set of predilections to be satisfied. Cratylism serves that need and offers satisfaction to the basic compulsion for resemblance between words and things, as does the whole modern aesthetic of literature which effectively caters to the frustration caused by linguistics. What has become the standard theory clearly prefers symbol to allegory, metaphor to metonymy, equivalence to dissonance, and generally promotes the idea that literary form should exhibit or somehow exemplify its meaning. The demon of analogy and the demand for motivation are still current and even dominant in our poetics, yet they may well be on the wane, not so much because their notions are false in some realist sense, but rather because they have faded and now look tired. That general idea of poetic language corresponds to the language in a certain kind of poetry, and that poetry coincides with a specific period in history. It is resolutely modern yet no longer very modern and certainly not immutable, even if so familiar as to seem natural or necessary. Ideas about literature have changed more than once in the past and will probably change again in the future, perhaps quite soon.

So it is that Genette not only situates in time and place but also explains in the psychological, almost pathological terms of preference, the very naturalism of language that Barthes considered essential to literature. This counterversion of Cratylism is primarily historical and so contingent, optional or arbitrary, as against necessary. Yet in making it a matter of taste or choice, Genette can easily remain sympathetic, for he too feels the attraction of a naturalism that is admittedly aesthetic and nostalgic, whence innocent or at least innocuous, rather than wrongly epistemic and truly dangerous.

In the matter of reading Proust on the language of literature, de Man clearly agrees with Genette, for he says quite specifically that Genette has "shown" how Proust dismantles the very convergence of sound and meaning which Barthes had celebrated in Proust. And he even calls that Cratylism "a seductive temptation to mystified minds," yet he does not merely side with Genette against Barthes, as one might expect, for he also says that Barthes can be read differently and read in a way that is perfectly consistent with what Genette has found to be the case in Proust. Though Barthes may well invite the kind of reading that supports the traditional aesthetic of adequation between form and content, there is still "part" of his statement that "moves in the opposite direction." Along that line in Barthes, naturalism is considered to be a mere *effect* of language, with no "substantial relationship" to anything beyond. It is a rhetorical effect, and so just one trope among others (paronomasis), which involves a correspondence between the name and the thing named that is "not phenomenal but conventional." Because that relation is conventional, indeed because what seems most natural is really conventional, language is autonomous and free from "referential constraint." Any word can refer or correspond to any thing quite easily and arbitrarily, but language is also fallible and unreliable as a result.

Autonomy simply means that language is not determined by anything else, whether it be true, good, or beautiful; rather, language has a rule of its own which is rhetoric, and not logic, ethics, or aesthetics. For de Man the autonomy of language marked by rhetoric is essentially literary in that literature as such is a matter of language, essentially a matter of using words in such a way as to exploit, exhalt, or enhance the autonomous potential of language as fully and as rigorously as possible. Literature is the most consistently rhetorical mode of discourse and therefore the most distinctively or definitely linguistic form of language. But literature is also, and for that very reason, the most suspect form of language because the least reliable, especially in matters of truth and knowledge. There is no natural or necessary connection between the language of literature and anything else, so that knowledge of literature does not entail knowledge of any other truth about the world. Rather, the truth of language exhibited in literature implies the very impossibility of arriving at truth through language. Accordingly, de Man identifies literature in general as "the place where this negative knowledge about the reliability of linguistic utterance is made available," and he concludes in particular that literature "involves the voiding, rather than the affirmation, of aesthetic categories" ("The Resistance to Theory," 10). On this negative or deconstructive version of poetics, all of literature as such is opposed to Cratylism or any other belief that still harbors the vain hope of discovering truth about the world through a knowledge of language.

It is easy to understand why de Man would find aesthetic theory so "aberrant" when applied to literature. Aesthetic categories are bound to falsify the basic facts about literature inasmuch as those facts are specifically linguistic and not just indifferent to aesthetic value but directly opposed to the whole idea. Theories based on history and ideology fare no better, according to de Man, since their bias is mimetic and no less alien. All such theories in effect deny the autonomy of literature and so deny its literariness; thus they defeat the very purpose of an appropriate theory which is to define the specific property that makes literature so distinctive as a form of language. Though he finds them aberrant, de Man admits that non-linguistic theories of literature are "inevitable" and quite significant in what they reveal about a crucial resistance to rhetoric in language. They are inevitable because that resistance is inherent to all language and further because any theory based on language and language alone is doubly fraught with tension and contradiction. Language as such produces contrary effects—some theoretical and referential, others practical and rhetorical—which can never be fully reconciled or simply eliminated. So it is that rhetoric always resists and eventually subverts the referential mode of theory, but so it is too that rhetoric maintains reference all the while.

Because language is divided against itself, as if by nature, any instance or utterance can be read in more than one way, in ways both aberrant and inevitable, both false and necessary. That difference in reading is crucial for de Man; it allows for the greater generality and accounts for the lack of sentimentality in what he says not only about Proust and literature but especially about literary criticism and its curious connection with literary language. Perhaps more relentlessly than any other recent critic, de Man has pursued a reflexive turn of thought leading from language back to the reading of literature. He has argued that the language characteristic of literature has troubling consequences which a true theory of literature must address in principle yet avoid in practice. Somehow literature implies a truth which it strangely denies, and that same truth also belies any ordinary claim about the nature of literature. A theory that is true *to* literature cannot be true *of* literature in the usual sense, but it would not be false all the same, and it would not be indifferent to truth either. All criticism as such both reveals and resists the very nature of literature in a figural or allegorical mode that repeats endlessly what it cannot represent outright.

What de Man says about criticism surely complicates the issue at hand by raising the same questions at a higher level and by making them even more difficult to resolve in any ordinary way that is not then open to further question. Obviously enough, first-order questions about the nature of literature and its language have always involved second-order questions about theories of language and literature, but not necessarily in a way that would render their resolution so problematic. Consider the differences between Genette and Barthes on the matter of Cratylism. Barthes advocated naturalism in poetics and conventionalism in linguistics without having to choose between the two because of a real difference between literary language and ordinary language. Genette agreed about linguistics but disagreed about poetics, where he found both naturalism and conventionalism equally justified by the diversity of literature and so open to choice as a matter of aesthetic preference. There is no such choice for de Man, since all language denies what it does in producing natural effects. And whatever we may want to say about it, we have no real choice in the matter because we have to operate with language in ways that defeat our best intentions. By reason of rhetoric, saying and meaning never match or simply coincide but displace each other in pursuit of an elusive and tantalizing adequation.

With his analysis of the problem de Man puts us in the predicament of having to consider not only *what* we should say or do about language but also *how* we could possibly say it or do it without saying or doing the very opposite and thus defeating our own purpose. If he is right, we cannot truly decide the basic issue of language, by choosing nature over convention or reference over rhetoric, nor can we simply avoid it, for the issue itself constitutes the very operation of language. Rather, the worst we could do would be to hope, expect, or even try to resolve it by reducing the tension in language between its aesthetic or mimetic effects and its rhetorical means, for that manner of simplification by elimination would falsify the most. But then we face the prospect of not being able to do anything that would make a real difference in the matter. Aporia can easily lead to apathy.

If language operates in essentially the same way at every level, and if the only important difference between literature and criticism, or the only significant difference among various types of criticism, is finally a matter of degree in rhetoric, then our range of effective choice seems relatively minor and merely formal. We are not given anything at all comparable to the absolute and substantial differences that are supposed to hold for true and false statements or good and bad actions. Both literature and criticism then seem more like a matter of style, which is really aesthetic after all. Yet de Man insists upon another kind of value in claiming, rather, that genuine instances of literary language deserve preference for their intellectual rigor, a form of rigor which is hardly trivial and which may even be moral. The advantage is that they are more reflexive and so more lucid because more willing or able to acknowledge their own scope along with its attendant limits. The most rigorous use of language would then be the most consistent in recognizing the basic fact of language, namely that language is only language, not something else, and especially not anything like a special relation or privileged access to something else. Rhetoric clearly promotes that recognition in drawing attention to the specifically linguistic properties of language, whereas a real concern for reference looks beyond language to something else. That pursuit is always subject to error in having to rely on some dubious relation between language and the world, a relation which nothing about language itself could possibly guarantee. Such is the inherent and therefore constant risk of aesthetics or any mimetics, while a poetics is relatively free from delusion when informed by the lucid though ironic mode of rhetoric that flourishes in literature as the truth of error.

However rigorous and reflexive, the rhetorical mode has its own problems, especially if applied to the practice of literary criticism or any other explicit use of language about language, where questions of truth and reference are particularly acute and very difficult to avoid. There is above all a serious problem of argument, quite simply because it is not easy to maintain full autonomy for language with consistency, and not easy to sustain a claim about language that lacks consistency. You could also say that the problem was one of rhetoric or even that the problem was rhetoric itself, insofar as it involves the choice of rhetoric appropriate for use in a theory of language as rhetoric. But that is again the point about consistency in any theory of language that does not admit differences in use of the kind supposed by traditional accounts of truth and reference as relations between language and some object. Consider for a moment the task of defending a radical because general claim that rhetoric constitutes the substance of language, including both truth and reference among other effects of usage alone.

When the difference between literature and criticism, as language and meta-language, has been reduced to a matter of rhetoric, since reference will only be recognized as a function of rhetoric or a difference in usage, there still has to be some property in and of language to account for reference and to assure the truth of any claim about language or literature. And so, for example, if it were indeed true that language was essentially rhetorical, there would have to be something about language not only to warrant but also to represent that truth. Naturalism for language and realism about language would solve the problem of truth by recourse to reference as a relation between words in language and things in the world. But that option is not open to a strict conventionalism that only allows rhetoric as a resource and only accepts rhetoric as a property of language. Somehow truth has to be found in language alone. The difference then between true and false theories about language can only be a matter of language itself, simply a matter of some difference in the language of the theories themselves, and for the purpose of establishing that difference language cannot be considered in relation to anything but itself. When it comes to truth, there is nothing else, on such an account.

It is not my purpose at this point to consider just how feasible or indeed how plausible would be a general account of truth and reference that made no appeal beyond language to any independent reality. Nor do I propose at present to consider how truly different that version would be from the naturalism or the Cratylism so readily taken for the very opposite. Yet both considerations are crucial to my argument, which not only defends a realist conception of truth for literary criticism but finally extends a naturalistic theory of language to cover a full range of aesthetic phenomena in literature, comprising even those examples offered as conclusive evidence to the contrary. It is also the purport of the same argument to establish a substantial connection between those different considerations by showing how questions about literature either demand or suppose answers about criticism.

Often the real issue seems to involve not so much the specific answer eventually given to some question about the nature of language in literature, as the very method originally chosen to decide. When that is indeed the case, criticism is best served by a form of self-criticism, by a reflexive turn which suspends belief in the matter of substance and doubles back with the idea to discover a hidden standard of evidence which has never been justified. But that is not always or only the case. Since the reflexive turn is likely to be linguistic, the question of method for literature as often repeats the question of substance about language. The issue has then come full circle. The original question of whether language in literature is natural or conventional, referential or rhetorical, leads to a question of how the difference can be decided and how the truth can be most adequately represented. But if that question were simply another version of the first, its answer would either beg or finally resolve the entire issue. To see just how that could be, compare what Barthes, Genette, and de Man suggest about the procedures for literary criticism.

Barthes does not say exactly what literary critics should think in the matter that opposes linguistics (words are arbitrary) and poetics (words are motivated), but he does say what they should do all the same. Critics should read literature according to the myth of Cratylism, for that is the way it is written, and clearly something they should respect. Since Barthes never really says whether the myth is not therefore true in a special sense, only that any reading of literature should be consistent with the basic principle of its writing, his advice remains equivocal. It can be construed in various ways, in all the different ways that a reading could possibly be consistent. First off, a critical reading can simply describe whatever the literary text says or does and thus be consistent in the empirical sense of being true to the facts. A reading can also say things very similar to what the text says and thus be consistent in the logical sense of not denying what has already been said. Along with the theoretical, there are practical ways of being consistent, such that different actions are taken to be consistent or coherent when they contribute to the same result. An act of reading could easily be consistent in that way by fulfilling whatever the text does rather than anything to the contrary.

In one form or other, Barthes conceives the standard of consistency as a relation between literature and criticism, rather than just a property they could have in common. His recommendation may have been theoretical and thus concerned with truth, or it may have been practical and then concerned with a different kind of result, but he wanted criticism to be consistent with literature in either case.

Genette wants literary criticism to be consistent with itself more than anything else. He thus commends the kind of integrity, both moral and intellectual, which appears when criticism shows the greatest lucidity and honesty about its own practice of interpretation. If every procedure indeed represents a preference that is neither true nor false, neither right nor wrong about literature, the cardinal virtue for any criticism is quite simply the capacity to recognize that preference for what it is, not only a choice but a valorization that would justify the choice. Genette can accept Cratylism as such and yet object to its abuse. The fault lies not with the preference so much as the ignorance that projects an incidental value of literature as an essential fact of language. Genette offers a correction and a cure. The discipline of history prevents that kind of mistake and develops a real sense of modesty, for it puts everything in perspective and everyone in place.

The integrity that results is a much better knowledge of oneself. For literary criticism, it comes as the rightful integration of theory and practice.

It may seem impossible to reconcile de Man with the others, quite simply because he contests their idea of consistency. He not only disputes it as a fact of language, he rejects it as a value for literature. He then argues that literary criticism cannot and should not hope to be consistent, especially if it is ever to acknowledge the duplicity of all discourse including its very own. And yet de Man finally defends an idea of consistency, one which subsumes as it denies the others. His is the consistency of permanent possibility, given the lack of any definite necessity. It is paradoxical in the sense that it is rhetorical, either theoretical or practical yet always equivocal if not indeterminate. As the basic principle of equivocation, rhetoric haunts every statement, even the most explicit, since they can all be construed in more than one way. Clearly there can be no decision about the meaning, let alone the truth, of a statement without some decision about its rhetorical force, which could be either literal or figural at the very least.

When de Man argues for the primacy of rhetoric, his statements can be read in various ways. They can be read as a recognition of the need for a more informed choice in reading, or as the negation of any valid choice in the matter. They can also be read as statements about what would ever count as decisive evidence for one reading against another. Among the many possibilities, there is a reading that de Man seems to prefer. He identifies literature with rhetoric as the most comprehensive theory and practice of language, then he attributes everything that involves language to literature, all the problems of reading as well as all the solutions, since literature includes every effect of language, whether syntactic, semantic, or pragmatic. When so construed, questions of method are really questions of substance, which already beg the question of literature by assuming the validity of any one reading. Because literature constitutes the possibility of several different readings and the necessity of none, it cannot have either a true theory or a valid reading that is both consistent and complete. The only way for criticism to be consistent with literature is to be inconsistent like literature, so that the difference between literature and criticism is reduced. They are equivalent when completely inconsistent and yet fully cognizant of their common predicament. Literature anticipates criticism as misreading, and criticism at best repeats the same.

Though Barthes and Genette demand consistency from criticism, they concede what de Man would refuse—an appropriate language that is not literary. They require criticism to be consistent in different ways, but they both allow literature to be consistent in a distinct way. While assuming the same possibility for literature, Barthes and Genette disagree about its necessity. Cratylism gives a name to that necessity and imposes the greatest consistency of form and meaning for truth in language. Though de Man clearly denies the need for such integrity, he insists upon the need for another. He requires that criticism represent the full complexity and real duplicity of literature, something that can only be done by replication and something already done by literature for language. Quite simply, de Man considers it impossible just to tell the truth about language, or anything else, because it is impossible to say just one thing. The force of rhetoric multiplies the meaning of every statement many times. If you could only say what you meant or say only what you meant, you could eventually tell the truth, at least to the extent that you could know it. When language only allows you to show the truth, it is difficult to know what is meant by the truth. We all share the burden of interpretation that results. If you cannot tell the difference between what has been shown to be true and what has been said to be true, then language is no more explicit about the truth than the world itself, for it requires the same effort of interpretation. Hence, the choice between literature and science is not so much the choice between objects of interpretation as the choice between different methods of representation. Science can be indifferent to language on both counts, literature cannot. The hardest question for criticism, as for any science of language or literature, is whether it is possible to split the difference.[5]

Notes

1. Roland Barthes, "Proust et les noms," in *To Honor Roman Jakobson* (The Hague: Mouton, 1967), 150–58.

2. Paul de Man, "The Resistance to Theory," *Yale French Studies* 63 (1982): 3–20.

3. Gérard Genette, *Mimologiques: voyage en Cratylie* (Paris: Le Seuil, 1976).

4. Genette, "L'Age des noms," in *Mimologiques*, 315–28.

5. This essay presents some of the opening argument for the case to be made in my book, *Onomatopoetics: Theory of Language and Literature.*

World Literature in an Age of Multinational Capitalism

Fredric Jameson

In these last years of the twentieth century, the old question of a properly world literature reasserts itself. This is due fully as much or more to the disintegration of our own conceptions of cultural study as to any very lucid awareness of the great outside world all around us. We may therefore—as "humanists"—acknowledge the pertinence of the critique of the present-day humanities by our titular leader, William Bennett, without finding any great satisfaction in his embarrassing solution, yet another impoverished and ethnocentric Graeco-Judaic "great books list": "the civilization of the West," "great texts, great minds, great ideas." And although one is tempted to turn back on Bennett himself the question he approvingly quotes from Maynard Mack—"How long can a democratic nation afford to support a narcissistic minority so transfixed by its own image?"—it is at least certain that the present moment offers a remarkable opportunity to rethink the humanities curriculum in a new way, on the shambles and ruins of all our older "great books," "humanities," "freshman-introductory," "core course" type traditions.

I will only imply in this essay that the reinvention of cultural studies in the United States demands the reinvention, in a new situation, of what Goethe long ago theorized as "world literature." In our context, more immediately, any conception of world literature necessarily demands some specific engagement with the question of Third World literature, and it is this not necessarily narrower subject about which I have something to say.

It would obviously be presumptuous to offer some general theory of Third World literature, given the enormous variety both

139

of national cultures in the Third World and of specific historical tra-
jectories in each of those areas. All of this is then provisional, and
intended to suggest specific perspectives for research on the one hand,
and also to convey a sense of the interest and value of these obviously
very neglected literatures for people who have been formed by the
values but also by the stereotypes of a First World culture. One great
initial distinction would seem to impose itself, which can itself in turn
be grasped only in the light of an even more preliminary fact of life,
namely that none of these cultures is to be conceived in a kind of
anthropological independence or autonomy; rather, all are in various
distinct ways locked in a life-and-death struggle with First World
cultural imperialism itself, a cultural struggle which is itself a reflexion
of the economic situation of such areas in their penetration by various
stages of capitalism, or as it is sometimes euphemistically termed,
modernization. This is then some first sense in which a study of Third
World culture also necessarily implies a new view of ourselves, from
the outside, insofar as we are ourselves (perhaps without fully knowing it) constitutive forces powerfully at work on the remains of older
cultures in our general, world-capitalist system. I will develop this
idea—that Third World cultures offer a more unvarnished and challenging image of ourselves—later on.

But if this is the case, the initial distinction that imposes itself
has to do with the nature and development of older cultures at the
moment of capitalist penetration, something it seems to me most
enlightening to examine in the light of the Marxian concept of "modes
of production" (you will recall the traditional list of these: primitive
communism, the polis or ancient society, the Asiatic mode of production or so-called Oriental Despotism, feudalism, capitalism, and so-
cialism or communism). Contemporary historians seem to be in the
process of reaching a consensus on the specificity of feudalism as a
form which, issuing from the breakup of the Roman Empire or the
Japanese Shogunate, is able to develop directly into capitalism. This
is not the case with the other modes of production, which must in
some sense be disaggregated or destroyed by violence before capitalism is able to implant its specific forms and displace the older ones.

My list will have made clear, then, that in the gradual expansion
of capitalism around the globe, our economic system will confront
two very distinct modes of production, which oppose distinct kinds
of resistance to its influence in the form of two very different types of
social and cultural relations. These are primitive, or tribal, society on
the one hand, and the Asiatic mode of production, or the great

bureaucratic imperial systems, on the other: African society and African culture as these become the object of systematic colonization in the 1880s provide the most striking example of the symbiosis of capital and tribal societies; while China and India (this last the object of a much longer colonizing process) offer the principal exhibits of another and quite different engagement of capitalism with the great empires of the so-called Asiatic mode. My examples in what follows, then, will be essentially African and Chinese; but I will also try to offer some proximate approach to the question of Latin America, which offers clearly yet a third kind of development, involving an even earlier destruction of imperial systems, now projected by collective memory back into the archaic or tribal, and whose earlier nominal conquest of independence opened them at once to a kind of indirect economic penetration and control, which Africa and Asia have come to experience only much more recently, since decolonization in the 1950s and 1960s.

Having made these initial distinctions, let me now, by way of a sweeping hypothesis, try to say what all Third World cultural productions seem to have in common and what distinguishes them radically from superficially analogous cultural forms in the First World. All Third World texts are necessarily, I want to argue, allegorical—and this in a very specific way: they are to be read as what I will call national allegories, even when, or perhaps I should say, particularly when their forms develop out of essentially Western machineries of representation, such as the novel. Let me try to stage this distinction in a grossly oversimplified way: one of the determinants of capitalist culture, that is to say, from our perspective, the culture of the Western realist and modernist novel, is a radical split between the private and the public, between the poetic and the political, between what we have come to think of as the domain of sexuality and the unconscious and that of the public world of classes, the economic, and secular political power—in other words, Freud versus Marx. Our numerous theoretical attempts to overcome this great split only reconfirm its existence and its shaping power over our individual and collective lives. We have therefore been trained in a deep cultural conviction that the lived experience of our private existences is somehow incommensurable with the abstractions of economic science and political dynamics. Politics in our novels therefore is, according to Stendhal's canonical formulation, a "pistol shot in the middle of a concert."

I will try to persuade you that, although we may retain for convenience and for analysis such categories as the subjective and the public or the political, the relations between them are wholly different in Third World culture. Those texts, even those narratives which are seemingly private and invested with a properly libidinal dynamic, necessarily project a political dimension in the form of national allegory: the story of the private individual destiny is always an allegory of the embattled situation of the public Third World culture and society. Is it necessary to add that it is precisely this very different ratio of the political to the personal which makes such texts alien to us at first approach and resistant to our conventional Western habits of reading?

I will offer, as something like the supreme example of this process of allegorization, the first masterwork of China's greatest writer, Lu Xun, whose neglect in Western cultural studies is a matter of shame which no excuses based on ignorance can rectify. "A Madman's Diary" (*Silent China: Selected Writings of Lu Xun*, ed. and trans. Gladys Yang [London, Oxford, and New York: Oxford University Press, 1973], 3–13) must at first be read by any Western reader as the protocol of what our essentially psychological language generally terms a "nervous breakdown." It offers the notes and perceptions of a subject in intensifying prey to a terrifying psychic delusion, the conviction that the people around him are concealing a dreadful secret, and that that secret can be none other than the increasingly obvious fact that they are cannibals. At the climax of the development of the delusion, which threatens his own physical safety and his very life itself as a potential victim, the narrator understands that his own brother is himself a cannibal and that the death of their little sister, a number of years earlier, far from being the result of childhood illness, as he had thought, was in reality a murder.

As befits the protocol of a psychosis, these perceptions are objective ones, which can be rendered without any introspective machinery: the paranoid subject observes sinister glances around him in the real world, he overhears tell-tale conversations between his brother and an alleged physician (obviously in reality another cannibal) which carry all the conviction of the real and can be objectively (or "realistically") represented. Since this is not the place to demonstrate in any detail the absolute pertinence to Lu Xun's case history of the preeminent Western or First World reading of such phenomena, I will only mention Freud's interpretation of the paranoid delusions of Senatspresident Schreber: an emptying out of the world, a radical withdrawal of libido (what Schreber describes as "world-catastrophe"), followed by the attempt to recathect by the obviously imper-

fect mechanisms of paranoia. "The delusion-formation," Freud
explains, "which we take to be a pathological product, is in reality
an attempt at recovery, a process of reconstruction" (*The Standard
Edition*, 12 [London: Hogarth Press, 1958], 457).

What is reconstructed, however, is a grisly and terrifyingly objective real world beneath the appearances of our own world: an
unveiling or deconcealment of the nightmarish reality of things, a
stripping away of our conventional illusions or rationalizations about
daily life and existence which is comparable, as a literary effect, only
to some of the processes of Western modernism, and in particular of
Western existentialism, in which narrative is employed as a powerful
instrument for the experimental exploration of reality and illusion, an
exploration which, however, unlike some of the older realisms, presupposes a certain prior "personal knowledge." The reader must, in
other words, have had some analogous experience, whether in physical illness or psychic crisis, of a lived and balefully transformed real
world from which we cannot even mentally escape, for the full horror
of Lu Xun's nightmare to be appreciated. Terms like "depression"
deform such experience by psychologizing it and projecting it back
into the pathological Other; while the analogous Western literary
approaches to this same experience (I'm thinking of the canonical
deathbed murmur of Kurtz, in Conrad's *Heart of Darkness*—"The
horror! the horror!") recontain precisely that horror by transforming
it into a rigorously private and subjective "mood," which can only be
designated by recourse to an aesthetic of *expression*—the unspeakable, unnameable inner feeling whose external formulation can only
designate it from without, like a symptom.

But not even this representational power of Lu Xun's text can
be properly appreciated without some sense of what I have called its
allegorical resonance. For it should be clear that the cannibalism
literally apprehended by the sufferer in the attitudes and bearing of
his family and neighbors is at one and the same time being attributed
by Lu Xun himself to Chinese society as a whole, and if this attribution is to be called "figural," it is if anything a figure more powerful
and "literal" than the "literal" level of the text. Lu Xun's proposition
is then that the people of this great maimed and retarded, disintegrating China of the late and postimperial period, his fellow citizens,
are "literally" cannibals: in their desperation, disguised and indeed
intensified by the most traditional forms and procedures of Chinese
culture, they must devour one another ruthlessly to stay alive—
and this at all levels of that exceedingly hierarchical society, from

Lumpens and peasants all the way to the most privileged, elite positions in the mandarin bureaucracy. This is, I want to stress, a social and historical nightmare, a vision of the horror of life specifically grasped through History itself, whose consequences go far beyond the more local Western realistic or naturalistic representation of cutthroat capitalist or market competition and know a specifically political resonance absent from its natural or mythological Western equivalent in the nightmare of Darwinian natural selection.

Now I want to offer four additional remarks about this text, which will touch, respectively, on the libidinal dimension of the story, on the structure of its allegory, on the role of the Third World cultural producer himself, and on the perspective of futurity projected by the tale's double resolution. I will be concerned, in dealing with all four of these topics, to stress the radical structural difference between the dynamics of Third World culture and those of the First World cultural tradition in which we have ourselves been formed.

I've suggested that in Third World texts such as this story by Lu Xun, the relationship between the libidinal and the political components of individual and social experience is radically different from what obtains in the West and what shapes our own cultural forms. Let me try to characterize this difference, or if you like this radical reversal, by way of the following generalization. In the West, conventionally, political commitment is recontained and psychologized or subjectivized by way of the public-private split I've already evoked: interpretations, for example, of the political movements of the 1960s in terms of Oedipal revolts are familiar to everyone and need no further comment. That such interpretations are episodes in a much longer tradition whereby political commitment is re-psychologized and accounted for in terms of the subjective dynamics of ressentiment or the "authoritarian personality," is perhaps less well understood, but can be demonstrated by a careful reading of antipolitical texts from Nietzsche and Conrad all the way to the latest Cold War propaganda.

What is relevant to our present context is not, however, the demonstration of that proposition, but rather of its inversion in Third World culture, where I want to suggest that psychology, or more specifically, libidinal investment, is rather to be read in primarily political and social terms. (It is, I hope, unnecessary to add that what follows is speculative and very much subject to correction by specialists: it is offered as a methodological example rather than a "theory" of Chinese culture.) We're told, for one thing, that the great ancient imperial cosmologies identify by analogy what we in the West analytically separate: thus, the classical sex manuals are at one with the texts that reveal the dynamics of political forces, the charts of the heavens are at one with the logic of medical lore, and so forth. Here already then, but in an ancient past, Western antinomies—and most particularly that between the subjective and the public or political— are refused in advance.

The libidinal center of Lu Xun's text is, however, not sexuality, but rather the oral stage, the whole bodily question of eating, of ingestion, devoration, incorporation, from which such fundamental categories as the pure and the impure spring. We must now recall, not merely the extraordinary symbolic complexity of Chinese cuisine, but also the central role this art and practice occupies in Chinese culture as a whole: the only very distant Western equivalent would be the culture of France. And when we find that centrality confirmed by the observation that the very rich Chinese vocabulary for sexual matters is extraordinarily intertwined with the language of eating, and when we observe the multiple uses to which the verb "to eat" is put in ordinary Chinese language (one "eats" a fear or a fright, for example), we may feel in a somewhat better position to sense the enormous sensitivity of this libidinal region, and of Lu Xun's mobilization of it for the dramatization of an essentially social nightmare— something which in a Western writer would be consigned to the realm of the merely private obsession, the vertical dimension of the personal trauma. The French analogy is instructive here, for in that progressive violation of literary taboos which characterizes Western literature generally in the 1960s—the sequential transgressions which open literary discourse to successive areas of the hitherto unnameable, from incest or Nabokov's nymphets to homosexualities and sadomasochisms—it is most striking to observe the approach in France to a last taboo unfamiliar to the rest of us, namely the transgression of the symbolic order of the menu—a wave of images of cannibalism and orgies of overeating that can only be taken as the collective expression of a peculiar new social crisis.

A rather different alimentary transgression can be observed everywhere in Lu Xun's works, nowhere quite so strikingly as in his terrible little story, "Medicine": the story of a dying child—the death of children is a constant in these works—whose parents have the great good fortune to procure an infallible remedy. At which point we must also recall, not merely that traditional Chinese medicine is "eaten" not "taken," as in the West, but also that for Lu Xun traditional Chinese medicine was the supreme locus of the unspeakable and exploitative charlatanry of traditional Chinese culture generally. In his crucially important preface to the first collective of his stories, he recounts the suffering and death of his own father from tuberculosis, while the declining family reserves rapidly disappeared into the purchase of expensive and rare, exotic and ludicrous medicaments. You will not sense the symbolic significance of this indignation unless you remember that for all these reasons Lu Xun decided to study Western medicine in Japan—the epitome of some new Western science that promised collective regeneration—only to decide that the production of culture (I am tempted to say, the elaboration of a political culture) was a more effective form of political medicine. As a writer, then, Lu Xun remains a diagnostician and a physician. Hence this terrible story, in which the cure for the male child, the father's only hope for survival in future generations, turns out to be one of those large, doughy-white Chinese steamed rolls soaked in the blood of a criminal who has just been executed. It is perhaps not necessary to add that the child dies anyway; but it is necessary to identify the hapless victim of a more properly state violence as a political militant, whose grave is mysteriously covered in flowers by absent sympathizers of whom one knows nothing. In the analysis of a story like this, we must rethink our conventional conception of symbolic levels of a narrative (where sexuality and politics might be in homology to each other, for instance) as rather a set of loops or circuits which intersect and overdetermine each other—the enormity of therapeutic cannibalism finally intersecting, in a paupers' cemetery, with the more overt violence of family betrayal and political repression.

   This new mapping process then brings me to the cautionary remark I wanted to make about allegory itself—a form long discredited in the West, and the specific target of the romantic revolution of Wordsworth and Coleridge, yet a linguistic structure which seems to be showing a remarkable reawakening of interest in contemporary literary theory. If allegory has once again become somehow congenial for us today, as over against the massive and monumental unifications of an older modernist symbolism or realism itself, it is because the allegorical spirit is profoundly discontinuous, a matter of breaks and heterogeneities, of the multiple polysemia of the dream rather than the homogeneous representation of the symbol. Our traditional conception of allegory—based, for instance, on stereotypes of Bunyan—is that of an elaborate set of figures and personifications to be read against some one-to-one table of equivalences: this is, so to speak, a one-dimensional view of this signifying process, which might only be set in motion and complexified were we willing to entertain the more alarming notion that such equivalences are themselves in constant change and transformation at each perpetual present of the text.

Here too Lu Xun has some lessons for us. This writer of short stories and sketches, which never evolved into the novel form as such, produced at least one approach to the longer form, in a much lengthier series of anecdotes about a hapless coolie named Ah Q, who comes to serve, as we might have suspected, as the allegory of a certain set of Chinese attitudes and modes of behavior. It is interesting to note that the enlargement of the form determines a shift in tone or generic discourse: now everything that had been stricken with the stillness and emptiness of death and suffering without hope—"the room was not only too silent, it was far too big as well, and the things in it were far too empty" (Lu Xun, *Tomorrow*, in *Selected Stories* [Beijing: Foreign Languages Press, 1972], 40)—becomes matter for a more properly Chaplinesque comedy.

Ah Q's resiliency springs from an unusual but, we are given to understand, culturally very normal and familiar technique for over-coming humiliation. When set upon by his persecutors, Ah Q—serene in his superiority over them—reflects:

> "It is as if I were beaten by my own son. What is the world coming to nowadays . . ." Thereupon he too would walk away, satisfied at having won. Admit that you are not even human, they insist, that you are nothing but an animal! On the contrary, he tells them, I'm worse than an animal, I'm an insect! There, does that satisfy you? In less than ten seconds, however, Ah Q would walk away also satisfied that he had won, thinking that he was after all "number one in self-belittlement," and that after removing the "self-belittlement" what remained was still the glory of remaining "number one." (*Tomorrow*, 72)

When one recalls the remarkable self-esteem of the Manchu dynasty in its final throes, and the serene contempt for foreign devils who had nothing but modern science, gunboats, armies, technology and power to their credit, one achieves a more precise sense of the historical and social topicality of Lu Xun's satire.

Ah Q is thus, allegorically, China itself. What I want to observe, however, and what complicates the whole issue, is that his persecu-tors—the idlers and bullies who find their daily pleasures in getting a rise out of just such miserable victims as Ah Q—these are *also* China, in the allegorical sense. This very simple example then shows the capacity of allegory to generate a range of distinct meanings or messages simultaneously, as the allegorical tenor and vehicle change places: Ah Q is China humiliated by the foreigners, a China so well versed in the spiritual techniques of self-justification that such humiliations are not even registered, let alone recalled. But the persecutors are also China, in a different sense: the terrible, self-cannibalistic China of "A Madman's Diary," whose response to powerlessness is the ceaseless persecution of the weaker and more inferior members of the hierarchy.

All of which slowly brings us to the question of the writer in the Third World, and to what must be called the function of the intellectual, it being understood that in the Third World situation the intellectual is always in one way or another a political intellectual. No Third World lesson is more timely or more urgent for us today, among whom the very term "intellectual" has withered away, as though it were the name for an extinct species. Nowhere has the strangeness of this vacant position been brought home to me more strongly than on a recent trip to Cuba, when I had occasion to visit a remarkable college-preparatory school on the outskirts of Havana. It is a matter of some shame for an American to witness the cultural curriculum in a socialist setting which also very much identifies itself with the Third World: over some three or four years, Cuban teenagers study both poems of Homer, Dante's *Inferno*, the Spanish theatrical classics, the great realistic novels of the nineteenth-century European tradition, and finally, contemporary Cuban revolutionary novels—of which, incidentally, we desperately need English translations. But the semester's work I found most challenging was one explicitly devoted to the study of the role of the intellectual as such: the cultural intellectual who is also a political militant, the intellectual who produces both poetry and praxis. The Cuban illustrations of this process—Ho Chi Minh and Augustino Nieto—are obviously enough culturally determined: our own equivalents would probably be the more familiar figures of DuBois and C. L. R. James, of Sartre and Neruda or Brecht, of Kollontai or Louise Michel. But as this whole essay aims implicitly at suggesting a new conception of the humanities in American education today, it is obviously appropriate to add that the study of the role of the intellectual as such ought to be a key component in any such proposals.

I've already said something about Lu Xun's own conception of his vocation and its extrapolation from the practice of medicine. But there is a great deal more to be said, and specifically about the preface I've already referred to, which is not only one of the fundamental documents for the understanding of the situation of the Third World artist, but also a dense text in its own right, fully as much a work of art as any of the greatest stories and the supreme example in Lu Xun's work of the very unusual ratio of subjective investment and a deliberately depersonalized objective narration. In the space of this essay, I cannot do justice to those relationships, which would demand a line-by-line commentary. Yet I will quote the little fable by which Lu Xun, responding to requests for publication by his friends and future collaborators, dramatizes his dilemma:

> Imagine an iron house without windows, absolutely indestructible, with many people fast asleep inside who will shortly die of suffocation. But you know that since they will die in their sleep, they will not feel the pain of death. Now if you cry aloud to wake a few of the lighter sleepers, making those unfortunate few suffer the agony of irrevocable death, will you imagine that you are thereby doing them a favor?

The seemingly hopeless situation of the Third World intellectual in this historical period shortly after the founding of the Chinese Communist Party, but also after the bankruptcy of the middle-class revolution had become apparent—in which no solutions, no forms of praxis or change, seem conceivable—will find its parallel, as we shall see shortly, in the situation of African intellectuals after the achievement of independence, when once again no political solutions seem present or visible on the historical horizon. The formal or literary manifestation of this political problem is, to be sure, that of the possibilities of narrative closure, something we will return to more specifically.

But it can also be discussed in a more general theoretical context, and it is this theoretical form of the problem I would at least like to thematize and to set in place on the agenda at this point. We must, I have felt lately, recover a sense of what in its strongest form "cultural revolution" means in the Marxist tradition. The reference is not to the immediate events of that violent and tumultuous interruption of the "eleven years" in recent Chinese history, although some reference to Maoism as a doctrine is necessarily implicit. But the term, we are told, was Lenin's own, and in that form explicitly designated the literacy campaign and the new problems of universal scholarity and education—something of which Cuba, again, remains the most stunning and successful example in recent history.

We must, however, enlarge the conception still further to include a range of seemingly very different preoccupations, the scope and focus of which the names of Antonio Gramsci and Wilhelm Reich, Frantz Fanon, Rudolph Bahro, and Paolo Freire may give an indication. Overhastily, I will suggest that "cultural revolution" as it is projected (and not necessarily under that designation) in such works turns on the phenomenon of what Gramsci called "subalternity," namely the mental inferiority feelings and the habits of subservience and obedience necessarily and structurally developed by situations of domination—most dramatically in the experience of colonized peoples. But here, as so often, the subjectivizing and psychologizing habits of First World peoples such as ourselves can play us false and lead us into misunderstandings. Subalternity is not in that sense a psychological matter, although it governs psychologies; and I suppose that the strategic choice of the term "cultural" aims very precisely at restructuring that view of the problem and projecting it outwards into the realm of objective or collective spirit in some nonpsychological, but also nonreductionist, noneconomistic, and nonvulgar/materialistic fashion. When a psychic structure is objectively determined by economics and political relationships, it cannot be dealt with by means of purely psychological therapies; yet it is equally impossible to deal with it by means of purely objective transformations of the economic and political situation itself, since the habits remain and exercise a baleful and crippling residual effect. This is a more dramatic form of that old mystery, the unity of theory and practice; and it is very specifically in the context of this problem of cultural revolution (now so strange and alien to us) that the achievements and failures of the Third World intellectuals, writers, and artists must be replaced in order to grasp their concrete historical meaning.

We have allowed ourselves, as First World cultural intellectuals, to restrict our consciousness of our life's work to the narrowest professional or bureaucratic terms, thereby encouraging in ourselves a special sense of subalternity and guilt which only reinforces the vicious circle. That a literary article could be a political act with real consequences is for most of us little more than a curiosity of the literary history of czarist Russia or of modern China itself: but we should perhaps also take into account the possibility that as intellectuals we ourselves are presently sleeping soundly in that indestructible iron room, of which Lu Xun spoke, on the point of suffocation.

The matter of narrative closure, then, and of the relationship of a narrative text to futurity and to some collective project yet to come, is not any merely formal or literary-critical issue. "A Madman's Diary" has in fact two distinct and incompatible endings, which it is instructive to examine in light of the writer's own hesitations and anxieties about his social role as we have just listened to them. One ending, that of the deluded subject himself, is very much a call to the future, in the impossible situation of a well-nigh universal cannibalism: the last desperate lines launched into the void are the words, "Save the children . . ." The second ending is disclosed on the opening page, when the older (supposedly cannibalistic) brother greets the narrator of the frame with the following cheerful remark: "I appreciate your coming such a long way to see us, but my brother recovered some time ago and has gone elsewhere to take up an official post." So, in advance, the nightmare is annulled; the paranoid visionary, vouchsafed his brief and terrible glimpse of the grisly reality beneath appearance, gratefully returns to the realm of illusion and oblivion therein again to take up his place in the space of bureaucratic power and privilege. I want to suggest that it is only at this price, by way of a complex play of simultaneous and antithetical messages, that the narrative text is able to open up a concrete perspective on the real future.

Now, before examining the African texts mentioned earlier, I must advise the reader that this essay is concerned to honor the memory of Robert C. Elliott and to commemorate his life's work. The very center of that work is to be found in his pathbreaking association of satire and the utopian impulse as two seemingly antithetical drives (and literary discourses) which in reality replicate each other such that each is always secretly active within the other's sphere of influence. All satire, he taught us, necessarily carries a utopian frame of reference within itself; all utopias, no matter how serene or disembodied, are driven secretly by the satirist's rage at a fallen reality. When I tell you that in writing of futurity earlier in the essay I took pains to withhold the word *utopia*, which is to my mind the proper name of this particular subject, you will perhaps understand that we have already begun to enter this central region, in which Elliott's master texts are the markers and the monuments.

But now I can be more explicit, and I want to take as my point of focus the concluding lines of an astonishing passage from the novel *Xala*, by the great contemporary Senegalese novelist and filmmaker Ousmane Sembène (Westport, Conn.: Lawrence Hill and Company, 1976). The title designates a ritual curse or affliction of a very special kind, which has been visited on a prosperous and corrupt Senegalese businessman just as he reaches the height of his fortune and takes to himself a beautiful young (third) wife—shades of *The Power of Satire!* The curse is of course, as you may have guessed, sexual impotence. The Hadj, the unfortunate hero of this novel, desperately explores a number of remedies, both Western and tribal, to no avail and is finally persuaded to undertake a laborious trip out into the hinterland of Dakar to seek out a shaman of reputedly extraordinary powers. Here is the conclusion of his hot and dusty journey in a horse-drawn cart:

> As they emerged from a ravine, they saw conical thatched roofs, grey-black with weathering, standing out against the horizon in the middle of the empty plain. Free-ranging, skinny cattle with dangerous-looking horns fenced with one another to get at what little grass there was. No more than silhouettes in the distance, a few people were busy around the only well. The driver of the cart was in familiar territory and greeted people as they passed. Sereen Mada's house, apart from its imposing size, was identical in construction with all the others. It was situated in the center of the village whose huts were arranged in a semi-circle, which you entered by a single main entrance. The village had neither shop nor school nor dispensary; there was nothing at all attractive about it in fact [Sembène concludes, then adding as if in afterthought this searing conclusion:] Its life was based on the principles of community interdependence. (*Xala*, 69)

Here, then, more emblematically than virtually any other text I know, the space of a past and future utopia—a social world of collective cooperation—is dramatically inserted into the corrupt and Westernized money economy of the new post-independence national or comprador bourgeoisie: indeed, Sembène takes pains to show us that the Hadj is not an industrialist, that his business is in no sense productive, but that he functions as a middleman between European multinationals and local extraction industries. To this biographical sketch must also be added a very significant fact indeed: that in his youth, the Hadj was political and spent some time in jail for his nationalist and pro-independence activities. The extraordinary satire of these corrupt classes (which Sembène will extend to the person of Senghor himself in another novel) is then explicitly marked as the failure of the independence movement to develop into a general social revolution.

The fact of nominal national independence—in Latin America in the nineteenth century, in Africa in the midtwentieth century—

puts an end to a movement for which national independence is the only conceivable goal. Nor is this symbolic myopia the only problem; the African states also had to face the crippling effects of what Fanon prophetically warned them against: to receive independence is not the same as to take it, since it is in the revolutionary struggle itself that new social relationships and a new consciousness is developed. Here again the history of Cuba is instructive: it was the last of the Latin American nations to win its freedom in the nineteenth century, a freedom which was immediately usurped by another greater colonial power. We now know the incalculable role played in the Cuban Revolution of 1959 by the protracted guerrilla struggles of the late nineteenth century (of which the figure of José Martí is the emblem): contemporary Cuba would not be the same without that laborious and subterranean (one wants to say Thompsonian) experience of the mole of History burrowing through a lengthy past and creating its specific traditions in the process.

So it is that after the poisoned gift of independence, radical African writers like Sembène or like Ngugi in Kenya find themselves back at square one (in the dilemma of Lu Xun), bearing a passion for change and social regeneration which has not yet found its agents. I hope it is clear that this is also very much an aesthetic dilemma, a crisis of representation: it was not difficult to identify an adversary who spoke another language and wore the visible trappings of colonial occupation. When those are replaced by your own people, the connections to external controlling forces are much more difficult to represent. The new leaders may of course throw off their masks in turn and reveal the person of the Dictator, whether in its older individual or new military form; but this moment also determines problems of representation, and it is a pity the scope of this essay does not allow me to examine the dictator novel in detail, as it has become a virtual genre of Latin American literature and has known significant analogues in Aimé Cesaire's Christophe play, in Salman Rushdie's *Shame*, and in far fewer African texts. These works are marked above all by a profound and uneasy ambivalence, a deeper ultimate sympathy for the Dictator which can perhaps only be properly accounted for by some enlarged social variant of the Freudian mechanism of transference.

The form normally taken by a radical diagnosis of the failures of contemporary Third World societies is, however, what is conventionally designated as "cultural imperialism," a faceless influence without representable agents, whose literary expression seems to demand the invention of new forms: Manuel Puig's *Betrayed by Rita Hayworth* may be cited as one of the most striking and innovative of those. One is led to conclude that under these circumstances traditional realism is less effective than the satiric fable—whence to my mind the greater power of certain of Sembène's narratives (besides *Xala*, I should mention *The Money-Order*) as over against Ngugi's impressive but problematical *Petals of Blood*.

With the fable, however, we are clearly very much back into the whole question of allegory. *The Money-Order* mobilizes the traditional *Catch–22* or *Captain from Koepenick* dilemma: its hapless protagonist cannot cash his Parisian check without identity papers, but since he was born long before independence there are no documents; meanwhile the money order, uncashed, begins to melt away before the fact in an accumulation of new credits and new debits. I am tempted to anachronistically suggest that this work published in 1965, prophetically dramatized the greatest misfortune that can happen to Third World countries in our time, namely the discovery of vast oil resources—something which, far from representing salvation, economists have shown, sinks them incalculably into a sea of foreign debts they can never dream of liquidating.

On another level, however, this tale raises the issue of what must finally be one of the key problems in any analysis of Sembène's work, namely the ambiguous role played in it by archaic or tribal elements. Viewers may perhaps remember the curious ending of his first film, *The Black Girl*, in which the European employer is inconclusively pursued by the little boy wearing an archaic mask; meanwhile such historical films as *Ceddo* or *Emitai* seem intent on evoking older moments of tribal resistance, either to Islam or to the West, yet imbed this in a historical perspective which with few exceptions tells the story of their defeat. Sembène cannot, however, be suspected of any archaizing or nostalgic "cultural nationalism"; so it becomes important to determine the worth of this appeal to older tribal values, particularly as they are more subtly active in modern works like *Xala* or *The Money-Order*. For I suspect that the deeper subject of this second novel is not so much the evident one of the denunciation of a modern national bureaucracy, but of the historical transformation of the traditional Islamic value of almsgiving in a contemporary money economy. A Muslim has the duty to give alms—indeed, the work concludes with just such another unfulfilled request—yet in a modern economy, this sacred duty to the poor is transformed into a frenzied assault by freeloaders from all levels of society (at length, the cash is appropriated by a Westernized and affluent, influential cousin). The hero is literally picked clean by the vultures; even more significantly, the unsought for, unexpected treasure fallen from heaven at once transforms everyone around him into ferocious and insatiable petitioners in something like a monetary version of Lu Xun's cannibalism.

The same double historical perspective—archaic customs radically transformed and denatured by the superposition of capitalist relations—seems to me demonstrable in *Xala* as well, in the often hilarious results of the more ancient Islamic and tribal institution of polygamy. This is what Sembène has to say about that institution (it being understood that authorial intervention, no longer tolerable in realistic narrative, is still perfectly suitable to the allegorical fable as a form):

> It is worth knowing something about the life led by urban polygamists. It could be called geographical polygamy, as opposed to rural polygamy, where all the wives and children live together in the same compound. In the town, since the families are scattered, the children have little contact with their father. Because of his way of life the father must go from house to house, villa to villa, and is only there in the evenings, at bedtime. He is therefore primarily a source of finance, when he has work. (*Xala*, 66)

Indeed, we are vividly treated to the spectacle of the Hadj's misery when at the moment of his third marriage, which should secure his social status, he realizes he has no real home of his own and is condemned to shuttle from one wife's villa to the other, suspecting each of them in turn as being responsible for his ritual affliction. But the passage I have just read shows that—whatever one would wish to think about polygamy in and of itself as an institution—it functions here as a twin-valenced element designed to open up historical perspective. The more and more frenzied trips of the Hadj through the great city secure a juxtaposition between capitalism and the older collective tribal form of social life—here alluded to by the reference to "rural polygamy," but in the visit to Sereen Mada's desert fastness openly identified as such.

These are as yet, however, by no means the most remarkable features of *Xala*, which can be taken as a stunning and controlled, virtually textbook exercise in what I've elsewhere called "generic discontinuities." The novel begins, in effect, in one generic convention in terms of which the Hadj is read as a comic victim: everything goes wrong all at once, and the news of his disability suddenly triggers a greater misfortune, as his numerous creditors begin to descend on someone whose bad luck clearly marks him out as a loser. A comic pity and terror accompanies this process, which does not imply any very great sympathy for the personage, but certainly a greater revulsion against the privileged new Westernized society in which this rapid overturning of the wheel of fortune can take place. Yet we have all been in error, as it turns out: the wives have not been the source of the ritual curse, and in an abrupt generic reversal and enlargement (comparable to some of the mechanisms Freud describes in "The Uncanny"), we suddenly learn something new and chilling about the Hadj's past:

> "Our story goes back a long way. It was shortly before your marriage to that woman there. Don't you remember? I was sure you would not. What I am now" (a beggar in rags is addressing him) "what I am now is your fault. Do you remember selling a large piece of land at Jeko belonging to our clan? After falsifying the clan names with the complicity of people in high places, you took our land from us. In spite of our protests, our proof of ownership, we lost our case in the courts. Not satisfied with taking our land you had me thrown into prison."
> (*Xala*, 110–11)

Thus the Ur-crime of capitalism is set in place: less wage labor as such, or the ravages of the money form, or the remorseless and impersonal rhythms of the market, than this primal displacement of the older forms of collective life in a land now seized and privatized—the oldest of modern tragedies, visited on the native Americans yesterday, on the Palestinians today, and significantly reintroduced by Sembène into his film version of *The Money-Order* titled *Mandabi*, in which the protagonist is now threatened with the imminent loss of his dwelling itself.

The point I want to make about this terrible "return of the repressed," however, is that it determines a remarkable generic transformation of the narrative: suddenly we are no longer in satire, but in ritual. The beggars and the Lumpens, led by Sereen Mada himself, descend on the Hadj and require him to submit, for the removal of his *xala*, to an abominable ceremony of ritual humiliation and abasement. The representational space of the narrative is lifted up into a new generic realm, which reaches back to touch the powers of the archaic even as it foretells in the mode of prophecy the utopian destruction of the fallen present. The word *Brechtian*, which inevitably springs to mind, probably does very inadequate justice to these new forms which have emerged from a properly Third World reality. Yet in the light of this unexpected generic ending, the preceding satiric text is itself retroactively transformed: from a satire whose subject matter or content was the ritual curse visited on a character within the narrative, it suddenly stands itself revealed as a ritual curse in its own right—the entire imagined chain of events becomes Sembène's own curse upon his hero and the people like him. No more stunning confirmation could be adduced for Elliott's great insight into the anthropological origins of satiric discourse in real acts of shamanistic malediction.

I want to conclude with a few thoughts on why all this should be so and on the origins and the status of what I have identified as the primacy of national allegory in Third World culture. We are, after all, very familiar with the mechanisms of autoreferentiality in contemporary Western literature: is this not simply to be taken as another form of that, in a structurally distinct social and cultural context? Perhaps, but then in that case, our priorities must be reversed for proper understanding of this mechanism. The disrepute of social allegory in our own culture, the well-nigh inescapable operation of social allegory in the West's Other—these things are finally to be grasped, I think, in terms of situational consciousness, an expression I prefer to the more common term, "materialism."

Hegel's old analysis of the Master-Slave relationship may still be the most effective way of dramatizing this distinction between two cultural logics: two equals struggle, each for recognition by the other. The one is willing to sacrifice life for this supreme value. The other, a heroic coward in the Brechtian-Schweykian sense of loving the body and the material world too well, gives in in order to continue life. The Master—now the fulfillment of a baleful and inhuman feudal-aristocratic disdain for life without honor—proceeds to enjoy the benefits of his Recognition by the other, who is now become his humble serf or slave. But at this point, two distinct and dialectically ironic reversals take place. Only the Master is now genuinely human, so that "recognition" by this henceforth subhuman form of life which is the Slave evaporates at the moment of its attainment and offers no genuine satisfaction. The truth of the Master, Hegel observes grimly, is the Slave; while the truth of the Slave, on the other hand, is the Master. A second reversal is in process as well, for the Slave is called upon to labor for the Master and to furnish him with all the material benefits befitting his supremacy. But this means that, in the end, only the Slave knows what reality and the resistance of matter really are; only the Slave can attain some true materialistic consciousness of his situation, since it is precisely that to which he is condemned. The Master is, however, condemned to idealism: the luxury of a placeless freedom in which any consciousness of his own concrete situation flees like a dream, like a work unremembered on the tip of the tongue, a nagging doubt which the puzzled mind is unable to formulate.

It strikes me that we Americans, we masters of the world, are in something of that very same position. The view from the top is epistemologically crippling and reduces its subjects to the illusions of a host of fragmented subjectivities—to the poverty of the individual experience of isolated monads, of dying individual bodies without collective pasts, and futures bereft of any possibility of grasping the social totality. This placeless individuality, this structural idealism which affords us the luxury of the Sartrean blink, the welcome escape from the "nightmare of history," and at the same time condemns our culture to psychologism and the "projections" of private subjectivity—all of this is denied to Third World culture, which must be situational and materialist, as it were, despite itself. And it is this, finally, which must account for the allegorical nature of Third World culture, where the telling of the individual story and the individual experience cannot but ultimately involve the whole laborious telling of the experience of the collectivity itself.

I hope I have suggested the epistemological priority of this unfamiliar kind of allegorical vision; but I must also admit that old habits die hard and that, for us, such unaccustomed exposure to reality—or to the collective totality—is often intolerable, leaving us in Quentin's position at the end of *Absalom, Absalom!* murmuring the great denial: "I don't hate the Third World! I don't! I don't! I don't!"

Even that resistance is instructive, however; and we may well feel, confronted with the daily reality of the other two-thirds of the globe, that "there was nothing at all attractive about it in fact." But we must not allow ourselves that feeling without also acknowledging its ultimate mocking completion: "Its life was based on the principles of community interdependence."

'Parler Sans Parler': The Rhetoricity of Fictional Discourse

Clayton Koelb

"**I**s There a Problem about Fictional Discourse?" asks the title of a valuable essay by the philosopher Richard Rorty.[1] One would suppose that there must be a problem, since the topic has received so much attention, particularly from Anglo-American analytic philosophy. Rorty argues effectively, however, that the question about fictional discourse is really a question about "what to say about truth in general. If truth is 'correspondence to reality,' we seem to have a problem. . . . If truth is simply 'warranted assertability,' however, [as Rorty maintains] we have what may seem a less difficult problem . . ." (110).

Rorty proposes that the difficulty of fictional discourse arises only when we adhere to a correspondence-theory of truth. He is able to make this assertion because indeed the questions about fictional discourse proposed by analytic philosophy have centered upon the truth-status of sentences like "Sherlock Holmes lived in Baker Street." We readily assent to the truth of this statement; but the analytic philosopher wonders how we can do so when there is no reality to which the name "Sherlock Holmes" corresponds. Various solutions have been proposed: that is, various philosophers have posited ways of understanding the sentence so that its truth-value can be maintained in spite of its fictionality. Rorty gives a lively account of some of the most important of these solutions, returning finally to his major point—that the whole problem ceases to exist, in a sense, if we accept the notion of truth as "warranted assertability." Under the proper circumstances, the assertion that "Holmes lived in Baker Street" is clearly warranted and therefore true, notwithstanding the nonexistence of any genuine person named "Sherlock Holmes."

159

Rorty is thus able to dispose neatly of the problem of fictional discourse as it has been formulated by analytic philosophy. But the ease with which Rorty disposes of the issue ought to make us a little suspicious—not of Rorty, who does admirably just what a pragmatist ought to do with the problem presented, but with the very presentation of the problem. The fact is, the most interesting questions about fictional discourse have not even been raised in the debate in which Rorty is participating. The sentence "Holmes lived in Baker Street" is indeed a good example of the kind of discourse that has received the attention of philosophy recently, but is it—in any fundamental sense—*fictional* discourse? It is, on the contrary, *genuine* discourse about a fictional object. (By "genuine" I do not mean something like "true," but rather, something like "bona fide." I use it as the opposite of "fictional," not as the opposite of "false.") Rorty is able to talk about the "warranted assertability" of this sentence because it is understood to be a real assertion. It is presumed that someone—we do not know or care who—is, in uttering the words "Holmes lived in Baker Street," claiming that Holmes (a fictitious person) lived (in the manner that fictitious persons may be said to "live") in Baker Street. But we might think of "fictional discourse" more radically and wonder how to treat sentences to which we cannot clearly attribute an intention to "say" anything at all. "Fictional discourse" in this more radical sense, where it is the act of saying itself that is fictional, will have to be defined on the fly, as it were, in the course of my discussion of it; for it is a complicated topic that goes far beyond the boundaries of the discussion cited by Rorty. It is a question of some interest to philosophers, perhaps, but of more urgent concern to literary critics. It is the question of what we are doing when we utter fictions. Instead of wondering what it means to say something like "Holmes lived in Baker Street," it might be more profitable to wonder what it means to say, with Randy Newman, "I love L.A.," or, with Faust, "Verweile doch! du bist so schön!"

Let me illustrate with an example taken from an authority on the philosophy of language in general and the problems of rhetoric in particular: Jim Ignatowski. While not often heard from in the pages of *PMLA*, Jim developed something of a reputation while serving as a regular on the television show "Taxi." He was a refugee from the drug culture of the sixties, one who had turned on, dropped out, but was never quite able again to tune in. But he tried. He wanted to get his driver's license in order to drive a cab, and though he studied hard, he still needed some help from his friends on the written test. One of the questions was, "What does a yellow light mean?" He asked his friend Bobby: "What does a yellow light mean?" Bobby replied, " 'Slow down'." And Jim repeated, "What . . . does . . . a . . . yellow . . . light . . . mean?" "'SLOW DOWN'!" "Whaaaat . . . dooees . . . aaaa . . . yeelllloow . . . liiiight . . . meeaan?" And so on.

Jim's problem here is really no laughing matter. It wasn't to him, of course, and while under these circumstances it might be to us, we might spend a few moments considering the nature of his difficulty. What it comes down to is the question of what Bobby was doing when he uttered the words *slow down*. Jim obviously thought he was *saying* "slow down" and acted accordingly. We find it odd that Jim thought so, but why? Didn't Bobby in fact say "slow down"? The answer is . . . well, yes and no, and thereby hangs the argument of this essay.

Before going on to the specific development of that argument, however, some initial discussion of a general theoretical framework is necessary. We find a useful framework for the kind of discussion undertaken here in speech-act theory, not only in the form first proposed by J. L. Austin in *How to Do Things with Words*,[2] but also in the surprising direction it takes in the work of Paul de Man. Austin's considerations are obviously of central relevance here, for the question I have formulated has to do with the relation between saying something and doing something, the very issue Austin first brought to the attention of philosophy. When we ask what Bobby was doing in uttering the words *slow down*, we are inquiring after the illocutionary force of his utterance. Under what we might call, with some trepidation, "normal" circumstances,[3] these words have the force of a command or request. By saying "slow down," in other words, one is ordinarily telling someone to slow down. What is obvious to us, if not to Jim Ignatowski, is that Bobby, in uttering "slow down," was *not* telling anyone to slow down. What he was doing, or trying to do, was instead to give the requested information about the meaning of a yellow light. His sentence was a kind of shorthand for "The meaning of a yellow light is that the driver should slow down," or even, "A yellow light issues the command: 'Slow down'." The intended illocutionary force of Bobby's "slow down," then, was not to command but to inform. He could have said, if he had wanted to avoid all ambiguity, "I hereby inform you that the meaning of a yellow light is a command to slow down." Then even Jim would have known what he was doing, though his utterance would have seemed to Jim, and to us, more than a little peculiar.

The fact is, we do not ordinarily have to be this specific about what we are doing with our words, because context usually acts to keep things clear. It is the audience's knowledge of the context, and Jim's inattention to it, that makes for the joke about the yellow light. We know perfectly well that, in such a situation, Bobby's "slow down" is an act of informing and not of commanding, that in uttering these words Bobby is not himself issuing a command, but citing the command issued conventionally by a yellow traffic light. We must also recognize, however, that there are no *textual* but only *con*textual clues to decide the illocutionary status of Bobby's remark, and that contextual clues are not wholly reliable. The context that is essential to determine the illocutionary force of any utterance is never wholly determinable, though it is never wholly lacking, either.[4] It is in the gap between the necessity for and impossibility of reliable context-determination that rhetoric prospers. Even in the relatively well defined context at issue here, the ground is not entirely firm: Bobby *could* have been telling Jim to slow down his speech because Bobby could not understand his question. Jim has wide experience of people not understanding him; and in this wider context of Jim's experience, his interpretation of Bobby's words makes a certain sense. Only the context, including especially our assumptions about that context, provides a basis for a decision. The words themselves, though, will not and cannot decide the issue.

In this respect (and seen from the perspective of Jim Ignatowski rather than the rest of us) Bobby's statement must be understood as *rhetorical* in the sense developed by de Man out of his consideration of the so-called rhetorical question.[5] De Man points out that, in the absence of a clarifying context or extratextual intention, there is no way to tell whether a given question is an actual question or a rhetorical one; that is, any question suspected of being rhetorical both affirms and denies its own illocutionary mode. He cites as an example the famous last lines from Yeats's "Among School Children":

> O chestnut-tree, great-rooted blossomer,
> Are you the leaf, the blossom or the bole?
> O body swayed to music, O brightening glance,
> How can we know the dancer from the dance?

While it has been the regular practice of critics to take these lines as rhetorical and not genuine questions, de Man's notion of rhetoricity suggests that both possibilities are open. Yeats's poem might be profitably understood as genuinely seeking to know how we could distinguish the dancer from the dance, while at the same time apparently denying the possibility of such a distinction.

As Jim's response demonstrates, Bobby's "slow down" has at least the potential for this same rhetoricity, as indeed does all fictional discourse. Because we cannot be absolutely certain of the quotation marks around his utterance, we cannot decide for certain whether to attribute to Bobby or to someone else (the yellow light) the intention to perform the illocutionary act of commanding. To put it more briefly, we cannot be certain whether or not Bobby is *saying* "slow down" "in the full sense of 'say'," as Austin puts it (92). Of course he is saying something, but as the audience understands him it is not he but the yellow light that "says" "slow down." What he "says," in this view, is that the yellow light "says" something. We must realize that, if the context is not clear—as it is not here for Jim—or if it is lacking altogether, there is no way to be sure what is being "said" in the case of fictional utterance. There are endless possibilities for what de Man calls referential aberration. Take the notorious case of Nietzsche's notebook entry, "'Ich habe meinen Regenschirm vergessen'." The possibility for commentary and debate, already partially realized in Derrida's *Spurs*,[6] that inheres in this sentence is for the most part the result of the quotation marks Nietzsche put around the sentence. Does this mean that someone else, not Nietzsche, is affirming the loss of his or her umbrella? Does it mean that Nietzsche is citing the sentence as an example of some sort? Because of those quotation marks we cannot simply assume that Nietzsche is reporting the loss of his umbrella, but we cannot on the other hand deny the possibility that he is doing so. He might be quoting himself. But if so, why would he thus distance himself from his own utterance? The questions can be multiplied at will.

Such questions are not relevant only to philosophers engaged in the development of high-level language theory. The rhetoricity of fictional utterance is something we meet with, and even at times use, in daily life. A particularly telling example—perhaps because it cuts so near the bone of our personal concerns—is this: a candidate is being interviewed for a position as a beginning assistant professor at a prestigious university. The interview is conducted by the department chairman, a person widely known to be extremely proud of his department, especially its record of recruiting faculty. "Nobody ever turned down an offer from us," he is reputed to have said. At the end of the interview, the chairman says:

> I want you to know that we had hundreds of applicants for this position. The department selected just three out of that group to be interviewed and authorized me to choose the best on the basis of these interviews. I have now seen all three candidates and must tell you that you are clearly the most qualified to fill our needs. What would you say if I were to tell you, here and now, "The job is yours"?

Has the candidate (let us call her "she") been offered a job? She has reason to believe both that she has and has not. Much in the context suggests that the chairman is really offering the job and using the fictional format merely for dramatic effect. After all, he does have the authority to offer the job, and he has stated that she is the most qualified candidate. On the other hand, it could be that the chairman wants to have assurances that any offer that *might* be made would be accepted and is with his question seeking a response in advance of any commitment on his part.

We can sympathize with the candidate's dilemma while at the same time recognizing the chairman's strategy as one which, at one time or another, many of us have used. There are many situations in which it is convenient to be able to say something and not say it at the same time, and the mode of fictional utterance stands ready to serve our need. Probably the sphere of activity most often pressed by this kind of obligation is diplomacy, where conflicting political and policy demands often make it necessary to present an utterance that can be both asserted and denied depending on what circumstances, or constituencies, dictate. Probably all of us can think of examples of rhetorical fictional discourse used in this very way by diplomats and politicians, the enumeration of which goes beyond the scope of this essay.

Such examples, as well as the one from the television show "Taxi," serve to show that even the most everyday instances of fictional utterance are capable of becoming rhetorical and generating referential aberration. In the belletristic use of language (in poetry and stories), however, this capability is almost always perceptible and often consciously exploited. The problematic is clearly visible not only in literary works of high culture but in popular forms as well. I remember seeing otherwise quite capable people scratch their heads with the mystified stare of a Jim Ignatowski upon hearing sung, over and over again, on every radio station in the country, the sentiment that "short people got no reason to live." It was with considerable relief that these listeners realized, most of them, that Randy Newman was not in fact expressing this view, but that there were invisible quotation marks around it, and that indeed the song worked ironically as a satire on racism. There are still those, however, who aren't quite sure, who harbor a suspicion that Newman would happily witness the eradication of everyone under, say, sixty-six inches tall. The song itself can never provide definitive evidence to refute such a view, because nothing but a fragile convention puts those unwritten and unheard quotation marks around Newman's words.

How unreliable that convention is can be readily seen in another of Newman's songs, "I Love L.A." Here it is simply impossible to determine whether the authorial voice is or is not asserting his love for Los Angeles. True, the L.A. landmarks the song singles out for praise are not exactly the ones the Chamber of Commerce would take us to see. On the other hand, Newman fans note—as does Newman himself, when asked—that the songwriter does by choice live in L.A. When we come to think about it, we realize that our inability to determine just how to understand this phrase, "I love L.A.," is the very thing that makes the song interesting. If we were sure one way or the other, if we knew that the song was either affirming (directly) or denying (ironically) a love of L.A., it would be tedious in the extreme. We can only love the song, as it were, because we can't know whether or not Randy Newman loves L.A.

Undoubtedly the most famous literary display of the problematic of fictional utterance appears in Goethe's *Faust*. Goethe transforms the traditional material of the Faust legend at the crucial point of Faust's contract with Mephistopheles: instead of a pact with a fixed term of twenty-four years, Faust proposes a bet. The terms of this bet, broadly conceived, turn upon the issue of Faust's becoming satisfied. Faust is betting that he will never find satisfaction, promising that if he does, the devil can have him then and there. The matter of central importance to the bet, then, is supposed to be Faust's satisfaction (or lack of it); but as the terms are actually worded, the central issue turns out to be something else. A world-famous quatrain sets forth the essence of the agreement:

Werd' ich zum Augenblicke sagen:
Verweile doch! du bist so schön!
Dann magst du mich in Fesseln schlagen,
Dann will ich gern zugrunde gehn! (1699–1702)

The point on which the contract turns is not Faust's satisfaction, but whether or not he *says* something, specifically the phrase, "Verweile doch! du bist so schön!" If and only if Faust does this thing, *says* this sentence, does Mephisto have the right to take his soul.

The question is, What does *sagen* mean? One thing is clear: neither Faust nor Mephisto understands it to mean "utter certain words." If they did so understand it, we realize, Faust would already have lost his bet, since in the very act of formulating the pact he had to utter the words "Verweile doch! du bist so schön!" If any utterance of those words constituted a *sagen*, a "saying" of them, Mephisto could legitimately claim that Faust's soul was then and there forfeit. Mephisto does not do so, and we readily understand why not: we know that Faust was not "really" *saying* at that moment "Verweile doch! du bist so schön!" but merely quoting the words so as to make them a part of the bet. They are, in this context, not genuine but fictional, and their utterance does not constitute a real act of "saying." Nothing in the context would lead us to believe that Faust, at this moment, would be expressing satisfaction: quite the opposite, since much of the surrounding discourse presents a Faust who is not only quite unsatisfied but also proud of and committed to his dissatisfaction. This Faust might, as he does, utter the phrase "Verweile doch! du bist so schön!" but he would never *say* it. The sentiment expressed by the words is not appropriate to the situation.

There is, of course, a real speech-act taking place here, but it is not an act of "saying" so much as of "promising." That this act of promising is a genuine action, undertaken deliberately and freely, is emphasized by Faust's defense of the "gesprochenes Wort" as something living and eternal in an impassioned speech just a few lines later in the scene (1716ff.). The devil wants it in writing, to be sure, but for Faust this is an unnecessary, and somewhat insulting, replication of the real promise made in the act of speaking. In a metaphor closely related to Plato's defense of the spoken word in the *Phaedrus*, Faust calls writing "ein Gespenst, vor dem sich alle scheuen" and maintains that "Das Wort erstirbt schon in der Feder" (1727–28).

The pact scene thus underscores the importance of "saying" things while, at the same time, it demonstrates how one may engage in discourse without in fact "saying" the words one speaks. Faust is right in taking Mephisto to task for not honoring his spoken word in the contract, since the issue of that contract is itself a set of spoken words. Mephisto is perfectly willing to take Faust's word (the proposed "Verweile doch! du bist so schön!") as sufficient occasion to bring about his damnation. Why, then, should he not be willing to accept Faust's word of promise?

Perhaps Mephisto suspects, correctly, that he is somehow in danger of losing the fish he thinks he has just caught. The devil's insistence upon the written contract, signed in blood, is a misdirected attempt at achieving clarity about the genuineness of discourse. Mephisto is, unfortunately for him, pinning down the wrong thing. In the context presented, there is no doubt that Faust has really performed the act of promising—the only issue clarified further by the written document—but there is considerable doubt about just what it is he has promised. He seems on the one hand to be promising to give himself up to Mephisto if he is ever satisfied, but on the other to be promising to give himself up only if he *says* certain words implying satisfaction. Mephisto has reason to think he can win the bet in the former case. He might at the same time dimly realize, however, that the latter case is a very hazy one, fraught with ambiguities potentially damaging to a literal-minded devil.

As we all know, Mephisto ends up losing the bet in the very moment when he apparently wins. The old Faust dies with the fateful words on his lips, but doubt remains as to whether or not he has actually *said* them:

> Zum Augenblicke dürft' ich sagen:
> Verweile doch, du bist so schön! (11581–82)

The mode is subjunctive and hypothetical: not "Zum Augenblick sag' ich hiermit . . ." (which would be a clear and enforceable instance of "saying"), but "Zum Augenblicke *dürft'* ich sagen. . . ." The implication is strong that this is no more a genuine "saying" of the crucial words than their citation at the time Faust made the contract. Once again, he seems to be quoting a prospective Faust of his imagination rather than actually performing the command "Verweile!" Once again, the discourse is fictional.

But there is an important complication in this instance of fictional utterance, because the context discloses a Faust who, unlike the Faust of the pact scene, really is expressing satisfaction. Although his words clearly enough belong inside quotation marks and are thereby attributed to an imaginary other, they express a sentiment appropriate to the situation. We have in this scene a character who could very well actually *say* "Verweile doch! du bist so schön!" even though he does not. Faust's apparently genuine satisfaction sharply alters the impact of his fictional utterance. We are no longer able, as we were in the pact scene, to disregard the sentiment expressed in the fictional discourse. The sentiment is simply too appropriate to the context—as it was not before—to permit such a move.

To put it bluntly, Faust seems here to have *both* said and not said the crucial sentence. His discourse has been rhetorical, for the utterance in its context both affirms and denies its illocutionary mode of "saying." The subjunctive mode and implied quotation marks deny it, while the situation and the surrounding text affirm it. We are no better able to decide here what Faust has actually done in speaking as he has than we were in the cases of "The job is yours," "Slow down," and "I love L.A." In terms of the letter of the contract, the point at issue has to be whether or not a genuine act of "saying" has taken place, since that determines Mephisto's right to Faust's soul. Evidently the high court of divinity decides this in Faust's favor, since the chorus of angels removes Faust's immortal part from Mephisto's grasp. But it could just as easily have gone the other way. The play ultimately makes clear that the issue of Faust's salvation or damnation has had little to do with the letter of the pact anyway, so from that point of view the issue is moot. That being the case, one is led to wonder why Goethe went to such trouble to set up a situation in which a rhetorical act of saying something produces the apparent climax.

One does not have to press very hard to see the answer to this question in the poetic reflexivity of Faust's situation. That Faust is a figure for the poetic spirit is a critical commonplace in no need of further defense or elaboration. That this is particularly true of the "Großer Vorhof" scene, the one in which Faust dies, is also evident. Faust's discourse is a pure "Dichtung," a poetic castle in the air with no more foundation than his mistaking his "Grab" for a "Graben"— the digging of his grave for the excavation of a canal.[7] The earnestness of Faust's wish "Auf freiem Grund mit freiem Volke stehn" (11580) is undercut by the real facts of his situation, in which neither "freier Grund" nor "freies Volk" are to be seen. Faust's final speech is both ironic and rhetorical in that it is both genuine (since it represents a real desire on Faust's part) and not at all genuine (since Faust is pathetically mistaken in the crucial assumptions underlying his discourse).

The rhetoricity of Faust's dying utterance as a whole, together with the rhetoricity of his utterance of the words of the pact, suggests strongly that Goethe was consciously foregrounding here the problematic of all fictional discourse, including particularly his own. This scene, and by extension the whole play, raises the question of what a poet is actually doing in composing a fiction. Do poets "say" anything in their compositions? Goethe seems to be rejecting both easy answers—the easy and naive affirmative answer and the equally easy, though somewhat more sophisticated, negative answer. The negative answer has been given particularly memorable form by Sidney in his observation that the poet "nothing affirmeth" and therefore cannot be accused of lying, even when seeming to make statements he knows to be untrue. This same position has been taken by I. A. Richards, in his assertion that the statements of poetry are "pseudo-statements," and by numerous others in similar formulations. The affirmative response claims that, while it may be true that the constituent elements of a fiction cannot be said to affirm anything, a literary work as a whole must be understood as some kind of act of communication—some act of "saying" something to us—else we would cease altogether from reading and interpreting such works.

I am arguing here that, to the degree that poetry is an act of fictional utterance, poets both do and do not say something in their fictions and that this "both-yes-and-no" situation is one of the most fundamental features of poetic discourse. I am also arguing that Goethe, aware of this characteristic of his own writing, dramatized it and put it in the most prominent possible position in *Faust*. The terms of Faust's bet with the devil, the question of whether he does or does not *say* something, may not be of crucial importance from the point of view of the salvation of Faust's soul, but it surely is of crucial importance when looked at as part of an allegory of poetic activity.[8]

Let me cite in support of this view another writer who saw the Faust story as an allegory of poetic activity. In the "Walpurgisnacht" section of the fifth chapter of Thomas Mann's novel *Der Zauberberg*,[9] Hans Castorp has a long and passionate conversation with Clawdia Chauchat. (That the title of this section is a reference to one of the most famous scenes in *Faust* hardly needs pointing out: the lengths to which Mann went in his *imitatio* of Goethe are well known, and the degree to which Mann's conception of the artist was dominated by the figure of Goethe is widely recognized.) Most of the conversation is in French, a language which Hans says he prefers in these circumstances, "car pour moi, parler français, c'est parler sans parler, en quelque manière,—sans responsabilité, ou comme nous parlons en rêve" (356). Hans shares, in a modest way, the linguistic gifts of another of Mann's Goethe-figures, Felix Krull. Felix, in his parodistic revision of *Dichtung und Wahrheit*, confesses that his ability with foreign languages

> was always amazing and mysterious. Universal in my endowments and possessed of every possible potentiality, I did not really need to learn a foreign language, once I had acquired a smattering of it, to give the impression, for a short time at least, of fluent mastery. . . . The imitative, parody element in my performance did not lessen its credibility but actually enhanced it, and with it came a pleasant, almost ecstatic feeling of being possessed by a foreign spirit. Plunged in this, or rather taken captive by it, I was in a state of inspiration, in which, to my astonishment (and this in turn increased the daring of my performance) the vocabulary simply flashed into my head, God knows from where.[10]

We recognize the imagery of possession and inspiration by which Felix describes his gift as essentially identical to that by which Plato has Socrates describe the poetic gift in the *Ion*. Indeed, the audience of Krull's demonstration of his linguistic abilities, the *Generaldirektor* Stürzli, restrains the ceaseless flow of language by calling out: "Stop! . . . You're slipping into poetry again and you know that makes me ill" (123). The equation Mann is making between the confidence man's glibness in foreign languages and poetic talent could not be any clearer. Poetry—and its sister art, foreign-language speaking— is a kind of speaking-with-the-voice-of-another, a "parler sans parler," as Hans Castorp puts it.

This is just how one might describe the artifice of fictional discourse, whereby, in the act of putting quotation marks around an utterance, we propose that it is perhaps not our speech but the speech of another. We cannot be sure what the quotation marks mean, or if they are "really" there: we have only a never-to-be-completely-determined context to help us decide. But their presence, even if only suspected,[11] does something peculiar to the discourse within them. Poets, dramatists, and novelists make use of this artifice all the time, gaining for their utterances a special privilege. They speak without a certain sort of responsibility, without having to answer for their words in quite the same way one has to in other circumstances. It is the solution to a crucial problem faced by most of us at one time or another, but some of us more acutely and regularly: the need to speak without *saying* anything. As Samuel Beckett once said, or did not say, "But it seems impossible to speak and yet say nothing." There are times, however, when it seems essential to try.

Poets are not alone in feeling this need. Philosophers feel it very often. To take some examples from both early and late in our tradition, one need only think of Plato, Nietzsche, and Derrida. Whether erecting or attempting to deconstruct the edifice of Western metaphysics, there is a need to speak without speaking, write without writing, to use the available tools of language in an effort to cast doubt upon those tools. How can you use a language and "get outside it" at the same time? Only by speaking and not speaking—that is, only by engaging in fictional discourse. The poet's motives may be different in detail, but in essence they are the same: the need or desire to use language as means and object at the same time, to take the boat apart, as it were, while sailing in it. Fictional utterance is a way of having your cake and eating it, too.

This mode of discourse that allows one to offer a job *and* not offer a job at the same time, to say something and not say something in a single breath, is problematic in a fruitful way. When we ask whether or not Hans was really saying all those passionate things to Clawdia, we find that there is no simple answer, just as there was not when we asked whether or not Faust really *said* "Verweile doch! du bist so schön!" or when we asked whether or not Randy Newman loves L.A. But the lack of such an answer does not diminish these texts; on the contrary, it is one of the most important elements enriching them.

Felix Krull, a parodistic and comic version of Goethe and of Goethe's Faust, can stand as a kind of emblem of rhetorical, fictional discourse. Felix both does and does not speak English, French, and Italian. Felix is and is not a nobleman. We can even say that he is and is not a criminal, because it is clear that his "victims," if they be such, more or less consciously collude with him. This sometimes comic, sometimes sinister ambiguity in his character seems to enthrall those around him. They love him, and they particularly love the problematic nature of his activity. In this vein, I can only conclude by answering Richard Rorty's question, "Is There a Problem about Fictional Discourse?" with an affirmative, but a somewhat restrained affirmative. There *is* a problem, but it is a problem very much like L.A.: we love it.

Notes

1. Richard Rorty, *Consequences of Pragmatism: Essays 1972–1980* (Minneapolis: University of Minnesota Press, 1982). Further references appear in the text.

2. J. L. Austin, *How to Do Things with Words*, ed. J. O. Urmson and Marina Sbisà, 2nd ed. (Cambridge: Harvard University Press, 1975). Further references appear in the text.

3. Stanley Fish, "Normal Circumstances and Other Special Cases," in *Is There a Text in This Class?* (Cambridge: Harvard University Press, 1980), 269ff. Fish's argument forces one to be careful about this notion. I use it here advisedly.

4. On this topic see Derrida's essay "Signature Event Context" and John R. Searle's reply to it in *Glyph 1* (Baltimore: Johns Hopkins University Press, 1977). Contrary to what some have thought, Derrida never claims that context-determination is not necessary, merely that *exhaustive* determination is impossible. Derrida comments on Nietzsche's "umbrella" fragment (quoted in the text), an utterance as close to "context free" as we are likely to encounter:

> One must not conclude, however, . . . that any knowledge of whatever *that* means should be abandoned. On the contrary, if the structural limit and the remainder of the simulacrum which has been left in writing are going to be taken into account, the process of decoding, because this limit is not of the sort that circumscribes a certain knowledge even as it proclaims a beyond, must be carried to the furthest extent possible. (133)

5. For more on the complex issue of rhetoricity, see Paul de Man, *Blindness and Insight* (New York: Oxford University Press, 1971), 102–41; and *Allegories of Reading* (New Haven: Yale University Press, 1979), 3–19; as well as Clayton Koelb, "Kafka's Rhetorical Moment," *PMLA* 98 (1983): 37–46.

6. Jacques Derrida, *Spurs* (Chicago: University of Chicago Press, 1979). See especially pages 123ff.

7. This speech, taking off as it does from a purely verbal circumstance, is a mild form of the "logomimesis" discussed in detail in Clayton

Koelb, *The Incredulous Reader* (Ithaca: Cornell University Press, 1984), 41ff.

8. The central position of the bet and its far greater relevance to the issue of *poesis* than to that of salvation tends to support the view that *Faust* is more urgently concerned with questions of rhetoric than of theology.

9. Thomas Mann, *Der Zauberberg*, 2 vols. (Frankfurt am Main: Fischer, 1972).

10. Quoted from the English translation of Denver Lindley, *Confessions of Felix Krull, Confidence Man* (New York: New American Library, 1963), 121.

11. There are numerous conventions that have been established to help prevent this suspicion: the convention of scientific and scholarly discourse is one of them. In such discourse it is ordinarily unwarranted and unproductive to suppose that the author is not asserting what appears under his/her name. But such conventions can never absolutely prevent the suspicion of the presence of fictional discourse (in the form, perhaps, of irony)— as de Man and others have suspected in the case of Derrida—any more than one can make absolutely certain that a given utterance will be understood as fictional. (Lucian tried to guarantee the absolute fictionality of his *True History* by announcing at the outset that his book was all lies. It didn't work. Cf. *The Incredulous Reader,* 143ff.) The opposition genuine/fictional stands always already deconstructed by the limitless rhetorical potential of language, while examples of literary rhetoric (from a Goethe or a Jim Ignatowski) simply thrust that deconstruction before our eyes. Such deconstructions have the power to hold our attention, however, precisely because the opposition being deconstructed is one which is absolutely essential to the communicative function of discourse. The deconstruction by no means dissolves or eliminates the need for the distinction between genuine and fictional utterance.

The Return of
William James

Frank Lentricchia

William James is on his way back:
under the banner of a "New Pragmatism," and what they are calling
"against theory," he may be on the verge of recapturing the imagination of the American literary humanist from its fascination with
the French intellectual scene—even though the canons of social responsibility say that James is not responsible, that he lacks something
in genuine seriousness. The return of James is all the more surprising
in the light of our preoccupation with theory, because what the canonical standards of seriousness declare that James lacks is nothing
other than the proper sense of theory, which George Santayana, his
younger colleague and competitor at Harvard, defined in its traditional Arnoldian setting when he wrote that theory is "a steady
contemplation of all things in their order and worth. . . . No one can
reach it who has not enlarged his mind and tamed his heart. A
philosopher who attains it is, for the moment, a poet; and a poet
who turns his practice and passionate imagination on the order of all
things, or on anything in light of the whole, is for that moment a
philosopher."[1] If the very sound and rhythm of Santayana's phrasing
makes us a little uncomfortable, that's because James or James-like
attitudes have already carried the day against traditional theory and
the theorizing posture. What is a little rankling about Santayana's
writing is not the traditional idea of the theorist, *per se*, which he
describes, but his unruffled performance of that idea, his commanding vocal assumption of the referential object of his sentences: such
authority seems to us epistemologically self-deluded—no one can
know *that*—and politically scary. The political force of James's writing is directed against the politics of that kind of voice from on high:
Santayana (European, urbane, aristocratic, catholic, and so cool)
can tell us what a theorist is because he is the theorist of theorists. He
can observe the moment of the intersection of the disciplines of phi-

losophy and poetry because he knows the difference (being neither a philosopher nor poet and above both). And he knows the order of things with such confidence that he can speak the declarative sentence from its ur-space, *ex cathedra:* "No one can reach it. . . . ," says Santayana, who has already reached it—"it" being the theoretical consciousness for which Santayana, Pope of Theory, establishes the conditions of attainment.

What Santayana says openly is what traditional theorists generally only imply when they define their activity as theorists: that to think theoretically is to concern yourself with "wholes," with "totalities"; it is to think beyond the parochialisms of the schools and to achieve some ultimate humanity of inclusive broad-mindedness by rising above the particular involvements of passionate commitment. Becoming nobody, no place, no time, we achieve the theorist's ideal, which Santayana's phrasing reminds us is the very ideal of reason as it has been traditionally conceived in the West since the Greeks. In this serene, epistemologically and morally secure space, beyond ideology, one has knowledge of the real order and value of all things. Early modern philosophical commentators on this view of theory—those for and those against it—called it "absolute," as in "absolute idealism" (they were thinking mainly of Hegel); recent Marxists and anti-Marxists alike (thinking of Lukács in his Hegelian mode) say "totalizing"; and more recently (after Richard Rorty, a Jamesian of sorts), the tendency is to say "foundational"—Rorty, when he uses that word, is thinking of all of philosophy with the exception of a few names: Hegel, Dewey, Wittgenstein, Heidegger, himself. James's coded synonyms for both theory and traditional philosophy are "reason" and "rational," close cousins to his pejorative of pejoratives— "abstract."

My central point will be this: independently of Marx, and as the founding gesture of his work, James in effect accepts the most famous of Marx's theses on Feuerbach—that philosophy should be trying to change, not interpret the world—but James out-Marxes Marx by saying that all the interpretive efforts of philosophy are always simultaneously efforts to work upon and work over things as they are. All intellectuals play social roles, whether they like it or not, James believed, because interpretation is always a form of intervention, a factor in social change or in social conservation. The recurring double point of James's pragmatism is that all theory is practice (situated intellectual involvement with real local effects) and that all practices are not equally worthy. If all thought is a mode of action, a tool, not a representation—an instrument for doing work—then the key consequence forced upon us by this philosophy of consequences would not be recognition (James's banal and potentially dangerous starting point) that there is nothing but practice. The key consequence of Jamesian pragmatism would be the urgent directive that we attend to the different consequences of different practices, for only in their different consequences can we know and evaluate such practices as different epistemological and political alternatives. No difference in consequences, no difference in practice. No difference in consequences, no difference in belief.

"Belief"—which is what a pragmatist prefers to "theory"—boils down to a "set of rules" for the action of changing-by-interpreting the world's various texts, verbal and otherwise.[2] Belief shapes our interpretive conduct—a redundancy: all conduct is interpretive—and conduct is the sole significance and real content of belief. It is a strong implication of what James believes about "belief" that the rules synonymous with belief are open to reflection and revision. Whether the set of rules which constitutes belief is knowable in advance of the conduct it shapes, or whether such rules are extrapolated from conduct, after the fact, the ethical and political imperative embodied in pragmatism tells us that we must evaluate the consequences of belief—action in the world—by evaluating the conduct-structuring rules of belief and, in doing so, become responsive to and maybe responsible for the future of a belief (the conduct and consequences that belief *will* produce), not from some transcendental standpoint in "theory" but from within a situation that is both primal and recurrent: the situation of emergency (*Pragmatism*, 98). We are lost in the woods, we need to find our way home, but we have no map. Then we see a path, choose to believe (maybe because of what we take to be irrefutable olfactory evidence) that it is a cow path which if followed will lead us to the safety of the farmhouse. Surfacing here in James's representative anecdote of cognitive emergency, which is at the same time an existential emergency, is the temporal character of belief. As tools for getting done the various works of liberation, beliefs are instruments of desire; they are born locally in crisis and have local consequences only. When they do not lead us out of the cognitive woods, we revise them—still in the woods, still in crisis, we remeasure our context—for other beliefs that might work. If it is the case that the triggering emergency (or the occasion for belief), the actual work of belief, and the consequences (or future) of belief are always bound to local contexts, then it is also the case that all efforts to escape temporal and geographic locality are expressions of a passion that is the traditional theoretical impulse par excellence. The desire to move to theory in James is the desire to move over the arena of work to a place where all possible situations of work can be surveyed in a single glance, and gathered up, and mastered. The site of theory turns out to be the totalitarian site of imposition where all local situations are coerced into conformity, and where the future itself (in the form of consequences) is known and therefore controlled and manipulated in advance. Theory is not belief because theory never sees itself restrained by its occasional status, it does not think its status occasional. With its global conception of itself, with its metaphysical confidence, theory has no need for self-revision. But if theory is in some sense like belief because it is also a form of practice, then the work of theory can only be the work of trying to convert (shape, force) experience into what theory wants to see in the world: an adequate object of its totalizing desire to rig the game of interpretation. Like belief, theory emerges from historical ground; unlike belief, theory cannot bear to live with history.

As Stanley Fish put it in an essay whose "New Pragmatist" conclusions I want eventually to challenge, theory would work as a general (rather than a "local") hermeneutics, an interpretive procedure which would always yield correct results if the proper steps were strictly followed. Fish argues convincingly that the model for "theory" (I'd say "traditional theory") is mathematics, a "rational activity" whose "constraints are not acquired through experience (education, historical conditioning, local habits) but are innate." The constraints of theory so conceived are necessarily abstract, general, and invariant. Fish's New Pragmatist definition of theory is pure William James. His conclusion that theory cannot succeed because "it cannot help but borrow its terms and its content from that which it claims to transcend, the mutable world of practice, belief, assumptions, point of view," manages to be Jamesian while at the same time missing what I read as James's ironic political theme: that theory's very inability to be successful in its own terms has powerful historical consequences, that it is precisely its failure to leave history that insures that theory is a practice and that theory always marks history with it imposing ambition.[3] The fully articulated pragmatism we find in James says that there is not only nothing but practice, but that practice carries with it the obligations of revision, that practice tends to force constant scrutiny of one's work in its context. This is so because the historical pressures at the site of practice produce a reflective (and dialectical) moment, let's call it *ad hoc* theory with a lower case *t*, which is in turn tested by the practice to which it is necessarily returned.

Pragmatism teaches nothing if not responsiveness to contexts of work. When not so accompanied, our practice, including theoretical practice, becomes mindless work, something like Charley Marlowe's with his rivets: which is to say that such work is not really mindless, but the hopeless effort of bad faith to escape from reflection on the situation of work and a form of intellectual cowardice. For Marlowe this means the hopeless desire to escape from reflection on the imperialist site of his activity and his responsibility at and for that site of work. The New Pragmatist demolition of theory is useful to a point: it shows us that theory, including its varieties after the New Criticism, conceived and held in the traditional way, is not only defined by a-historical hunger but is doomed to perpetual inability to satisfy such hunger. But the New Pragmatist analysis, once it has uncovered that defining contradiction of theory (formalist desire, contingent setting of desire) concludes its own work too soon, not seeing that theory-desire's contingent setting is the ground of theory's real work, the ironic (because unwanted) object of its intention. The premature closing of New Pragmatism's own analysis has a double effect: it produces a style of dismissiveness which then comes around to haunt and seize antitheory, turning it into precisely the sort of theory that antitheory ought not want to be—historically and politically blind praxis, theory (try to imagine it) as blithe-spirited Charley Marlowe.

Expressed most resonantly in key metaphoric moments, James's vision of pragmatism is irreducibly a vision of heterogeneity and contentiousness—a vision strong for criticism, self-scrutiny, and self-revision that never claims knowledge of a single human narrative because it refuses the belief and the often repressive conduct resulting from belief in a single human narrative. James's fully committed pragmatism has no way of settling once and for all the questions it constantly asks: Does the world rise or fall in value when any particular belief is let loose in the world? When we act upon others or when others act upon us? (*Pragmatism*, 122–23). By insisting that the question be posed that way, in nonacademic form (Does the *world*, not literature, not philosophy, rise or fall in value?), James is insisting that the consequences of belief reveal themselves most fully outside the immediate domain (in his case, the discipline of philosophy) of any particular belief's application. Like the father of pragmatism, C. S. Peirce, James is no philosophical ostrich with his head in the sand. He starts with the recognition that others believe differently and just as strongly.[4] James thereby puts us in a world of different and sometimes competing choices and conducts, and of different and sometimes competing stories, a world in which resolution could be achieved only in a final solution of criticism: by the forcible silencing of the competitor.

So the world according to James is a geography of practices adjacently placed: a heterogeneous space of dispersed histories, related perhaps by counterpoint, or perhaps utterly disrelated—a cacophony of stories—but in any case never related in medley. "The world we live in exists diffused and distributed, in the form of an infinitely numerous lot of eaches" (*Pragmatism*, 126). Overarching metanarratives, say Marxist or Christian, which would make all the "eaches" cohere (and so eliminate heterogeneous plurality) never tempt James. He is no utopian. He believes that history conceived as teleological union is a late and nostalgic expression of classical aesthetics—the proleptic imaging forth in the rigorous causal perfections of Aristotelean plot, of desired historical order, the harmony of time itself. Better, he believes, to think against Aristotle's preference for drama over romance, better to prefer romance to drama, better to think that the "world is full of partial stories that run parallel to one another, beginning and ending at odd times. They mutually interlace and interfere at points, but we cannot unify them completely" (*Pragmatism*, 71). Together with his literary metaphor of narrative richness, James levels this backyard metaphor at the dogmas of monism: "It is easy to see the world's history pluralistically, as a rope of which each fiber tells a separate tale; but to conceive of each cross-section of the rope as an absolutely single fact, and to sum the whole longitudinal series into one being, living an individual life, is harder" (*Pragmatism*, 71). "It is easy," if you are James: James himself knew that the seeing of plurality, and the letting be of what you see is not a matter of just opening your eyes to the facts and having a good attitude. His philosophical project is dedicated to the cause of getting others to see it his way while showing us, at the same time, the violent effects of seeing it otherwise, the bad attitude that necessarily accompanies seeing it otherwise.

History in James, as in his master, Emerson, is no monument that demands mimetic awe. Rationalism (a key word for "theory" in James) would force a mimetic role upon the text of the world: "On the rationalist side," James writes, "we have a universe in many editions, one real one, the infinite folio, or *edition de luxe*, eternally complete; and then the various finite editions, full of false readings, distorted and mutilated each in its own way." The effort of the rational textualist must be to make all finite editions somehow "correspond" to the *edition de luxe*. But the pragmatist gives us history in a complex metaphor as both text and as the liberation of textual work—a text, James writes, "in only one edition of the universe, unfinished, growing in all sorts of places, especially in places where thinking beings are at work" (*Pragmatism*, 124). For the pragmatic textualist, who is the bibliographer's version of the devil, there is only one text: the forever unfinished, decentralized text of history—forever supplemented, new chapters being written in all sorts of places by all sorts of people not especially in touch with one another. There is no work of "correspondence," only of "production." James's textual metaphor is an effort to speak against the political authority which masks itself in rationalist certitude and self-righteousness, which demands mimetic fealty, and which he specifically and frequently evokes—after his involvement in the New England Anti-Imperialist League—in royalist, militarist, aristocratic, and papal terms.[5] James's textual metaphor speaks *for* the liberation of the small, the regional, the locally embedded, the underdog: the voice that refuses the elocutionary lessons of cosmopolitan finishing schools. His unfinished (and unfinishable) text of history, authorized by no single author, is the text of American history as it ought to be—the multiauthored book of democracy in its ideal and antinomian form.

For James, then, there may be nothing more ugly than theoretical consciousness in the rational practices it authorizes. The lectures he delivered in late 1906 and early 1907 in Boston and New York, and then shortly after published as the book *Pragmatism*, bear the mark of a decisive moment in U.S. history: our first fully launched imperialist adventure, in the last years of the nineteenth century, in Cuba and the Philippines. Though inchoately present in his *Principles of Psychology*, he began to know his philosophy as pragmatism only after he found the political terminus of his thought in his anti-imperialist activism at the turn of the century. In the New England Anti-Imperialist League, James experienced a direct and codeterminative connection between his philosophical principles and his political life. It was at that point—after his political turn and not before, when it was abstractly possible for him to do so—that he began freely adapting from Peirce; it was at that point, and not before, that he began to understand empire as theory (as a kind of theoretical impulse) and theory or traditional philosophy as empire (as a kind of imperialist impulse). For James, the two impulses are measured and joined by the effects they produce in trying to cure the world of diversity.

James's anti-imperialism becomes the first effort in a hidden history of oddly connected American refusals of imperialism. The second was Wallace Stevens's "Anecdote of the Jar" of 1919 as read by a third, that of Michael Herr in his book on Vietnam of 1970, *Dispatches,* in which the entire focus of American military power that was concentrated in the fortification at Khe Sanh was crystallized by Herr with (of all things) Stevens's poem. Stevens, who found Dwight Eisenhower radical, is made by Herr to speak directly against the ideology of imposition and obliteration coactive in Vietnam with a strategy of defoliation. The textual expression of that strategy is the literal remapping of a country—"the military expediency," in Herr's ironic reflection on the sometimes mad and deadly relations of sign and referent, "to impose a new set of references over Vietnam's truer, older being, an imposition that began with the division of one country into two and continued . . . with the further division of South Vietnam into four clearly defined tactical corps. . . ." Herr concludes by glossing Khe Sanh via the imaginative imperialism that was acti-vated and subtly evaluated in "Anecdote of the Jar." "Once it was all locked in place, Khe Sanh became like the planted jar in Wallace Stevens's poem. It took dominion everywhere."[6]

James had written his own anecdote of the jar in the opening lecture of *Pragmatism:*

> The world of concrete personal experiences to which the street belongs is multitudinous beyond imagination, tangled, muddy, painful and perplexed. The world to which your philosophy professor introduces you is simple, clean and noble. The con-tradictions of real life are absent from it. Its architecture is classic. Principles of reason trace its outlines, logical necessities cement its parts. Purity and dignity are what it most expresses. It is a kind of marble temple shining on a hill. (*Pragmatism,* 17–18)

The marble temple shining on a hill is James's metaphor for tradi-tional philosophy in its traditional project of representation: mind as correspondence, thought as reflection of real ontological structure, thought emptied of the messes of social time, thought historically uncontingent. But philosophy so conceived, James says, is not, despite its claim, an "account of this actual world." It is an "addition built

upon it": a "sanctuary," a "refuge," a "substitute," a "way of escape," a "monument of artificiality"—"cloistral and spectral." All
negative qualities, of course, and quite harmless, until we add one
other characteristic which gives ominous point to all the others—
James's shining marble temple of philosophy, like Stevens's jar of
aesthetics, like Khe Sanh, is also a "remedy" (*Pragmatism*, 18). In
this dismantling of the classic project of reason, what James wishes to
show is that the product of rationalist method is not cool, contempla-
tive representation—"theory" above the battle—it is *purity in action.*
The shining marble temple is "round upon the ground" and it does
not give "of bird or bush." Like the defoliating jar in Stevens's
Tennessee, or the imposed references of military need in Vietnam
which attempted to recreate the referent (we had to destroy that
village in order to save it), theory classically conceived is the desire
for a "refined object." And theory-desire, the desire for refinement,
is a "powerful . . . appetite of the mind" which gets expressed as the
will to refine: a chilling process when considered in the political
contexts within which James writes (*Pragmatism*, 18). In an eerie
prolepsis of both Stevens's poem and Herr's reading of Khe Sanh as
the "planted jar," James evoked his sense of the perversity of the
American presence in the Philippines by describing it as an effort to
"plant our order" (*The James Family,* 626).

I have to this point been emphasizing what I have called, a little
misleadingly, James's political period, the late phase of his career
when he could with some justice refer to himself as an anarchist.
Actually this late phase represents a substantial change of heart which
if ignored would obscure by suppressing not the nonpolitics but the
more familiar American politics of his earlier career. Two historical
points may be made, the first more or less factual, the second more
or less speculative. In the late 1880s James responded to the protests
of exploited labor in this country by telling his brother not to be
"alarmed by the labor troubles here" (Henry was not "here").
Brother William went on to explain, in all seriousness, that the turmoil
of strikes was "simply a healthy phase of evolution, a little costly, but
normal, and sure to do lots of good to all hands in the end." If that
response to the emergence of organized labor deserves to be characterized as academic in the worst possible sense of the word—how else
to understand his application of Darwin?—then his remarks on the
Haymarket Riot of May 1886 need another, less kind evaluation: in
his response to that violent moment in our labor history James gave
voice to American xenophobic paranoia. "I don't speak," he contin-

ues in the same letter to Henry, "of the senseless 'anarchist' riot in Chicago, which has nothing to do with 'Knights of Labor,' but is the work of a lot of pathological Germans and poles [*sic*]" (*The James Family*, 622).

The missing political link in the journey from "a lot of pathological Germans and poles," to James's critique of philosophy's shining marble temple on a hill, to Stevens's critique of the jar on the hill in Tennessee, to Herr's meditation on Vietnam (Khe Sanh upon a hill), may actually be the first link—John Winthrop's vision of puritan community as a "city upon a hill" and his unwittingly ugly interpretation of that city when, years after he had coined the phrase, he banished Anne Hutchinson for antinomian heresy. Hutchinson: "I desire to know wherefore I am banished." Winthrop: "Say no more, the court knows wherefore and is satisfied."[7] The city upon a hill, a metaphor of community self-consciously visible and vulnerable, is revised in Winthrop's retort to Hutchinson into a metaphor of the imperial city rigorously and violently exclusionary—a structure of male authority, purity (puritanism) in action, poised as a "remedy" against a radically individualist principle of resistance whose most famous American representative is female. Winthrop's revision, and its impersonal authoritarian devastation of an insurrectionary female conscience, just may be (more on this later) the political unconscious of Jamesian pragmatism at its radical edge.

If Hutchinson is the hidden moral and political mother figure behind James's pragmatism, then the not-so-hidden moral and political father figure behind his pragmatist celebration of sovereignty (personal and national) is Emerson—for intellectual and biographical reasons it could not have been anyone else—the Emerson who wrote that "whenever I find my dominion over myself not sufficient for me, and I undertake the direction of my neighbor also, I overstep the truth, and come into false relations with him. . . . This is the history of government—one man does something which is to bind another."[8] Emerson found the history of the word *politics* to be the history of a pejorative, coincidental with *cunning*, the indenturing of others to the imperatives of power not their own, and (as Stevens would put it) the taking of dominion everywhere (*Emerson*, 427). In his essay "History" (1841), Emerson argued by metaphorical sleight of hand that in the self's true (presumably American) domain there are no medieval relations of economic and political coercion, that the privileges of the spirit are radically open to all: "He that is at once admitted to the right of reason is made a freeman of the whole estate.

What Plato has thought, he may think; what a saint has felt, he may feel; what at any time has befallen any man, he can understand; who hath access to this universal mind is a party to all that is or can be done, for this is the only and sovereign agent" (*Emerson*, 123). And with the agility of the socially critical punster, Emerson trained his wit in his famous "Nature" essay (1836) on private property in the capitalist system, writing in a famous passage that though Messrs. Miller, Locke, and Manning may claim ownership of the physical property of their farms, their warranty deeds give them no title to the very best part of those farms: the "property" of vision is "owned" by the integrating eye of the visionary capitalist, the poet who alone can "possess," because he creates, the "landscape" (*Emerson*, 5–6).

The point of Emerson's compressed metaphoric recollections and attacks on feudal and capitalist modes of production is that the great human values are preserved only in the world of culture, because in that world the power that accrues from economic privilege— whether lordly or bourgeois—is presumably annulled, even though apparently culture can at no point annul the actual unfreedom and oppression that obtains in material society which, in Emerson's memorable phrasing, "everywhere is in conspiracy against the manhood of every one of its members" (*Emerson*, 148). "Society" for Emerson is synonymous with the surrender of "liberty and culture," with a process of coercion that sanctions the binding of many for the benefit of a few (*Emerson*, 148). But culture is not a way of life intervening upon and shaping social, economic, and political relations: rather, "culture" is an alternative to "society," wherein governments will continue to underwrite relations of domination. So culture for Emerson is simultaneously an idealist affirmation of freedom and truth in a democratic intellectual world of equal opportunity, and an implicit denial that actual collective life can be the ground of those values. At its worst, and by virtue of what Herbert Marcuse would call its affirmative inward turn, Emersonian culture becomes an implicit validation (via benign neglect) of the real injustices rooted in real economic inequalities.[9]

What now appears most dated in Emerson's American repugnance for our European social origins, where the dream of America was hatched, was perhaps for his audience the most thrilling and the most duplicitous element in his writing. His clarion call for intellectual independence, sounded on numerous occasions—"We have listened too long to the courtly muses of Europe"—was intended to urge his fellow Americans on to the cultural end of the adventure, political independence presumably having already been secured (*Emerson*, 62). But the overt message of "The American Scholar" and other essays which touch political themes directly is subverted time after time in Emerson's American revenge against the history of economic privilege. The American poet and the American scholar are the representative men who stand in for the desire of history's dispossessed and excluded to come into possession—for possession is power, and power is freedom. In taking his revenge, the Emersonian poet asserts on behalf of all the mute and all the inglorious of all times solidarity in the transhistorical community of noble spirits and brilliant minds, for it is the Emersonian poet who underwrites the proverb of American proverbs that it is not where you come from that counts, but who you are; it is he, the Emersonian poet, who celebrates the natural ground of privilege. But the retreat to the interior enacted by Emerson's various metaphors against ownership in both feudal and capitalist systems of production carries the unhappy message that cultural independence will not be the grace note of American history—in the citadel of subjectivity, where we contact the "sovereign agent," it will be the only independence we know.

In spite of Emerson's obvious delight in trumping the card of capitalism, neither the poet nor any other isolable individual finally owns anything, not even himself. The primary fact of Emerson's transcendental economy is not owning but belonging, not possessing but being possessed. That to which we belong ("the only and sovereign agent") and that by which we are possessed is no individual. What Emerson liked to call the "universal soul," or "Reason," or the "oversoul" he defined strategically, with a perfection of vagueness, as an "immensity not possessed and that cannot be possessed"—"we are its property." Whatever *it* is, whatever more specifically the word *immensity* signifies in Emerson's discourse, we can say that *it* is not quantifiable, that it cannot be economized as a "commodity." *It* is precisely that which cannot be made precise, specific, an object. It neither buys nor sells; it controls no labor power. It is instead a condition of release from possessive selfhood and the commodified consciousness of liberal political vision. *It*—this "immensity," a cliché in the rhetoric of the sublime—is revalued on American political ground as our possession by freedom, which Emerson (at his most hopeful) calls "the background of our being" (*Emerson*, 263).

In the crucial definition of personal consciousness that he offers in the first volume of *Principles of Psychology*, James chooses to ignore Emerson's rejection of all economic conceptions of selfhood.

James finds (or thinks he finds) truly inalienable private property located at (and *as*) the core of selfhood. So the price of James's anti-imperialist vision of human heterogeneity may be the most radical of all possible alienation and disconnection, which he expresses as the first commandment of his capitalized psychology—Thou Shalt Not Steal Individuality:

> Each of these minds keeps its own thoughts to itself. There is no giving or bartering between them. . . . Absolute insulation, irreducible pluralism, is the law. It seems as if the elementary pyschic fact were not *thought* or *this thought* or *that thought* but *my thought*, every thought being *owned*. Neither contemporaneity nor proximity in space, nor similarity of quality or content are able to fuse thoughts together which are sundered by this barrier of belonging to different minds. The breaches between such thoughts are the most absolute breaches in nature. . . . The worst a psychology can do is so to interpret the nature of these selves as to rob them of their worth.[10]

Or, more emphatically still: *"In its widest possible sense . . . a man's self is the sum total of all that he can call his*, not only his body and his psychic powers, but his clothes, and his house, his wife and his children, his ancestors and friends, his reputation and works, his lands and horses, and yacht and bank-account" (*The Principles of Psychology*, 291). But all of the things that we think we "own," James says, are "transient external possessions" with the sole exception of the "innermost center within the circle," that "sanctuary within the citadel," the *"self of all the other selves,"* of which we can never be dispossessed: the "home," the "source," the "emanation" of "fiats of the will"—a feeling of an "original spontaneity," an active power within, without constraining ground, that becomes the ground of our personal freedom to say yes or no, to open and shut the door, and a point of departure for James's anti-imperialist pluralism (*The Principles of Psychology*, 297–98, 299–305). That feeling of original spontaneity is James's phenomenological postulate for the inviolability of self, or of a self that should be responded to as if it were and deserved to be inviolable.

What I think James knew is that his intellectual father's transcendentalist commitment to a community of justice and dignity beyond all those historical powers of oppression that Americans like to associate with the Old World could have no material site, not even here in the so-called New World. Emerson's "active soul," an ideal instrument working directly, if at all, from mind to mind, never works in, on, or through the mediations of actual social arrangement. In the heat of James's anti-imperialist activity, Emersonian nonconformity was simply not enough—it lacked (my anachronism is the point) James's muscular pragmatism—for the disturbing implication of Emerson's divestiture of agency and sovereignty from the individual was political passivity, not political action. What James knew is that there can be no Emersonian practice. Any act of personal will over and above the organic act of transcendental selfhood is more than neither necessary nor appropriate; it is dangerous. Any act of would-be anti-imperialist will might become (ironically) a trace of the will of the imperialist that James and Emerson abhorred. But James's pragmatism is nothing if not a philosophy of will, of personal not transcendental agency, of personal not transcendental sovereignty that would and did risk (without guarantee of moral purity) frightening appropriation of its tenets. James took that risk because, unlike Emerson, he could not be satisfied with the interiorization of cultural power and the subjectification of freedom. James would make culture instrumentally powerful; he would make intellect politically decisive to the fate of society.

What ran deep in James and what beyond argument was altogether there in Emerson (let's call it the American instinct against the imperial social gesture), but which did not surface in James until late in his career, after he had been politicized, is a sense of American history and society as severely ruptured from its European origins and from European institutions synonymous with oppression: the Roman Catholic Church, the army, the aristocracy, and the crown. James named these institutions as the true enemy of his philosophic method, which he sometimes late in his career associated with a Whitmanesque, unbuttoned, even anarchic notion of self-determination. Especially after 1900, James conceived the role of the intellectual in specific American terms as one of guarding our freedom from those European institutionalizing impulses which might and *did* insidiously rebirth themselves here from the ("theoretical") "passion of mastery" and in the form of "national destiny," a slogan which speaks for efforts to organize—first on native ground—in a "big" and "great" manner (James hated those words) against the "molecular forces that work from individual to individual," then *over there* in the form of bringing light to the uncivilized: "national destiny" as the will to impose our sense of national history—plant our order—on foreign soil (*The James Family,* 624, 626, 633). It was the American intellectual's duty, James wrote in numerous letters to the *Boston Transcript* in protest against our imperialist policies, to expose the empty but murderously effective abstractions of the party of Roosevelt (like our "responsibility" for the islands, like the "unfitness" of the Filipinos to govern themselves), and James was convinced that this could be done only if intellectuals in America developed a class consciousness as intellectuals: a class with presumably no reason to align itself materially with special interests because it stood, or should stand, for ideal interests only—by which he meant the preservation of radical individual freedom. Even in the United States this cannot but be characterized as an innocent view, but it is a view borne aloft in the morning freshness of the founding American myth—the democratic hope that with nothing resembling an aristocracy to encumber them, Americans in the new Eden had the right to think of the individual as truly prior to society. But at the same time, James saw that in such presumably fluid social circumstances we could have no equivalent to a permanent presence (like an aristocratic class) responsible for overseeing the integrity of the social process as a whole. (Who, anyway, aside from Emerson, could oversee the integrity of antinomianism?) James nominated intellectuals for that role because he thought that in a society without those entrenched institutions within which European intellectuals found themselves, the American intellectual could wield "no corporate selfishness," and "no powers of corruption" (*The James Family*; 633, 635). James underrated, though he did not ignore, the corruptive power of capital in fluid democratic contexts—he did not imagine that capital could bind intellectuals; he could not imagine American intellectuals giving voice to the impulses of imperialism.

James *did* imagine the American intellectual as defender of a self that is, or should be, inaccessibly private property: a self that is, or should be, the motor principle of American anti-imperialism. Each of us, he writes in an essay called "On a Certain Blindness in Human Beings," is bound "to feel intensely the importance of his own duties and the significance of the situations that call these forth. But this feeling is in each of us a vital secret, for sympathy with which we vainly look to others. The others are too much absorbed in their own vital secrets to take an interest in ours. Hence the stupidity and injustice of our opinions, so far as they deal with the significance of alien lives" (*The James Family*; 398). The elaborate but symptomatic difficulty in making sense of James is coming to see that his overt commitment to the inalienable private property of selfhood, the original feeling of spontaneous action, the freedom felt within, is an inscription of a contradiction at the very heart of capitalism (and theorists of capital like Adam Smith) because property under capitalism can be property only if it *is* alienable—only if it can be bought, sold, stolen, and, when necessary, appropriated. James's political turn taught him that nothing is inalienable in the coercive world of imperialism, not even the secret self that we think we possess beyond alienation. He employs the language of private property in order to describe the spiritual nature of persons and in an effort to turn the discourse of private property against itself by making that discourse literal in just this one instance: so as to preserve a human space of freedom, however interiorized, from the vicissitudes and coercions of the marketplace.

James's anti-imperialism is American anti-imperialism; his philosophical term "pluralism" is an antithetical word signifying not so much what *is*, but rather resistance to the imperialist context of his work in the modernist moment. In other words, pluralism signifies what "is not" and what should be. His major effort is to combat the hegemonic discourse of a capitalism rooted in a democratic political context by appropriating the cornerstone economic principle of capitalism to the advantage of his counterdiscourse and a vision of human sanctity and difference central not only to his pragmatism, but also to the originating myth of American political history. What James says in all but words is that if imperialism and capitalism on their own are capable of destroying the self, then in their unified American form they represent a global principle of structure, a world-historical menace of unparalleled proportions. In the name of pragmatism and the American dream, James wanted to turn America against the self-pollution of its foreign policy at the end of the nineteenth century; in such an act of self-criticism, he thought, we would subvert the economic and political postures which, by treating all human subjects as if they were objects, for all practical purposes convert us into objects who suffer degradations that nonhuman commodities cannot suffer. So James's quasi-Cartesian postulate of an interior spontaneity is not ontological but thoroughly instrumental. It is his great heuristic principle, the energy of his criticism, and the basis of his anti-imperialism.

After his political turn, James could in the same breath speak against the rationalizations of theory and traditional philosophy as well as the theorizations of society—those political and economic arrangements of power that rob the self of itself by rationalizing the self in the name of capitalism and the commodification of human labor. Against the in-house economic imperialism which appropriated the self for capital in America, against his own earlier reaction to the Haymarket Riot, and against the international imperialism which denied self-determination to the Philippines and to Ireland, James brought his pragmatism as an emancipating critical force which would liberate the particular, the local, the secret self from intellectual, economic, and political structuralizations which would consume, control, deny all particularity, all locality, and all secret selfhood. James, to say it again, is no utopian: he has no vision of a future social arrangement that would insure the safety of the self, no vision of the good collective. His pragmatism is emancipatory—it would lead us out of suffocating and tyrannous theorizations; it has nothing to say about where we should be, only about where we do not want to be.

Does James's stance on the issue of traditional theory have any consequences of the sort that would bind intellectuals to the social contexts of their activity? Not an innocent question: my professional context is theory-conscious, even theory-obsessed. Passion for and against theory seems unavoidable among those who come in contact with it: in the profession of literary studies as we know it, that means most of us. For since the late 1950s and the publication of Frye's *Anatomy of Criticism*, the American scene in literary criticism has been constituted by a controversy over the role of theory carried on with theological fervor by believers and scoffers alike. And since the summer 1982 issue of *Critical Inquiry* and the publishing of an article called "Against Theory," a new breed of scoffers, much to the delight of the old breed, has dominated the conversation. Unlike the old breed, however, this new breed comes cunningly armed with the intellectual skills associated with theorists in order to slay the dragon of theory and offer it up, lo!, on the altar of the good old American philosophy, pragmatism itself. The movement in the United States drawing most attention now, even threatening to become fashionable, is the "against theory" movement; it is being associated everywhere with the names of Peirce, Dewey, and James; it is called the "New Pragmatism."[11]

I think James would have found the "against theory" position beside the point (to put it gently) because he knew that there is no sense in being for or against what you cannot escape from. There is no escape from theory because, in James's characterization of rationalism, the theory of theories, theory is "an appetite of the mind"—

part of the self (*Pragmatism*, 18). We are all beset by the theoretical impulse—or theory-desire, as I have called it—by the need to make the place clean and well ordered. In its simplest and yet most far-reaching implications, theory is the need to generalize, to overcome, to forget, to obliterate differences: a description I'd offer as an equally fair characterization of concept-formation (the obliteration of per-cepts) and of imperialism both as foreign policy and as a feature of the ordinary—the casual imperialism of everyday life (the oblitera-tion of persons). Since James's temperament is shaped by nominalist, empirical, and skeptical philosophical traditions, he believes that when theory-desire expresses itself by offering itself as an explanation of the concrete world, it must necessarily fail as theory, as explanation of the way things are at all times and in all places. The world just isn't the way theory says it is. So theory cannot have the conse-quences that it wishes. But it does have consequences because in an effort to make over into an image of its desire the heterogeneous world of history—the romance world of many stories that do not cohere—theory acts for worse upon the world.

The jaunty little dismissal of theory by the authors of the essay called "Against Theory" is irrelevant—but it is also something more: it is self-deluded. Knapp and Michaels say that "theory is not just another name for practice. It is the name for all the ways people have tried to stand outside in order to govern practice from without." They conclude that since no one can actually achieve that transcendental perch, no one should "try" to, and "therefore" the "theoretical en-terprise" should come to an end.[12] That sort of conclusion, which seems so Jamesian, is not. What James says is that though no one can actually get outside practice, the impulse to get outside is un-avoidable because the practice of theory takes its point of departure not from a special venture of literary business—a "theoretical enter-prise," as Knapp and Michaels suppose—but from the constitution of mind itself. One cannot "try" or "not try" to be a theorist. Theory is not simply a matter of intention or will or conscious agency. It is a matter of necessity: an impulse, an appetite. The effects of such unavoidable theoretical impulse can be the most heinous form of practice, with the most ugly sorts of political consequences. Theory—whether we call it structuralism or capitalism—is the desire which would be the "remedy" of difference. It cannot be dismissed. It can, however, be guarded against, and the method of vigilance is James's pragmatism, not "New Pragmatism." Jamesian pragmatism is noth-ing less than the strategy for taking away rationalist theory's theoretical ambition, for encouraging us, in our impulses to theory, to recognize that we must live with differences, provisional utility, and the necessities of revision. Theory, so conceived by the old pragmatism, tentatively holding itself as *belief*, becomes a tool for getting our work done, for exploring the shifting situations we call history. But pragmatism (the vigilante within) is always on the verge of vanquishment, of giving belief over to theory (the totalitarian within).

In an effort to tame theory in the name of pragmatism, James seems to allow himself one theoretical moment, the sentimental essentialization of mind as Manichean battlefield—a struggle between traditional philosophy, or "theory," a male principle, and "pragmatism" (homage to Anne Hutchinson), which is a woman: the principle that "unstiffens" all theories and makes them useful, and a synonym for "himself" as woman in his untraditional philosophic activity. But James's essentialist portrait of mind as a conflicted androgeneous unit is intended pragmatically, not theoretically, as a useful way to view, guard against, and maybe curb the aggressivity he found theoretical: aristocratic, churchly, European, and male, but not identical with the male gender. It is his way of encouraging self-critique, the braking of the ego; of saying that we have unshakeable reason to worry; of encouraging the desire for the responsible life (the life that is responsive to its contexts) while specifying the content of responsibility with American liberal vision. James's figurative language tells us that pragmatism is a woman, but not identical with the female gender: pragmatism is democratic, pragmatism is Protestant, pragmatism is inseparable from the dream of America. Pragmatism is an epistemology for *isolatos* who experiment at the frontier, who work without the kingly privileges of tradition and the a priori, who in refusing the a priori of rationalism would also refuse all of the encrusted precapitalist social contexts that James associates with the history of philosophic rationalism. Theory, on the other hand, is a social elitist; theory is a masturbatory old-world gentleman who never gets his hands dirty, who cannot "unstiffen" himself. As the tool of tools, theory-erect would make unnecessary all other tools, all thinking, all revision, all worry, because it is the machine for allegorizing and rationalizing and coercing all texts and all humans as instances of the same.[13]

The New Pragmatists flounder on one of James's strongest insights—that theory cannot be identified with agency and the self-conscious individual, that theory is the sort of force that tends to control individuals by speaking through them. And so does James.

What unifies and binds both ends of the pragmatist tradition is its political pivot, the ideology of liberalism. In the New Pragmatism, the liberal commitment surfaces in the sentiment that theory can be dismissed, as if one could, as an autonomous individual, either will it away or will oneself into it. In James the liberal commitment surfaces in the belief that the central resistance to the hateful impositions of imperialism is generated autonomously in the molecular individual: molecular individualism is the great thing and can be saved only by efforts of molecular will. The problem is that James treats epistemological and political rationalizations as if they were the same thing. The epistemological move to generalization may well be an "appetite of the mind," well-nigh unavoidable except in moments of radical Bergsonian cherishing of perceptual particularity. And the late James is very Bergsonian. But the economic and political move to generalize—the global generalization of labor known as capitalism—is not an unhistorical appetite; it is a locatable, historical phenomenon whose role tends to be blurred and repressed by James's liberal ideology of the autonomous self. The most powerful enemy of the self is not an irrepressible impulse but the economic imperative of capital rooted in and projected from collective interests. The category missing in new and old pragmatism is the category of class which tells us, among other things, that "individuals," including intellectuals, are also representations—vessels of power not originating in themselves and directed against themselves.[14]

The typical liberal response to the destruction of selfhood that is synonymous with the commodification of labor at the economic level and the commodification of human relations in everyday life at all levels of human interaction is to ignore the historical action of capital in the American scene: the steamrolling of the individual in the name of individualism. The problem is collective, the antidote would seem to be collective; but it is precisely the decent collective that is unimaginable to the liberal mind, maybe because the underground of the liberal mind is really antinomian. When collectives are imagined by James, they tend to be represented as life-denying "system." James's celebration of individualism, whether in its modest liberal or its wild antinomian forms, must remain at the mercy of the systematic, capitalist appropriation of the individual that he laments. Since radical individualism in America can be seen, by definition, in no cooperative venture, it would appear that James needs to keep alive a threatening principle of generalization (always at the doorstep of individualism) in order that the radical individual may feel the isolated purity of its freedom. The idea of radical individualism in America derives much of its energy from the memory of our European origins—and capitalism, in James's America, is an ironic aid to that repressed memory of the *ancien régime*. If in one way James out-Marxes Marx, in another he un-Marxes him.

The really ironic thing about the recent "against theory" position, even in its latest and most clever formulation in a recent essay by Fish called "Consequences," in which it is argued that neither theory nor belief can have "necessary" and therefore powerful consequences that we need to be responsive to and responsible for—is that its effort to bury theory has the consequence of reinstating theory-desire in its most naked form. The "against theory" position turns out to be the "for theory" position—a powerful expression of the very theory impulse that James so eloquently contextualized, but with none of James's feeling for its insidious and necessary impact on human behavior. The "against theory" phenomenon turns out to be a repetition, this time around in the name of *practice*, of the escape from history and political accountability so characteristic of the various formalisms that have dominated American critical thought since Frye. Whereas James counsels vigilance for the enemy within, the voices "against theory" counsel a dismissal of a nuisance from without, of recent academic origin, not realizing that they, too, like the rest of us, are the enemy, and in disturbing garb, especially when they write, as Fish now writes, without apparent awareness of the action that theory-desire takes upon their own discourse: i.e., when Fish offers as an example of the irrelevance of theory "the case of two legislators who must vote on a fair-housing bill."

Fish offers this case hypothetically, as if such an example might conceivably have occurred to anybody (say to Locke or Hegel) or in any place (say in classical Athens or in feudal Europe). He argues that a legislator voting on behalf of equal access just might be a libertarian typically committed to individual freedom, that said libertarian might not side with the lobby which works for landlords and all others who like to rest their case on the rights of private property; while the utilitarian, who would ordinarily be committed to arguments on behalf of equal access just might side with advocates of property rights as the only way to insure in the long run the greatest good for the greatest number.[15] Fish's example is confusing because it is abstract; it never touches historical earth; it is an example offered in the analytical style of Anglo-American philosophy—a philosophical style which routinely rarifies "examples" like abortion, nuclear weapons, and capital punishment. Nowhere does Fish indicate awareness of what his language indicates against his intention—what his language speaks. At the level of his example's historical unconscious we find a discourse inscribed which must be made to say, against Fish's intention, that fair housing became an issue in the United States in the heat of the Civil Rights movement in the 1950s and 1960s. Within that historical locale, the position of the libertarian was almost always the position of the covert segregationist, the position that gave comfort, energy, and ideas to the racist who clothed his arguments with the rhetoric of property rights; while the utilitarian was almost always, within that historical locale, a proponent of social change who advocated fair housing as a way of making civil rights socially concrete for blacks—a position, in other words, that gave comfort, energy, and ideas to advocates of civil rights.

Fish's abstract antagonists on the issue of fair housing *might* conceivably, as he argues, have changed sides, *might* conceivably have taken each other's typical stance, thus demonstrating Fish's point—that it *might* not matter a damn what your position is, your practice *might* be otherwise. But in historical fact, these antagonists almost never *did* change sides because their beliefs or theories or positions were politically and historically rooted, politically and historically determinate, in a moment which militated against such possibilities, in a moment which extracted determinate consequences from the antagonists. Thus in his discourse on the problem of fair housing in which the problem is reconceived so as to have no necessary relation to any concrete historical scene, Fish's discourse becomes theoretical—it would prove some general point about the impotence of self-conscious position taking, applicable for all times and all instances, and in so doing it would elide the differences between the positions that produced the particular and potent forms of agony this country has experienced since the fifties and sixties. History exacts its revenge within Fish's discourse, and against his Anglo-American philosophical abstractness, and says not only that all ideas are rooted in specific social situations, but expressing ideas bears specific political consequences, and Fish's discourse on consequences is a prime example, especially at the moment when it denies the consequential nature of having belief and theory.

What I am saying about Fish's most recent critical incarnation amounts to this: his treatment of the issue of fair housing is a betrayal of the strong historicism that he would elaborate, and it is a particularly destructive sort of betrayal which cancels out the only sort of political responsibility that an historicist can live with. Not the Kantian sort, which makes appeals to an ahistorical world of rights and moral imperatives; not the utopian sort, which appeals to a global community-to-be grounded in no particular time or locale. The political responsiveness that Fish betrays is to the very persons and historical community within which his nexus of terms—"fair housing," "utilitarianism," "libertarianism"—takes on determinate and powerful significance: not just *any* historical community, but the very community within which Fish writes and within which his readers must receive him.

But the commanding question about the New Pragmatism's consequences cannot really be pursued with justice at this moment. It is too new. I'll conclude, then, not with any statement about its consequences, which are not especially clear at this point, but with some remarks about its stance and its omissions. 1) However misled by the allurements of formalism, what was called theory in the United States in the 1960s, 1970s, and early 1980s has been the site in our profession of basic and often explosive questioning about the nature and role of literature. Marxism, deconstruction, feminism, psychoanalysis: these are the current terms of opposition to the status quo of the institution of literary study; these are terms of resistance that in various ways would take literature out of the vacuums of traditional humanism and traditional formalism and into the world of economics, power, gender, and class. The rhetoric of "against theory," therefore, at this juncture, cannot help but bring comfort, energy, and ideas to the enemies of change. The rhetoric of "against theory" is reactionary. 2) The "against theory" proponents are representative of a claustrophobic form of professionalism. They speak of "theory" as if it were the invention of literary critics and philosophers, a phenomenon merely of the academic institution. But the lesson of James is that theory is a phenomenon of everyday life in history and society, a phenomenon of all of society's institutions, and the name of a disposition whose consequences are revealed in oppression. The overly narrow, single-institutional focus of the "against theory" proponents trivializes the social issues of theory as James never did, and in the process it trivializes the broader social role of literary study. In the name of practice, "against theory" gives us, once more, the ivory tower. 3) The constant accompaniment to James's criticism of theory and traditional philosophy is a commitment to anti-imperialism and an extended and troubled meditation on the fate of persons in a capitalist context. Fish's example of the two legislators and the question of fair housing looks like a splendid invitation, another social document calling for the intervention of historicized Jamesian conscience, but it is not. Despite the fact that his example has everything to do with the obsessive and intertwined themes of James's critique of theory—the sanctity of selves and the rights of property—Fish's point is that we can dance away (with impunity, if we like), and keep on dancing away, from the determinate responsibilities of belief that history thrusts upon us.

Since theory of the sort that James, Fish, and I are talking about works in the realm of probability on culture and history, not on nature, presumably the realm of rigorous causality and the classic object of scientific inquiry, it would follow that Fish's major point— that cultural theory has no "necessary" theoretical consequences—is logically correct. But his point is a trivial tautology unless pressed beyond its tautological truth that culture is not the realm of necessity. In other words, after all of contemporary theory's hermeneutical suspicions have been registered, after we have once again followed the lead of the early Roland Barthes, who encouraged us to break the conspiracy of silence by refusing to let culture be naturalized by the attitude of "it goes without saying," the question of probability remains. What might be the effect of a literary theorist working to get to that transcendental perch, getting scientific? What has been the effect of imposing our will in Central America? Making them hew, in James's terms, to our story? Or, in Fish's case, where the issue is also political, what might be the (probable) effect on readers and students of his homogenization of the terms of struggle in the Civil Rights movement, especially in the context of the 1980s, when so many of our students (with the aid of Reagan's justice department) seem convinced that racism in the United States was utterly routed everywhere by the late 1960s and that its last bastion is South Africa? The question about the literary theorist who would be scientific, the question about our political relation to the Third World, and the question about Fish are not questions of the same order. But they all involve the effects of theorization: the costs of working to wipe out differences and otherness; the costs of trying to move over the realm of history, and command it from above. These costs are not the costs, or consequences, of theory as theory imagines itself and its effects; they are instead the costs, or consequences, organic to the effort of trying to succeed in the futile and inevitable adventure of theory. And they are real.

The New Pragmatists maybe could learn a lesson from our godfather, Vito Corleone, who believed that one (preferably someone

else) had to "answer" for one's actions. Don Corleone was a con-
noisseur of reason (as in "I will reason with him"; or, as in "But no
one can reason with him"). But the don was no Kantian. Unlike the
New Pragmatists who assign self-consciousness no historical role, he
knew that the sort of worry synonymous with self-reflection takes
place in a context of other wills—not in some self-contained transcendental inner sphere, but in a context of situations that make vivid,
sometimes vividly red, the consequences of taking "unreasonable"
positions. Critical self-consciousness, in other words, is not a pointless
activity of intellectuals too enamored of philosophical idealism, but a
necessity for getting on with others in the world—a necessity even for
intellectuals.

If the political unconscious of the New Pragmatism is liberal (in
its wild phase, antinomian), its explicit political content runs all to
indifference and the professionalism that would make itself a world
apart. James, an integrated intellectual—a professional with an organic sense of the relation of philosophy and all other institutions—
who called himself a meliorist because he thought his world needed
changing and could be changed for the better, would find in the New
Pragmatism the thoroughgoing satisfaction that he had excoriated in
Josiah Royce: the confidence that this is the best of all possible worlds.
James not only thought otherwise, but he thought that the process of
change must be initiated close to home, in self-worrying critique. The
New Pragmatism, on the other hand, would stand one of the most
ancient of Western maxims on its head. It says in all but words: "The
unexamined life is the only life worth living." Here at last, moving
with the tides of the times, is the basis for a literary criticism of the
eighties.

Notes

1. *Selected Critical Writings of George Santayana,* ed. Norman Hen-
frey (Cambridge: Cambridge University Press, 1968), 1: 149–50.
2. William James, *Pragmatism & The Meaning of Truth,* introduction
by A. J. Ayer (Cambridge: Harvard University Press, 1975), 28–29. Page
numbers for further references to *Pragmatism* appear in the text.
3. Stanley Fish, "Consequences," *Critical Inquiry* 11 (March 1985):
435.

4. C. S. Peirce, *Selected Writings*, ed. Philip P. Weiner (New York: Dover Publications, 1966), 103.

5. See, for example, pages 31, 40, and 125 of *Pragmatism* and F. O. Matthiessen, *The James Family: A Group Biography* (New York: Alfred A. Knopf, 1961), 633. Page numbers for further references to *The James Family* appear in the text.

6. Michael Herr, *Dispatches* (New York: Alfred A. Knopf, 1977), 92.

7. Quoted in volume 1 of *American Literature: The Makers and the Making*, ed. Cleanth Brooks, R. W. B. Lewis, and Robert Penn Warren (New York: St. Martin's Press, 1973), 10n.

8. *The Selected Writings of Ralph Waldo Emerson*, ed. Brooks Atkinson and foreword by Tremaine MacDowell (New York: Random House, 1968), 430–31. Page numbers for further references to *Emerson* appear in the text.

9. See Herbert Marcuse, "The Affirmative Character of Culture," in *Negations: Essays in Critical Theory*, trans. Jeremy J. Shapiro (Boston: Beacon Press, 1968).

10. William James, *The Principles of Psychology* (New York: Dover Publications, 1950), 1:226. Page numbers for further references to *The Principles of Psychology* appear in the text.

11. The relevant documents are collected in *Against Theory: Literary Studies and the New Pragmatism*, ed. W. J. T. Mitchell (Chicago: University of Chicago Press, 1985).

12. Steven Knapp and Walter Benn Michaels, "Against Theory," *Critical Inquiry* 8 (Spring 1982): 742.

13. For pragmatism as a woman, see pages 43–44 of *Pragmatism*; on rationalism as an old-world gentleman, see pages 38 and 40 of *Pragmatism*. The metaphor of pragmatism as a woman is infrequent in James; rationalism as a gentleman is common.

14. I allude to the classic treatment of intellectuals in *The German Ideology*.

15. Fish, 444.

"The Return of William James," copyright 1986, Frank Lentricchia. Reprinted with permission.

Contextualizing the Either/Or:
Invariance/Variation and Dialogue in Jakobson/Bakhtin

Virgil Lokke

One way of reading contemporary literary theory and philosophy, particularly the newer French theories, is to imagine these theories reinscribed in an older discursive exchange between Roman Jakobson and Mikhail Bakhtin—not, of course, to imply that the issues under examination by these two figures of the early twentieth century have remained identical, but rather to use and misuse these two figures as structuring metaphors for displaying the postmodern challenges to the authorizing force of the "either/or."[1] Bakhtin's texts can function as the contrastive anti-formalist response whose refracted spectrum finds contemporary expressions in writers such as Lyotard, Derrida, Deleuze and Guattari, and Bourdieu, thus illustrating the post-structuralist challenge to the formalist structures and their proliferating disjunctions.

My own discourse, with its transparent agenda, chooses Jakobson as a magnet around which I can cluster certain notions of a formalist analytic, a structuralist hope, and a more or less benign "scientism." Here we find a linguistics which would be simultaneously "scientific" and "humanistic," a linguistics which seeks to accommodate classical literary and poetic conventions: Jakobson, then, plays the role of the genial formalist.[2] Bakhtin functions as the equally congenial antiformalist challenger, as the contrastive reminder of the decisive force of exclusionary cuts, of the "as if" conditions which provide the forgotten or suppressed foundations of Jakobson's "linguistic" arguments.

In addition, my narrative points in incidental ways to a story of the decay and dissemination of two or three faculties which were competing for the most powerful voice of translator of literary texts. Literary languages—like religious, philosophical, political, sociological, and mathematical languages—have made and still do make their own imperialist bids for power. That it is a power move is evident in the eagerness to see the translation as a unidirectional process, a nonreversible reaction, and in the persistence with which one language is privileged as being "literal" and the other demeaned or patronized as merely "figurative."

The languages of linguistics, the rhetorical and foundational strategies of linguistic discourse, occupy such a central position in the formalist/antiformalist debate, largely, it seems, because the language of linguistics is presumed most stridently to be the voice of "science" as monitor and judge of the discordant voices of the humanities and the social sciences. Linguistics became the leading candidate for domination principally because of the further assumption that "linguistics" spoke "scientific"—that linguistics offered the most faithful translation of science, which was in turn the most faithful translation of the language of the world. Such, in brief, is a genealogy of one authorizing process.

But many other languages which we speak offer tempting opportunities for translation projects; that is, each may be viewed as a candidate for some universalizing, totalizing project. To the extent that authorizing projects can be viewed as translation projects, any language which resists translation into another language can, from the view of the chosen language, be regarded as inauthentic, unauthorized, a nonlanguage, mystic, primitive, or perhaps even an attempt to "speak in tongues."

The two particular languages I will focus upon here are the language of science—empiricism of the late nineteenth and early twentieth centuries—and the language of linguistics. The former, although many-voiced, nevertheless was assumed to have a monologic voice, and as such it became ideological by almost any usage of the term. This monologic voice spoke as if there were both a constituted scientific language and a constituted method. The "method," however, was in effect only another language, the "authorizing" subset of the language of science. This authorizing subset (the scientific method), this monologic voice, rejected any area of interest, any language which could not translate itself into *the* foundational language. Any language failing to meet these conditions was deauthorized and marginalized as "subjective" or worse.

▼

Jakobson's communications model can well serve as an illustration of an authorizing project which depends upon its presumption of having successfully translated "linguistic" into "scientific." That this "scientific language" was an admixture or conglomerate is probably transparent enough to render explication unnecessary. What I wish to stress for the moment, however, is the language and strategic deployment of Jakobson's model, which presumes that the scientific and rational procedure to be followed is: (1) to find and label all the constituent parts of something called "communication," (2) to isolate the parts from each other with restrictive and context-controlling names, and (3) to locate the names of the parts on a horizontal time scale that has the Message suspended momentarily between the Addresser and the Addressee.

Jakobson's essay "Linguistics and Poetics" exemplifies most of the problematic features of the model. There he displays the communications model which even in the present day still maintains a vestige of its initial authoritative potency (*Selected Writings*, 3:18–51). Herein is a taxonomy which became for many a powerful authorizing agency for empirical research and for utopian hopes of offering to literary studies, composition, and communications studies a means for escaping charges of irresponsible subjectivity. On the horizontal axis, then, the model can be viewed as a description of the simple transfer of energy from addresser to addressee, from left to right. The vertical scale can simultaneously indicate such determinate synchronic essences as "context," "message," "contact," and "code"—introducing hierarchy and value, and thus "meaning," into the construct.

When Jakobson's model identified the "six basic aspects of language," (*Selected Writings* 3:23), few enough asked the serious questions such enumerations raise, such as, Why six? What is the presumed status of each unit? How discrete is each unit? and What kind of ontological status, if any, does such a unit have? Jakobson sometimes refers to the units as "factors" or "aspects," and again these units have "functions," which may be multiple or singular. The unit Message has a "predominant function," yet not an exclusive function which is "referential," "denotative," and "cognitive." Herein lies the message's positive linking to a "real" and a "rational" world. Jakobson assures us, at least, that "numerous messages" have such a function. In addition, however, the Message has an "emotive" function which implicates the Addresser: and, of course, the "emotive" function may also carry cognitive information. Furthermore, a focus upon or "orientation toward" the Addressee reveals the Conative function, that is, in vocative and imperative expressions. What seems to be exemplified in Jakobson's descriptive maneuvers is the search for the exhaustive detailing of the full range of "possible" functions of Messages. In this detailing operation, the terms are "referential, denotative, cognitive and emotive, conative, vocative and imperative."

So far the model is very similar to the older Buhler model, with its total dependence upon a grammatical structure reflecting first person (addresser), second person (addressee), and third person (the someone or something spoken of or about). Jakobson adds three more constitutive units, the Contact, the Code, and the Context, each having a proper function. The Contact tests whether the circuit is open or closed; the Code has the metalinguistic function of testing whether the Code is shared by Addresser and Addressee; and finally, the Context acts as "a set toward the referent." Each of these constituent elements has a function, and Jakobson's circuitry begins to expand and multiply. The emotive function is connected to the Addresser: the conative function is connected to the Addressee: and the referential, phatic, metalingual, and poetic functions are all connected to the Message! The sheer mathematical potentiality for combinatory possibilities of the Jakobsonian model is impressive, even without noting that each function may contain internal divisions. The poetic function, for example, differs from its allied message-related functions such as the referential, phatic, and metalingual in that the poetic function foregrounds the Message for its own sake. It is the poetic function which, while not at all confined to poetry, is the "dominant, determining function . . . of verbal art." (Here Jakobson invokes the credo of Russian Formalist aesthetic theory; here is the selfless, autonomous, potentially nonideological credo of a formalist aesthetic, fully installed in communication itself.) It must be added, of course, that the poetic function "acts as a subsidiary, accessory constituent in all other verbal activities (*Selected Writings*, 3:25).

The awesome permutational complexity of the model must, however, yield to a more basic problem designated, and in part obscured, by the feature or constitutive element Context, in that what appears to be a closed and exhaustive series—"referential, phatic, metalingual (self-reference to language)"—becomes infinitely self-referential with the inclusion of the poetic. This function, which seems only to act as a "subsidiary, accessory constituent in all other verbal activities," in fact renders the constitutive factor Context an infinitely open series. Jakobson's Context, in its inclusion of the poetic function, includes not merely a literary, fictional, or aesthetic domain, but potentially all that has not yet been said and will always remain to be said.[3]

Perhaps the model itself illustrates why it authorized so many imitative deployments in literary theory, semantics, and communications theory. Even this bare-bones description illuminates the almost infinite opportunities it offers for being at once "scientific" and "poetic," while still maintaining the authorizing voice of a "scientific linguistics." One kind of reader found great empirical solace in such terms as "constitutive factors" and found in the listed elements of Addresser, Context, Message, Contact, Code, and Addressee a set of clearly identifiable entities from the object world. Furthermore, it permitted one to view the whole middle block, Message, as an entity that shuttled endlessly from left to right, from Addresser to Addressee, as an energy transmission that could be submitted to measurement. Another reading would welcome an escape from a more primitive scientism of identification of entities with the notion of functions, even shall we say as having the potentiality of some more "neutral," mathematical function. Here we move into the possibility of avoiding any naive attribution of tangibility to the "constitutive factors" by reading the model as simply a description of relational sets.

I do not wish, however, to exhaust the possible readings of the Jakobson model, nor do I wish to offer a "correct" one. I wish merely to point out that the success of the model, its reputation as an authorizing device, rests on its ability to evoke the aura of the "scientific." Such an aura relies upon a taxonomy whose generation is dependent upon the force of the exclusive disjunction, the "either/or." Like the linguistics of Jakobson's time, Jakobson's model too was dependent for its "scientificity" upon its use of the "undistributed middle," its particular binarism, and its concerted efforts to maintain itself as a strong theory.

The model loses its general authoritative force unless it also retains the metaphysics of a grammar which foundationally asserts that "communicative praxis is *about* something, *by* someone, and *for* someone."[4] For all practical purposes, this traditional grammatical formulation may be a privileging of those positional languages that become the foundational norm for just such assertions. Note also that communication is about a *thing*, a *one*, and a *body*—terms which historically engrave notions of self, external objects, and others—all embodiments of the metaphysics of presence, and, as such, providing an exclusion of nondiscursive features of experience which are operative in all of our social contexts. There is, for example, no recognition of the not-yet-sayable, no evidence of the social processes generative of meanings. What appears in this model is always already constituted. In short, the structuring operations, the operational processes, are all obscured by this model. The Jakobson model thus represents a reincorporation of a very traditional metaphysical and grammatical model which is designedly incapable of dealing with practice and process and is totally dependent upon a highly traditional metaphysics of the self and the other, the "inside" and the "outside," the privileged and the estranged.

It is no surprise that the historical forces which constituted "science" in opposition to the "humanities" have never maintained a stable opposition. The division itself is a product of a historical moment; the position of privilege has changed, and the terms themselves have been in the constant process of changing themselves. There is no surprise either in the use by apologists of science of the features and foundational premises of the hermeneutic discursive practices, as there is no surprise in the use by theologians, philosophers, linguists, historians, anthropologists, and literary scholars of the foundational premises of selected scientific discourses. What is more surprising, perhaps, is the extent to which such fraternal borrowing is concealed under the rubric of the exclusive binary.

Jakobson is much concerned with the binary; he uses this exclusive disjunction as a central move, yet he knows that it is not a universally reliable strategy. He expressly rejects the firm distinction between synchrony and diachrony, and between poetics and linguistics:

> Since my earliest report of 1927 to the then new born Prague Linguistics Circle, I have pleaded for the removal of the alleged antinomy synchrony/diachrony and have propounded instead the idea of permanently dynamic synchrony, at the same time underscoring the presence of static invariants in the diachronic cut of language. (*Verbal Art, Verbal Sign, Verbal Time*, 6)

Here indeed is a reflection of Jakobson's abiding concern with the binary which for him is the most central: "Invariance and Variation."

We can also see the highly problematic mode of reconciliation, the mode in which the oppositional binary is made to collapse, to become a nonexclusive binary whose function is simply to reincorporate history, process, change under the privilege of the synchronous, the universal. Or is it the other way? Is the synchronous being collapsed under the privilege of the "permanently dynamic"? Perhaps Jakobson's strategy here is similar to the reconciliatory move made by the positivists of the Vienna Circle when they discovered that they could label their universalizing syntheses as either "logical empiricism" or "empirical positivism."[5] Such a convergence of rationalism and empiricism under one umbrella may be the equivalent of Jakobson's somewhat indecisive governance of ultimate stasis, in light of his conjoining of the synchronic and the diachronic in such a way that he can still look forward to a linguistic scene heavily populated with the determinate and the axiomatizable. So much then for the false dichotomy of the synchronic and the diachronic. But this is only part of the story. Jakobson characterizes his own career as follows:

> My continuous studies in aphasia can be summed up as follows: "The basic binary concepts viewed in the linguistic quest as the key to understanding the obvious dichotomy of aphasic disturbances, namely dyads such as encoding/decoding, syntagmatic/ paradigmatic, and contiguity/similarity, gradually found access to the advanced neuropsychological treatment of aphasic enigmas." . . . The multifarious linguistic and poetic manifestations of the last dyad which may be outlined as metonymy/metaphor . . . , urgently demand a deeper and wider scrutiny. . . . To conclude, I avow that binary solutions attract me and I believe in the mutual salutary influence of linguistics and philology. (*Verbal Art, Verbal Sign, Verbal Time*, 6–7)

While binary solutions do indeed attract Jakobson, it is equally evident that not all binaries are equally attractive. Here the burden must be shifted from the particular, specific binary to the more comprehensive category of the good or bad binary. Thus, for those who seek good binary solutions, it seems necessary to identify and specify the criteria for the discrimination of universal binariness, the binary of the binaries. This ultimate discriminatory operation can be regarded as at least problematic. The features of the good and the bad binary are not, shall we say, "distinctive."

It is the presumptive distinctiveness of the "distinctive features" of phonology that is foundational for much of Jakobson's theorizing. He depends upon the presumed scientific solidity of phonology with its foundational rock, "distinctive features," a rock which shadowed forth its presence against all "undistinctive features." Here we are confronted with the *touch*-stone of linguistics itself. For the unquestioning, "distinctive features" provided a missing link between language and the nonlinguistic world, between utterance and verifiability of utterance; it was a "fact" which ran beyond the conventions of usage, exemplifying, in short, a firmly undisputable "literal" statement rescued from the sea of metaphoricity.

If, however, the binary literal/figural is not an ontological binary, and no more than another illustration of a sociolinguistic convention, then the claim of linguists to have discovered a piece of the rock in "distinctive features" is, to say the least, problematic. A likely condition is that the "distinctive feature" is no more than a highly attractive metaphor.[6]

Jakobson's text, then, seems firmly dependent upon its "scientificity." This particular science, the linguistics of Jakobson, is dependent upon the presumptive "literalness" of its phonological descriptions. The aura of a linguistics so envisioned grounds the authority of Jakobson's pronouncements. Within this generalized context lies the communications model itself, which has been the focus of my exploration. Models, diagrams, sketches—the pictorial arrangement of words with drawn or implied boxes around them—all supply visual signs of the authoritative "real" and provide the evidence of closure, definition, and certainty, while offering at the same time the necessary elusiveness for elaboration and application. So also, of course, Jakobson's model skillfully deploys key terms which identify units in the model in such a way that these terms remain ambiguously operative in a multiplicity of senses. Jakobson can, with his model, imply but not assert an overt causality, imply but not assert measureability, and thereby offer a model which can provide the necessary, and still properly authorized, slippage.

This model itself is, however, embedded in another context which has a range of dimensions—institutional, academic, and political—thus authorizing Jakobson's voice in a transparent abundance of signals. Such an overwhelming display (within the confines of thirty-odd pages of the essay where the model is offered) of linguistic competence in a range of twenty different languages—including Lithuanian, classical Chinese, Efik, and American Indian Pima-Pogo—and with an equally impressive set of references to some fifty authors—literary critics, linguists, painters, and film producers—may have set a bench mark for future aspirants to the authorization of discursive practice in linguistic texts. Finally, however, the whole essay "Linguistics and Poetics," as perhaps is the whole corpus of Jakobson's impressive textual production, seems itself to be comfortably nestled in the master narrative inherited from the eighteenth century, that is, the story of progress and of the relentlessly humanizing benefits of the accumulation of information.

▼

The Russian Formalists and Jakobson, as one of their most distinguished exemplars, are almost inconceivable without their dependence upon a linguistics, which was governed in its course by a positivistic moment in the history of the philosophy of science. The most powerful dissenting voice, challenging a positivistic or structuralist linguistics[7] and formalist analytical strategies themselves, was that of Bakhtin. Bakhtin's vigorous antiformalist position has, within the last decade, spread throughout the American academy of letters. We are now forced to recognize the formalist position as only part of a dialogue which took place in the intellectually charged atmosphere of postrevolutionary Russia of the 1920s. This dialogue laid out in almost schematic form, with a clarity rarely achieved since, an almost complete set of the theoretical concepts which, up until comparatively recently, has constituted the principal arena of contention within literary theory.

To the extent that literary theory in America has been theoretical, it has been predisposed toward formalism *à la* New Criticism or an "emancipated" theological structuralism as illustrated by Northrop Frye. One can, of course, deny that New Criticism was ever theoretical in any strong sense, and some would even exclude Frye as a theorist. Without taking time at this juncture to describe the available literary theory on the American scene, one can only mention the neo-Kantianism of Wellek, the logico-empiricism of Beardsley and Wimsatt, the Aristotelianism of Crane. Suffice it to say that American criticism had access to a number of formalist positions and that it could have availed itself, for example, of the antiformalist features of Kenneth Burke—a resource that would have made the impact of New French Theory less traumatic had Burke been more carefully read rather than treasured as a maverick.

Bakhtin's antiformalism was, however, simply not available to American literary studies. His "translinguistics," his foregrounding of the social aspect of text generation, his notions of the processes of text consumption, his reconstitution of the self and objects in language and in society—all are alien to our native and imported formalisms. As a theorist, Bakhtin relied less upon separation and closure as explanatory and analytical procedures than he did upon a narrative description of discursive practices which, among other things, implicated his theory of the novel as well as his more general theory of genre.

In *The Formal Method in Literary Scholarship*, Bakhtin-Medvedev[8] describes the formalist assumption:

> In their interpretation the formalists tacitly presuppose a completely ready and static intercourse and communication that is just as static.
>
> This can be schematically expressed thus: given are two members of a society, A (the author) and R (the reader); the social relations between them are constant and stable at the given moment; also given is the ready communication X, which will simply be transmitted from A to R. The "what" (content) of this message X differs from its "how" (form) and the "orientation toward expression" ("how") is characteristic of the artistic word.
>
> This scheme was shaped in the first period of formalism when the poetic word was opposed to the practical, ready-made, and automatized utterance. The word became the converse of such an utterance.
>
> This scheme is radically incorrect. (152)

Bakhtin argues that all communication, poetic or ordinary, is always "generating in the process of intercourse," and further, that aesthetic or poetic works cannot be differentiated on the basis of any deautomization—for the description of the "ordinary" communication process as automatized is faulty. "Ready-made work objects," poetry, etc., cannot be prized simply because presumably they are generated by a special isolating function of aesthetic utterance.

What Bakhtin attacks is the binary "literary/ordinary" as a feature immanent in a text, or in the language of a text, unless it be made clear that the binary is itself a socially constituted construct. One does not, in short, improve the faulty communications model by positing a "literary" communications model in which some of the originally excised complexity is restored in order to simultaneously elevate and insulate "literariness." Along with the "literary/ordinary" dyad also falls the "intrinsic/extrinsic" configuration, which Bakhtin sees not as an autonomy/dependence ratio but rather as a conflict between two social orientations. The "art for art's sake" stance is a social stance, and the basically "social nature of art is no less sharply evident in these formulations than it is in cases of direct agreement of art and the social demands of the epoch" (*The Formal Method in Scholarship*, 155).

Bakhtin's assault upon the exclusive binary finds targets in philosophy and linguistics as well. His criticism of Saussure argues that language is not abstract; it is not a system, much less a rule-bound structure; it is not passively assimilated, and as it comes to us, it is conflictual, stressful, processual, live, open. He argues that the *langue/parole* distinction, the synchrony/diachrony pairing, the differentiation between written and oral language in their manifestations as exclusive binaries, are frequently employed as buttressing structures for more or less authorizing, centralizing modes of sociocultural patterns.

None of his own key terms are in fact proposed as exclusivities. Perhaps his opposition to exclusive binarism can be illustrated by a key pairing in Bakhtin's discourse, the monologic and the dialogic. These terms define each other but not by exclusion. In Bakhtin, these terms are defined by mutual dependence and not by a presumptive exhaustion of categorial possibilities. A monologic world, for Bakhtin, is one in which a thought is "either affirmed or repudiated." The result of this mode of thought, the attempt to achieve a full monologism, is that the heteroglot features of thought are suppressed, fail to achieve representation, and implicate the violence of denial, by the confining of alternative modes of expression "harshly and implacably." Bakhtin sees much of our discourse, our philosophy, our art in Western culture as being articulated within the constraints of a monologic ideology:

> Ideological monologism found its clearest and theoretically most precise formulation in idealistic philosophy. The monistic principle, that is, the affirmation of the unity of *existence* is, in idealism, transformed into the unity of the *consciousness* . . . The unity of consciousness, replacing the unity of existence, is inevitably transformed into the unity of a *single* consciousness; when this occurs it makes absolutely no difference what metaphysical form the unity takes: "consciousness in general" (Bewusstsein uberhaupt), "the absolute I," "the absolute spirit," "the normative consciousness," and so forth . . . In the ideal a single consciousness and a single mouth are absolutely sufficient for maximally full cognition; there is no need for a multitude of consciousnesses, and no basis for it . . .

In an environment of philosophical monologism the genuine interaction of consciousness is impossible, and thus genuine dialogue is impossible as well. In essence idealism knows only a single mode of cognitive interaction among consciousnesses: someone who knows and possesses the truth instructs someone who is ignorant of it and in error; that is, it is the interaction of teacher and a pupil, which, it follows, can only be a pedagogical dialogue. (*Problems of Dostoevsky's Poetics*, 80–81)

Bakhtin's monologic/dialogic pairing is not an exclusive binary in that the terms are not equivalent; they do not exclude each other, for the monologic is only a special case of the dialogic. The monologic defines itself by excluding particulars of its environment in order to constitute itself. It is a system which constitutes itself by the intensity of its foregrounding of exclusivity. In short, Bakhtin's dyads are essentially asymmetrical, interdependent, and thus become hierarchical only to the extent that environment as "inclusiveness" is privileged over the systems it relates to. Inclusiveness, however, constitutes only some ever-receding horizon.

Such an explanation of Bakhtin's argument does not presume that his discourse is free from privileging elements of his own dyads. In fact most of his explanations and analyses are based on finding more satisfactory explanations in terms of the *social* over against the *individual*, for the social is more inclusive and constitutes the environment for the individual:

> The idea—as it was *seen* by Dostoevsky the artist—is not a subjective individual-psychological formulation with "permanent residence rights" in a person's head; no the idea is inter-individual and inter-subjective—the realm of its existence is not individual consciousness, but dialogic communion *between* consciousnesses. The idea is a live *event*, played out at the point of dialogic meeting between two or several consciousnesses. In this sense, the idea is similar to the *word*, with which it is dialogically united. Like the word, the idea wants to be heard, understood, and "answered" by other voices from other positions. Like the word, the idea is by nature dialogic, and monolog is merely the conventional form of its expression, a form that emerged out of the ideological monologism of modern times characterized by us above. (*Problems of Dostoevsky's Poetics*, 88)

Language and consciousness are participatory interrelationships, separable only by taxonomic artifice; word and idea are themselves the products of dialogic interplay and isolatable only in the interests of some monologic game. Language itself is not a system or a whole or even a system in the mind of the speaker. It is a system neither for the collective nor for the individual. Language is always composed of many different languages that constantly compete for ascendancy, a phenomenon Bakhtin calls heteroglossia. Moreover, each of these languages contains random elements. Language, literature, and culture proceed by dialogues among systems and by dialogues between all systems and the unsystematic. The dialogues insure that language will always have enough consistency to be comprehensive and enough inconsistency to produce surprise. Openness, then, unfinalizability, and the resistance to all that purports to be fixed and stable, is characteristic of Bakhtin's stance.

On page 54 of *Mikhail Bakhtin: The Dialogical Principle*, Tzvetan Todorov attempts to set up two contrasting communications models, Jakobson's and Bakhtin's:

Bakhtin	**Jakobson**
object	context
speaker	sender
utterance	message
listener	receiver
intertext	contact
language	code

Todorov's modeling strategy here calls particular attention to the absence of "contact" in Bakhtin's model, and the absence of any equivalent of "intertext" (Todorov's label) in Jakobson's model. Todorov's comparative modeling serves to display the basic, and in a sense irreconcilable, difference between the formalist, linguistic, information-engineering concepts of Jakobson and the antiformalist, dispersive, and aggressively sociological analytics of Bakhtin. Jakobson, Todorov reminds us, seeks to present "the constitutive factors of any verbal event, of any act of verbal communication." Jakobson's model operates within a linguistics, a rule-bound structure which must always protect its self-sufficiency, its decontextualized existence as a systematic structure with units and features such as "words and grammatical rules [which can end up] with sentences" (54).

In strong contrast, the "translinguistics" of Bakhtin "starts with sentences and the context of enunciation and . . . obtains utterances. Thus to formulate propositions concerning any verbal event, an event of language as well as of discourse would be, in Bakhtin's perspective, a useless enterprise" (54). Language, Todorov continues, does not, for Bakhtin, constitute a "code." Discourse does not maintain a uniform relation with its object; it does not "reflect" it, but organizes, transforms or resolves a situation. To remind us that Bakhtin remained firm in his early critique of the communications model of language, Todorov quotes from Bakhtin's notes made in 1971: "Semiotics prefers to deal with the transmission of a ready-made message by means of a ready-made code, whereas, in living speech, messages are, strictly speaking, created for the first time in the process of transmission, and ultimately there is no code" (57). What is concealed in the hypostatized categories of the communications model, Bakhtin reminds us, is that it could at very best apply only to a dead language; thus, it creates an illusory stability whenever applied to living language, an unwarranted deadness obscuring what well may be a radically unsystematic feature of our language world, thereby silencing an anarchic aspect of our very texts in order to proceed with the totalizing and systematizing game which has characterized aspects of linguistics as well as literary studies. For Bakhtin, these abstracting models have been powerful and influential in our humanistic disciplines—serving as supportive agents for authoritarian ideological configurations.

One of the many reasons Bakhtin finds the communications model irrelevant is that it ignores dialogue and reported speech. Not only is communication, for Bakhtin, essentially dialogic, but he also finds that most speech is *reported speech*. David Carroll's essay, "The Alterity of Discourse," quotes Bakhtin's reminder that the situation between addresser and addressee is complex because speech is most commonly reported speech, "speech within speech, utterance within utterance, and at the same time speech about speech, utterance about utterance" (70).

Dogmatic utterances—including those which populate this essay—are utterances which seek to preclude, to exclude, to deny the community of voices, the "speech within speech" and thus disallow active response. Bakhtin-Voloshinov suggests "the more dogmatic the utterance, the less leeway permitted between truth and falsehood, good and bad, in its reception by those who comprehend and evaluate, the greater will be the depersonalization that forms of reported speech must undergo" (*Marxism and the Philosophy of Language*, 120). What is exhibited in Bakhtin is a rather thorough analysis of the possible implications of any system, structure, or model which has reified the triadic configuration of AUTHOR-TEXT-READER + WORLD. Bakhtin's alternative explanation, however, resists the label of model or system. It seeks always to pose itself against finalization and closure.

Bakhtin's description may be thought of in two ways: first, it establishes itself, temporarily, in contrast with centralizing, logocentric, dogmatic models as being decentralizing, disseminationist, dialogic, and antiauthoritarian; but secondly, it must be remembered that Bakhtin's alternative modes are always present as nonexclusive binaries such as the logocentric/disseminationist, the monologic/dialogic, and the centripetal/centrifugal. These pairings are always present, contestatory, operative and alive—just as the systolic and diastolic rhythm of the heart, the inhalation and exhalation of the lungs, and the death-in-life and life-in-death processes in mind and body proceed endlessly as long as there is process, as long as there is life.

A recognizable openness, a constant reminder of the carnivalesque and the unfinalizable, pervades Bakhtin's own discourse: "Nothing conclusive has yet taken place in the world, the ultimate word of the world and about the world has not yet been spoken, the world is open and free, everything is still in the future and will always be in the future" (*Problems of Dostoevsky's Poetics*, 166).

One ought not to forget, Bakhtin reminds us, that the law of formal identity ($A \equiv A$) does not apply to the historical individual; a man "never coincides with himself." Nor should one forget that in history and society, "[i]f we produce my words, then I do not know what I am going to say until I have said it." That is, each utterance is constituted not simply as a projection of a private psyche, but, rather, belongs to the two speakers and all the voices of society that speak within their speech. Such openness, such emphasis on flux and process, subverts all authorizing principles as only passing moments.

———————▼———————

Closely related to a more generalized analysis of problems of authorization is the argument of Lyotard in *The Postmodern Condition: A Report on Knowledge*. Whether the focus is upon "legitimation" or "authorization," the question remains the same. What kind of ranking order exists among classes of statements embedded in different generic contexts of discourse? How do we differentiate the true from the false, the important from the trivial, within each of the genres of discourse that confront us in these present moments of our history? In our epoch there is no longer available to us any single judgmental criterion, nor even any cluster of criteria that have an acceptability across the whole domain of discursive practice. What we are left with is the attempt to describe, from wherever we stand, the differences that obtain among the contestants, to determine, tentatively, some genealogical descriptions of the ascension and declension of the various modes of "legitimation," and, finally, to suggest some of the possible consequences of such shifts in authorizing modes.

Lyotard's initial move is a dyadic one: the separation of *narrative* knowledge from *scientific* knowledge. Such a cut may seem to be based on an exclusive either/or. However, Lyotard's analysis proceeds to explain why his cut is a nonexclusive one. Narrative knowledge does not, for example, exclude scientific knowledge. It is scientific knowledge that insists on its exclusivity and its essentially deauthorizing function with respect to narrative knowledge.

Lyotard argues "against the unquestioning acceptance of an instrumental conception of knowledge" and adds that "knowledge is not the same as science, . . . and science, far from successfully obscuring the problem of its legitimacy, cannot avoid raising it with all of its implications, which are no less sociopolitical than epistemological" (*The Postmodern Condition*, 18).

"Scientific" discourse seeks to "obscure the problem of legitimacy" by isolating and differentiating itself from narrative discourse. Through the conventions of "literal" language with its presumptions of tight referentiality, the employment of "causal," syntactical, and lexical practices, along with other *rhetorical* "scientific" discourse, suppresses clues to its kinship with parallel functions in narrative. Or, if one prefers, "narrative" language obscures its similarity of functions with "scientific" language. In any event, what we can be concerned with is the translation process, for surely the process can be viewed as translation, and the product of translating "narrative" into "scientific" is a foregrounding of the hierarchical, judgmental, exclusionary, and unidirectional flow of the "scientific" translation process in opposition to the bi-directional potentiality of flow always implicit in narrative. Narrative can abide more comfortably with the awareness of its loss of innocence, with its impurity. Some scientific discourse still impatiently resents any reminder of the "as-if-ness" of its own virginity.

Lyotard defines *knowledge (savoir)* as broader than and different from "learning" and science. Knowledge is not merely a set of denotative statements. It also includes notions of "know-how"— "knowing how to live" and "knowing how to listen." Narrative knowledge is not only rooted in custom and practice; it is the "quintessential form of customary knowledge" (*The Postmodern Condition*, 20). But the decisive rule, the pragmatic legitimation of all narrative knowledge is illustrated by the following condition:

> The narrative "posts" (sender, addressee, hero) are so organized that the right to occupy the post of sender receives the following double grounding; it is based on the fact of having been recounted oneself, by virtue of the name one bears, by a previous narrative—in other words, having been positioned as the diegetic reference of other narrative events. The knowledge transmitted by these narrations is in no way limited to the functions of narration; it determines in a single stroke what one must say in order to be heard, what one must listen to in order to speak, and what role one must play (on the scene of diegetic reality) to be the object of a narrative. (21)

It is, in Lyotard's view, the condensation of these posts or functions within narrative that marks it as a practice which does not depend upon the taxonomic cuts (sender, addressee, subject or referent or message) for its effectiveness or authority. Its authority rests on its embedment in, its lack of differentiation from, the community and the society in which it is enacted. "What is transmitted through these narratives is the set of pragmatic rules (social practices, if you will), that constitute the social bond" (21).

In contrast, the pragmatics of scientific knowledge, according to Lyotard, exhibits several important differences. Here I mention only the idea that scientific discourse "requires that one language game, denotation, be retained and all others excluded," and that scientific discourse "sets itself apart from the language games that combine to form the social bond" (25).

Without entering into a description of the full range of differences between the narrative and the scientific modes, I must note how important it is for Lyotard to emphasize that

> Both are composed of sets of statements; the statements are "moves" made within the framework of generally applicable rules; these rules are specific to each particular kind of knowledge, and the "moves" judged to be "good" in one cannot be

of the same type as those judged to be "good" in another, unless it happens that way by chance. (26)

The dyad "narrative knowledge" versus "scientific knowledge" thus becomes an exclusive either/or from the point of view of scientific discourse but nonexclusive from the stance of narrativity. Narrative knowledge does not give priority to its own legitimation:

> That is why its incomprehension of the problems of narrative discourse is accompanied with a certain tolerance; it approaches [scientific discourse] primarily as a variant in the family of narrative cultures. The opposite is not true. The scientist questions the validity of narrative statements and concludes that they are not subject to argumentation or proof. He classifies them as belonging to a different mentality: savage, primitive, underdeveloped, backward, alienated, composed of opinions, customs, authority, prejudice, ignorance, ideology. Narratives are fables, myths, legends fit only for women and children. . . . This unequal relationship is an intrinsic effect of the rules specific to each game. We all know its symptoms. It is the entire history of cultural imperialism from the dawn of Western civilization. (*The Postmodern Condition*, 27)

The "imperialism" of specific taxonomic cuts to which Lyotard refers can be related to the kind of segmentation that is required to generate the communications/information theory model. The model is itself dependent upon such key concepts as identity, unity, and hierarchy. First of all, the model is seen as "identical with" or "equivalent to" or "imitative of" or "representative of" something external to the model. Second, it is self-contained, a "unity." Third, it is made up of parts related to each other on the basis of their relation to a center, and such a hierarchical relationship insures unity and effective closure. These modeling modes have developed a tedious monotony in that the "authorization" or "legitimation" is always some univocal notion of "science"—a notion frequently enough expressive of an embedded Baconianism, Newtonianism, logical positivism, or some Husserlian phenomenology advanced in quiescent unawareness of the deauthorizing plurality of the voices of a Popper, Polanyi, Toulmin, or Feyerabend. Thus we continue to bully each other with our batteries of exclusive "either/or's"—our selective cuts from our multiple "philosophies of science" which have already distanced themselves irrevocably from the *practice* of any of the existing sciences in our purview.

Crucially implicated, then, in investigations of authorization is the practice/theory dyad. Various attempts have been made to explore, and speculate about, the relations between theory and practice, and the problematics of this relationship continue to concern us. My own preference reflects Bourdieu's suggestion (discussed below) that theory as theory and practice as practice cannot speak to each other because practice has no voice. Too often the word *practice* in discourses on theory and practice remains a transparent and feeble gesture exemplifying a gross unawareness of the radical potentiality of practice as a signal of the function of some estranged other. Practice does not attain voice when it is introduced into some discourse as "practice." Rather, what follows only too frequently from this generous gestural token of the theorist or philosopher is that since "practice" has now been introduced in the discourse, business can continue as usual.

A significant portion of practice lies, for me, outside of discursive analysis, and whenever it is brought into discourse, it is either consciously or unconsciously brought in as a "theory of practice," for it is only in this way that interaction is possible.

▼

What is taking place, then, in post-structuralist discourse is a reminder, a calling to our attention, of the probability that "theory" is a particular type of discursive practice, and that "practice" is the large and in some sense inaccessible generative force which is resistant to total incorporation within discourse. For example, deconstruction is itself recognizable as a discursive practice which has inbuilt resources resistant to codification or stabilization. One of its functions is to question the very grounds of the theory/practice distinction, or at least to show the processes at work in the generation of such differentiation.

Derrida's essay, "Signature Event Context," places most of the problems discussed in the present discourse in a readily accessible cluster. In its opening paragraph, the essay poses the following question:

> Is it certain that there corresponds to the word *communication* a unique, univocal concept, a concept that can be rigorously grasped and transmitted: a communicable concept? Following a strange figure of discourse, one must first ask whether the word or signifier "communication" communicates a determined content, an identifiable meaning, a describable value. But in order to articulate and propose this question, I

already had to anticipate the meaning of the word *communication:* I have had to predetermine communication as the vehicle, transport, or site of passage of a *meaning,* and of a meaning that is *one.* If *communication* had several meanings, and if this plurality could not be justified to define communication *itself* as the transmission, assuming that we are capable of understanding one another as concerns each of these words (transmission, meaning, etc.). Now the word *communication,* which nothing initially authorizes us to overlook as a word, and to impoverish as a polysemic word, opens a semantic field which precisely is not limited to semantics, semiotics, and even less to linguistics. (*Margins,* 309)

Derrida's question concerning the term "communication" is not at all a reminder of the term's metaphoricity. Rather, it is a matter of the violence of making it a center, of the construing cuts that have created its presumed determinacy, it univocality. What has been foregrounded is the relation between "polysemy and communication," and "dissemination and communication." To press the issue for but a moment is to be reminded of the role played by the terms "communication" and "context." Derrida adds:

It seems to go without saying that the field of equivocality covered by the word *communication* permits itself to be reduced massively by the limits of what is called a *context.* . . . Are the prerequisites of a context ever absolutely determinable? Is there a rigorous and scientific concept of the *context?* Does not the notion of context harbor, behind a certain confusion, very determined philosophical presuppositions. . . . I would like to demonstrate why a context is never certain or saturated [and mark] the theoretical insufficiency of the *usual concept* of (the linguistic or nonlinguistic) *context* such as it is accepted in numerous fields of investigation, along with all the other concepts with which it is systematically associated . . . (310)

Almost any one of Derrida's works, such as "White Mythology" (located in *Margins*) or *La carte postale,* contains both appropriate instructions for dismantling the communications model and examples of its generative prowess, that is, certainties achieved through the employment of the exclusive disjunction of practice/theory.

In the pursuit of the problematic features of the practice/theory dyad, I have pressed a bias, a perspective, and this perspective, transparent enough, has created a focus which obscures the many and significant differences which obtain among such independent minds as those of Lyotard and Derrida as well as those semiautonomous speculations of Deleuze and Guattari, and Bourdieu, which I now propose to examine. Nevertheless, through the perils of paraphrase, condensation, and translation, I will be pointing to a congeniality of concern, a dialogic and contestatory community of interest, that tentatively, loosely, and occasionally links the post-structuralist figures I have mentioned.

With Deleuze and Guattari, structuralism as found in psychoanalysis, Marxism, capitalist apologetics, and linguistics becomes the focus of the rupturing of the theory/practice dichotomy. Structuralism in all its forms manifests for Deleuze and Guattari its dependence upon a "majoritarian" or "sedentary" thinking—a thinking whose essence is a certain strain of Platonism. Deleuze and Guattari would invert Platonism, or, if not that, at least make room for "minoritarian" or "nomadic" thinking. This latter mode derives from an analytic strategy dependent upon both Nietzsche and, most specifically, a concept of unity arising out of Spinoza.[9]

Two basic terms, the "rhizomatic" and the "arborescent," provide a contestatory but not exclusive dyad: the arborescent can be described as a strongly centered, binary-ridden plane of organization in contrast with the rhizomatic, which involves an "a-centered plane of existence which embraces multiplicities, collections, open-ended adjacencies, and, in short, utterly impermanent connections." Such terms and phrases as "body without organs," "machine assemblages," "collectivities of heterogenous elements which function together," clusters whose "sole unity is that of co-function" provide a sense of that immanence or "plane of consistency," which is the *rhizome.* The *arborescent,* in contrast, is characterized as a "majoritarian," "sedentary," essentializing mode of discourse or perspective which operates in terms of exclusive binaries. Its tree-like structure is the product of aggressive dyadic proliferation:

> One becomes two: each time we encounter the formula . . . we find ourselves before the most classical and overworked, the oldest and tiredest of ideas. Nature does not work like this: in reality roots themselves are not dichotomic, but form taproot systems and are multiply ramified both laterally and radically. ("Rhizome," 51)

In the above passage, Deleuze and Guattari are comparing a rhizomatic book with an arborescent one. Their comments are directed in specific toward structuralist texts (including those of Freud,

Marx, Chomsky, Saussure, and Levi-Strauss, among others) and
in general toward all those literary, economic, and linguistic texts
which so heavily depend upon a presumed imitation, mimesis, or representation of the world or a facet of it. "The book," Deleuze and
Guattari assert, "is not an image of the world. It forms rhizomes with
the world." They add that "mimeticism dependent upon binary logic
is a very poor concept when applied to phenomena of a quite different
nature" ("Rhizome," 51). At each turn in the Deleuze and Guattari
text, the concepts of re-presentation, hierarchy, unity, and identity
are brought under inspection. It is not as if, of course, the arborescent
could be displaced by a processual, actively constructivist assemblage
of particulars which have "neither subject or object, but only determinants. One does not escape binaryism—at least in the West—for
such dyads are the basic elements of power." As Paul Patton, one of
the authors' translators, explains:

> How could one think without drawing distinctions? To suppose
> that this should be even attempted is only the first step toward
> the conclusion that we cannot escape the confines of our own
> system of rationality and still continue to think. We are already
> trapped, in thought as in reality, in the web of power. ("Rhi-
> zome," 46)

The answer then is not to presume to supplant the dyadic mode, but
rather to deauthorize specific deeply entrenched dyadic structures by
generating alternate dyads, again and again. One does not dispose
of, but rather deploys, "guerrilla tactics." In Deleuze and Guattari's
words, we "only invoke one dualism in order to refute another" (48).

The Jakobsonian communications model and the generative
taxonomy it is linked with is viewed by Deleuze and Guattari as
dyadic, linear, and hierarchical. Based as it is on part-whole sche-
matics, it is, in the eyes of Deleuze and Guattari, a "tracing," and
tracings are always constrictive. Rhizomes can be mapped but not
traced:

> The map is open, it is connectible in all its dimensions,
> detachable, reversible, susceptible to constant modification. It
> can be torn, reversed, adapted to any kind of setting, it can be
> set to work by an individual, a group, a social formation. It can
> be drawn on a wall, conceived as a work of art, constructed as
> a political action or as a meditation. . . . A map is a matter of
> performance, whereas the tracing always refers to an alleged
> "competence." (58)

But "tracings" and "authorized models" share the more generalized "representational model of the tree." The analysis of the congeniali-ties of those disciplines which depend so heavily upon the potentially infinite dyadic exfoliation of structuralism—Chomskian linguistics, Freudianism, Marxism, and capitalist apologetics, etc.—is pursued with untiring enthusiasm throughout the texts of *Anti-Oedipus* and *Mille Plateau.*

Those articulations which give preference to segmentation, cut-ting up into "manageable" units, whether they proceed by straight-forward binaries, by the dialectical strategy, by bi-univocal "relations between successive circles," or by the "fasciculated root"—all invite the same opportunity for distortion (51). That is, each "time a multiplicity is caught in a structure, its growth is compensated for by a reduction in the laws of combination," and we face yet another manifestation of "the abortionists of unity" (52).

Two points in the Deleuze and Guattari examination of struc-turally oriented model making need to be brought more sharply into focus. The first is the question of power and how structurally oriented discursive modes implicate certain types of power. For example, De-leuze and Guattari contend:

> in linguistics, even when one claims to confine oneself to the explicit and to assume nothing about language, one must re-main inside the sphere of discourse which implies particular modes of assemblages and types of social power. Chomsky's "grammaticality," the categorial symbol S set over all sentences, is first of all a power marker, and only secondly a syntactic marker. Thou shalt constitute grammatically correct sentences, thou shalt divide each statement into a noun phrase and a verb phrase (first dichotomy). . . . (53)

What Deleuze and Guattari focus upon is all that must be excluded, ignored, taken out of play in the forgotten "as if" of the discursive formulation. The further somewhat covert implication is that all the omitted particularities will be fitted in by a further expan-sion of the system or by the results of a proper distribution and allocation of unfinished tasks. The second point of focus is the co-relative stress of Deleuze and Guattari upon a partial listing of fea-tures which the dyadic construct has excluded, particularly those semantic and pragmatic "assemblages of enunciation" which have been severed from "a whole micropolitics of enunciation" (53).

The "as if" status of the initial taxonomic moves in defining the discipline of linguistics is occasionally forgotten, and the trichotomy of syntactics, semantics, and pragmatics is viewed as all-inclusive, self-evident, and objective. It is not that some theoreticians in linguistics are not troubled by the possibility that this trinity was not made in heaven or that it might be another variant of the form/content dichotomy—with the third term "pragmatics" as the wastebasket category for all the "relations" and otherwise excluded data that do not fall neatly into either form or content. Nor are they unaware of the problems that beset the term "pragmatics," both in its initial formulation by Morris and in its revision by Carnap, which still retains its "systematic three way ambiguity" (Stephen Levinson, *Pragmatics*, 3), or in its equally inadequate formulation by Montague. The confining of pragmatics to the study of indexicals or deictic terms involves at best the establishment of another tree-game—this time at the expense of the theme/rheme game, whose terminological problems have, according to Levinson, left "little that is salvageable" (x). In addition to these problems of definition, pragmatics must also exclude any "systematic remarks on prosody, and intonation" as well as any "systematic observation about the relations between pragmatics and syntax" (x).

At stake here is the more generalized awareness that the game of pragmatics as it is played within the larger game of linguistics is in most exemplary ways elegantly irrelevant to anything called practice. Linguistics is, in the sight of Deleuze and Guattari, quite perfectly suited to illustrate the wondrous exfoliation of dyadic proliferation into arborescence. By way of contrast, a rhizome:

> endlessly connects semiotic chains, power organizations, occurrences relating to the arts, the sciences, or to social struggles. A semiotic chain is like a tuber agglomerating quite different kinds of acts—linguistic, but also perceptual, mimetic, gestural, cognitive ones: there is no language in itself, nor any universality of language, but a concourse of dialects, patois, slangs, special languages. (53)

Certain concepts specific to some formulations of linguistic theory are directly challenged by Deleuze and Guattari:

> There exists no ideal "competent" speaker-hearer of language, any more than there exists a homogenous linguistic community. Language, according to Weinreich, is "an essentially heteroge-

nous reality." (1) There is no mother tongue, but a seizure of power by a dominant tongue within a political multiplicity. Language stabilizes around a parish, diocese, a capital. It forms a bulb. It develops by stems and underground flows, advances along river valleys or railroad lines, like oil on water. (2) It is always possible to decompose language into its component structures—this is not fundamentally different from a search for roots. There is always something geneological about the tree; this is not a democratic method. (53)

The rhizomatic method, "on the contrary, can only analyze language by decentering it on other dimensions and other registers. It is only in the movement of becoming impotent that a language can become closed in on itself" (53). The argument developed in the basic texts of Deleuze and Guattari finds in linguistics and other allied fields only examples of that face of Western philosophy which struggles strenuously to obscure the "face of Otherness." Western philosophy in its proclaimed search for the real, and then the "really real," has tended to assume that the "really real" consists of a circle which "already contains an installed philosopher" (64). What needs to be repeated here, perhaps already too tediously, is that for Deleuze and Guattari all structuralist operations, early and late, are seen as illustrations of a specific kind of metaphysics, so that Freudianism, Marxism, capitalism—all become exemplary functions of a metaphysics of the *same*, a metaphysics which reinscribes itself in our sciences, our social science, our literary studies, etc., a metaphysics which seeks always to retain its circularity, to give priority to identity over difference, to deny the possibility of symbiosis, and to mask that difference that lies within identity.

Deleuze and Guattari speak in voices which, if heard, destabilize those structural articulations, those ancient circularities which philosophy once laid claim to in offering the services of its transcendent neutrality to the status quo. Deleuze and Guattari remind us of those philosophies which have given aid and comfort to all those discursive practices whose very existence depends upon the effacement of the other, and the erasure of particularities in all discourse.

Such an effacement, through the deployment of the exclusive binary, is the project of the communications model, the information theory model, the formalist literary model. These models are prime examples of a strategy which has been employed with some degree of success as a universal, objective, classificatory schema, presumptively free from political, economic, or institutional embedment—

functioning, shall I say, as a means of subduing the otherness which threatens all our taxonomic devices.

———————▼———————

The destabilization of the communications model implicated in the philosophical texts of Lyotard, Derrida, and Deleuze and Guattari is reinforced by the analytics of Bourdieu's anthropological and sociological text, *Outline of a Theory of Practice*. During the course of Bourdieu's argument, the whole panoply of binaries, such as synchrony/diachrony, objectivism/subjectivism, structure/history, culture/personality, model/performance, *langue/parole*, determinism/ freedom, rule/improvisation, system/event, becomes the target of analysis, but the initial move in Bourdieu's text which seeks to give visibility and attention to "the theorization effect" does so by giving voice to practice. First, Bourdieu makes clear that practice is a process and that practice is governed by a "dialectic of strategies" rather than a "mechanics of the model." The semi-formalized "repertoire of rules" which is supposed to *represent* practice, in fact, according to Bourdieu, *guarantees* distortion:

> Knowledge does not merely depend, as an elementary relativism teaches us, on the particular standpoint of an observer "situated in space and time" takes upon the object. The "knowing subject", as the idealist tradition rightly calls him, inflicts on practice a much more fundamental and pernicious alteration which, being a constituent condition of cognitive operation, is bound to pass unnoticed: In taking up a point of view of the action, withdrawing from it in order to observe it from above and from a distance, he constitutes practical activity as an *object of observation and analysis, a representation.* (*Outline of a Theory of Practice,* 2)

That which cannot become an object of observation and analysis and thus cannot become a representation without distortion is the *habitus,* which, for Bourdieu, is a "socially constituted system of cognitive and motivating structures lying outside of articulation." Doxa, which is "that which goes without saying," is a manifestation of the habitus; and while the habitus itself is a theoretical construct, it refers to those nonarticulated learned strategies which are supplementary to the articulated rules. The habitus is composed of:

> systems of durable, transposable dispositions, structured structures, predisposed to function as structuring structures, that is, as principles of the generation and structuring of practices and

representations which can be objectively "regulated," and "regular" without in any way being the product of obedience to rules, objectively adapted to their goals without presupposing a conscious aiming at ends or an express mastery of the operations necessary to attain them and, being all this, collectively orchestrated without being the product of a conductor. (72)

Bourdieu is urging a supersession of "methodological objectivism" through the "displacement of the mechanical model" in order to escape the *"realism of the structure":*

> It is necessary to abandon all theories which explicitly or implicitly treat practice as a mechanical reaction, directly determined by the antecedent conditions and entirely reducible to the mechanical functioning of the pre-established assemblies, "models," "roles,"—which one would, moreover have to postulate in infinite number. (73)

Bourdieu adds that we should not, in our rejection of mechanistic theories, "bestow on some creative free will the free and willful power to constitute, on the instant, the meaning of the situation by projecting the ends aiming at its transformation," nor should we "reduce the objective intentions and constituted significations of actions and works to the conscious and deliberate intentions of their authors" (73).

To see in Bourdieu's work a mysticism or a regression into the unknowable and unanalysable in the use of the term "habitus" is, however, to read Bourdieu against his expressed intention. The habitus is not otherworldly, nor is it a subjective condition.[10] Rather, the habitus is a reminder that the totality of our experience is not confined entirely to language, that there is a nondiscursive feature of human experience, and that what Bourdieu calls the habitus may well consist of a set of objective structures which, in part because of the very multiplicity of their nature, may escape articulation. Once again, these structures may well be in such a relatively processual flux that determinacy would, to say the least, be difficult.

Habitus manifests doxa—doxa manifests the habitus. A feature of the habitus is that, once it achieves articulation, it becomes either orthodoxy or heterodoxy. Orthodoxy seeks to become *straightened* opinion, to become "that which goes without saying," to escape utterance, to escape the condition of possible negation and to operate in a realm where the logic of statements, exclusion, and identity do not function. In short, orthodoxy seeks the impossible goal of becoming doxa—that extralinguistic system which operates without identifying itself. An acceptance of Bourdieu's postulates about the habitus does not render the study of culture inaccessible; it does, however, militate against the employment of any simple causal model, and it does enjoin the anthropological observer to a radical awareness of the complexities inherent in his/her "observational" methodologies. Bourdieu's *Outline* invites, but does not provide, tangential speculation about alternatives to a model too heavily freighted with a bias toward language itself.

Equally important is Bourdieu's criticism of those "observational" methodologies which seek in their modeling constructs to "take care of " problems of context, recursivity, and self-reference by adding little boxes, squiggles, and arrows, for example, to the communications model. In language, for Bourdieu, it becomes increasingly clear that "the meaning of a linguistic element depends at least as much upon extra-linguistic factors as on linguistic factors." Bourdieu notes the extent to which "hierarchies of age, power, prestige, culture determine the very content of expression" (25). He quotes from Charles Bally's *La Langage et la vie:*

> When I talk to someone, or talk about him, I cannot help visualizing the particular type of relationship (casual, formal, obligatory, official) between that person and myself; involuntarily I think not only of his age, sex, rank, and social background; all these considerations may affect my choice of expressions and lead me to avoid what might discourage, offend, or hurt. If need be, my language becomes indirect and euphemistic . . . (26)

The point being stressed in Bourdieu's argument is the essentially "gestural" behavior of those "linguists and anthropologists who appeal to 'context,' or 'situation' in order, as it were, to 'correct' what strikes them as unreal and abstract in the structuralist model [and who] are in fact still trapped in the logic of the theoretical model which they are rightly trying to supersede . . ." (26). Bourdieu cites Van Velsen's *The Politics of Kinship* as an example of the attempt to "integrate variations, exceptions, and accidents into descriptions of regularities" or to show "how individuals in a particular structure handle the choices with which they are faced—as individuals are in all societies." Such moves lead Van Velsen to "regress to the pre-structuralist stage of the individual and all his choices, and to miss the very principle of the structuralist error" (26).

Such classification systems, initiated and revised to accommodate "observed" differences from "practice," reveal, for Bourdieu,
another aspect of an "objectivism [which] constitutes the social world
as a spectacle presented to an observer." Taxonomies, whether in
literary theory, linguistics, anthropology, history, or sociology, are
often made by those who

> forget that these instruments of cognition fulfill as such func-
> tions other than those of pure cognition. Practice always implies
> a cognitive operation, a practical function of construction which
> sets to work, by reference to practical functions, systems of
> classifications (taxonomies) which organize perception and
> structure practice. (97)

Bourdieu's summarizing statement reveals the extent to which the
erasure of the context of any taxonomy denies its dependence on its
social matrix:

> Practical taxonomies, instruments of cognition and communi-
> cation which are the precondition for the establishment of
> meaning and consensus on meaning, exert their *structuring*
> efficiency only to the extent that they are themselves *structured.*
> This does not mean that they can be adequately treated by
> "structural," "componential," or any other form of strictly *in-*
> *ternal* analysis which, in artificially wrenching them from their
> conditions of production and use, inevitably fails to understand
> their social functions. (97)

Bourdieu's protest against those discourses which are "artifi-
cially" wrenched "from their conditions of production and use" entails a complex nest of problems, most of which will be temporarily
postponed; but, for the moment, the protest can be seen as a rejection
of those discourses which seek to authorize or to obscure a decontex-
tualization through the use of the exclusive either/or. Other discourses
which focus intently upon such an exclusionary device include
preeminently most feminist discourse. In the majority of feminist
analytics, the specific sensitivity to the man/woman, active/passive
binary has served as the generative relationship which determines the
thematic drift of the argument, the differentiating mode of the particular "feminism." However, the marking and differentiating of the
wealth of strategies and complexities of stance *vis à vis* the exclusive
disjunction in feminist discourse is a task well beyond the scope of
this essay.[11]

The communications model as initially framed by Jakobson has been the focus of such concerted post-structuralist attacks, already described, because it embodies such a full range of logocentric assumptions and because its deployment has been so widespread. Because its presumptions have so long gone unchallenged, and because it has served so unobtrusively as an authorizing foundation for such a wide diversity of humanistic discourses in philosophy, linguistics, economics, sociology, psychology, psychoanalysis, and literary studies, its underlying assumptions are under close scrutiny.[12] In the communications model, post-structuralist criticism has found a focus, an example so rich in hierarchical, logocentric, exclusionary strategies that its availability for service in the maintenance of the status quo seems transparent. The model itself, post-structural critics argue, has offered a foundational strategy, custom-made, especially for those disciplines needing a constant valorization of the "same," a strategy doubly empowered through a repetition in the model's structure of the very doublet (subject/object) it endlessly reconstitutes as its product.

If the communications-semantic-semiotic-literary-information theory model with its varying substitute formulations for the elements of its triangular configurations has lost its authorizing power and whatever pretensions it had as the embodiment of the scientific and empiric voice, it seems that its deauthorization will also endanger those particular concepts of identity, unity, and representation which are so essential to its functioning. However, such a loss does not simultaneously signal the ascendancy of another model or an alternate and satisfactory representation.

What seems to be occurring is the recognition, as in Derrida, that the logocentric and disseminating moves within discourse, like the centripetal and centrifugal alternations between the monologic and dialogic in Bakhtin, can be thought of as systolic and diastolic flows and not necessarily as separable or exclusive alternatives. They are, rather, wholly symbiotic. For Bakhtin, heteroglossia and polyglossia are but the cloth out of which monoglossia is cut. With Deleuze and Guattari, the arborescent and the rhizomatic constitute, once again, symbiotic relationships. How they are identified depends upon the strategy of differentiation. Practice and theory can, or so it seems, be conceived not as exclusive binaries, but rather as nonexclusive dependencies, identifiable as tentative markings upon discursive practice as an interacting process.

Just as formalism and antiformalism can represent perspectives reflecting the necessary conditions of utterance, of meaning, of truth conditions, of an epistemology, and of an ontology, so also, at least within language, formalism and antiformalism are functions of changes in time and space. These two are flexible conceptual generations involved in multiple ratios of interdependent flux. Time and space are themselves dependent not only upon each other and upon the ways in which each hides in the other to define itself, but also upon the kinds and ratios of such dependencies which are always contingent upon their own sociocultural embedment.

To privilege "context" can, in one sense, be to privilege the social and perhaps to suggest that there is really after all only one queen of the disciplines—sociology. Such a notion is foreign to the direction of this discourse, which urges only that all cuts, all categorizations, are necessary but tentative moves, and that sociology is only one of the narrowed definitions of context; for we can speak only of sociologies among the spectrum of more or less adjacent members of a nontotalizable class.

What needs emphasis here, however, is that (at least from the perspective of this essay) each of these loosely labelled "deconstructive" projects displays its own structurally implicated exclusive disjunction, a disjunction projected in the articulation of its own "position." Whenever the exclusive disjunction becomes more than a temporary, limited, and necessary linguistic function, it would seem appropriate to observe with care any tenacity with which the exclusionary utterance is held and any sustained or terminal reluctance to deauthorize its own exclusions. It is necessary then to scrutinize with care the "foundationalism" of its exclusionary binary, to mark strongly the degree to which the particular privileged term of the pair becomes totalizing, the degree to which it is no longer confined to a "local" analytic operation.

Bourdieu's attack upon Derrida in his recent text *Distinction*, wherein Bourdieu analyzes Derrida's interpretation of Kantian aesthetic theory, can be examined for evidence of a "totalizing" move alien in some senses to his own cautionary arguments. What can be focused upon is the practice/theory binary, which Bourdieu destabilizes in *Outline*. In *Distinction*, Bourdieu charges Derrida with a "sovereign indifference" to anything that lies outside of philosophy. Such an indictment is hardly new; it is a stock-in-trade charge that some critics of Derrida use to justify their preference for Foucault, for example. In the attack on Derrida, Bourdieu has reinstituted certain binary cuts such as "truthful discourse/philosophical game" and real/unreal. What Bourdieu's discourse suppresses is that while it seeks to stake out a new post-structuralist field, it risks a somewhat strident naming of itself as "true" discourse, a discourse having achieved "objectivity," having escaped the difficulties of being merely "objectivist." Bourdieu here risks being read as a purveyor of the populist thesis of the purer insights of the common, nonphilosophical, non-academic man, as a defender of an inside/outside dichotomy, as grounding a view which aggressively privileges the "outside" perspective. Such a move would ignore that what he places "outside" of philosophy may well be seen as "inside" of sociological, anthropological discourse and thus subject not only to the "bias" of "objectivism" but also to the particular taxonomic segmentation of these disciplines which, in short, guarantee distortion. Succumbing to a need to display the credentials of his own discipline, Bourdieu here faces his own charges against structuralism, making his own charges against Derrida seem more like an intradepartmental dustup than an exhaustive searching of the limits of his own foundational utterances.

Still, the strong temptation, or need, to foreclose, to differentiate, to authorize an utterance with exclusionary strategies tends to dominate some discourse. In Bourdieu's case this move has perhaps both positive and negative motivations. The central role played by the habitus which is placed both outside and inside language, and which has a powerful role as a "structuring structure," invites—despite Bourdieu's strong disclaimer—the charge that some "mystical" element has been introduced into the otherwise "rational," "empirical," and "objective" realm. The charge, if it is a "charge," has been stated clearly by Michel de Certeau in his essay "On the Oppositional Practices of Everyday Life," where he notes that the "habitus" which "solves," as it were, the theory/practice relationship is itself and must remain "unverifiable and invisible":

> Habitus becomes a place of dogma, if by that term we understand the affirmation of a certain "real" which discourse requires in order to make totalizing claims . . . Texts of Bourdieu use their analytic content to fascinate and their theoretical content to polemicize. . . . His style also knows its contrasts, perverse and labyrinthine in its pursuit, massively repetitive in its affirmations: a peculiar combination of an "I know, I know" (this proliferating and transgressive ruse) and a "still and all" (there *must* be some totalizing meaning). In order to escape

this aggressive seduction, I will suppose (in my turn) that something essential for the analysis of tactics *must* be at stake in this contrast. The blanket characterization Bourdieu's theory casts over these tactics, as though to extinguish their flames by certifying their subsumption under socio-economic rationality, or by declaring them unconscious and thus in some sense inoperative as agents, ought to teach us something about their relationship to all theory. (21)

The point, however, of introducing a critique of Bourdieu's reading of Derrida's interpretation of Kantian aesthetic theory (see *Distinction*, 494–95) is clearly not to find the most "logocentric" culprit in the discourse, but rather to pursue the persistence of the complementary functions—the centripetal and centrifugal, the logocentric and the disseminational features of discourse itself—a complementarity which manifests itself so stridently in theory, philosophy, and, need I add, the social sciences. It is the "inside/outside" pairing that provides so many opportunities for exploration, analysis, polemic, and new theoretical constructions in the post-structuralist moment of academic discourse. More specifically, given the "linguistic twist" of both structuralist and post-structuralist theory, it is the examination of extralinguistic/intralinguistic relationships that determines the specifics of the textual discourse, of the shape of theory in most of its post-structuralist configurations. What lies within language? What lies without language? Do we deal with an exclusive and exhaustive disjunction? Having abandoned an empiric Cratylism, left with a pragmatic need, an "unverifiable belief," we still must deal with the problem of what kind of relationship between the linguistic and nonlinguistic seems credible. Certain key terms within post-structuralist texts—"differance" (Derrida), "plane of consistence" (Deleuze and Guattari), and "habitus" (Bourdieu)—come immediately to mind. We are confronted with terms which are operative, functional, yet not in any strict sense definable. In a significant sense, as Derrida insists about "differance," they are not strictly speaking terms. "Habitus" as a "structuring structure" constitutes an interacting function with that which lies outside of language and yet is itself implicated within language. Part of its function is to abrogate, or more appropriately to contextualize, the "exclusive disjunction" framed in attempts to mark and remark upon the inside and the outside of language—to recognize, as it were, that the powerful disjunction is itself inside language and cannot thereby govern the relationship of that which language defines as being outside itself.

One recognizes in the discourses of other postmodern figures the deployment of loosely allied pivotal terms which bear similar but not identical functions. In Foucault we find "procedures," in Kristeva the "chora," in Jameson the "political unconscious," in Cixous the "undifferentiated woman," in Irigaray "womanspeak." In each, one can, according to disposition, reject or applaud the success with which the theorist resists or succumbs to the temptation to positivize, and thus restore, the very binary which the key term itself was intended to suspend, to contain, to suppress, or to avoid.

The principal function of my discourse has been to describe the range of analytic strategies which have arisen to challenge the either/or's, the exclusive disjunctions of aggressively formalizing discursive practices, and to identify the kinship among a group of deauthorizing voices. The notions of practice, dissemination, the dialogic, heteroglossia, and the rhizomatic, while not all "identical," do display a cohesion of function, as do, on the other hand, such terms as theory, the monologic, the logocentric, and the arborescent. Each of the nonexclusive dyads reflects a specific plane or axis of projection. With Derrida, the projection results in a mapping of traditional philosophical discourse; with Bourdieu, the field of cultural anthropology is traversed; with Bakhtin, language as a social domain is charted; with Deleuze and Guattari, a particular philosophical-psychological domain is the focus.

To the extent, then, to which one holds the formalist/antiformalist confrontation as the very condition of discourse, as its constitutive feature, this contention becomes an antiformalist thesis—and the fulfillment of such a contention would require a reopening of the closure which permitted this essay to begin. A resulting complementary essay, filled with reversals, could seek to identify the formalism of Bakhtin and the antiformalism of Jakobson. Each contemporary member of the Bakhtin family needs, then, a story of the twistings and the turnings that yielded its interminable flux. So also each member of the Jakobson family needs a story told of how it achieved its terminable stability. Fortunately, Jakobson, in his characteristic rhetorical deployment of the chiasmus, has provided his readers with a fascinating clue and an inexhaustible resource. Each energetic pursuit of this device in his discourse could bring new life into his own texts as well as into those of his valuable opponent, Bakhtin.

Notes

1. "Strong" theories are centrally dependent upon exclusionary strategies. Aggressive formalists need them. Their chief weapon for the exclusion of ill-formed or unwanted fringe speculations and competitive explanations is the exclusive disjunction. The "either/or" may well be the rhetorical principle *par excellence* of the discursive strategy of "maleness," for surely its centering display in argument is most singularly *macho*.

2. The "geniality" of Jakobson, which I attribute to a perspectivism, represents the characteristic thrust of phenomenology. Descombes, paraphrasing Michel Serres (*Le Système de Leibnitz*), points out that "by definition, perspectivism means to find *order* in diversity, *invariables* in change, *identity* in difference. It tells how, in such and such a case, such and such an 'appearance' is produced" (*Modern French Philosophy*, 188). The case for Jakobson as Husserlian phenomenologist is advanced persuasively in Peter Steiner's *Russian Formalism*.

If Jakobson's geniality is to be viewed even more genially, it can be contextualized within the domain of Kristeva's remarks in *Desire in Language*, where she reminds us of Jakobson's ill-suppressed antiformalism. Quoting from Jakobson's "What is poetry?" she states clearly that Jakobson understands that the poet "wants to make language perceive what it doesn't want to say, provide it with material independent of the sign, and free it from denotation" (31). Jakobson states in the essay:

> The word is experienced as word and not as a simple substitute for a named object nor as the explosion of emotion [. . .] beside the immediate consciousness of the identity existing between the object and its sign (A is A), the immediate consciousness of the absence of this identity (A is not A) is necessary; this antinomy is inevitable, for, without contradiction, there is no interplay of concepts, no interplay of signs, the relationship between the concept and the sign becomes automatic, the progress of events comes to halt, and all consciousness of reality dies [. . .] Poetry protects us from this automatization, from the rust that threatens our formulation of love, hate, revolt and reconciliation, faith and negation. (*Desire in Language*, 31–32)

Kristeva identifies the "genial" in Jakobson: "Whoever understands them [the 'wasted poets'] cannot 'practice linguistics' without passing through whole geographic and discursive continents as an impertinent traveler, a 'faun in the house' " (31–32).

3. Derrida's comment ("This is my starting point; no meaning can be determined out of context, but no context permits saturation. What I am

referring to is not richness of substance, semantic fertility, but rather structure, the structure of the remnant or of its iteration" [*Margins*, 81] is summarized by Culler: "Meaning is context bound, but context is boundless" (*On Deconstruction*, 123).

4. Calvin O. Schrag's *Communication Praxis and the Space of Subjectivity* employs such a definition as a point of departure. The developing argument seeks to deconstruct and recuperate the key terms, such as "subject," in such a way as to rehabilitate "humanism" and "hermeneutics." A problem perhaps is, Why try to salvage "terms" so firmly embedded in a paternalistic, logo- and ethnocentric context? How effective can a cleansing operation be on terms so central to the traditional vocabulary—and, again, will such an operation be viewed as merely strategic multiple voicing? As cosmetic? Or is Schrag opting for the Derridean strategy of paleonymy?

5. Steiner in *Russian Formalism* quotes from Husserl:

We start out from that which antedates all standpoints: from the totality of the intuitively self-given which is prior to any theorizing reflection, from all that one *can* immediately see and lay hold of, provided one does not allow oneself to be blinded by prejudice, and so led to ignore a whole class of genuine data. If by "Positivism" we are to mean the absolutely unbiased grounding of all science on what is "positive," i.e., on what can be primordially apprehended, then it is *we* who are the genuine positivists. (78)

6. Language, of course, is what it is. The "literal/figural" binary is a sociocultural convention of a particular discursive mode. However, only the privilege of a "presumptive" ontological literalness need be noted.

7. For Jakobson, "structuralism" represented some sort of oscillatory synthesis between "science and philosophy."

8. The problem of properly identifying the unique voice of Bakhtin in texts attributed to Medvedev or to Voloshinov is a problem for those who need such discriminations in order to solve their problems. I avoid the problem, here, by an indiscriminate use of the hyphen and by grammatically reconstituting an "indeterminate" Bakhtin.

Some kind of differentiation is suggested by those texts authored (Voloshinov or Bakhtin and Medvedev), coauthored, "ghost-written," or generated by the Bakhtin Circle (such as *Marxism and the Philosophy of Language, Freudianism: A Marxist Critique,* and *The Formal Method*) from those specifically attributed to Bakhtin (that is, *Rabelais and His World, Problems of Dostoevsky's Poetics,* and *The Dialogic Imagination*). In the first group, perhaps, there is a more intense foreground of critique of formalist rhetorical strategies. In the texts identified as Bakhtin's, the reader seems to face a significantly different order of complex interplay.

Virgil Lokke

▼
237

Whether or not, for example, Bakhtin's monologic/dialogic binary avoids falling into a "terminal" either/or-ness can, of course, be questioned. As long as manifestations of the monologic in Bakhtin's own discourse can be regarded as necessary concessions to a formal feature of language, then we have one sort of problem. However, if, as Paul de Man suggests, Bakhtin by way of extopy uses "the radical experience of voiced otherness as a way to a regained proximity," then we have not only a "technician of literary discourse," but a "metaphysician." More to the point, it is in the analysis of the differences between the "polysemy of poetry" and the dialogism of prose that Bakhtin sets up the "binary opposition between trope as object directed and dialogism as social-oriented that is itself tropological in the worst possible sense, namely as reification" (de Man, 106–14).

9. Questions involving the concepts of "unity," "identity," "part-whole relationships," the "either/or," and the infinitely extending "either/or, or, or . . ." are explored in Deleuze's *Nietzsche* and *Différence et répétition* as well as in *Spinoza et le problème de l'expression, Spinoza: philosophie pratique*, and "Rhizomes." Constantin Boundas in his dissertation, *The Theory of Difference of Gilles Deleuze* (unpublished), offers a detailed analysis of Spinoza's expressivist model as viewed by Deleuze. Deleuze, Boundas explains, points out that for Spinoza,

> the individual substance is not the sum of its attributes. The "complexity" of the substance which expresses itself through the internal diversity of its attributes does not make it composite. It is simple in its complexity, to the extent that it is not divisible into parts. The unity of Spinoza's substance is not an arithmetic unity: it does not designate the existence of one individual whose simplicity sets it apart from all others. It is not a being: it is all there is and can be understood, and which has itself as its own cause. Spinoza's substance is the multiple in itself. This is the reason why it has no numerical value, and the infinity of the expressive attributes is more a way to affirm the absolute positivity of Being, and less a mathematical symbol. Perhaps against the traditions, one must say that Spinoza was not a monist, any more than he was a dualist. God is not one or two or three, because numbers do not quantify the substance. (57–58)

For a full and contextualized discussion, see Boundas's chapter, "Spinoza: When One Is Not a Number" (44–75).

Another way to suggest how Deleuze can challenge the traditional concept of unity is to refer to Descombes's description of the relation between perspectivism and phenomenology in *Modern French Philosophy*: Descombes quotes Merleau-Ponty's view that perspectivism is then "no aberration but a projection of existence and an expression of the human condition." Contemporary French philosophy challenges this notion. The intimate relations among such terms as the center, order, invariance, and identity and their reinforcing energy is indicated in Descombes's citation from Serres (*Le Système de Leibnitz*), who explains that

> perspectivism is the same thing as phenomenology . . . [Perspectivism shares] the aim of descriptive geometry [in seeking] to determine the unvarying properties of any figure *for all perspectives*, for all projections of this figure on a plane (where it "appears"). . . . [He once again reminds us that] by definition, perspectivism means to find *order* in diversity, *invariables* in change, *identity* in difference. . . . The French Nietzscheanism of the last twenty years has tried to understand perspective in precisely the opposite way—not to impose order on variety, but, on the contrary, to make order one possible figure of variety, or to see the invariable simply as one perspective among others. (*Modern French Philosophy*; 188)

For Deleuze, both Spinoza and Nietzsche offer a critique of that genteel pluralism or "perspectivism" which can listen to the multitude of perspectives in the quiet comfort of knowing that they will all serve to reveal the true perspective, which is already silently and charitably known by the humble pluralist.

10. However, an interesting problem seems involved in an examination of Bourdieu in light of de Certeau's description of "Mystic Speech" in *Heterologies: Discourse on the Other* as practices rather than "a body of doctrines," an "epistemic foundation of a domain within which certain procedures are followed: a new space, with new mechanisms" (81). For a more thorough discussion, see de Certeau's "On the Oppositional Practices of Everyday Life."

11. Feminist criticism has been particularly sensitive to the aggressive deployment in older discourse of the exclusive and exhaustive disjunction. Carol Gilligan's *In a Different Voice* at first differentiates between a male "ethic" which is primarily concerned with "what goes first" and a feminine response concerned with "what is left out," and she contrasts an ethic which constantly demands the foregrounding of the "either/or" in making choices based on "rules," "logic," "laws," "deduction," and "codes" seeking "clarity," "autonomy," "individuation," "separation," and "quantification," with one which is based on the recognition of a network, a community of relationships, and a defining of self through an identified relatedness, "a world cohering through human connection." Helene Cixous and Catherine Clement spell out in typographic excess how "thought has always worked through opposition." They indicate clearly how the setting up of "the" couple, man/woman, has engendered "a movement through which the couple is destroyed. A universal battlefield. Each time a war is let loose.

Death is always at work . . . We see that 'victory' always comes down to the same thing: things get hierarchical. Organization by hierarchy makes all conceptual organization subject to man" (*The Newly Born Woman*, 64).

Irigaray wrestles with the problem in her attempt to avoid the trap of creating a simple reversal of male/female dominance. And some feel that Kristeva in her refusal to "specify" the "feminine" in her determined avoidance of a reconstituted either/or has left "feminism" altogether. Needless to say, the problem of discourse—the problem of language and its investment in the exclusive disjunction—is a strongly foregrounded feature of most feminine discourse.

12. One of the most exhaustive attacks upon the communications model as well as upon the exclusive "either/or" appears in the "systems/environment—difference" theory of Niklas Luhmann. Luhmann reformulates the form/content dyad as a form/context relationship. Form, then, is always a tentative, momentary stabilization of some features of a context. No permanent form exists—only forms with variable degrees of stabilizing intensity. Systems, yes, but not as stabilized structures, for structures are always some kind of stabilizing context that is being imposed upon another system. Systems, for Luhmann, do not necessarily require centers or internal hierarchies, nor do systems need "unity" in any of the older senses of the word. Systems have boundaries, temporary horizons. They are portions of the environment which have generated framing configurations. In short, by the differentiating operation itself, Luhmann's general systems theory "supplants the classical conceptual model of a whole made up of parts and relations between parts with a model emphasizing the difference between systems and environment" (*The Differentiation of Society*, 190). The energizing factor for system generation is the intensification of differentiation. Once the differentiating process is developed, self-reflexive features operate to create an inside and an outside of the system.

Supporters of Luhmann see in his systems theory yet another perspective which subverts, deconstructs, and offers an alternative to the grammar-based model of the communications triangle. A significant point of contrast between Derrida and Luhmann is the relation between "differance" and Luhmann's "difference." Luhmann argues that Derrida is still dependent upon the "communications model." In Luhmann's eyes, Derrida *deconstructs* the communications model and is still dependent upon "the concept of structure." Luhmann *excludes* the model and constructs an alternate theory of communication dependent upon difference. See in this volume Schwanitz's essay, "Systems Theory and the Environment of Theory."

Works Cited

Bakhtin, Mikhail. *Rabelais and His World*. Translated by Helene Iswolsky. Cambridge: MIT Press, 1968.

———. *The Dialogic Imagination*. Edited by Michael Holquist and translated by Caryl Emerson and Holquist. Austin: University of Texas Press, 1981.

———. *Problems of Dostoevsky's Poetics*. Edited and translated by Emerson. Minneapolis: University of Minnesota Press, 1984.

Bakhtin, Mikhail, and P. N. Medvedev. *The Formal Method in Literary Scholarship*. Translated by Albert J. Wehrle. Cambridge and London: Harvard University Press, 1985.

Bourdieu, Pierre. *Outline of a Theory of Practice*. Cambridge and New York: Cambridge University Press, 1977.

———. *Distinction*. Cambridge: Harvard University Press, 1984.

Carroll, David. "The Alterity of Discourse: Form, History and the Question of the Political in M. M. Bakhtin." *Diacritics* (Summer 1983): 65–83.

Certeau, Michel de. "On the Oppositional Practices of Everyday Life." *Social Text* 3 (Fall 1980): 3–43.

———. *Heterologies: Discourse on the Other*. Minneapolis: University of Minnesota Press, 1986.

Cixous, Helene, and Catherine Clement. *The Newly Born Woman*. Minneapolis: University of Minnesota Press, 1986.

Culler, Jonathan. *On Deconstruction*. Ithaca: Cornell University Press, 1982.

Derrida, Jacques. *Margins of Philosophy*. Translated by Alan Bass. Chicago: University of Chicago Press, 1982.

Deleuze, Gilles. *Nietzsche*. Paris: Presses Universitaires de France, 1965.

———. *Différence et répétition*. Paris: Presses Universitaires de France, 1968.

———. *Spinoza et le problème de l'expression*. Paris: Les Editions de Minuit, 1968.

———. *Spinoza: philosophie pratique*. Paris: Presses Universitaires de France, 1970.

Deleuze, Gilles, and Felix Guattari. *Anti-Oedipus: Capitalism and Schizophrenia*. New York: Viking Press, 1977.

———. *Capitalisme et schizophrénie: mille plateau*. Paris: Les Editions de Minuit, 1980.

———. "Rhizome." Translated by Paul Patton in *Ideology and Consciousness: Power and Desire; Diagrams of the Social* 8 (1981): 40–71.

Descombes, Vincent. *Modern French Philosophy*. London and New York: Cambridge University Press, 1982.

Gilligan, Carol. *In a Different Voice*. Cambridge and London: Harvard University Press, 1982.

Jakobson, Roman. *Selected Writings*. The Hague, Paris, New York: Mouton, 1981.
————. *Verbal Art, Verbal Sign, Verbal Time*. Minneapolis: University of Minnesota Press, 1985.
Kristeva, Julia. *Desire in Language*. New York: Columbia University Press, 1980.
Levinson, Stephen C. *Pragmatics*. Cambridge and New York: Cambridge University Press, 1983.
Luhmann, Niklas. *The Differentiation of Society*. New York: Columbia University Press, 1982.
Lyotard, Jean-François. *The Postmodern Condition: A Report on Knowledge*. Minneapolis: University of Minnesota Press, 1984.
Man, Paul de. *The Resistance to Theory*. Minneapolis: University of Minnesota Press, 1986.
Schrag, Calvin O. *Communication Praxis and the Space of Subjectivity*. Bloomington: Indiana University Press, 1986.
Steiner, Peter. *Russian Formalism: A Metapoetics*. Ithaca and London: Cornell University Press, 1984.
Todorov, Tzvetan. *Mikhail Bakhtin: The Dialogical Principle*. Minneapolis: University of Minnesota Press, 1981.
Voloshinov, V. N. *Marxism and the Philosophy of Language*. New York: Seminar Press, 1973.
————. *Freudianism: A Marxist Critique*. Translated by I. R. Titunik. New York: Academic Press, 1976.

An Uncertain Semiotic

Floyd Merrell

Our recent past is strewn with
what threatens to become a logarithmic expansion of theories and
countertheories—which is news to hardly anyone these days.[1] What
too often does go unacknowledged is that it might well be futile to
expect any definitive criteria of choice for this apparent entanglement,
for it is slowly becoming evident that each and every choice can be
no more than arbitrary . . . or culturally transparent. In this light,
after briefly attempting to lay bare the core problematics of some of
the more noteworthy contemporary critical postures, I will contextualize them within the general milieu of twentieth-century intellectual endeavors; and with a lateral move, I will then introduce a
hitherto overlooked but important aspect of C. S. Peirce's semiotic,
arguing for its relevance to the issue at hand.

▼

One familiar critical approach, presumably resting on rational
foundations, is that of the meaning determinists (E. D. Hirsch, et
al.), whose fundamental tenet goes something like this: start with the
evidence at hand, and with well-reasoned critical encounters it is
possible to adjudicate between less adequate and more adequate
interpretations, for how effectively a literary work "fulfills particular
criteria of excellence is not easily decided, but at least decidable"
(Hirsch, *The Aims of Interpretation* [Chicago: University of Chicago
Press, 1976], 110). This dictum implies that an interpretive goal can
be established by the objective evaluation of different meanings advocated by the community of interpreters. Stemming from a fear of
interpretive subjectivity, meaning determinism is intended to counter
the emergence of each interpreter as his/her own expert, which would
presumably lead to disorder in a world without any centralized authority toward which all interpretations could defer. Authorial meaning, which, argue the determinists, remains a possibility, must be the
consensual goal; it is certainly preferable to the unconstructed, undisciplined, and fragmented morass that would inevitably evolve out of
interpretive subjectivism, with no obvious standards.

243

This appears at the outset to be an admirable hard-nosed response akin to Karl Popper's program of "conjectures and refutations."[2] Of course the notion of rationality and the growth of knowledge by means of clear-headed, give-and-take deliberation has attracted some of the greatest minds throughout history. Indeed, it affords an enviable degree of security. Unfortunately, however, it also entails the *tu quoque* argument: since rationalism rests on an irrational commitment to rationalism, it is as irrational as any other commitment. Or at best the implications of the argument are circular: meaning determinism can be validated if, and only if, it is believed to be valid. The option exists, then, either for a leap of faith or for an irrationalist version of rationalism. One may choose between the two and remain naive, which is ordinarily the case; or preferably, one may choose while nurturing an awareness of one's necessarily tenuous base—but, unfortunately, this move may breed a most uncomfortable skepticism. Either way, the paradox tends to be gently pushed under the rug, and the game felicitously goes on. We might pardon this maneuver were it not for the fact that rationalism often gravitates dangerously toward intellectual imperialism, which in critical theory cannot be defended by any stretch of the imagination. So much for the rational base of meaning determinism.[3]

A problem with "New Criticism" lies in the assumption that a few key rhetorical devices—paradox, irony, and ambiguity being foremost among them—constitute the formal structure of all poetry. This seems to be a fiat, which does not always bear up under scrutiny. The truth of the matter is that paradox, irony, and ambiguity in literary and discursive texts did not become prevalent until the Renaissance—though there were a few obvious precursors—when mathematicians first began seriously entertaining infinity, imaginary numbers, and other such mysteries, and when the irresolvable conflicts between temporality and eternity, the sacred and the profane, man and God, etc., began to surface in religious debates. The "New Critics," of course, have conveniently limited themselves ordinarily to post-Renaissance texts. When they occasionally decide to test their skills with earlier texts, the results often suspiciously appear to be either too cute or too ingenious.[4]

I raise the issue of "New Criticism" to demonstrate that such text chopping so as to squeeze it into a Procrustean bed is also common to the early structuralists, who (like the Russian Formalists in general) adopt an ahistorical approach in their well-meaning but feeble imitation of the sciences. Of course, for structuralism the putative universal model is usually binary, derived from information theory, Boolean logic, linguistics, or wherever else binarism can be disinterred. The first problem with this model is that it comes from foreign disciplines and hence it can be only tentative at most (especially in light of such disasters as Herbert Spencer's dog-eat-dog Darwinian model of human societies, to mention only one example). The second problem is that, when "applied" to texts, the binary model usually becomes reductionistic to the extreme—which is not unbearably pernicious if that is what the structuralists desire. But, whether they like it or not, reductionism has little chance of winning any prizes at a science fair these days: the presumably sound foundations of structuralism are actually rooted in an archaic positivistic conception of science. A third problem is that demonstration of binarism's validity eventually ushers in a dilemma comparable to the "paradox of induction." Carl Hempel demonstrates that "All ravens are black" and "All non-black things are non-ravens" are logically equivalent statements ("Studies in the Logic of Confirmation," *Mind* 54 [1945], 1–26 and 97–121). Whatever confirms or disconfirms one confirms or disconfirms the other. Hence to verify the blackness of ravens one must observe not only all ravens past, present, and to come, but all nonravens as well. Commensurately, try as they may, the structuralists can never confirm their model short of demonstrating the validity of the binarist thesis with respect to each and every text and, in addition, demonstrating that all nonbinary things are nontexts. A tall order indeed; in fact, it is impossible, as we are aware at least since Hume. (It hardly needs saying that the same fallacy applies to the meaning determinists' validation of their authorial center, or to the validation of any theory or method by traditional means so far as that goes.)[5]

Of the current meaning indeterminisms, deconstruction would win hands down in a fashion show. Deconstructionists counter meaning determinism with the claim that every reading misses the mark. From another angle, the hermeneutical relativists (Hans-Georg Gadamer, et al.) make a remotely comparable claim: our beliefs and values are necessary "preconditions" for our understanding, but since these beliefs and values are historical products, they could always have been something other than what they are; hence, understanding is indeterminately variable. As for deconstruction, texts are considered to be undecidable: at their very navel, where *aporia* is to be discovered, they are plurivocal, even paradoxical, to the extreme— strange that this premise should be mandated on no undecidable terms. And stranger yet, Derrida once reprimanded John Searle in so many—perhaps too many—words for having misread him.[6] Are we to believe Derrida's text itself is univocal, unique, decidable, and determinate? Conveniently forgetting one's own premises when critiquing another's premises can place one in such a quandary. But then, perhaps this is no worse than the textual determinists' forgetting or being unaware of the *tu quoque* argument. Here, we can at least entertain the idea that the indeterminists and the determinists are inversely related to one another. One places indeterminism on dogmatic, tacitly assumed, or at best conventionally founded premises; the other dogmatically argues for a rationalism based on irrational grounds.

Focusing more specifically on a key aspect of the deconstructionist controversy, J. Hillis Miller, one of the apostles among North American deconstructors, asserts that the language of criticism "is subject to exactly the same limitations and blind alleys as the language of the works it reads" (*Deconstruction and Criticism*, ed. H. Bloom, et al. [New York: Continuum, 1979], 230). Of course, it might be contended that the author of this statement presumably exists *outside* the language of criticism in order to comment *upon* it. But Hillis Miller quickly makes a strategic move to cover his rear flank, conceding that deconstruction "does not provide an escape from nihilism, nor from metaphysics, nor from their uncanny inherence in one another, there is no escape." Deconstruction can and does, however, oscillate within this inherence in such a way that "one enters a strange borderland, a frontier region which scans to give the widest glimpse into the other land ('beyond metaphysics'), though this land may not by any means be entered and does not in fact exist for Western man" (231).

So at the borderland, alluded to occasionally by Nietzsche, one can be neither inside nor outside, but, beyond all formalism, all logic, one is wherever one is, within the text, wherever that is, for one cannot know. This daring avowal, interestingly enough, entails the essence of Bertrand Russell's "Barber of Seville" who declared, "I shave all those, and only those, who do not shave themselves," to which the obvious question arises, Does he shave himself? If he does, then he is damned, and if he doesn't, he is damned. Assuming our hapless barber to remain within the textual confines of his statement, he will most likely continue with his daily pruning, oblivious of the quandary into which he has placed himself. The question concerning his logically applying his razor to himself, on the other hand, comes from without, from which perspective the paradox potentially becomes eminent. So it appears that the forbidden land in the case of the barber paradox in some strange way *is* entered, that the previous state of innocence *is* forever lost, and that the supreme vantage point from which the question was raised in the first place *does* lie outside.[7] But if outside, it still remains within the prison house of language, so it is still inexorably inside: there is no legitimate metalanguage, only words *qua* words.[8] Now, this conception of things is analytical, yet it subverts itself, but on so doing it also seems to testify to the validity of the deconstructionist premise: the deconstructive activity validates itself by invalidating itself. Obviously we have now taken a giant step ahead of our naive barber who apparently believes his statement to be valid even though he might shave himself. But, upon his being made aware that on so doing he invalidates his own claim, he is not thus liberated from his dilemma. So it appears that deconstruction is having its day.[9]

Hillis Miller, however, goes on to admit, quite appropriately it might seem at the outset, that the "ultimate justification" for deconstruction is "that it works" (*Deconstruction and Criticism*, 252). This is indeed remarkable. One is given the impression that Hillis Miller has exercised a carefully guarded pragmatic move. But, in the first place, it also entails a leap of faith, an irrational commitment to irrationalism, so to speak. This, as we have observed, is relatively benign, so it can generally be disregarded. In the second place, however, a circular argument is implied. Deconstructors not only claim to be able to deconstruct any and all texts, they at times also wisely admit that the deconstructive act subverts itself in the same operation, and since the procedure "works," it is thereby validated. The question might arise, Does it "work" on its own activity, that is, on itself? To which the likely response is, Yes, since it subverts itself. Then one might wonder, Does it subvert its own "working" on itself? To which query the answer must be, Of course, if it "works," and it *does* "work," so it subverts itself. Perhaps a conclusion, if there be any, is none other than this: if deconstruction "works," then it does not "work"; but if so, then this is evidence that it "works." . . . Or perhaps simply: deconstruction's "workability" is, itself, undecidable, paradoxically. The wily deconstructor will most likely applaud such sequiturs. In fact, against his/her splendid "negative theology" any argument one might generate falls into insignificance. Rather than the critic of deconstruction winning the last round of the argument, then, a draw invariably ensues. We must briefly return to this problem later.

The hermeneutical relativists tell us that we are trapped within our own historical "horizon"—to use Gadamer's term. There can be no context-free subject, for the subject is bound to a particular tradition with all its implied "prejudgments" (*Truth and Method* [New York: Crossroad, 1984], 235–44). Hence we can understand other-cultural texts solely from within the context of our own culture. Understanding, consequently, involves two contexts—that of the author and that of the interpreter. The latter can adequately derive meaning from the text only by means of "horizon fusion" (273). That is to say that one should not merely interpret texts from within one's own horizon: a statement circumscribing the limitations of any and all interpretations. The problem is that since two radically distinct cultures do not share the same fundamental prejudgments, logically speaking, we cannot understand other-cultural texts—that is, unless a transcendental perspective is assumed, but hermeneutical relativist theory bars such a perspective.[10] So, *ipso facto*, we cannot understand other-cultural texts. Yet since the hermeneuticists lay claim to be able relatively adequately to do so by "horizon fusion," they must exempt themselves from the limitations of their own horizon; somehow they alone must be at some context-free level, while other interpreters remain context-dependent. This problem, of course, is common to all relativist hypotheses. For instance, consider, in light of Kuhnian "relativism," the proposition: "All knowledge is generated from within a paradigm."[11] Is it paradigm-generated or not? If so, then it refers to itself and is historically situated; therefore it is not a universal and hence is inapplicable to itself. If not, then its objectivity can be maintained only by positing a perspective which contradicts that very proposition. On the other hand, the relativists can claim their knowledge to be generated from outside all paradigms, but this transcendental position places them on equally contradictory grounds (given their own premises), for who are they—but no one else—to be privileged to such a God's-eye view?[12]

Nor are the interpretive subjectivists free of problematics. Fish, to mention only one, posits an interactive approach between reader and text: the reader does something to the text and vice versa (for example, "Interpreting the *Variorum*," *Critical Inquiry* 2 [1976], 465–85). Here, though at the outset it might appear that the critic has unbounded freedom to choose between interpretive heuristics and strategies, he/she in reality becomes committed—albeit at a tacit level—to an interpretive community. And although this might appear similar to a Kuhnian "subjective" or "intersubjective" paradigm, it is not. Kuhn sees scientists as a guild of masters and their apprentices.

Fish's interpretive community, on the other hand, bears greater commonality with Michael Polanyi's a-critical community of scientists whose knowledge is tacitly embedded such that they tend to follow authoritative canons of thought.[13] And how do they acquire this tacit knowledge? Why, in the classroom, we must suppose, perhaps somewhat akin to the manner Culler's ideal scholar acquires "literary competence." Reliance on authority, however, often becomes stifling. Besides, what makes the present canons of acceptability valid in a world of chance and change where what was yesterday's truth can become today's nonsense, and vice versa? Interestingly, Polanyi views dissent from the canon and against the community of scientists as undesirable strife, while Popper sees it as proper recognition of the masters. This seems to be an about-face, for Popper is supposedly the rationalist and Polanyi is—though he would probably deny it—over the long haul apparently as "irrationalistic" as Kuhn. By the same token, might not the self-critical meaning determinist actually be as open as the interpretive subjectivist or relativist?

But this might be unfair. Perhaps, in the final analysis, it *does* come down to the classroom. Whatever is taught there should always be open to questioning, to change, and therein lies the source of interpretive intersubjectivity. I suppose Fish might agree. But what threatens to take place in the knowledge grinder might well be another story. Galileo taught Ptolemaism in the classroom while independently believing in his own interpretation. In this respect, I've heard more than a few critical theorists admit they teach literature in a rather traditional fashion; that way the pedagogical chore becomes less of a nuisance. Significantly, Bacon called classrooms kingdoms of the mind, and teachers tyrants and conquerers. Perhaps following his advice—though actually he never practiced what he preached—we should eschew our ideas of all theoretical frameworks and interpretive communities. Then we could simply look at the "facts" in the text. The "facts," naturally, must bear us out. And now we are back to the Dark Age of the positivist-inspired scholarship of yesteryear. And the positivists, it is well known, also pushed a few of their own anomalous presuppositions conveniently under the rug.

▼

It might appear that I have placed some sophisticated formulations in an all-too-convenient nutshell. This, I submit, is at times advisable: reactions against nutshell summaries tend to breed cults of devoted hagiographists who spend lifetimes paying homage to their chosen authors. I present these brief exposures in order subsequently to place current theoretical frameworks in a broader context, the underlying assumption being that the present proliferation can in no conceivable manner culminate in a Monolithic Theory to end all theories. This should evoke more than a little concern, for the atmosphere generated by these theories seems occasionally to have bred confidence-building programs among eager young scholars, which in the long run could prove to be detrimental. Unfortunately, rather than concern over wider issues, including complex interdisciplinary relationships, too often energy is expended in unproductive squabbling over trivial differences. Those who recoil in horror at radical statements by subjectivists, relativists, indeterminists, and so on, apparently do not at times realize that they are a symptom of the very crisis confronting us. On the other hand, those who would like to be iconoclasts, such as the deconstructionists, presumably the most revolutionary group around, are actually engaged in dismantling a structure which is rapidly disintegrating anyway.

Between the meaning determinists and the indeterminists, the scales at present weigh in favor of the latter. But, as I shall argue, this is actually to be expected. Each century in the West, artistic structures have patterned the structure of science and, more generally, the cultural mode of viewing the world; this is especially true since the Baroque period. I am by no means asserting that there are vague isomorphisms or bilateral influences between art and science, or between art, science, and "reality." Neither am I alluding to any bleary-eyed notion of *Weltanschauungen*.[14] I am speaking of modes of organization, entailing broad conceptual frameworks by means of which the world is ordered. A certain temper of the times, I suggest, pervades all facets of human intellectual endeavor. To illustrate this phenomenon, I now briefly turn to science and mathematics.

Though rumblings were felt toward the end of the nineteenth century, emanating particularly from James Clerk Maxwell's electromagnetic field theory, Nietzsche's philosophy, and Stéphane Mallarmé and other artists, a new world-perspective finally began to emerge around 1905 with Albert Einstein's special theory of relativity. Shortly thereafter, Russell's "Theory of Logical Types" in the *Principia Mathematica* proved to be only a stopgap measure to prevent the breakdown of any sufficiently rich conceptual system. And David Hilbert's dream of reducing the whole of mathematics to a small set of indubitable axioms was shattered when in 1931 Kurt Gödel published his unexpected, and rather unwanted, theorems: either (a) the truth-value of a system cannot be determined from its own set of axioms but only from some outside axiom (the "incompleteness principle"), or (b) a given system cannot be totally free of hidden contradictions (the "inconsistency principle"). In the years that followed, other equally unpleasant theorems were presented. Howard De Long (*A Profile of Mathematical Logic* [New York: Addison-Wesley, 1971]) calls them "limitative theorems," a somewhat deceptive label if not a misnomer, for they are limitative in the sense that they bar closure, but they are unlimited in that any set of axioms of complexity comparable to that of number will generate propositions whose truth or falsity cannot be known except by making that set part of a larger system, which will in turn generate further undecidable propositions within an even larger system, and so on. There can be no end.

This epistemological uncertainty was paralleled by turmoil in physics, particularly during the 1920s. Werner Heisenberg's uncertainty principle, roughly the physical equivalent of Gödelian undecidability—according to Popper's extension of the proof—demonstrated conclusively that we cannot describe reality faithfully; we can do no more than inquire into our own knowledge of reality. Niels Bohr's complementarity rules out the possibility of knowing different behavioral patterns of nuclear particles simultaneously. And Einstein's relativity, which has resisted alignment with quantum mechanics, thus perpetuating the reigning uncertainty of scientific knowledge, is predicated on a field concept of the universe which demolishes Newtonian physics. But what is more important to the present concerns, as we shall see, David Bohm's attempt to reconcile once and for all quantum mechanics with relativity envisages the universe as a vast interconnected web, which he calls the *implicate* order or a potentiality, from which actual events, composing the *explicate* order, are drawn. Relativity, it is well known, implies frames of reference, be they compatible in varying degrees or mutually exclusive. This notion of relative frames of reference, which will have a bearing on later sections in this essay, was placed under the rubric of "perspectivism" by José Ortega y Gasset with respect to sociocultural contexts (*El tema de nuestro tiempo* [Madrid: Revista de Occidente, 1923]). "Perspectivism" presupposes a plural universe, from the quantum level to broad sociocultural conceptual frameworks. Clarity, determinism, and closure—the hallmarks of science from Galileo to Bacon to Boyle—appear to be a dream forever lost.

Physical phenomena aside, the classical theory of communication has also been undermined. Classical theory was deterministic. Contemporary theory, or better, the Emergent Perspective, is compatible with the "new cybernetics," which is based statistically rather than determinately on the principle of negentropy: a measure of order drawn from the impending disorder, or entropy.[15] The question arose, during the 1940s and 1950s, that if the universe according to statistical probabilities should be so unordered, then why do we find so much order? The answer, found after much investigation and more than a few failures, lies in a push—on the part of all organisms from the genetic code level to "consciousness"—against the Second Law of Thermodynamics, which dictates progressive degrees of chaos. The genetic code, which entails a set of statistical rules for open and incomplete generation in an unbounded system, organizes matter into islands of negentropy surrounded by an inorganic sea in incessant degeneration. The code's operation, as is now commonplace, is roughly analogous to the use of language, where two or more interlocutors exchange messages. The verbal message of the speaker is indeterminate, and it can or cannot change the listener's knowledge or behavior in diverse ways. And the listener is in a state of uncertainty concerning the message he/she will hear. I say uncertainty rather than ignorance, for he/she *does* know (or expect) that the message will be one of a range of possibilities. Once again we have probabilities. Any "exact" model can be no more than statistical, hence it will forever remain to a degree uncertain.

Just as quantum theory has superseded classical physics, so the "new cybernetics" approach has superseded the classical theory of communication. In this new era, and speaking generally of the reigning conceptual framework, incompleteness, openness, inconsistency, statistical models, undecidability, indeterminacy, complementarity, polyvocity, interconnectedness, and fields and frames of reference are the order of the day. Some scholars have recently attempted to discover lines of correspondence between this Emergent Perspective and trends in the arts.[16] Yet the import of the Emergent Perspective by and large remains obscured in the humanities: obviously feared by some, and mentioned only in passing by a handful of scholars.[17]

Why the general unwillingness to come to grips with this new Emergent Perspective? Embracing it is not, contrary to many warnings, a retreat into nihilism or irrationalism. Actually, in the broadest possible terms it is akin to the essence of Gödel's proof. It forces a choice between completeness (closure) and consistency. A mathematical system can be axiomatized only by accepting paradox (inconsistency), or it remains forever open. But such paradox need not be construed as global. It is, rather, local. The deconstructor's disclosing the undecidable (illogical) in the presumably decidable (logical) text is itself a logical operation, but on distinguishing between the frame of the text, the whole of intertextuality, the deconstructor's surgical operation, and his/her own frame of reference, we can potentially become aware that closure at one level is openness at another, determinacy reverts back to indeterminacy, and so on. Actually, mathematicians and theoretical scientists are usually more straightforward than most humanists about all this, for they demonstrate how intuitively obvious and natural is the path leading to paradox, and how devious, *ad hoc*, elusive, and unnatural it is to attempt eliminating any and all paradoxes. Indeed, acceptance of the Emergent Perspective may illuminate the virtues of this intuitively obvious path which, if not elegant, at least affords us a degree of learned ignorance.

Finally, I turn to a discussion of semiotics (and here I intend to be more specific, the reasons for which will become obvious), before I return to the so-called Emergent Perspective.

▼

For Peirce, the sign—synonymous with what is also called a representamen—is, stated very generally, something which stands to somebody for something in some respect or capacity. A sign creates in the mind of the recipient an equivalent sign, or perhaps a more developed sign, which is the interpretant of the first sign. The sign also stands for its object, which can be either intensional or extensional, as a sort of idea rather than a referent to a "real" object. This interpretant, upon interaction, is no longer an idea but another sign, which has its own interpretant, and so on, *ad infinitum*. In this sense the object of representation

> can be nothing but a representation of which the first represen-
> tation is the interpretant. . . . [And the] meaning of a represen-
> tation can be nothing but a representation. In fact, it is nothing
> but the representation itself conceived as stripped of irrelevant
> clothing. But this clothing never can be completely stripped off;
> it is only changed for something more diaphanous. So there is
> an infinite regression here. Finally, the interpretant is nothing
> but another representation . . . and as representation, it has its
> interpretant again. Lo, another infinite series.[18]

Of course we have in this image the equivalent of Zeno's paradox with which Peirce remained fascinated to the end. What are the implications of such an infinite regress of signification? The first one entails Umberto Eco's contention that the problem of semiotics is the problem of referring back *(aliquid stat pro aliquo)*. And referring back bears on the ability to lie, for to lie is to say something in the present which refers back to that which the statement is *not* (Eco, *A Theory of Semiotics* [Bloomington: Indiana University Press, 1976], 6ff.). Negation is most obviously a precondition for lying. But we must regress further, much further, to the very foundations of modern logic: called Sheffer's "stroke function," its approximate equivalent is also to be found in Peirce's "logic of relatives," and both are predicated upon the notion of a primordial "cut." A "cut" in what Peirce calls the original "sheet of possible assertions," is necessarily finite, and it is an incomplete disclosure whose pattern is more definite in terms of what it excludes (i.e., what is negated) than what it includes (i.e., what it *is*), therefore breeding vagueness (inconsistency) upon which the edifice of logic is erected. The logical form of negation, as well as of inference, can be generated from this primordial inconsistency, which introduces the notion of the finite, and thus "the whole movement of logic is provided for" (Alfred North Whitehead, *Modes of Thought* [New York: Macmillan, 1938], 52).

Significantly, E. H. Hutten, philosopher of science, remarks with respect to Sheffer's "stroke function" that "it is the very essence of rationality to abolish contradictions; but logic—being the most rational thing in the world—is generated by contradiction" (*The Origins of Science: An Inquiry into the Foundations of Western Thought* [London: George Allen and Unwin, 1962], 178). In addition, this foundation of inconsistency dictates that two propositions, *p* and *q*, cannot exist in simultaneity; there can be either one or the other but not both. Such a discrete state of affairs is offset, however, by the Peircean notion of sign continua, for a continuum escapes the exclusions of inconsistency; it is the immanence of the infinite interjected into the finite; it dissolves inconsistencies. In other words, if, as Peirce asserts, all signs constitute a continuum, then any break is merely an ephemeral ripple in the pond. So even here we encounter the roots of indeterminacy. It appears that the indeterminists, and especially the deconstructors, are correct, but at least in part for the wrong reason; for logic, our own Western World logic, is edified upon the cornerstone of contradictory principles.

Now Eco's referring back, which likewise implies inconsistency and potentially generates the lie, is nowhere better illustrated than in the Cretan paradox, which is significantly employed by Jacques Lacan in his discussion of analysis (*The Four Fundamental Concepts of Psycho-Analysis* [New York: W. W. Norton, 1981], 136–48). Lacan maintains that "I am lying" entails no antinomy if contextualized, for in such case it is directed to the addressee with reference to a past or future statement. On the other hand, if the "I" of "I am lying" in formal thinking is construed to be both that of the enunciator and of the statement, then a paradox ensues; but such analytical thinking, asserts Lacan, is absurd anyway. More significant still, the Möbius strip, which underlies Lacan's various schemata, is a worthy visual counterpart to the liar paradox. A one-dimensional line (Truth) on the strip is folded into itself to produce two-dimensionality (Truth *and* Falsity), but since the line on the strip is neither inside nor outside, there is, metaphorically speaking, *neither* Truth *nor* Falsity.

As I have argued elsewhere, all fiction making is dependent upon the primordial possibility of the lie.[19] The fiction, of course, is "nonreal," but since the reader must necessarily possess a degree of "real world" knowledge to understand it, a proper reading demands awareness—tacit at one level and conscious at the other—of both the "real" *and* the "nonreal"; but since an absolute line of demarcation can never exist between the two, there can be *neither* the "real" *nor* the "nonreal"—in an absolute sense, that is. Hans Vaihinger and Nietzsche, from their own perspectives, have said as much. It would appear, then, that rigorously logical thinking is incompatible with contextualized utterances, but, trapped within our cultural imperatives, we cannot resist the compulsion of trying to make them compatible (i.e., R. D. Laing's hypothesis).

Inconsistency, in sum, lies at the heart of semiosis, coiled like a worm, doubled back onto/into itself. This is by and large inescapable, in spite of our efforts to establish viable criteria of choice.

———————▼———————

It may be said that Peirce is a methodological realist (like the fiction maker) but an ontological idealist (Nicholas Rescher and Robert Brandom, *The Logic of Inconsistency* [Totowa, New Jersey: Rowman and Littlefield, 1979], 113–17 and 123–26). This is not quite the conflict of terms it might appear to be. The objects of knowledge are the *product* of inquiry, not the *cause*. Hence the methodologically real is the ontologically ideal, and for Peirce, at the interface of the two lies inconsistency and incompleteness, or what he usually terms *vagueness* and *generality*. This now brings us directly to Peirce's notion of continuity. Peirce maintains that continuity is of central importance to philosophy. Ideas or interpretants—that is, signs—consist of a continuous flowing or "spreading out" to affect other ideas, and as an idea spreads, its power to affect others loses intensity, though its quality remains virtually unchanged. This accounts for Peirce's maxim that there is no cognition that is not determined by previous cognitions. Ideas, then, have continuous extension both in space and in time, insofar as "the present is connected with the past by a series of real infinitesimal steps" (*Collected Papers,* 6.109). This continuity "is shown by the logic of relatives to be nothing but a higher type of that which we know as generality. It is relational generality" (6.190). And this higher type is one to which our own classical logic aspires. But since the continuum is far beyond our range of comprehension, we can hardly expect adequately to grasp it.

True: a continuum is incomprehensible if we attempt to relate it, by finitistic reasoning, to any given multitude of individuals. Consider, for instance, a line. No point can actually exist along it, for if it does, the continuum is breached, or better stated, "cut." There is an infinity of potential "spots" where a point can be abstracted, but this potential remains no more than indeterminate, at least until a specific point is made; but then the line, as a continuous totality, has been mutilated. In this light, the notion that syntax is discrete while semantics (i.e., meaning) is continuous should become apparent. Signs as marks on paper or sounds in the air are easily differentiated for the competent speaker: written signs are marked off by spaces and punctuation and their spoken counterpart by periods of silence and distinctive phonetic features. It is obvious that meanings are not so marked. We might even entertain the idea that there are not many meanings but One meaning, like Peirce's sign continuum, which is divisible but not divided. Utterances might make "cuts" in this meaning space in a way comparable to a physical object making a "cut" in space without destroying it.

W. V. O. Quine significantly observes that the class of all sentences should include not only those which have been uttered/written but also those that *could have been* but were *not* (*From a Logical Point of View* [New York: Harper and Row, 1953], 1–19). Of course, this class of sentences is imperative for the possibility of Eco's lying. In a roundabout manner, Quine uses his assumption to refute synonymy and translatability, which are dear to the meaning determinists. Quine's contrary-to-fact conditional is also picked up, independently we must assume, by Whitehead, who calls it the possible in contrast to the actual. The actual is atomistic, discrete; the possible is continuous, potentially infinite in extension. Since, with varying contexts over time and space, meanings entail a vast range of possibilities past, present, and future, they must have the properties of a continuum. Replace Peirce's ideas, interpretants, thoughts, and even mind—signs all—by meanings, and we have virtually the same image!

Furthermore, some would argue that ideas—or meanings—are inherent in real objects, for if a dog and the idea of a dog were separate, then there would be a relation between them, and therefore an idea of this relation, and so on, *ad infinitum*. But this is precisely Peirce's and Whitehead's contention, following their "relational" philosophy. Given the vast universe of signs past, present, and future, for all intents and purposes meanings can most adequately be described as composing a dense nondenumerable continuum. Signs are not things, they are process; they do not *have* meaning, nor do they point *to* meaning, they *are* meaning, as they incessantly do their dance before us. And more importantly, says Peirce, there is no beginning or final sign. Signs, as process, are like an infinite series of chinese boxes, with no largest or smallest box. They are *flow:* reminiscences of Deleuze and Guattari's *Anti-Oedipus.* However suggestive this meaning-as-continuum idea may be, Mortimer Taube, who has briefly touched on it, remarks that it remains vague (*Computers and Common Sense* [New York: Columbia University Press, 1961], 115). However, I believe, in light of the Emergent Perspective, that it is more than mere speculation.

------------▼------------

No lesser an abstract thinker than Heisenberg has also used the quasi-Aristotelian potential-actual trope (*Physics and Philosophy* [New York: Harper and Row, 1958]). More significantly still, Bohm demonstrates, in his radical interpretation, how quantum theory demands a need for a totally new view of what we call "reality" (*Wholeness and the Implicate Order* [London: Routledge and Kegan Paul, 1980]). Quantum theory has in part retained the Cartesian view of the world as constituted by an infinite set of points in three-dimensional space. Bohm replaces it with a "holographic" trope, which is inspired by the hologram (from the Greek *holo* = "whole" and *gram* = "to write"). As is well known, a laser beam can be split by passing it through a half-silvered mirror. Part of the reflected beam strikes an object so that it diffracts from it and comes back to overlap with the original beam, producing a very complex pattern, the hologram, on a photographic plate. When the processed plate is then illuminated by a laser beam, the object is reproduced exactly as before, apparently with three-dimensional qualities. The important property of the hologram is that each part of the plate can reproduce the entire image, although the smaller the part, the more vague the image.

Bohm, in his hypothesis of the quantum interconnectedness of the universe, relates the hologram to the implicate, or enfolded, order (the realm of possibilities). The Cartesian coordinates, then, are capable of expressing the explicate, or unfolded, order (the actuals). The first cannot be expressed but only known implicitly, the second can be expressed by classical laws. The first is smooth, a continuous, seamless fabric, the second is discontinuous, grainy. The analogy between quantum theory and the hologram rests in quantum theory's stipulation that, at a deep level, matter can be understood neither as constituted of localized particles nor of fields of wave motion in space. It has the attributes of both, and at the same time, strictly speaking, there are neither particles nor fields. Interestingly, Bohm's "holographic" universe is in a manner of speaking logically inconsistent, and it is incomplete, for it is eternally in flux. And we cannot know it; hence it is indeterminate. Bohm's model quite adequately fits the Emergent Perspective I have mentioned. Moreover, if we think of intertextuality as neither the field of all possible textual meanings nor a given set of actual readings at a particular time, we have an enlightened view of the metaphor. Intertextuality is neither the localized text before the reader nor the web of textual meanings; it is both at once, and the text is as much a part of the field as the field of the text. Now I return to Peirce, who develops a similar image.

Peirce notes that "an endless series of representations, each representing the one behind it, may be conceived to have an absolute object as its limit" (*Collected Papers*, 1.339). Peirce rightly calls this absolute object the final interpretant, but he appears to be contradicting himself here, especially in light of his inclination toward infinity and Zeno's paradoxes, for which there can be no end. This final interpretant, or sign, we might conjecture (and as Eco claims), "is not really a sign, but is the entire semantic field as the structure connecting and correlating signs with each other" (*A Theory of Semiotics*, 69). I would suggest that, given the Peircean continuum, this global semantic field must itself be a sign, perhaps a hypersign, as Peirce calls a set of conglomerated signs—in fact, we might call this vast conglomeration the "cosmic hypersign." If so, then the continuous web of signs can be the set of possibles (an "implicate order"), and discontinuous signs the actuals (an "explicate order").

So everything seems to be wrapped into a neat package. Peirce, Bohm, intertextuality: meaning as a continuum.

Charles Hartshorne, however, argues that Peirce did not anticipate the quantization of modern physics ("Charles Peirce and Quantum Mechanics," *Transactions of the Charles S. Peirce Society* 9, no. 4 [1973], 191–201). Peirce, he rightly observes, affirmed the *actual* continuum, and he justified it by the argument that continuity keeps all the possibilities open in simultaneity. Hartshorne counters this argument by asserting that discreteness excludes portions of the range of possibilities, and therefore the continuum could at no point be actualized; discreteness rules out nothing *except* continuity. However, Hartshorne makes no mention of Bohm's interpretation of quantum theory, which includes both the continuous web *and* discreteness.[20]

Peirce provides a model to account for this interconnectedness. We can imagine the total realm of possible "assertions," he tells us, as a "book of separate sheets, tacked together at points, if not otherwise connected" (*Collected Papers*, 4.512). The first sheet in this book is the standard "sheet of assertion," a "universe of existent individuals [i.e., actuals]"; different sections of it represent sentences asserted concerning that particular subuniverse. A "cut" in this sheet enables one to pass into a successive sheet, into areas of conceived sentences which are not yet actualized. Further "cuts" in this and successive sheets then allow one to "pass into worlds which, in the imaginary worlds of the other cuts, are themselves represented to be imaginary and false, but which may, for all that, be true, and therefore continuous with the sheet of assertion itself, although this is uncertain" (*Collected Papers*, 4.512).

Peirce invites us to regard the "ordinary blank sheet of assertion" as a film upon which there exists the as-yet-undeveloped photograph of the actuals of the universe. But this is not a literal picture, for when we consider historically the range of actuals which have been asserted to be true, we must conclude that this "book" can be none other than a continuum which "must clearly have more dimensions than a surface or even than a solid; and we will suppose it to be plastic, so that it can be deformed in all sorts of ways without the continuity and connection of parts being ever ruptured" (*Collected Papers*, 4.512). Peirce goes on to compare this pliable topological image to a map in which all points of a surface correspond to points on the next surface—and so on, successively—and the continuity is preserved unbroken. In this manner, each point, each "cut," corresponds to the initial "sheet of assertion" where the actualized state of things is represented. All successive sheets, then, represent a set of possibles—many of which can, at another time and place, become actualized.

Peirce's "book of assertions" is also a metaphor for what Eco has called *unlimited semiosis (A Theory of Semiotics*, 69ff.). I would suggest an even more labyrinthine image, which mirrors either Laplace's Superobserver or the idea of God, take your pick. Consider each sign possibility to be a point (potentially the Cartesian factor) with an infinite set of lines connecting it to all other points in the universe (the non-Cartesian factor). Each sign-point is like a chimerical octopus whose body is the point and whose tentacles are the infinite number of lines emanating from that point ready to suck in one or more of all the other sign-points, which will then become its interpretant and hence another sign-point. (Actually, more in accord with Laplace and God, each tentacle would have an eye at its extremity enabling it to "see" all other sign-points simultaneously.)[21]

This entire conglomeration of lines, to be true to form, will have certain characteristics: (a) the whole can be "cut" at any point and reconnected along any one of its lines, like Peirce's amorphous "book of assertions"; (b) at a given instant the conglomerate is static (the synchronic dimension), but it holds the possibility for all future connections (the diachronic dimension)—this instant is not the Saussurean slice out of the semiological salami, it is the entire conglomerate given "en bloc," holding all past, present, and future possibilities; and (c) the conglomerate is self-contained, twisting and doubling back on itself, like Einsteinian space-time (called the "block" universe), or like an infinity of infinitely thin Möbius strips intersecting each other at the point of their twist. However, (d) with respect to finite sign users, unlike point-octopuses, all observations and relations must remain inside; there is no global vision, for immanence rules—commensurate with quantum theory, which has demolished the classical view of subject/object and observer/observed.[22] And (e) there can be no complete description of the whole, since, commensurate with Peirce's plastic "book of assertions," logical connections do not remain the same over time, and since, with our own finite number of appendages and sensory organs, we can never process all signs in an instant.

Now this *IS* intertextuality with a vengeance! And yet it is, I submit, an adequate though unformalizable image insofar as: (a) it avoids the problematics of a Saussurean based semiology, of that synchronic slice which freezes the signifying process; and (b) *indefinite semiosis*, which is implied by it, is compatible with indeterminacy, incompleteness, undecidability, complementarity, plurivocity, intertextuality, and meaning continua—all of which are prevalent in the Emergent Perspective.

▼

All these uncertainties, surfacing at the end of the nineteenth century and falling upon us with full force in the last half of the twentieth, present an option. One can acquiesce. If not, one must adopt another conceptual framework. But which one? As was pointed out in the beginning of this essay, the prevalent "isms" are, each and every one, inextricably rooted in a contradictory assumption or two anyway. So at this bottom level there is no choice accompanied by a guarantee. Those who want absolutes may have no recourse but to take refuge in the monasteries. But actually, there's no need for despair. Gödel's proof, the other "limitative theorems," quantum theory, and relativity didn't put all the mathematicians, logicians, and scientists in the unemployment lines. In fact, the game became more adventurous once they discovered they shouldn't be so serious about it. In other words, they have accepted in essence the implications of the Octopus Thesis. In so doing, they lost the certainty of a great resolutive power; but, on the other hand, vast and previously unconceived horizons opened before them. In this sense, deconstruction, and post-structuralism in general, are to a large degree compatible with what I have called the Emergent Perspective.

Notes

1. Of particular interest are the debates in *Against Theory: Literary Studies and the New Pragmatism*, ed. W. J. T. Mitchell (Chicago: University of Chicago Press, 1985).

2. Popper, *Conjectures and Refutations* (New York: Harper and Row, 1963), chap 1; and *Objective Knowledge* (Oxford: Oxford University Press, 1972), chap. 1.

3. For a comparable critique of the rationalist view of science, including Popper's, see Joseph Agassi, *Science in Flux* (Dordrecht, Holland: D. Reidel, 1975); and *Science and Society* (Dordrecht, Holland: D. Reidel, 1981).

4. For further relations between the "New Criticism" and other critical approaches discussed here, see T. K. Seung, *Structuralism and Hermeneutics* (New York: Columbia University Press, 1982).

5. The problem here involves not only the induction fallacy, which structuralism shares with other outmoded views of science, but, in addition, structuralism fails Popper's test of falsification. One might argue, following Popper's critics, that falsification is not a viable prescription for scientific activity and that the sciences have always been interpretive rather than descriptive-explanatory. I will briefly address myself to this issue in footnote 12.

6. I refer to the Derrida-Searle debate found in *Glyph 1* (Baltimore: Johns Hopkins University Press, 1977).

7. Just as Jorge Luis Borges reiterates in "Garden of Forking Paths" (*Labyrinths, Selected Short Stories, and Other Writings*, ed. D. A. Yates and S. E. Irby [New York: New Directions, 1962]) the apothegm that the only prohibited word in a riddle is its answer—a word from "outside" the riddle—so the solution to a paradox must lie "outside" the system from within which the paradox was generated.

8. Significantly, the view that there can be no neutral metalanguage, commonly held in deconstructionist circles, has been a focus of fierce debate in the philosophy of science for some time, one of the foremost antagonists of the metalanguage thesis being Paul Feyerabend (*Against Method* [London: NLB, 1975]).

9. For further discussion of deconstruction along these lines, see my *Deconstruction Reframed* (West Lafayette, Ind.: Purdue University Press, 1985), especially chap. 3.

10. I am here presupposing relatively incommensurable perspectival frameworks between two given cultures, akin to Feyerabend's incommensurability formulation of scientific theory making. See *Against Method*, especially chap. 17.

11. In defense of Kuhn, it must be admitted that he denies he is a relativist. See, for example, the debates in *Criticism and the Growth of Knowledge*, ed. Imre Lakatos and Alan Musgrave (London: Cambridge University Press, 1970); and *The Structure of Scientific Theories*, ed. Frederick Suppe (Urbana: University of Illinois Press, 1977).

12. Gadamer (*Truth and Method*, 308–9) summarily admits to the relativity paradox, but he becomes—apparently willingly—a victim of it anyway. It bears mentioning also that in general the hermeneutical movement has been beneficial insofar as it has directed attention to the role of interpretation and understanding in the humanities. However, Stephen Toulmin observes, and rightly so, that this movement "has done us a disservice also because it does not recognize any comparable role for interpretation in the natural sciences and in this way sharply separates the two fields of scholarship and experience. Consequently, . . . the central truths and virtues of hermeneutics have become encumbered with a whole string of false inferences and misleading dichotomies" ("The Construal of Reality: Criticism in Modern and Postmodern Science," in *The Politics of Interpretation,* ed. W. J. T. Mitchell [Chicago: University of Chicago Press, 1982], 99–100). Toulmin concludes:

> Critical judgment in the natural sciences, then, is not geometrical, and critical interpretation in the humanities is not whimsical. In both spheres, the proper aims should be the same— that is, to be perceptive, illuminating, and reasonable. In the sciences, formal rigor is not the same as rational soundness; in the humanities, idiosyncrasy is not the same as originality. In either case, a successful interpretation will combine *soundness* and *centrality* in its general approach with *relevance* and *sensitivity* in its specific details, and the task of judging any such interpretation requires us to pay attention to its claims in both respects. (117)

Concerning the hermeneutical character of scientific research, Patrick Heelan's *Space-Perception and the Philosophy of Science* (Berkeley: University of California Press, 1983) is excellent.

13. Polanyi, *Personal Knowledge* (Chicago: University of Chicago Press, 1958). The enterprising reader will most likely discover an interesting conjunction between Polanyi and the notion of scientific hermeneutics outlined by Toulmin—see footnote 12.

14. Nor, I might add, any social determination of knowledge such as that of Luien Goldmann (*The Human Sciences and Philosophy* [London: Jonathan Cape, 1969]), who posits an isomorphism between intellectual, artistic, and social structures.

15. I do not speak here of the cybernetics, accompanied by general systems theory, of the 1950s and 1960s which provoked—as is evident in retrospect—much ill-advised enthusiasm. I refer to a recent and rather more sober assessment of the relations between information and the material world as recently summarized by David J. Bolter, *Turing's Man* (Chapel Hill: University of North Carolina Press, 1984); Jeremy Campbell, *Grammatical Man* (New York: Simon and Schuster, 1982); and Heinz R. Pagels, *The Cosmic Code* (New York: Random House, 1983).

16. To mention only a few: Leonard Meyer, *Music, the Arts, and Ideas* (Chicago: University of Chicago Press, 1967); Wylie Sypher, *Loss of the Self in Modern Literature and Art* (New York: Random House, 1962); and, in his own way, Douglas Hofstadter, *Gödel, Escher, Bach* (New York: Basic Books, 1979).

17. Admittedly, there are a few who, I believe, have recently proceeded in the appropriate direction. In the first place, the work of Derrida reveals what, in humanistic studies, might well be the ultimate import of the general loss of certainty in contemporary mathematics, logic, and physics, as I argue in *Deconstruction Reframed.* Michel Foucault's suspicion of global

theories in *The Order of Things* (New York: Pantheon, 1971) and his contextualization of them to demonstrate that there is no external position of determinacy—no universal understanding which remains outside history—implies a view in large part commensurate with that of Derrida. And Jean-François Lyotard's *The Postmodern Condition* (Minneapolis: University of Minnesota Press, 1984), which is a penetrating look at science, technology and the arts, and the dissolution of metadiscourse, is a giant step toward the world-vision implied by the "new physics." And I mention several others briefly: Gilles Deleuze and Felix Guattari's *Anti-Oedipus* (New York: Viking Press, 1977) outlines quite effectively what I would term the "new cybernetic" view concerning individual and social behavior; Alex Comfort's *Reality and Empathy* (New York: State University of New York Press, 1984) establishes relations between the "new physics," mathematical and computer models, and the mind; J. E. Loveluck (*Gaia* [London: Oxford University Press, 1979]) has constructed a fascinating and radically novel model of earth as a complex, interacting, interconnected system; and Nobel Laureate Ilya Prigogine and Isabelle Stengers's *Order Out of Chaos* (New York: Bantam Books, 1984), drawing from thermodynamics, offers a creative disquisition on "man's new dialogue with nature." Finally, I cannot overlook Hofstadter's *Gödel, Escher, Bach*, which is a staggering display of interdisciplinary conjunctions.

    18. Charles S. Peirce, *Collected Papers*, ed. C. Hartshorne and P. Weiss (Cambridge: Belknap Press of Harvard University Press, 1960), 1.339. Hereafter references to this book will be incorporated directly in the text.

    19. See Eco, *A Semiotic Theory of Texts* (Berlin: Mouton de Gruyter, 1985), and *Pararealities* (Amsterdam: John Benjamins, 1983).

    20. This is not to imply that Hartshorne is necessarily wrong and Bohm and Peirce right, for there are various competing interpretations of quantum mechanics.

    21. Eco, incidentally, uses a comparable but less cumbersome and less mathematical image, the "rhizome," taken from Deleuze and Guattari's book by the same title (Paris: Minuit, 1976). See Eco's *Semiotics and the Philosophy of Language* (Bloomington: Indiana University Press, 1984), 81–82.

    22. The dilemma here is that Einstein *was* able, by a stroke of imagination, to step outside the universe to construct his image of the "block," but that is another story.

Systems Theory
and the Environment
of Theory

Dietrich Schwanitz

The purpose of this essay is to acquaint an American audience largely unfamiliar because of language barriers with the brand of systems theory formulated by Niklas Luhmann and to articulate the implications of that theory for the study of literature and culture.[1] Because of its status as an unknown quantity in this country, I will begin with an outline of its systematic framework; but in order not to lose sight of literature, I will make a few anticipatory claims (temporarily deferring their substantiation) about the relevance of systems theory for the humanities.

1) Systems theory operates with a claim to universality with reference to both the totality of its scope and the depth of its foundations. Starting with a radical break with the tradition of Western thought, it reorganizes almost every central concept used by literary theory such as language communication, meaning, subject, individual, society, temporality, experience, action, structure, process, art, history, etc.

2) As applied theory, it has developed a wide range of practical research in the fields of historical sociology, sociology of knowledge, intellectual history and cultural theory.

3) As a theory of society, systems theory also contains a theory of the social subsystem of art production and consumption, from which insights may be derived concerning the autonomisation of art, the development of taste, the differentiation of professional artists and an appreciative public, the relation between individual works of art with a shared style, etc.

4) Over and beyond all identifiable theoretical consequences, systems theory contains a potential for stimulating literary and cultural studies if only because of its conceptual strategies. Though stringent, its mobility makes it profoundly adaptable, and its ability to break down the most taken for granted phenomena into separate elements matches its powers of recombination. A problem is invariably reconstructed as a common point of reference for the most divergent phenomena, which then can be compared as different solutions; problem orientation is the crest of systems theory, comparability its motto. Any literary theory seeking to bring the relation between micrological questions of textual organization and macrohistorical developments under theoretical control will welcome these conceptual strategies.

Epistemology—Evolution—Environment

Systems theory has severed all connections with the epistemological traditions of philosophy, adopting instead epistemological attitudes developed in the natural sciences, particularly in biology and the theory of evolution.[2] As to philosophical tradition, it shows at most a certain affinity with the historical turn of Hegel's philosophy of spirit. This epistemological attitude can be sketched as follows: like every accomplishment, quality or ability, human cognition also is a product of evolution, biological or social. As such an ability or faculty, cognition can be compared to other achievements attained through the evolutionary process of adaptation by which, for example, organic systems react to their environment. Thus the process of adaptation to the environment can be seen as a type of knowledge which allows information about the environment to enter into the system proper. In this sense, the structures developed as a consequence are "images" of the environment, just as the wings of a bird reflect the aerodynamic qualities of air. The image reflected within the system forms a sort of negative image of the environment, and its relation to it has been described as contrapuntal. As an immediate consequence, such concepts as information and knowledge lose the privileged position they had received through their exclusive reference to human rationality.

By means of self-reinforcement or feedback, whether positive or negative, systems develop entirely new qualities which cannot be explained with reference to the qualities of their elements. Control loops of various degrees of complexity exist in the organic world in countless varieties, and they are always a matter of self-reference. In other words, the empirical sciences, in discovering an increasing number of self-referential systems, have progressively undermined the royal prerogative of the human subject to assume the exclusive and privileged title of self-referentiality (in the sense of recursive knowledge about knowledge). This has led to a transition from transcendentalism to what has been termed natural epistemology.

With regard to self-referential systems, natural epistemology shifts the starting point of cognition from the analyzing subject to the reality under analysis with the instruction to continue research until research itself reappears as one of its own subjects, as a self-referential system. Science, as a self-referential system, is thus able to compare itself with the objects of its research and to use this comparison as a means for self-control. Similarly, evolution too becomes self-referential: it reaches the state of self-knowledge in systems theory as its own product. It is here that systems theory shows a certain affinity with Hegelian self-referentiality; however, it replaces history with evolution and makes a point of avoiding the Hegelian conclusion that, at the end of history, spirit merges with itself by its self-perception to become absolute spirit. The understanding of evolution is not identical with evolution itself. This difference between the perceiving and the perceived, embedded in all self-reference, is of decisive theoretical importance, for the basic concept of systems theory is the same one used by such post-structuralist theories as deconstruction—difference.

This rough sketch of the theoretical repercussions of self-reference on the theory which reconstructs it already points to a conceptual strategy in systems theory which colors its intellectual climate—the comparability of seemingly incommensurable subject matters. This comparability is effected across the concept of function, or functional equivalence, which determines the angle from which to compare various solutions to the same problem while disregarding the side effects. However, this forces one to maintain such a high altitude that every attempt to describe systems theory runs the risk of disappearing into clouds of theoretical abstraction. The conceptual patterns of comparability and self-reference which enforce this high level of abstraction are also at the basis of a misconception of systems theory centered on the status of the system consciousness. For the type of systems theory with which we are dealing here—in the main a theory of society—society and consciousness do not belong to the same system; they form two different systems and reciprocally constitute each other's environment. However, they mutually use each other for their self-constitution and cannot, of course, exist independently of one another.

In our culture, as Alvin Gouldner (*The Coming Crisis of Western Sociology* [London, New York: Basic Books, 1970]) has shown, the individual still experiences himself as a more densely structured system than everything else. According to this conception, society consists of individual people and the relations between them. Systems theory, however, opts for a different alternative: man may experience himself as a unity, but he is not, for all that, a system. On the contrary, the boundaries between his organism and his consciousness on the one hand and consciousness and society on the other run straight through him. Society is as autonomous in relation to consciousness as consciousness is to society. Yet this situation must not be thought ahistorical: this could only become manifest in contemporary society because modern society no longer derives its principle of differentiation from the categorization of whole people, as in the stratified societies of the past, but from social functions in which people participate only partially; society has now developed its own, social principle of differentiation and thus shows, as a manifestation of its greater autonomy, its qualifications as a system.

Here again we find that evolution becomes self-referential by leading to knowledge of its own principle. We find too, in this cognitive leap, a supersession of the humanist notion that man is the measure of society. On the contrary, because man is not the measure of society, social systems are free to evolve towards greater autonomy, and this autonomy of society allows evolution to pass from the basic biological existence of man to culture, so that all those ideas of social Darwinism which expect sociocultural evolution only from the evolution of man are particularly misleading.

Systems theory has been developed in two steps, and as a result, its two main parts have retained a certain systematic independence. The first part is systems differentiation, which deals with the combination of elements in systems; the second is *autopoiesis*, which deals with the constitution of elements by systems. These two parts are easily grafted because a system is separated from its environment by the quality of its elements but develops interior differentiation by their combination.

Systems Differentiation

The starting point of systems differentiation was a replacement of Parsonian structural-functionalism by the concept of system (organized on the basis of the difference between system and environment), which then allowed for a theory of system differentiation so conceived as to have the basic system/environment difference repeat itself by forming subsystems within the interior of the system. System boundaries separate the system from its environment; both the unity of the system and the unity of the environment result from the system proper. However, environment—unlike system—is not delimited by boundaries but by open horizons.[3] Its unity is relative to each system and is, therefore, different for each system because each system excepts only itself from the environment. A system may observe other systems in its environment, but their special system/environment relations are never completely at the disposal of the observing system. Each system, therefore, has an environment which appears both as a complex whole of different system/environment relations and as a homemade unity.

Each system's environment is more complex than itself, and each compensates its inferiority in complexity by reducing environmental complexity through strategies of selection. A system can only do this on the basis of its own complexity, for reduction of complexity only occurs when one relational pattern is reconstructed by a simpler one. Therefore, the concept of "reduction" means a relation between relations. Systems theory does away with the old relation between the indestructible simple and the destructible complex which had paved the way for so many "reductionisms"; for in a relation between relations there is no solid simplicity, and if systems constitute the units of which they themselves consist, one cannot play off the one against the other.

Here again, in both the concepts of reduction and selection, one notes the influence of Darwinian evolutionary theory, yet systems theory radicalizes the Darwinian paradigm by attributing everything to difference, in this case to the system/environment difference. On its basis, systems build up structural complexity by self-differentiation. The outward boundaries secure a sort of domesticated region within the interior of the system which, as a special environment of reduced complexity, makes further system differentiation possible. Interior differentiation can only proceed along lines of generic homogeneity; organic systems can only be differentiated into further organic systems, and social only into social subsystems. Thus, system formation becomes self-reflexive: it starts autocatalytically and not according to plan. The whole of the social system is represented at every boundary between system and subsystem, albeit from a different angle: that is, it appears as a confrontation between the political or economic or scientific subsystem with its respective internal environment, from which each subsystem can only except itself. Reduction of complexity receives the form that each subsystem is only oriented towards its own specific system/environment relation since other functions are taken care of elsewhere. In that sense, self-reference is restructured. Though a subsystem cannot identify itself without reference to a whole that includes it, which makes self-reference perfectly circular, the whole is reconstructed as an asymmetrical difference between subsystem and internal environment. Accordingly, internal differentiation reproduces outward boundaries by gradations within the system. The differences thus produced converge in relation to the outward boundaries and can only be maintained through them. If the principle of self-differentiation is not derived from the environment but chosen autonomously as in our own type of functional society, the difference between system and environment becomes even more obvious.

With this "controlling difference" between system and environment, the theory of system differentiation severs the connection to a tradition that reaches back to antiquity, in which society was conceived as the unity of the sum of its parts.[4] In systems theory, a differentiated system no longer simply consists of a certain number of parts or their relations to each other but is composed of a number of operational system/environment differentiations that reconstruct the entire system as the respective unity of each subsystem and its environment. The pivotal concept of this new paradigm is autopoiesis.

Autopoiesis

The concept of autopoiesis refers to an aspect of system/ environment difference which is theoretically more fundamental than systems differentiation: it refers to the system's basic elements by the constitution of which a system constitutes itself.[5] If we take into consideration that there exist two ways of decomposing systems, the difference to systems differentiation becomes immediately apparent. The theory of systems differentiation already presupposes the system's outward boundaries. However, these boundaries only result from the sudden appearance of new elements created *ex nihilo* by a system emerging simultaneously with its constitutive elements. This fulguration of new creation, of totally new phenomena that cannot be explained by reference to qualities in their material basis, is covered by the concept of emergence *(Emergenz)*. In addition, the theory of autopoiesis claims that creation is self-referential, that autopoietic systems create themselves because in the process of constituting both their elements and their elemental operations, they refer to themselves. In doing this they employ techniques of self-observation and self-description which thereby acquire a strategic importance for both the ways in which different systems constitute themselves and the design of systems theory itself.

The temporalization of the element and the introduction of an elaborated phenomenological concept of meaning were the two decisive innovations of Luhmann's which permitted the application of the theory of autopoiesis to social theory. These innovations are complementary: in their use of meaning, psychic and social systems are alike, but they differ with regard to the form of events which constitute their elements. As the elements are constituted only in a process of self-referential feedback and as the self-referentiality in both systems operates along the lines of self-observation, the observing elements and the observed elements must form two different levels which in psychic systems differ from those in social systems:

1) In the social systems, the observing elements are communications and the observed elements actions.

2) In psychic systems, the observing elements are thoughts and the observed elements ideas *(Vorstellungen)*.

As elements are defined by their functioning as indivisible units for their systems, systems can develop only through recombination of elements and not through their dissolution or reorganization. Therefore, social evolution proceeds by systems differentiation, meaning that consciousness can recombine ideas but cannot dissolve them into neural processes and that society can structure actions but cannot dissolve them into consciousness. As elements are constituted by the systems themselves, they are independent of any material base. They are units only for the system by which they are constituted. Furthermore, as the elements function as units only within the system which constitutes them, they are neither just analytical constructs nor do they rest in some ontological substance. They really do exist, but their existence is only brought about by self-reference and cannot in any way be explained by reference to preexisting ideas, substances or individuals. Self-reference, then, acquires a meaning which dissolves the subject's exclusive right to this title. The subject is just a special case of self-referentiality, and this signifies the fundamental break with both transcendental theories and all ontologies.

In the process of self-observation within psychic and social systems, the system/environment difference is reintroduced into the system to secure the elements' reproduction as the system's elements and not as elements of the environment. This is done by the application of meaning. Meaning is the condition for the possibility of the combination of self-observation and autopoiesis, for: 1) being self-referential, meaning can react only to meaning, and 2) only meaning includes the system boundaries in processes internal to the systems by continuous references to both system and environment. Only a system operating with meaning *(Sinnsystem)* can ascribe meaning to its environment though it has produced it itself. As meaning renders the self-referential structure of the system asymmetrical by its reference to the environment, it creates the possibility of combining self-referential closure with openness towards the environment, or, in other words, the self-referential closure becomes the means by which contact with the environment can be established.

System boundaries, then, only separate elements; they do not separate relations. Therefore, it becomes possible to distinguish between internal relations and system/environment relations, which makes it clear that system boundaries function as filters that both separate and connect system and environment. With reference to system boundaries, the theory of autopoiesis reenters the theory of systems differentiation. The impossibility for all relations between all the systems' elements to be realized enforces a selection of relations that depends on the system/environment difference. By means of its strategies of selection, the system compensates for its inferior complexity to the environment, which it reduces by the selectivity of its perception. This enables it to transform its own indeterminate complexity (the possibility that every element can be related to every other) into a determinate complexity (internal differentiation) which then again can recursively find its take-off conditions in the determinate complexity of its environment and build itself up until it is able to process even indeterminate complexity both in itself and in the environment.

Time and Meaning

The reference problem of this special form of autopoiesis, the condition for the emergence of new systems, is the transitoriness of events which have to be linked to build up structured complexity. Events are already system-constituted units, and by the continuous disintegration of events, systems reproduce themselves while inscribing time into themselves. Therefore, the following phenomena are all related: the self-constitution of systems by means of events, the problem of continuous disintegration, the special form of complexity reflected in the question of continuity, the special form of indeterminate complexity, and the solution of the problem through the buildup of structured complexity by means of the selection of possibilities.

The selection of possibilities proceeds by means of the self-referential reinforcement of selection which uses the duplication of time as irreversibility and reversibility. Time manifests itself in alterations, and self-referential systems articulate alterations as data, differences that make a difference. Against the background of contrary expectations, even absence, voidness or error can thereby cause alterations, and continuity can become the reason for change precisely because it shows that as of yet nothing has changed. The selective construction of order by selection can take two possible forms that differ in their relation to time: structure and process.

Processes are sequences of irreversible events in which one event functions as the premise for the selection of the next. Structures reduce the indeterminate complexity of unlimited relationality between elements by the selection of specific relations that, by their iterability, can be anticipated. This enables them to arrest time in the form of reversibility. Whereas processes are either probable or improbable, structures form a relational scheme according to the conformity/nonconformity opposition. Because of the transitoriness of system elements, only such structures are formed that can relate such passing and emerging elements. The structural problem of such systems lies in the necessity for constant reproduction of self-reproduction, and the continuous disintegration of the elements leads to the structuring of self-reproduction.

To be able to fulfill their purposes, the structures of self-reproduction have to differ from the events and their relations fixed in time. In this respect, stable structures and continuously disintegrating and newly created events complement each other to the effect that psychic and social systems become temporalized systems. As opposed to nontemporal systems, they do not age but can adapt to the irreversibility of time by joining in: they copy time into themselves. The system can exploit the fact that every event is indeterminate with regard to the next step for scouring the environment for information about the determination of the following events.

On the level of systems differentiation, systems can attain temporal autonomy in relation to their environment. Though they cannot completely detach themselves from any temporal agreement with their environment, they can abandon complete synchronicity-in-every-point. This is compensated by internal shifts in time such as the simulation of environmental events within the system, anticipation, postponement of reactions, etc. For now, it becomes clear how autopoietical systems connect reversibility and irreversibility by the combination of structure and process: by temporalizing their elements, they abandon themselves to irreversibility; by structuring reproduction, however, they selectively fix time as reversible.

On a fundamental level, time and meaning appear to be equal in systems theory: meaning is conceived as the difference between actuality and possibility. Everything actual acquires meaning only within the context of other possibilities; however, its relation to other possibilities renders the actual unstable and replaces it by one of the possibilities held in readiness, so that again the horizon of possibilities is rearranged. In this respect, there seems to be a relation to the instability of the event: meaning furnishes the event with a horizon of possibilities from which the subsequent event can be chosen. In this sense, meaning is temporal in that it bridges the temporal difference of a sequence of actualizations and virtualizations that continuously keeps itself going and, in this respect, is undoubtedly autopoietic. The differences with which meaning operates do not precede the constitution of meaning but emerge together with the constitution of meaning itself. Inasmuch as meaning can only relate to other meaning, it is closed off by self-reference. On the other hand, the self-reference of meaning also seems to operate in time. Events can only be related to other events by means of memory or foresight (and memories of foresight and foresight of memories) along the lines of temporal horizons, for this seems to be the only way by which the elements of a system can be condensed into events. And just this condensation enables the irreversibility of time to reappear in the system inasmuch as meaning lost in time is immediately replaced by a more recent meaning. Meaning and time mutually make each other possible. Their difference lies in the different forms of asymmetry, of irreversibility and the relation of possibilities.

This concept of meaning, as the combination of intentional actualization, and an accompanying horizon of possibilities is adopted from Husserl and connected to systems theory to explain that each selection can become conscious of its own selectivity by keeping the reference to other possibilities of selection at hand. Therefore, meaning reflects complexity, and only systems using meaning are able to reintroduce their own difference to the environment by means of reflexion and then use it within the system itself.

One way of doing this is by a self-description, which is not identical with the described but is an indication within a difference. The difference with regard to the self-description of meaning is the difference between the "world" and "meaning." Meaning describes itself as the "world," while "world" is, so to speak, a simplification of meaning. The relation between meaning and the "world" is characterized by decentrality *(Dezentrierung):* as meaning, the world is accessible from every possible point. But the "world" is not only the sum of all possible perspectives of meaning and, accordingly, of all system/environment differences; it is also their unity. In this respect, the world becomes each system's ultimate unity of all system/environment differences in which its own somehow merges with those of all the others. However, it is not by this unity of the world that the operation of meaning becomes comprehensible but only by the difference between this unity and meaning itself. Here, too, the general rule applies that all experience of meaning presupposes a difference.

The pure self-reference of meaning conceived as the difference between the actual and the possible undergoes a second differentiation that produces three forms of specific self-referentiality, three dimensions of meaning *(Sinndimensionen):* the dimension of objectivity *(Sachdimension),* the social dimension, and time. With that, we have reached the second level of time's emergence: it reappears as one of the three dimensions subsidiary to meaning. All three dimensions designate horizons that contract the universal self-reference of meaning and distinguish it from other contracted horizons. Each of these horizons is marked by a specific difference: time by reversibility/irreversibility, the dimension of object-ivity by the interior/exterior horizon, and the social dimension by consensus/dissent. In this respect, the dimensions of meaning are the differentiations of differences. Once established, the self-references specific to the dimensions close them off against each other: the future is the future only with respect to the past and not with respect to a social consensus. Crossing the boundaries between these dimensions is no longer possible. This, however, permits the establishment of relations between them which interrupts the tautology of a purely self-referential meaning by forming asymmetries: with regard to the system/environment difference, time becomes asymmetrical, and with regard to time, the system/environment relation becomes one of graded complexity, etc. Order can only be established by forming such asymmetries.

The differentiation of time as a specific and independent dimension begins with the detachment from the immediacy of experience. That is, time has to emancipate itself from the difference between presence and absence in order to make the idea accessible that the absent can be simultaneous to the present.[6] In the long run, time becomes so abstract and universal that all sequences detach themselves from the temporal horizons of the past, present and future and can, therefore, be brought into relations to these dimensions. This creates the condition for the multiple modalisation of time into the past present and the present past, etc.[7] By the same token, time as the continuous presence of change from the future into the past is now reduplicated: as a point in the process of becoming irreversible, and then as a continuous duration of this process itself. The present, therefore, is doubled so that it signifies the duration of change and can be conceived as the combination of stability and change.

Social Systems

In social systems, the possibility for negating created by meaning receives the form of double contingency due to its relation to ego and alter: ego acts/reacts on the assumption of the other's freedom and controls his own behavior on the basis of this insecurity by stabilizing it by means of expectations. However, behavior is not naturally free but is only rendered so by expectation. As soon as one has become aware of expectations, one has the alternative of either affirming or disappointing them. Thus, double contingency builds up a structure of expectations (which in their turn may also be expected) and reproduces double contingency. As social order is built up and maintained only under the pressure of the problem created by double contingency, it has to be continuously reproduced. Therefore, social order cannot be conceived as a result of consensus but of the consensus/dissent difference. And this determines the autopoiesis of social systems.

Insecurity is constantly reproduced in and by communication, which is the basic operation of the social system. It is realized as the unity of a triple selection: information, expression,[8] and understanding. For the comprehension of the structure of communication (not for the way it functions), the third selection is the decisive one: communication takes place when alter (who understands) imputes the difference between information and expression to ego (who expresses).

For the theory, it is decisive that all three selections should be conceived as unhierarchized, although at times one selection may predominate. The unpredictable changes in the dominance of the three selections prevent the determination of a definite direction for the reinforcement of selection (which is the definition of the process). Therefore, communication simplifies itself in its self-description by comprehending itself as action. This self-description sets up the dominant expression as a (speech-)act, attributes it to the communicator by rendering him responsible for the expression, and makes it asymmetrical by forcing it into the sequential mold of "addresser to addressee." By means of this simplification, the communication-act can be fixed in time and treated as an event.

The combination of asymmetry and its character as an event regulates the follow-ups, so that reaction to the communication by the addressee is also comprehended as an act of communication. In other words, in the continuous flow of autopoiesis, communication and action are articulated by a different interpunctuation. Communication is concluded only when alter has reacted to ego; action abbreviates communication to the attribution of expression to ego. Alter's reaction is then comprehended as a new act of communication. Only this difference—between communication as an elementary unit of self-constitution and the communication act as an elementary unit of self-description—allows communication to be conditioned as a sequence of events in which ego's act is considered to be the premise upon which alter can act, and all follow-up acts can only be determined in this manner.

Communication on its own leaves everything suspended. One may ask further questions, hesitate, misunderstand; but as long as discussion continues, nothing will be decided. Due to the self-description of communication as action, one act can become the premise for the next and thereby form a directional sequence. Communication fixes reversibility; action copies irreversibility into the social system. Both are necessary, and the difference between them enables the social system to emerge from the continuous flow of the autopoiesis of life, consciousness and communication. Communication provides a continuous hailstorm of stimulation by keeping up the pressure of problems.

Social evolution is conceived as the buildup of structures that relate to specific improbabilities of success in communication: the improbability of reaching the addressees, the improbability that once they are reached they should understand, and the improbability that they shall accept rather than reject what is communicated if they do understand. However, evolution may not be misunderstood as a continuous perfection of communication; rather, it must be seen as the continuous redistribution of probability and improbability. The continuous production of new conditions for improbability leads on social evolution by making it run after a problem which it can never catch up to. Accordingly, it progresses like the donkey that constantly tries to get hold of the famous carrot which is always just out of reach because it dangles from some contrivance fixed to the poor beast's own head. In social evolution, however, both donkey and carrot are continually being transformed in the process.

As an object of social analysis, it was the autonomy of the social subsystems which provided the stimulus for the development of systems theory. To begin with, the discovery of their self-referentiality was elaborated from the point of view of social systems' differentiation until, with the introduction of the concept of autopoiesis, it became possible to relate self-referentiality not only to the subsystems but to the social system as a whole. As we have seen, conceiving the elements of social systems as temporal and therefore insubstantial events provided the basis for the application of the concept of autopoiesis. If the system/environment boundaries are simply presupposed, one can begin to describe the internal differentiation of a system without having to determine the nature of its elements: internal differentiation does not refer to the elements but only deals with their combination. If one wishes to determine, however, the nature of a system with regard to its environment on the basis of its emergence in order to differentiate it from both the environment and other systems, one has to determine the nature of its elements. Therefore, it was only with the help of the concept of autopoiesis that it became possible for systems theory to differentiate the social systems from other systems, and from the system consciousness in particular.[9]

Before investigating the system consciousness itself, it would be best for us to linger momentarily on this point of its differentiation from the social system, concentrating on an aspect of systems theory that we must reconstruct as a relation between two differences: the difference between interaction and society and the difference between consciousness and society. The first difference still systematically belongs to the theory of social systems; the second is logically more fundamental and marks off a system boundary. But in spite of their logical distinctness, there is good reason for connecting these differences: the interpenetration of psychic and social systems occurs in interaction. However, the difference between interaction and society is transformed in the process of social evolution which, in its turn, subjects interpenetration to permanent change from the social side. Since this becomes manifest in cultural semantics, cultural developments can best be traced along these theoretical lines.

The difference between interaction and society leads us back to the improbability of successful communication. In a fundamental sense, language is a medium by means of which communication can differentiate itself and emerge from perception. This doubling of language and perception constitutes interaction—interaction being defined by the simultaneous presence of its participants. Perception contributes a far-reaching mode of nonnegotiable background agreements—its rate of information processing being extremely high—and thus provides a basis with which to relativize, weaken, disclaim, deny, ironize, turn about or reinforce all communication by language. Accordingly, interactional communication shows an intensity and multiplicity of dimensions that no other form of communication can offer.

The difference between interaction and society takes the form of society's transcendence of interaction. Even in societies that are very close to interaction, interaction and society are not congruent; here, too, interaction is episodic. Without the overall social coherence transcending the limits of interaction, interaction could never stop without also putting an end to society, and neither could it start off again somewhere else. Therefore, the boundaries of interaction are not those of society. The difference between them is, again, most clearly revealed in their relation to time: whereas society is the simultaneous coexistence of subsystems, interaction is a sequence of episodes that follow one after the other. Taken together, they connect synchronic and diachronic differentiation. The temporal organization of interaction stands laterally to the other two dimensions of meaning: socially it is closed off by restrictions as to admission of participants (but they have to speak one after the other), and object-ively it is regulated by admission of subjects and themes (but they too have to be treated serially). With the growing separation of interaction and society, the production of themes can no longer be expected from interaction alone, which would have to invent them in accordance to every new situation. Therefore, society provides a stock of thematic clusters that can readily be processed in interaction and thus organizes its self-articulation. This stock of themes functions as "culture" and, in its readiness for communicative uses, as "semantics." Thus, culture mediates between language, which imposes no restrictions on what may be said, and interaction, which requires a structure. However, culture emerges out of the difference between interaction and society. Accordingly, it is only the widening of the rift between them that sets off the accumulation of permanent and durable meaning surviving the transience of interaction.

In archaic societies, meaning still had to be constantly revised along with and by the ongoing interaction, which must have meant a complete abandonment to the respective present and a lack of distance from all experiences. In the course of social evolution, participants in interaction are increasingly forced to distance interaction by having to consider other situations with other role requirements. Thus society relieves the pressure of interaction, creates greater freedom, and thereby increases double contingency. As society forms a context to interaction which is not subject to its limitations, it provides a background for clusters of expectations such as persons, roles, programmes, and values, over which recursive interactions can then dispose themselves. Evolution is possible only as evolution of society, and interaction provides the material for its experiments—new forms of interaction ranging from sit-ins to revolutionary festivals can be created as occasion demands. Precisely because of its difference to society, interaction can be used up for risky experiments. Improbabilities such as barter or the incest taboo were probably created in and by interaction and have subsequently stood the test of social usefulness. In this sense, society selects interactions; however, it does not exist outside interactions but regulates the connection between them and constitutes the condition for their compatibility. In this respect, interactions also select societies, and they both form a context of self-conditioned selectivity along which the progress of evolution can take place.

Now, if consciousness and society interlock in interaction, evolution also changes the relation between consciousness and interaction. In order to form an idea about what this relation of interpenetration may be like, one has first to delineate the specificity of consciousness.

Consciousness

Like the social system, consciousness[10] also consists of events, but, *a fortiori*, events of a different nature: for want of a better term they are called thoughts *(Gedanken)*. They cannot be stored since that would overtax the capacity of consciousness; therefore, they have to disintegrate continually and be replaced by thoughts which must be distinguishable from their predecessors. In the face of its continuous disintegration, consciousness has to provide for its own continuity by means of self-observation.

As we have seen, self-observation in society is communication that treats itself as action. The operation of self-observation in consciousness effects the continuous transformation of thoughts into ideas. With its back to the direction of progression, a thought observes its predecessor and distinguishes it from itself by casting it in the mold of an idea. By means of this differentiation from itself, the thought refers to itself. Observation, as an idea of an idea, becomes self-referential. Each idea views itself, so to speak, from the back, from the temporal point of view of the next following thought, a location it had just occupied itself; hence, it views itself from a point of view located in its own past. Only by registering what has happened to it can it take notice of itself. Therefore, observation itself has no telos. Only after having observed itself in retrospect does it discover teleology as an idea in the ideas and then orient itself towards the future, bypassing itself in the direction of the future by reusing its retrospection. This permits the continuous self-continuation of consciousness on the basis of differences it discovers in itself.[11]

As to the observation of other thoughts, thoughts employ the difference between self-reference and extraneous reference and thereby constitute what Husserl had called intentionality. The handling of this difference ends as soon as the observing thought becomes the observed idea. This has a decisive consequence for consciousness: it is not even transparent to itself. The idea, therefore, is not a quality of consciousness but presents the unity of a difference for another thought which, as long as it is observing an idea, is not an idea itself. As an observing thought, it also differs from the difference between self-reference and extraneous reference (the unity of which is an idea). For this difference, however, it uses the same difference between self-reference and extraneous reference and then applies "self-reference" to itself. Only by subsuming itself to the same difference it has created in the idea can a thought offer a connection to the following thought. Thus, each thought determines itself only by observing other thoughts and noticing at the same time that it cannot do this by observing itself: it has to use the difference between self-reference and extraneous reference a second time in order to distinguish itself from the unity of this difference (idea). Accordingly, the self-continuation of consciousness is the continuous recombination of self-reference and extraneous reference.

Consciousness follows the differentiating boundary between these two forms of the same differences between self-reference and extraneous reference. That makes it possible to continuously redistribute the difference, and it is this continuous rearrangement of self-reference and extraneous reference which prevents consciousness from either completely losing itself in the world or from losing itself in itself. The world is accessible from each instant of consciousness, and consciousness is accessible from each place in the world. The option as to self-reference or extraneous reference is regenerated in each operation. That is why consciousness is neither predictable nor calculable—not even for consciousness itself. Since consciousness finds its own conditions inaccessible to itself, it has to found its own behavior on freedom. Surprisingly enough, the fact that consciousness is impenetrable to itself makes communication possible: in observing another psychic system, consciousness realizes its impenetrability to observation. And only because it is also impenetrable to itself, can it then assume that the other consciousness is like itself, that the other is as free as itself. In this respect, the opacity of the self becomes the condition for seeing the other as alter ego. This duplicated freedom is the double contingency we have already considered as prerequisite to the emergence of society.

In view of its freedom, consciousness has to condition itself by limiting its possibilities. It does this by structuring itself so that the equal probabilities of follow-up events are reduced in favor of specific events that can then be repeated. These structures are built up by learning. And that also proceeds in the known manner: by means of observation, a thought pinpoints another thought as an idea and thereby regulates the transition to the next idea. By means of the difference between self-reference and extraneous reference, certain sequences are routinized with the help of which consciousness then can build up and extrapolate identities. Then, one can continue with either the object or one's reaction to the object by committing oneself to one or the other. Thus, rudimentary structures are established that by epigenesis may become very complex. Experiences thus condensed can then be projected into the environment in the form of expecta-tions (without which the environment would not appear in the pure self-referentiality of autopoiesis) so that the system can obtain infor-mation about the environment by processing the differences experi-enced with the help of these projections. With reference to the controlling difference of expectation, all further experiences are either normal or deviant. Only deviance is so alarming that it enforces intensified attention to itself with the end to either normalize deviance so that it accords with expectations or revise the expectations.

In the social system, the maintaining of expectations leads to the emergence of law and morality which support and justify expec-tations even if they are disappointed in reality. Consciousness has to proceed in a different manner: it can build up expectations to the level of claims. Then, if it is thwarted, it does not know how to continue and uses its own frustration as a means to go on; that is to say, it switches to self-reference and drives itself into a crisis by having its autopoiesis continue to operate on the basis of the preoccupation with its own perplexity. As a means by which this adaptation is effected, it uses emotions. Emotions are symptoms of a crisis and by nature unstable. For consciousness they function as an immune sys-tem, just as conflict does for the social system. They are the means by which consciousness can continue on a reduced level of perception regardless of consequences. In themselves, emotions are undirected and diffuse, but they are culturally specified and linked to claims. Accordingly, emotions can be subdued if claims are replaced by expectations or if the claims are regularly complied with or frustrated. The articulation of fulfillment and frustration impresses episodes on autopoiesis.

With the relation of claims and expectations, we have already reached the interpenetration of consciousness and society, the social and psychic supports of which converge in expectations: the social supports being laws and morality, the psychic being claims and emotions.

Next to expectation, language plays a decisive role in the interpenetration of social and psychic systems. With regard to this function, language cannot be identical to consciousness because in the interior monologue, ego lacks the relation to alter which is prerequisite to double contingency and communication. Instead, language transforms social into psychic complexity by impressing sequences on the stream of consciousness and thereby giving form to autopoiesis by means of cesurae, themes, transitions, new starts, etc., without putting an end to it for good.

As language and expectation are not identical to consciousness, they do not serve to explain how a psychic system is unmistakably individualized with regard to itself. We are not concerned here with the answers provided by cultural semantics but with the conditions under which consciousness can use these cultural products. In this case, too, the idea of unity can only be observed, and that means that it has to reappear as an indication within a difference. Here the decisive difference is that between the psychic and organic systems. By means of this differentiation, a psychic system identifies itself with the help of something other than itself, its own body. Since within this identification it only distinguishes itself from its own body and not from the whole world, it distinguishes its body from the world and marks its body off as its own. And this, then, is the basis for all further aggregation of individuality.

Because of the difference between their elements and between their respective forms of self-referentiality, the social and psychic systems constitute disorder for each other. Accordingly, the autonomy of each system's selectivity as expressed in the way they use each other is not jeopardized, because meaning provides the basis for this. Consciousness can continue its own course when communication ends, and communication can transcend consciousness. Both can appear simultaneously, but neither can be traced back to the other. Evolution moves along the inferential line of interpenetration because only those structures are preserved that are acceptable to both psychic and social systems.

Information or Expression?
The Environment of Theory

With the concept of communication, we are in the center of both systems theory as a theory of society and literary theory. The decisive point in the concept of communication is its triadic articulation as information, expression, and understanding, which shows a certain analogy to similar triads in linguistics.[12] For systems theory, "understanding" occupies a strategical position because it decides in what way the difference between information and expression can become manifest. Only from the point of view of understanding can this difference be comprehended as a boundary between the subject which creates the information by expression and the objective world of information. Both contain each other: the subject is the source and origin of the information, the objective world of information is the sphere in which the subject has to locate itself. Nevertheless, this difference can in no way be suspended. By reference to this difference, Luhmann is able to characterize other theories of communication as to whether they opt for either the objective world of information or the expression of the subject, and to what extent the difference between the two plays a part in any such theory. Two examples which by virtue of their contemporary potency help articulate the specific difference of systems theory are the oppositions between Husserl and Derrida, between Luhmann and Jürgen Habermas, and between structuralism and deconstruction.

In accordance with the absolute position of the subject in his philosophy, Husserl sides with expression and then runs into the problem of how one subject reaches another. Inversely, Luhmann sees Derrida on the side of information because he develops his theory from the concept of the sign (which Luhmann defines as a designation of something else). Given the method of Derrida's microscopic analysis, the limitation of perspective to information would then break it up into presence and absence; but the temporal displacement of unity and "differance" would be nothing else but the difference between information and expression from the point of view of information, a difference which is, however, only clearly seen from the point of view of understanding.

If Derrida wants to curtail the phonocentric privileges of presence in favor of a "differance" anterior to the difference of presence and absence, Luhmann, too, wants to explode all transcendental a prioris, all ontological foundations, and all basic concepts like substance, identity, etc., in favor of difference. Hence, Luhmann reaches similar conclusions regarding the relation of language and writing as Derrida, and one reason for this can be derived from his social theory: insofar as writing transcends interaction in the direction of society, it is an evolutionary achievement of the first order. But this can be made more specific with reference to the model of communication: writing removes the interactional pressure of presence from communication which, by the contagious effect of oral communication, tends to cover up the difference between expression and information in favor of information. Only writing reveals this difference necessary for communication, which makes writing a more "communicational" form of communication, for it reinforces a difference by which communication is constituted. Since writing is a more distinct form of communication, it enables communication to react to itself and become self-reflexive. As with Derrida, writing is not a decayed form of oral language; on the contrary, oral language is a prefiguration of writing in which the possibilities of language are revealed.

Luhmann's controversy with Habermas, however, is a different story.[13] Though Habermas's attack may have been motivated by Luhmann's "cool" dismissal of moral commitment as an organizing principle for theory, and though the controversy touched upon all major issues, the theoretically decisive difference can be located in the concept of communication: for Habermas, society must be measured by the possibility of a consensus reached by free people in the process of rational argumentation in an interaction undeformed by domination. This utopia of communication is quite interactionist, and there is a vision behind it of healing social evils via an institution dedicated to this ideal of rational communication—the university. So it is not surprising that Habermas has exerted such a lasting influence on the student movement and on pedagogy.

From the point of view of systems theory, it is impossible to solve social problems by recourse to interaction or to comprehend the whole of society from the limited perspective of a subsystem. But beyond that, the very concept of communication excludes the possibility of securing consensus by communication—not because the condition of freedom from domination cannot be realized, but because of the structure of communication. The decision as to whether to accept or refuse a communication does not fall within the range of communication itself as a unit of social autopoiesis; rather, it is a question of sequential linking of several communications in which the second reacts to the first with either acceptance or refusal. But this sequential arrangement into a process can only be brought about by the simplified self-description of communication as action which provides the condition for one communication to become the premise of the next. However, this creates possibilities of acceptance and refusal, for the asymmetrical self-description of communication as action is the condition for the continuous reproduction of double contingency. Therefore, every theory that attempts to bring communication and consensus into congruence falls prey to two misunderstandings at once: it imputes a sequential direction to communication from sender to receiver which can only be attributed to action as a self-simplification of communication, and it imputes to the conditioning of action (by the necessity of building up social order) that it could exclude dissent. But this is impossible, for it would remove the pressure of contingency which alone enforces the evolution of order. On Habermas's premises, one would have to accept the paradox that society keeps going only through its failure and that its success would destroy it. For systems theory, communication has to reproduce the continuous possibility of dissent, the discrepancy of perspectives— i.e., double contingency. It cannot conceive society from the point of view of consensus. Here, again, the basic concept is a difference, the difference between consensus and dissent. And this excludes any social utopia, for the regulation of dissent presupposes a consensus that may produce dissent.

It may have become obvious that systems theory thinks the concept of structure to be indispensable but grants it only a second rank in the assembly of fundamental concepts like system, meaning, time, etc. For social systems, structures regulate the reproduction of events by the reduction of equal probability of any event (contingency); this reduction is brought about by self-selective self-commitment of action for the future. Hence, social structures are structures of expectations, because every action is conceived within the horizon of the possibility for further action. While events are located on the level of the constitution of systems, the concept of structure refers to the level of the selection of events. And here structure is only one form of selection (the other being process). In social systems, only those patterns of selection that reproduce double contingency have a chance, and therefore, structures are only built up by pressure of contingency which they themselves have to reproduce in order to keep up their right to exist. As the condition for self-reproduction of a system, structure is also the condition for self-observation.

For Levi-Strauss the concept of structure refers not only to reality but to a model of reality. That raises the question of what happens when analysis encounters a form of reality which works with models of itself. Since the decision whether to confirm or criticize other models cannot be controlled by the concept of structure, it must be left to one's critical or conservative predilection. The same ambivalence between its analytical models and the self-descriptions of its object organizes the relation of structuralism to reality: once one has encountered structured order, it can only be attributed to reality, not to the observer. Hence, structuralism's marked preference for self-descriptions like texts, myths and discourses. The very concept of structure is the guarantee of objectivity. From the point of view of systems theory, structuralism—like so many communication theories—presupposes that order, which is only created by self-description under the pressure of contingency. Structuralism is a sort of epistemological ontology; it always imputes an order to reality which can only be understood in relation to its opposite—contingency, insecurity, etc. The difference between both order and contingency becomes visible only in a theoretical context dominated by the concept of system, for then structure can be understood to result from the necessity of the autopoietical reproduction of transitory events. That is why the concept of system supplants structure in the position in which the object and the conditions of its analysis coincide. The crucial point is the question of self-description: for structuralism it disappears behind its result, order; for systems theory it produces the difference (order and contingency) behind the autopoiesis of self-referential systems.

Like systems theory, deconstruction uses, as a point of reference, the phenomena of boundaries that are retraced in the context of semantic variants of the binary opposition between inside and outside (picture/frame, text/signature, work/commentary, etc). One would expect this asymmetrical relation of inside/outside to suggest the idea of the system/environment relation; however, Derrida sticks to the concept of structure, and this drives him—in the process of the deconstruction of structures—into paradoxes. First the opposition is reversed; then in a second step, the boundary between the two terms is established as a logical third. If one has reached that point, one cannot decide in which direction (of the opposition) to proceed, and that makes the difference collapse.

Boundaries in systems theory function as a sort of dam for the gradient between the system's and the environment's complexity, which only the system can produce. From the point of view of the system, they are self-generated boundaries which function whenever the system uses its own means to refer events to the inside or to the outside, i.e., when communication determines what may count as communication and what may not. Boundaries function by interrupting processes that link systems and environment and enable the system to dispose itself over its own contact with the environment by differentiating between the respects with which the interruption is effected. In this sense, boundaries are a system's achievement in the process of self-constitution. If this achievement is not attributed to the system, theory gets bogged down in paradoxes. The production of a paradox means that determination in the sense of a possible follow-up of further operations (to the inside or the outside) is no longer possible. This can be confirmed when one relates the problem of autopoiesis to the problem of the definition of boundaries. In autopoiesis, self-reference uses the operation that constitutes the respective self (as element, operation, or system): the amount that contains itself, "containing" meaning the self-constitution of the amount. The paradox results from negations: one can play off the constituting against the constituted act (although they are identical) and then no longer be able to choose. The problems which arise from such constellations have been elaborated with reference to Russell's theory of types, especially by Paul Watzlawick and his Palo Alto Group.[14]

For Luhmann, this shows the need for the creation of systems: by drawing boundaries, system differentiation dissolves paradoxes by the asymmetry between environment and system. The main difference of opinion between Luhmann and Derrida is the former's use of the concept of system, which illustrates that boundaries are dependent on systems and in fact are their achievement. By sticking to the concept of structure, Derrida simply ends up destroying it by producing paradoxes; the paradoxes themselves, however, remain tied to the concept of structure. Systems theory replaces the paradoxes of deconstruction with the movement of rendering self-referentiality asymmetrical by the building of systems and the irreversibility of time.

In the same way in which systems theory subordinates the concept of structure to that of system, it subordinates sign to meaning. We have seen that it was meaning that made the application of the theory of autopoiesis to society possible, for meaning reintroduces the system/environment boundary into the system and thereby combines self-referential closure with sensibility towards the environment. This determines the relation between the concept of language and semiotics. A sign is conceived as something that refers to something outside and other than itself. Though Luhmann concedes that words are sometimes used as signs, he does not consider language as a whole to be a simple network of signs. Instead, he replaces "sign" with the term "symbolic generalization," for in language, meaning is symbolically generalized; pluralities are summarized into unities (all dogs > "dog") so that, as condensed meaning, they can be reutilized in other situations with other participants in the communication. Language becomes a form of reaccessibility and, therefore, of self-referentiality of meaning. Accordingly, generalized symbols are not signs that simply signify something else; they incorporate the generalization of meaning which they themselves produce. As a consequence, the generalizations relate to all three dimensions of meaning. It is generalizations which channel connections in the sense of further expectations of meaning so that meaning sustains itself—as language—by means of autopoietic self-reproduction. Precisely because meaning is self-referential and because it is prerequisite to the use of signs, sign and meaning cannot be identical (if signs are defined as signifiers of something outside themselves). Meaning provides signs with a context which does not consist of signs.

Exit to System

The discussion of systems theory by the academic community is currently in full swing. Its reception by literary theory in particular is just about to begin. In this, the vanguard consists of a circle of literary scholars who meet regularly for interdisciplinary conferences at the Interuniversity Center of Dubrovnik under the guidance of Hans-Ulrich Gumbrecht. The proceedings of these conferences are published under the serial title "Der Diskurs der Literatur- und Sprachhistorie."

A great obstacle to the reception of systems theory by literary scholars, however, is its forbidding level of abstraction, which is necessary and misleading at the same time: necessary in order to extend the range of comparability to the discovery of self-referentiality; misleading because, by this very comparative method, investigation can reach down to the most microscopically intricate subjects. Systems theory can only be fruitfully applied if one sees through its theoretical premises. It is a very mobile and adaptable theory, but it is a theory with such a strong structure that it prohibits eclectic use. Inversely, this makes it possible to take up theoretical propositions on the highest level of abstraction and develop them independently for the purpose of adapting them to one's own field of investigation.

Another obstacle to its reception has to do with the repulsive aura of the term "system," which connotes rigidity, coldness, and enmity to throbbing life. Though this is understandable, it is particularly misleading and may encourage repression of the following central propositions:

1) No system (or theory) can ever gain control over its own complexity or that of its environment; no plan can ever anticipate all reactions to itself; and nobody can ever foresee the future.

2) The closure of systems does not mean rigidity but freedom to use distinction from the environment for self-determination.

3) Self-referentiality allots a subsidiary position to causality and a high rank to the concepts of meaning and freedom. This implies delimiting the range of science: what is inaccessible to it appears in the form of complexity, contingency, chance, and the concrete. It is the form in which the inaccessible becomes tractable. This is of vital interest to literary studies and, at first sight, constitutes an implausible paradox: in order to make the concrete tractable, they have to be guided by theory. The concrete cannot be explained with reference to the concrete, but only by the answer to the question of what makes abstractions possible.

For itself, systems theory chooses the relation between system and environment in order to be able to compare itself to its other objects. In doing this, it acts very much like the painter Velásquez when he painted *Las Meninas:* he did not isolate his self-portrait but painted *Las Meninas* in a situation in which he discovered himself while painting them, which put him in a position from which he could control his painting. In the same way, the concept of self-reference replaces all last foundations and transcendental a prioris. It also explodes the transcendental/empirical polarity. The concept of subject is replaced by that of self-referential systems (of which it is just one case), for there are other self-referential systems in the world. This will make nonsense of the distinction between science *(Naturwissenschaft)* and the humanities *(Geisteswissenschaften)*, and it means that there is no more need for a special methodology for the humanities such as hermeneutics. The hermeneutical circle is replaced by the self-referentiality of autopoiesis. But self-referentiality, like God, will only appear to those looking for it long enough. On the basis of natural epistemology, self-referentiality can only be discovered by theories of a wide range and never by theories of a limited scope. This difference between theories will replace the old difference between science and the humanities. And this, in turn, implies the advice to literary theory to reach out beyond its self-limitation in order to discover itself among its objects.

Notes

1. This essay is based upon the complete published work of Niklas Luhmann. In addition to this material, I have drawn quite extensively upon two of his unpublished manuscripts and have clarified some details through personal discussion with him.

The book Luhmann considers his most important is *Soziale Systeme: Grundriss einer allgemeinen Theorie* (Frankfurt am Main: Suhrkamp, 1984). In a recent newspaper interview *(Frankfurter Rundschau,* 27 April 1986), he added the comment: "In any case, it will be the point of reference for publications from posthumous papers."

See the bibliography following these notes for a list of other important publications by Luhmann.

2. Cf. D. T. Campbell, "Evolutionary Epistemology," in *The Philosophy of Karl R. Popper,* ed. P. A. Schilpp (La Salle, Ill.: Open Court, 1974).

3. The logic of differentiation (between system and environment) operates with a theory of form which knows only one fundamental difference—form and everything else. For the foundation of the logic, see George Spencer Brown, *Laws of Form* (London: George Allen and Unwin, 1972), which also provided the foundation for Luhmann's theory of self-observation.

4. Cf. Plato: *Parmenides,* 495C–497C; 505C–506B; *Theaetetus,* 545B–547B; *Sophist,* 566A–D. Cf. Aristotle: *Physics,* I, 2, 260B–C; III, 6,

285B–D; IV, 3, 289B–C; *Metaphysics*, V, 6, 536A–537C; V, 26, 545E–D; X, 1, 578B, D–580A; *Nicomachean Ethics*, X, 4, 428B–429A; *Politics*, I, 1, 445B; I, 2, 446C.

5. Originally, theorists used the weaker term "self-organization." In order to include the meaning of "self-creation," it was increasingly replaced by "autopoiesis." Cf. Marshal C. Yovits and Scott Cameron (eds.), *Self-organizing Systems* (Oxford: Oxford University Press, 1960); and Heinz von Foerster and George W. Zopf (eds.), *Principles of Self-Organization* (Oxford: Oxford University Press, 1962).

6. Derrida has shown that the idea of presence (in contrast to absence) may nevertheless inhabit the temporal conception like a Trojan horse and thereby contract our idea of being to the third-person singular of the present tense.

7. This is the condition for the narrative technique of the novel to dramatize the past into present past.

8. To translate Luhmann's word *Mitteilung* as "expression" is certainly misleading because the English term carries the connotation of revealing the interior of the mind, which, according to systems theory, is quite impossible. However, in this context the point is to characterize *Mitteilung* as a selection of the subject dominated by its own communicativeness; therefore, "expression" serves the purpose much better than the literal "message."

9. Luhmann uses *Bewusstseinssystem* when he wants to distinguish it from *soziale Systeme;* but he seems to prefer *psychische Systeme* when he wants to indicate their individuality. Until now, we have disregarded the demands of strict terminology, but from now on we shall speak either of "consciousness" or "psychic systems."

10. This presentation of system consciousness relies upon an as yet unpublished manuscript by Luhmann entitled "Die Autopoiesis des Bewusstseins." This manuscript formed the basis for a lecture delivered during a conference on "Bekenntnis und Gestandnis: Formen der Selbstthematisierung," which was held in May 1985 at the University of Trier.

11. Historically, it seems symptomatic that the development of the philosophy of the subject was accompanied by a reflexion on ennui.

12. For example, Buhler's "Darstellung/Ausdruck/Appell" or Austin's locutionary/illocutionary/perlocutionary acts.

13. Apart from the collection of Habermas's and Luhmann's contributions under the title *Theorie der Gesellschaft oder Sozialtechnologie* (Frankfurt am Main: Suhrkamp, 1971), the contributions of further participants in the clash of systems theory and critical theory have been collected in three supplementary volumes under the same title between 1973 and 1975. More recently, Habermas has launched another attack on Luhmann in his survey of modern theory, published under the title *Der philosophische Diskurs der Moderne* (Frankfurt am Main: Suhrkamp, 1985). See pages 420–45. This shows, however, that Habermas has changed his attitude

considerably, having even adapted parts of systems theory to his own purposes; and he qualifies Luhmann's systems theory "to be incomparable as to its theoretical creativity, its conceptual cogency and the scope of its applicability" (411).

14. Cf. Watzlawick et al., *Pragmatics of Human Communication* (New York: Norton, 1967).

Niklas Luhmann's Publications

Funktionen und Folgen formaler Organisationen. Berlin: Duncker and Humbolt, 1964.

Vertrauen: Ein Mechanismus der Reduktion sozialer Komplexität. Stuttgart: Enke, 1968.

Zweckbegriff und Systemrationalität. Tübingen: Mohr, 1968.

Legitimation durch Verfahren. Neuwied am Rhein and Berlin: Luchterhand, 1969.

Soziologische Aufklärung. 4 vols. Opladen: Westdeutscher Verlag, 1970–81.

Politische Planung. Opladen: Westdeutscher Verlag, 1971.

Theorie der Gesellschaft oder Sozialtechnologie. With Jürgen Habermas. Frankfurt am Main: Suhrkamp, 1971.

Rechtssoziologie. 2 vols. Reinbek bei Hamburg: Rowohlt, 1972.

Macht. Stuttgart: Enke, 1975.

Funktion der Religion. Frankfurt am Main: Suhrkamp, 1977.

Theorietechnik und Moral. Edited by Luhmann and G. H. Pfürtner. Frankfurt am Main: Suhrkamp, 1978.

Reflexionsprobleme im Erziehungssystem. With K. E. Schorr. Stuttgart: Klett-Cotta, 1979.

Gesellschaftsstruktur und Semantik: Studien zur Wissenssoziologie der modernen Gesellschaft. 2 vols. Frankfurt am Main: Suhrkamp, 1980–81.

Liebe als Passion: Zur Codierung von Intimität. Frankfurt am Main: Suhrkamp, 1982.

Zwischen Technologie und Selbstreferenz: Fragen an die Pädagogik. With K. E. Schorr. Frankfurt am Main: Suhrkamp, 1982.

Soziale Systeme: Grundriss einer allgemeinen Theorie. Frankfurt am Main: Suhrkamp, 1984.

Ökologische Kommunikation. Opladen: Westdeutscher Verlag, 1986.

Engendering
Critical
Discourse

Patrocinio Schweickart

It is inevitable that *1984* should be invoked in the context of the current debate about the nature and the function of interpretation. According to Steven Mailloux, Winston Smith represents the "objectivist"/"foundationalist" camp: E. D. Hirsch, M. H. Abrams, and others who believe that the hermeneutic project has to be grounded on a stable, objective, verbal meaning, immanent either in the text or in the intention of the author. O'Brien, on the other hand, represents the "subjectivist"/"pragmatist" camp—people who believe with Stanley Fish and Richard Rorty that because the apprehension of objects and facts is always a function of belief, there can be no objective ground for interpretation and knowledge.[1]

Mailloux's commentary on *1984* underscores the two focal issues of the current discussion of the nature of interpretation: the issue of truth or validity, and the issue of power. The "naive realist ontology" and "simplistic commonsense epistemology" of the objectivist/foundationalist position have been under heavy attack in recent years. Meaning, according to reader-response theorists, is something that is constructed rather than discovered by the reader. Different readers will read the same text differently, and disagreements in interpretation cannot be settled by simply appealing to what is in the text. The objective constraints posed by the text, says David Bleich, are "trivial," since they can always be overruled by subjective action.[2] Fish argues that the meanings we read out of a text are always a function of the interpretive strategies we employ: "Strictly speaking, getting 'back-to-the-text' is not a move one can perform, because the text one gets back to will be the text demanded by some other interpretation—and that interpretation will be presiding over its production."[3] Walter Benn Michaels suggests: "Our beliefs are not obstacles between us and meaning, they are what make meaning possible in the first place."[4] While literary critics are most interested in the interpretation of texts, the terms of the discussion apply as well to the interpretation of reality. Rorty argues that the "notion of reality as having a 'nature' to which it is our duty to correspond is simply one more variant of the notion that the gods can be placated by chanting the right words. The notion that some one among the languages mankind [sic] has used to deal with the universe is the one the universe prefers—the one that cuts things at the joints—was a pretty conceit. But by now it has become too shopworn to serve any purpose."[5]

The second issue prominent in the critical debate concerns the political implications of these theories.[6] The appeal of the subjectivist/pragmatist position is based to a large extent on the cogency of its critique of the authoritarian implications of objectivist hermeneutics, and on the liberal, egalitarian and democratic values implicit in its advocacy of the prerogatives of the interpreter. If meaning/knowledge is something that is constructed rather than discovered, if there is no one stable "objective" text/reality that the knower is obliged to represent as accurately as possible, then, in principle, each person is free to act according to her own interests and needs: meaning becomes the responsibility of the reader. The decline of the authority of the text is associated, first of all, with an increase in the value accorded to the experience and perspective of the reader, and secondly, with greater respect for the multiplicity and variability of interpretive behavior.

Unfortunately, the moral argument in favor of pragmatism can easily be reversed. The demise of the objectivist hermeneutics does not necessarily make the interpretation into an anarchic free-for-all, because an individual never constructs meaning in isolation. Interpretation is always situated in an interpretive community and subject to its canons of acceptability. Moreover, the community—specifically, the profession or the critical establishment—sets the agenda for discussion. As Fish puts it: "Anyone who is able to advance the discussion of [the topics central to the institution's concerns] will automatically be accorded a hearing and be a candidate for the profession's highest rewards."[7] Fish does not say so explicitly, but the converse is equally true: anyone who does not adapt herself to the institutional agenda will be ignored, edged out of positions of professional influence, and possibly starved out—literally and meta-phorically—of the profession itself.

The example of *1984* accentuates the dangers implicit in a subjectivist hermeneutic. In his debate with Smith in the Ministry of Love, O'Brien argues that reality exists in the human mind and nowhere else—but not in the individual mind, "only in the mind of the Party, which is collective and immortal. Whatever the Party holds to be the truth *is* truth. It is impossible to see reality except by looking through the eyes of the Party."[8] If the notion of objective truth is rendered meaningless, so the argument goes, the individual is deprived of any independent ground for contesting the hegemony of the state. People will be "without any impulse to rebel," because they will be "without the power to grasp that the world could be other than it is" (173).[9] With the standard of truth gone, power becomes the sole arbiter of discourse. Mailloux calls attention to the affinity between O'Brien's theory of "collective solipsism" and Fish's theory of the authority of the interpretive community. In both cases, authority—the power to regulate the process of interpretation and therefore to define reality—is vested in the ruling institution (the Party in one case, and the interpretive community or literary and critical establishment in the other).

We see, then, that a commitment to truth and freedom lies at the heart of *both* the foundationalist and the pragmatist positions, but, at the same time, that a hermeneutic originally motivated by egalitarian ideals can become terroristic. Is the dystopian inversion inevitable? Is it possible to define the enterprise of interpretation so that it is a defense against rather than an instrument of oppression?

Interestingly enough, Orwell's novel revolved around similar questions: What is the reason for the inversion of the socialist dream into the nightmare of Ingsoc? "*Why* should human equality be averted? . . . what is the motive for this huge, accurately planned effort to freeze history at a particular moment of time?" (178). The answer given by O'Brien in the Ministry of Love is usually taken as authoritative: the key to the enigma of the dystopian inversion is the power-madness that drives all revolutions. "The Party seeks power entirely for its own sake. . . . Power is not a means; it is an end. One does not establish a dictatorship to protect a revolution; one makes a revolution in order to establish a dictatorship" (217). However, there is another reading latent in Orwell's text.

Recall that just as Goldstein is about to answer the questions posed above, Winston's reading is arrested in mid-sentence:

"The motive really consists . . ."
Winston became aware of silence as one becomes aware of a
new sound. It seemed to him that Julia had been very still for
some time past. . . .
"Julia."
No answer.
"Julia, are you awake?" (179)

Failing to get a response from Julia, Winston stops reading and
goes to sleep himself. The Thought Police arrive shortly after they
wake up. If I were to read *1984* as a tragedy, I would take the
moment cited above as the crucial point when disaster could have
been averted. We never know Goldstein's answer, but the arrangement of the text suggests that the key to the enigma of history is in
Julia's silence. Her silence interrupts the discourse of the brotherhood.
Unfortunately, to Winston's unaccustomed ears, this "new sound"
signifies nothing. His failure to attend to Julia's silence seals his cap-
tivity within the discourse of the brotherhood. The rest, as O'Brien
might say, is history.[10]

▼

It is clear to me that, at least in the domain of literary criticism,
it is pointless to reinstitute the objectivist point of view. The criticisms
against it are too cogent. Our best bet, I believe, is to develop the
utopian potential of the pragmatist position in such a way as to block
the dystopian inversion. Pragmatism offers two advantages. First of
all, it situates knowledge, truth, and meaning in human interests and
social practices. Pragmatism makes the interpreter into a participant
rather than a spectator and gives hermeneutics "an aim appropriate
to humans rather than to gods."[11] Freed from the obligation to find
the one language that cuts things or texts at the joints, we come to
appreciate the value of language as a means of "altering ourselves
and our environment to suit our aspirations."[12] Secondly, pragmatism has the advantage of consolidating our awareness that we are
social beings—that knowledge, meaning, truth, and reality are produced through discourse, and discourse implies an intersubjective
relation.[13] It follows that ethics and politics, rather than metaphysics,
is the proper object of inquiry for theorists of discourse. These two
advantages form the basis of the feminist interest in pragmatism.

Unfortunately, the greatest amount of energy has been expended on proving only that discourse, reading, and interpretation
are intersubjective activities that take place in the context of a community; the conversation tends to get mired in the tedious themes of

the objectivism/relativism debate. I will assume that the pragmatists have won the argument: knowledge and meaning make sense only if we think of them as something that is attained intersubjectively, through discourse. It is now time to inquire into the nature of the intersubjectivity implicit in discourse. Let me stress that my aim is to develop the utopian potential of the pragmatist position. Eventually, gender will emerge as a key issue. The utopian potential of discourse—the hopes that inspire the quest for truth and meaning—will remain illusory so long as discourse is constituted as the discourse of brotherhood.

Among theories of discourse, the work of Jürgen Habermas is distinguished by its explicit linking of pragmatics and ethics. According to Habermas, truth or validity is not a property intrinsic to propositions, but a *claim* implicitly made in the act of uttering an assertion. He advocates a consensus theory of truth: "In order to distinguish true from false statements I make reference to the judgment of others. . . . The condition of the truth of statements is the potential agreement of all others."[14] On the surface, he appears to concur with Fish. The process of validation proceeds along the model of persuasion rather than the model of demonstration. However, Habermas is careful to distinguish two terms that Fish conflates— *truth* and *belief. Belief* is a subjective "certainty-experience," but *validity* or *truth claim* is something that is meant to be tested intersubjectively. One cannot assert meaningfully that something is true or valid only for oneself. I *have* beliefs, prejudices, or presuppositions; but I *make* validity claims.

When I make a validity claim, the horizon of my assertion extends beyond *de facto* consensus. The *de facto* approval of the community—indicated, say, by the awarding of professional honors—is not a sufficient warrant of truth. The warrant for truth is consensus attained under conditions of an *ideal* speech situation, where the outcome of the discussion is determined only by the "unforced force of the better argument." An ideal speech situation satisfies two structural requirements:

1) Universal symmetry must obtain: the opportunity to select and employ speech acts must be equitably distributed among all the participants of the discourse. In addition, there should be no internal or external structures that impose nonreciprocal obligations on the participants or allow some of them to dominate others.

2) There must not be any constraints on communication that prevent the progressive "radicalization of discourse." Everything—

specific assertions, theoretical explanations, language-systems, and theories of knowledge—must be open to question.

Habermas is aware that actual conversations often fail to meet the requirements of an ideal speech situation, since structures of domination are endemic in our present reality. However, this does not nullify his argument. Domination-free discourse is a legitimate regulative ideal: it can be more or less approximated in reality, and it can serve as a guide for organizing discourse and as a critical standard against which actual conversations can be measured. Furthermore, Habermas argues, the ideal speech situation is constitutive: it "is neither an empirical phenomenon nor a mere construct, but rather an unavoidable supposition reciprocally made in [argumentative] discourse. This supposition can, but need not be counterfactual; but even if it is made counterfactually, it is a fiction that is operative in the process of communication."[15] The idea of settling a truth claim "on its merits" becomes meaningless unless we adopt the fiction that discourse is free of structures of domination that can interfere with the force of the better argument.

The debate between Smith and O'Brien in the Ministry of Love looks different in light of Habermas's theory. O'Brien is intent on persuading Smith that "whatever the Party holds to be truth *is* truth." For his part, Smith is intent on contesting the Party's control over the truth. He rests his case on the claim that objective reality is external to human subjectivity; it exists in its own right, and is compelling and self-evident to all impartial minds. He believes, for example, in the innocence of three men who were executed for treason because he has seen a photograph indicating that their confessions were false. To prove this, all he has to do is produce the photograph. Similarly, he insists that two and two are four because he cannot "help seeing what is in front of [his] eyes" (207).

O'Brien counters by demonstrating that neither documentary evidence nor sense-certainty is decisive. He taunts Smith by showing him a slip of paper that appears to be the photograph proving the innocence of the three men:

> For only an instant it was before his eyes, then it was out of sight again. But he had seen it, unquestionably he had seen it! He made a desperate, agonizing effort to wrench the top half of his body free. . . . All he wanted was to hold the photograph in his fingers again, or at least to see it.
> "It exists!" he cried.
> "No," said O'Brien. (204)

At this he lifted the grate covering the memory hole, and soon "the frail slip of paper . . . was vanishing in a flash of flame." "Ashes," says O'Brien triumphantly. "Not even identifiable ashes. Dust. It does not exist. It never existed" (204). Similarly, O'Brien shows that if the Party says two and two make five, then that is the case. Of course, his persuasiveness is a function of his power to inflict pain. As the pain intensifies, Winston is unable to cling to the evidence of his senses. Eventually, O'Brien is completely victorious. Winston *agrees* that if the Party says two and two make five, then it must be so.

Mailloux argues that Smith was bound to lose the debate, not only because "he confronts the overwhelming power of the state but because he presents such a weak case for his hermeneutic position. He fails to understand that his commonsense 'facts' are as much a product of interpretation as are the Party's; and he clings to a naive realist ontology and a simplistic commonsense epistemology" that is no match for O'Brien's more sophisticated hermeneutic argument.[16] Given Orwell's lurid description of torture, I wonder how Mailloux can calmly discount O'Brien's power to intimidate and inflict pain. From the point of view of Habermas's theory, O'Brien's command of the instruments of torture is decisive. The relative merits of validity claims cannot be determined under conditions of domination. However, Habermas would agree that the objectivist position is untenable. Winston's faith in objective reality is misplaced. The notion of truth is rendered meaningless in Oceania not because of the Party's power to manipulate historical documents—Orwell's paramount symbol for objective reality—but because of its power to control discourse. As O'Brien puts it: "The real power, the power we have to fight for night and day, is not power over things, but over men" (219).

The example of *1984* also corroborates Habermas's contention that even when it is counterfactual, the fiction of an ideal speech situation is constitutive of discourse. We note first of all that this fiction is implicit in Smith's discursive behavior. He struggles desperately to construct an argument that will persuade O'Brien. That is, he tries to muster the only force he has at his disposal—the unforced force of the better argument. In spite of the actual situation, he behaves as if discourse were free of structures of domination. Given the (counterfactual) supposition of an ideal speech situation, Smith's behavior makes sense (even if it seems silly of him to think that the force of the better argument can be much help against a torturer). The rationale for O'Brien's behavior, however, is less clear. His principal interest is to dominate, and he certainly has the means to do so. Why, then, does he bother to construct arguments? To answer this question (assuming that O'Brien's behavior is realistic) we need to know something about the psychology of torturers and of ideological domination. The point I want to make, however, is that our reaction to O'Brien's behavior also illustrates Habermas's contention that the ideal speech situation is constitutive of argumentative discourse. O'Brien's discursive behavior is puzzling because its argumentative character leads us to think that he is operating under the assumption that discourse is domination-free even though such an assumption is inconsistent with his personality and his function. This example suggests that in its own perverse way, even the discourse of domination presupposes the ideal of domination-free discourse.

The two issues prominent in current discussions of interpretation—the issue of validity and the issue of politics—are simultaneously addressed by Habermas's model of an ideal speech situation. In light of this model, validity becomes not the property of interpretations in themselves, but a claim implicit in the act of advancing an interpretation. When I propose a reading of a text, I am implicitly submitting my sense of the meaning of the work to the judgment of others, and I am signalling my willingness to have the merits of my reading examined and tested through rational discourse that is governed only by the force of the better argument. In other words, my confidence that my interpretation will be vindicated in domination-free discourse is the measure of my confidence in its validity. In Habermas's view, the notion of truth or validity hinges on the notion of domination-free discourse.

————————▼————————

It might appear at first glance that Habermas's solution to the problem of validation represents the full elaboration of the utopian potential of pragmatism. However, at this point we must recall Julia's silence. The ideal speech situation described by Habermas is an exemplary embodiment of the ideals of the enlightenment. It links rationality and truth with liberty, equality *and* . . . fraternity. It is, in short, an ideal that has been abstracted from the discourse of the brotherhood. As such, it embodies masculine interests and intuitions—a masculine sense of self and the intersubjectivity of man-to-man relationships.

The abstract argument against Habermas is easy to see: an ideal that excludes half the human race is clearly suspect.[17] However, the problem cannot be remedied by stipulating simply that women should be encouraged to develop argumentative skills and to participate in discourse. Going back to *1984*, we notice that, on the face of it, Julia's silence cannot be blamed on sexual discrimination. Oceania under Ingsoc appears to be a sex-blind society. In fact, Winston tries very hard to include Julia: "You must read it [Goldstein's contraband book]," he says to her. "You too. All members of the Brotherhood have to read it" (165). But the discourse of the brotherhood fails to engage Julia—it puts her to sleep. Women's relative lack of enthusiasm for the argumentative mode exalted by Habermas is as significant as the discrimination against them, and this lack of interest is a sign not only of a deficiency in women, but also of a flaw in the model itself. What is at issue, as much as the exclusion of women, is the exclusion of the perspectives, interests, values, and modes of interaction associated (historically, socially, and culturally) with women.

Thanks to feminist theory, our understanding of gender has advanced far enough so that we can be more specific about what is bracketed out of androcentric accounts of discourse. Evidence has been accumulating that there are fundamental differences in the "interactive competence"[18] of males and females and that these differences are developed at an early age.[19] For example, markedly different interactive patterns are evident in children's play. Girls' play tends to be organized in terms of a community of equals. Girls prefer to form leaderless groups, while boys tend to create a structured hierarchy of peers (this is consistent with Orwell's insight that the emergence of Big Brother follows from the logic of brotherhood). Moreover, much of girls' activities and interactions are mediated by talk. "Girls learn to do three things with words: 1) to create and maintain relationships of closeness and equality, 2) to criticize others in acceptable ways, and 3) to interpret accurately the speech of other girls."[20]

Boys, on the other hand, learn to use language: "1) to assert a position of dominance, 2) to attract and maintain an audience, and 3) to be assertive when other speakers have the floor." There is a sharp contrast between girls' well-developed sensitivity to others and their preference for shared storytelling and boys' ability to sustain a monologue even in the absence of overt support. "The storyteller is frequently faced with mockery, challenges, and side comments on his story. A major sociolinguistic skill which a boy must apparently learn in interacting with his peers is to ride out this series of challenges, maintain his audience, and successfully get to the end of his story."[21]

Researchers have found that these differences are carried into adulthood. Men's discourse often takes on the quality of a verbal tournament, characterized by monologic storytelling, arguing, and verbal posturing:

> (1) women see questions as part of conversational maintenance while men see them as requests for information;
> (2) women explicitly acknowledge previous utterances and try to connect with them while men have no such rule and often ignore preceding comments;
> (3) women interpret aggression as personal, negative, and disruptive while men view it as simply one conventional organizing structure for conversational flow;
> (4) men shift topics quickly while women develop them progressively and shift gradually;
> (5) women share experiences, offer reassurances, and give mutual support; men hear problems as requests for solutions and respond by giving direction and advice, acting as experts, or lecturing their audience.[22]

Studies of teaching style consistently report that in general there is more student participation in women's classrooms regardless of department, course level, sex ratio, or class size. Men lecture more, and they tend to emphasize mastery of course content. Women teachers tend to be less direct in their reprimands, and they prefer to avoid the appearance of the assertion of authority when correcting or criticizing their students, while men are more often "direct, harsh and ridiculing."[23]

Studies of cross-sex conversations show "gross asymmetries" in the frequency of interruptions (defined not simply as speech overlaps, but as "deep intrusions into the internal structure of a speaker's speech," which "have a potential to disrupt a speaker's turn"): an overwhelming majority of the interruptions observed (96 percent in one study) were done by males to females; "in every conversation, the male interrupted the female more frequently than the converse."[24] At the same time, it appears that there is "an unequal distribution of work in conversation." The data in a study of male/female couples showed that "women tried more often and succeeded less often in getting conversations going, whereas the men tried less often and seldom failed in their attempts." The women introduced considerably more topics than the men, but most of the topics introduced by the women were dropped; almost all of those introduced by the men were picked up and developed into conversations.

We can see from the differential use of strategies that the women are more actively engaged in insuring interaction than the men. They ask more questions and use more attention beginnings. Women do support work while the men are talking and it is the women who generally do active maintenance and continuation work in conversations. . . . The failure of the women's attempts at interaction . . . [is due] to the failure of the men to respond, to do interactional work. The success of the men's attempts is due to the women doing interactional work in response to remarks by men. . . . [Thus] what part of the world the interactants orient to, construct, and maintain the reality of, is his choice, not hers. Yet the women labor hardest in making interactions go.[25]

Carole Edelsky's study of interaction in mixed-sex faculty committees is worth mentioning. Edelsky found that there are two models of discursive interaction. The first is the "stereotypical kind where one speaker at a time holds the floor, so that a single speaker is on center stage." The second involves a "collaborative floor developed by several people operating on the same wave length or engaged in a seeming free-for-all." The first model is characterized by monologic, single-party control of talk and features the sorts of interactions "where floors are won and lost." They resemble "other contexts in which women have learned they had best not assert themselves." The second model of faculty discussion is more congenial to women. Edelsky suggests that these more informal cooperative situations "provide a cover of anonymity for assertive language use and a comfortable backdrop against which women can display a fuller range of language ability."[26]

Gender-differences in discursive behavior are consistent with the differences in moral and cognitive development found by Carol Gilligan. According to Gilligan, the moral and cognitive development in males is informed principally by the drive toward individuation and autonomy, in women by the need to form and sustain relationships. Of course, the difference is complex, subtle, and difficult to pinpoint, but Gilligan's theory owes much of its persuasiveness to the shock of recognition elicited by her examples. One pair in particular capture the gist of her claim that men operate according to an "ethic of rights," and women according to an "ethic of care" (or "responsibility").

Text A

[Morality] is recognizing the right of the individual, the rights of others, not interfering with those rights. Act as fairly as you would have them treat you. I think it is basically to preserve the human being's right to existence. I think that is the most important. Secondly, the human being's right to do as he pleases, again without interfering with somebody else's rights.[27]

Text B

We need to depend on each other, and hopefully it is not only a physical need but a need of fulfillment in ourselves, that a person's life is enriched by cooperating with other people and striving to live in harmony with everybody else, and to that end, there are right and wrong, there are things which promote that end and that move away from it, and in that way it is possible to choose in certain cases among different courses of action that obviously promote or harm that goal. . . . There are certain things that you come to learn promote a better life and better relationships and more personal fulfillment than other things that in general tend to do the opposite, and the things that promote these things, you would call morally right.[28]

▼

Text A comes from a 25-year-old man. It was one of the responses that formed the basis for Lawrence Kohlberg's theory of moral development. The central theme in this text is the passage from the recognition of the principle of individual rights to the definition of human rights as a reciprocity of rights. According to Kohlberg, this young man's definition of morality exemplifies the highest stages (stages five and six) of moral development. "Moving to a perspective outside of that of his society, he identifies morality with justice (fairness, rights, the Golden Rule), with recognition of the rights of others as these are defined naturally and intrinsically. The human being's right to do as he pleases without interfering with somebody else's rights is a formula defining rights prior to social legislation."[29]

Text B comes from a 25-year-old woman who participated in Gilligan's study. When asked to describe herself, she said that she valued "having other people that I am tied to, and also having people that I am responsible to. I have a very strong sense of being responsible to the world, that I can't live just for my enjoyment, but just the fact of being in the world gives me an obligation to do what I can to make the world a better place to live in, no matter how small a scale that may be on." The woman's "very strong sense of being responsible to the world," and of being "tied to" others contrasts with the young man's concern with the individual's "right to do as he pleases." While he worries about interfering with other people's rights (and with others interfering with his own), she worries about "the possibility of omission, of your not helping others when you could help them."[30]

Gilligan's terminology, which contrasts a concern with *rights* to a concern with *responsibility* can be misleading. It is often pointed out that the notion of rights is connected to the notion of responsibilities—the assertion of certain rights implies the assumption of certain responsibilities. I would like to point out the confusion that arises from the different meaning "responsibility" assumes in male and female discourse. In the context of an ethic of rights, "responsibility" is bound up not only with the notion of being in charge of something, but also with the notion of liability. The "responsible party" is the one who is liable for damages if things go awry. Being a responsible father means accepting the obligation for the financial support of your offspring; being responsible for fathering a child means that you could be sued for support payments.

In the context of an ethic of care, "responsibility" has different connotations. When a woman says she feels burdened by family responsibilities, she is generally not thinking of the possibility of being sued; and even though financial considerations may be a major component of her anxiety, the obligation to pay is seldom experienced subjectively as the only or even the central concern. For a woman, the weight of responsibility is, in general, experienced in connection with feeling overwhelmed by the needs of others, with being pulled in opposite directions by conflicting needs, with anxiety about whether she can meet these needs adequately. When one thinks of "responsibility" in the context of an ethic of care, one should keep in mind that the accent is on *responsiveness*.

▼

According to Habermas's reconstruction of communicative competence, the act of making an assertion involves a truth claim put forth by the speaker with the expectation that she will be able to obtain the agreement of others. The ideal speech situation is concerned above all with discourse oriented toward the production of understanding, which, further, is to be taken principally to mean the attainment of agreement. Agreement, or more specifically, "rational consensus" is the privileged mode of intersubjectivity in Habermas's theory of discourse; all other forms of intersubjectivity are bracketed out. The bare-bones intersubjectivity of Habermas's ideal speech situation evades both the problems and the promise implicit in the intersubjective construction of cognition and of the notion of validity.

Habermas's concept of ideal discourse is an exemplary expression of interactive competence that has been shaped by an ethic of rights. He links the idea of truth and validity with the ideal of free speech. Notice that the most distinctive feature of this model—the principle of nondomination—is the translation of the principle of reciprocity and noninterference from the personal to the discursive dimension. However, the model does not incorporate the obligation to be responsive to the voice of the other, to protect and nurture fragile speech, to assume responsibility for doing "interactive labor," to draw out, to facilitate, to engender and cultivate the speech of the other. What is more, Habermas's tough-minded allegiance to the force of the better argument and his obsession with formal schematization serves to bracket out behavior and values associated with an ethic of care—that is, feminine traits which in the discourse of the brotherhood are often disparaged as sentimentality. In *1984*, Orwell warns against the ever-present danger of the dystopian inversion of the utopian project. The lesson is applicable to Habermas's reconstruction of a universal pragmatics that affirms and promotes the emancipatory potential of speech. To see what the dystopian inversion of the ideal speech situation might be like, let me invoke another literary example, Sartre's *No Exit*.

The play is set in hell, and it features a conversation involving three characters—a man and two women. Notice that the structural conditions of Habermas's ideal speech situation hold. In Sartre's hell, men and women are equal. There are no apparent structures of domination, and there are no constraints on discourse. The opportunity to speak is uniformly distributed among the participants, and each is free to argue, to explain, to question, to criticize, to appeal, to interrupt, to intimidate, etc. There are no asymmetrical obligations, and everything is open to question. And yet, clearly, the speech situation presented by Sartre is far from ideal. It is also worth noting that although the play is set in hell, its effectiveness depends on the realism of the interaction between the characters—on the audience's recognition that the frustrating, aggravating (in a word, hellish) conversation they are watching is reminiscent of real-life conversations they have experienced.

No Exit illustrates that the absence of structures of domination is a necessary but by no means sufficient condition for an ideal speech situation. Habermas's model stipulates the negative condition—non-domination—but this does not imply that the social relations required for the collaborative production and validation of meaning would ensue. The obvious problem in hell is that the participants in the conversation lack "good faith." However, for the purpose of this essay, I will set aside the issue of good faith except to note that although Habermas stipulates a sincerity requirement for the participants of an ideal speech situation, his discussion of the issue of good faith or sincerity seriously underestimates its ramifications. What I want to do now is to focus on another issue raised by Sartre's play, namely, the issue of intelligibility. Habermas disposes of this issue quickly. The redemption of validity claims through discourse presupposes that speakers can comprehend each other, but this is taken to be a simple matter: they must use a language that is mutually intelligible, and each must be willing to explain obscure terms. The assumption here is that language is representational and transparent, that meaning is given in utterances. *No Exit* illustrates the idea of the indeterminacy of utterances and of the active role of the reader or hearer in producing meaning.[31] The text does not insure that the hearer's interpretation will correspond to the intention or the expectation of the speaker. In Sartre's play, communication is blocked not by disagreement, but by the failure of speakers to obtain a good hearing. Hell is being trapped forever in conversation not with people who disagree with you, but with people who cannot or will not be good listeners.

In Habermas's model, discourse is construed entirely from the point of view of speech. The participants in the ideal speech situation are regarded only in their capacity as speakers; as such, they have reciprocal rights and obligations. Each has the right to speak as he sees fit; each has the obligation to protect (or at least not to obstruct) the right of others to speak freely. Nothing is stipulated about subjects in their capacity as hearers. The assumption, of course, is that nothing needs to be stipulated. Meaning is transmitted through language. In the ideal case, it is transmitted intact from speaker to hearer. The hearer passively receives the message in the utterance—i.e., the propositional content and the implicit validity claims. His subjective activity is restricted to testing claims, judging the cogency of arguments, and deciding which ones merit agreement. The process of interpretation is left entirely out of consideration.

Of course, interpretation is not simply a matter of taking out of an utterance whatever the speaker has put in. Interpretations of texts, like interpretations of reality, are shaped by the interests, experience, and point of view of the interpreter. Hearers/readers (I am deliberately ignoring the difference) are producers of meaning, and what they hear/read out of a text depends at least in part on what they put in. The same text can call forth divergent interpretations, and we cannot determine the validity of these interpretations by appealing to a correspondence theory of meaning any more than we can determine the validity of a claim about reality by appealing to a correspondence theory of truth.

Discourse involves not only the interaction between different subjects, but also that between different modalities of subjectivity. All speech acts presuppose hearers as well as speakers. When I speak, I do so with the expectation of being heard. Any theory of communicative action and interactive competence must take account of the role of the hearer no less than that of the speaker, and any conception of an ideal speech situation must include an account of the norms and values implicit in the ideal of being a good listener.

The inadequacy of the bare-bones intersubjectivity emphasized by Habermas becomes apparent as soon as we look at the role of the hearer. As hearer, I encounter the voice of an other, expressing interests, experiences, intuitions, perceptions, ideas, needs, that are not my own. I am expected to be a good listener—but what does it mean to be a good listener? A universal symmetry requirement is useless here. Little is gained by stipulating the uniform distribution of the opportunity to obtain a good hearing, since this can mean no more than the uniform distribution of the opportunity to speak without interference, and, as everyone knows, one can speak freely, but this does not mean that anyone will listen. In fact, the interactive competence implicit in being a good listener eludes the conceptual scheme of an ethic of rights.

There are two obvious models of the role of the hearer/reader: a text-dominant model which invests control and authority on the text, and a reader-dominant model which emphasizes the subjective activity of the reader. Pragmatism is based on the argument that the first alternative is impossible. My own perspective, interests, needs, and predispositions necessarily color and shape the meaning that I attribute to the speech of the other. At the same time, an interpretation that completely assimilates another's utterance into my own subjective interests is at odds with the idea of being a good listener. Being a good listener requires attentiveness to the needs and interests of two subjectivities. It means not only getting the speaker's arguments straight, but also trying to adopt his perspective, discern his assumptions and motives, identify with his feelings, feel his needs, understand what is at stake for him. In effect, the hearer must perform a service. She must put her subjectivity at the disposal of the speaker; she must cultivate and entertain, play host to, another subjectivity. At the same time, she must retain a lively sense of her own subjectivity; otherwise she risks losing the capacity for autonomous response and judgment necessary for validating the speaker's claims, or of imposing her own subjective predispositions surreptitiously on the other. The idea of being a good listener to another involves a richer conception of intersubjectivity than agreement, since it requires a commitment to the realization of two subjectivities and to a process that coordinates the need to establish connection with the need to preserve difference.

The contrast between the intersubjectivity of Habermas's ideal discourse and the intersubjectivity of discourse which involves genuine listening is clearest when we consider conversation that cuts across structural difference such as gender (or race, class, and sexual orientation). In conversations between men and women, gender is a locus both of difference and power. Women often complain that men don't listen, and the problems are especially acute when gender is the topic of discussion. Take, for example, the way men react to feminist theories of gender difference—say Gilligan's theory that male development revolves primarily around issues of individuation and autonomy, and men tend to think of morality in terms of rights, while female development revolves around issues of relationship and connection, and women think of morality in terms of caring for and being responsive to the needs of others. My experience leads me to expect the following responses. One likely response is hostility: some men would dismiss the claim out of hand as feminist and therefore antimale; others would resent the suggestion that men are deficient in caring; and still others would be annoyed at being "lumped in" with men in general ("Why should a person be defined by their genitals? Why can't we look at people simply as people?"). Another likely response is disagreement: one points out that the evidence and the arguments presented cannot survive scrutiny, therefore, the claim is invalid. A third response is agreement: yes, women are different; they are more concerned with relationships than with personal autonomy, with caring rather than rules. Women have been oppressed; they have been deprived of the right of self-definition and of the opportunity to express their values. Men should *allow* them to define themselves and to express their own perspectives.

The second and third responses indicated above fit into Habermas's ideal speech situation. Notice, however, that whether the result of the examination of claims is agreement or disagreement, the resolution means the end of discourse. Moreover, the intersubjectivity between speaker and listener stops short of genuine collaboration. The speaker has the responsibility to present cogent arguments, the listener to examine and judge. The speaker must be articulate and persuasive, the listener judicious. The assumption is that claims and arguments are fully formed when uttered. There is no stipulation that the participants in discourse be engaged in a collaborative discovery process, where ideas and arguments may not be fully formed when uttered, where each participant may be striving to understand and to formulate her own perspective. In reality, especially where the topic is complicated and potentially distressing, arguments are often not fully formed when they are uttered, and speakers are not entirely transparent to each other and to themselves. Ideally, discourse would involve a discovery process, with each participant trying to realize— discover no less than understand—her own position and commitments. Being a good listener in this situation is to lend oneself to the project of an other. Thus, instead of challenging the arguments, instead of merely agreeing or disagreeing, the listener will strive to "lean into" the position of the other.[32] A man would try to comprehend the issue of gender difference from the point of view of women, to listen with the ears of a woman, to hear what remains unspoken— to intuit the experiences, values, motives, and mode of being that forms the substance of the claims. At the same time, he would be attentive to his own position. The discussion of gender would problematize not only woman's gender but also his own. He would understand what it means to be, like woman, a gendered being rather than the paradigmatic human. In this sort of discussion, there would be mutual recognition that utterances are necessarily tentative and vulnerable—that each participant has the right to speak freely *and* the obligation to perform the interactive labor that would enable the speech of others, and to be responsive to the needs and perspectives they are striving to express. In short, each will be able to count not only on having equal access to the floor, but also on having good listeners. Validation would be an open-ended process oriented not only toward persuading others, but more generally toward engaging them in discourse. The goal is mutual understanding: not necessarily agreement, but the making of connections between diverse experiences and perspectives, and the production of an intersubjectivity that would allow the conversation to flourish.

The incorporation of the problematics of listening (or reading) into a theory of the ideal speech situation would require the supplementation of the ideal of domination-free discourse with the ideal of responsiveness to the needs and appeals expressed in the speech of the other—in other words, with the interactive competence and the ethic of care that is currently associated with the discourse of women. *No Exit* illustrates the dystopian inversion of Habermas's ideal speech situation. The characters in hell speak and argue, but they do not listen. Each is deaf to the needs and appeals expressed by others. They are in hell because they are incapable of caring for other people. Discourse bereft of the ethic of care sets the stage for the famous conclusion of the play: "There is no need for red hot pokers. Hell is—other people!"

Although gender differences in interactive competence may be very deeply ingrained, it does not follow that they are essential sexual characteristics. There are good reasons to believe that gender differences could be bridged. In particular, the work of certain male theorists of discourse indicates that the muted structures of the ethic of care are "there"—to use Ardener's phrase, "in the wild"—even though they could not be realized within the discourse of the brotherhood. Habermas's own work is a case in point. I have in mind specifically his emphasis on communicative action and his strong interest in building an ethical theory around the discursive resolution of conflicts. His revision of Kohlberg is particularly interesting in this regard. Habermas argues that the latter's schema for moral development is a special case of the development of interactive competence. Then he offers a developmental schema which has seven rather than six stages. The highest stage (the sixth) for Kohlberg is characterized by the attainment of individual moral autonomy. Habermas adds a seventh stage because "only at the level of a universal ethics of language can the need interpretations themselves—that is, what each individual believes he ought to understand and to represent as his 'true' interests—also be the object of practical discourse [i.e., discourse oriented toward the determination of moral norms]." At the highest stage of moral development, "the principle of justification of norms is no longer the monologically applicable *principle* of generalizability, but the communally followed *procedure* of discursive redemption of normative validity claims."[33]

It is apparent, then, that for Habermas, moral issues are not to be referred to rules and principles, but rather negotiated and worked out through human interaction. Both the recognition that "need interpretation" is crucial to moral deliberation and that the emphasis on communication and negotiation rather than the monologic interpretation and application of general principles are—according to Gilligan—hallmarks of an ethic of care. I might also mention that H. P. Grice's idea of the "collaborative principle" informing the logic of conversation is similarly laden with promise.[34] Unfortunately, with Grice as with Habermas, the values and interests connected with the ethic of care are censored out in the process of articulation into fraternal discourse. What Grice gives us—his five maxims: be perspicuous, avoid obscurity of expression, avoid ambiguity, be brief, and be orderly—is a pale shadow of what a truly collaborative intersubjectivity could be.

The sense of an intuition straining to break through the inhibiting structures of the discourse of the brotherhood becomes most poignant in *1984*. Apparently, Orwell had a dim intimation of a way to block the advent of the nightmare state of Big Brother: to realize the utopian ideal implicit in discourse, Julia and her sisters must take their place in the conversation; men must learn to listen to us—better still, they could learn to draw us out, to facilitate the articulation of values and interests associated with female experience.

Notes

1. Steven Mailloux, "Truth or Consequences: On Being Against Theory," *Critical Inquiry* 9 (1983): 760–66. This essay is a reply to Steven Knapp and Walter Benn Michaels, "Against Theory," *Critical Inquiry* 8 (1982): 723–42.

2. David Bleich, *Subjective Criticism* (Baltimore: Johns Hopkins University Press, 1978), 112.

3. Stanley Fish, *Is There a Text in This Class? The Authority of Interpretive Communities* (Cambridge: Harvard University Press, 1980), 354.

4. Michaels, "Saving the Text," *Modern Language Notes* 93 (1978): 780.

5. Richard Rorty, "Texts and Lumps," *New Literary History* 17 (1985): 3.

6. E. D. Hirsch, Jr., "The Politics of Theories of Interpretation," *Critical Inquiry* 9 (1982): 235–47; and Gerald Graff, "The Pseudo-Politics of Interpretation," *Critical Inquiry* 9 (1983): 597–610.

7. Fish, 371.

8. George Orwell, *1984* (New York: Harcourt Brace Jovanovich, 1949), 205. Page numbers to further references appear in parentheses throughout the text and are taken from this edition.

9. Milton Fisk's argument about the connection of metaphysics to nonphilosophical practices is germane here: "Philosophies in [the constructivist] phase reassure people about ways of doing things. If old views of the world make doing things in a new way seem impossible, then there is need for reassurance about how in fact the new way is after all possible. A metaphysical philosophy reassures us that a practice can realize its goals by drawing the lines of the world in a way that makes it possible for this practice to fit into the world" ("The Instability of Pragmatism," *New Literary History* 17 [1985]: 25).

10. For a thorough and authoritative documentation of the misogynist and sexist attitudes underlying Orwell's works, see Daphne Patai, *The Orwell Mystique: A Study of Male Ideology* (Amherst: University of Massachusetts Press, 1984). See also my review of Patai's book, "Orwell Revisited," *Women's Review of Books* 2, no. 2 (November 1984); and my essay, "Why Big Brother: The Maternal Sub-Text of *Nineteen Eighty-Four*," *Papers in Comparative Studies* 4 (1985): 69–80.

The theme of woman's silence has been prominent in feminist theory during the last decade. The most influential theoretical formulation of this theme was proposed by the anthropologist Edwin Ardener. Ardener distinguishes between "muted" and "articulate" groups. An articulate or dominant group has the prerogative of producing and controlling the ideological structures that define social reality. In patriarchal society, women constitute a muted group (there are others: homosexuals, children, criminals, "the lower classes," oppressed racial and ethnic groups, etc.). Ardener makes a point of invoking the double meaning of "muted": women are rendered inarticulate (silent) by the dominant male structures, and their experience and sense of reality assumes "a reduced level of peceptibility." "The muted structures are 'there' but cannot be 'realized' in the language of the dominant structure" ("The Problem Revisited," in *Perceiving Women*, ed. Shirley Ardener [New York: Halsted Press, 1975], 22). See Edwin Ardener's "Belief and the Problem of Women" in the same volume, and Shirley Ardener's discussion of muted groups in her introduction, xii–xv. See also Cheris Kramerae's excellent account of this issue in *Women and Men Speaking* (Rowley, Mass.: Newbury House Publishers, Inc., 1981), 1–32.

11. Fisk, 26.

12. Rorty, 5.

13. See Bleich ("Intersubjective Reading," *New Literary History* 17 [1986]: 401–21) for the logical sequel to *Subjective Criticism.*

14. Jürgen Habermas, "Wahrheitstheorien," in *Wirklichkeit und Reflexion: Walter Schulz zum 60 Geburtstag* (Pfullingen: Neske, 1973), 219; or, as translated by Thomas McCarthy, in *The Critical Theory of Jürgen Habermas* (Cambridge: MIT Press, 1978), 299. I am also indebted to Alan Soble's unpublished translation of this work.

15. Habermas, "Wahrheitstheorien," 258–59; or McCarthy, *The Critical Theory of Jürgen Habermas*, 310.

16. Mailloux, 762.

17. Actually, Habermas's scheme is eurocentric as well as androcentric. For a discussion of the problem of eurocentricism, see McCarthy, "Rationality and Relativism: Habermas's 'Overcoming' of Hermeneutics," in *Habermas' Critical Debates*, ed. John B. Thompson and David Held (Cambridge: MIT Press, 1982), 57–78.

18. This very useful term comes from Habermas—"Zur Entwicklung der Interaktionskompetenz" (unpublished manuscript). Cf. McCarthy, 333–36. The concept is analogous to Chomsky's notion of linguistic competence and central to Habermas's theory of communicative ethics.

19. For an excellent summary of work in this area, see Barrie Thorne, Kramerae, and Nancy Henley, "Language, Gender and Society: Opening a Second Decade of Research," in *Language, Gender and Society*, ed. Thorne, Kramerae, and Henley (Rowley, Mass.: Newbury House Publishers, Inc., 1983). The annotated bibliography entitled "Sex Similarities and Differences in Language, Speech, and Nonverbal Communication" included in *Language, Gender and Society* is a good indication of the volume and variety of research in this area.

20. Daniel Maltz and Ruth Borker, "A Cultural Approach to Male-Female Miscommunication," in *Communication, Language, and Social Inequality*. Quoted by Paula A. Treichler and Kramerae, "Women's Talk in the Ivory Tower," *Communication Quarterly* 31 (1983): 119.

21. *Ibid.*

22. *Ibid*, 120.

23. *Ibid*, 121.

24. Candace West and Don H. Zimmerman, "Small Insults: A Study of Interruptions in Cross-Sex Conversations between Unacquainted Persons," in *Language, Gender and Society*, 102–17. See also Zimmerman and West, "Sex Roles, Interruptions and Silences in Conversations," in *Language and Sex: Difference and Dominance*, ed. Thorne and Henley (Rowley, Mass.: Newbury House, 1975), 105–29.

25. Pamela M. Fishman, "Interaction: The Work Women Do," in *Language, Gender and Society*, 98–99.

26. Carole Edelsky, "Who's Got the Floor?" *Language and Society* 10 (1981): 383–422. See Treichler and Kramerae, 123.

27. Carol Gilligan, *In a Different Voice: Psychological Theory and Women's Development* (Cambridge: Harvard University Press, 1982), 19.

28. *Ibid*, 20–21.

29. Lawrence Kohlberg, "Continuities and Discontinuities in Childhood and Adult Moral Development Revisited," in *Collected Papers on Moral Development and Moral Education* (Cambridge: Moral Education Research Foundation, Harvard University, 1973), 29–30. Quoted on page 20 of Gilligan.

30. Gilligan, 21. See also Nancy Chodorow, *The Reproduction of Mothering: Psychoanalysis and the Sociology of Gender* (Berkeley: University of California Press, 1978); Joyce Trebilcot, ed., *Mothering: Essays in Feminist Theory* (Totowa, N.J.: Rowmann and Allanheld, 1983), especially the essays by Ruddick and Kuykendall; and Nell Noddings, *Caring: A Feminine Approach to Ethics and Moral Education* (Berkeley: University of California Press, 1984).

31. Today one is likely to associate the idea of the indeterminacy of the text with deconstruction and reader-response theory. However, the same idea is evident in Sartre's *What Is Literature?*—especially in the famous essay "Why Write?"

32. "Leaning into the text" is the key operation in Jean Kennard's model of polar reading. See Kennard, "Ourself Behind Ourself: A Theory for Lesbian Readers," in *Gender and Reading: Essays on Readers, Texts and Contexts*, ed. Elizabeth A. Flynn and Patrocinio P. Schweickart (Baltimore: Johns Hopkins University Press, 1986), 63–82.

33. Habermas, "Moralentwicklung und Ich-Identitat," in *Zur Reconstruktion des Historischen Materialismus* (Frankfurt: Suhrkamp, 1976), 84–85; quoted by McCarthy, *The Critical theory of Jürgen Habermas*, 351.

34. Grice, "Logic and Conversation," in *The Logic of Grammar*, ed. D. Davidson and G. Harman (Encino, Calif.: Dickinson Publishing Company, 1975), 64–75.

Imperialism
and Sexual
Difference*

Gayatri Chakravorty Spivak

Feminist criticism can be a force
in changing the discipline. To do so, however, it must recognize that
it is complicitous with the institution within which it seeks its space.
That slow labor might transform it from opposition to critique. Let
me describe a certain area of this complicity in a theoretical and
historical way.

My theoretical model is taken from Paul de Man. De Man
suggests that a critical philosopher initially discovers that the basis of
a truth-claim is no more than a trope. In the case of academic
feminism, the discovery is that to take the privileged male of the
white race as a norm for universal humanity is no more than a
politically interested figuration. It is a trope that passes itself off as
truth and claims that woman or the racial other is merely a kind of
troping of that truth of man—in the sense that both must be understood *as* unlike (nonidentical with) it and yet *with* reference to it.
Insofar as it participates in this discovery, even the most "essentialist"
feminism or race-analysis is engaged in a tropological deconstruction.[1] De Man goes on to suggest, however, that even as it establishes
the truth of this discovery, the critical philosopher's text begins to
perform the problems inherent in the very institution of epistemological production, of the production, in other words, of any "truth" at
all. By this logic, varieties of feminist theory and practice must reckon
with the possibility that, like any other discursive practice, they are
marked and constituted by, even as they constitute, the field of their
production. If much of what I write here seems to apply as much to

*I am grateful to David Bathrick for a critical reading of my essay.

319

the general operations of imperialist disciplinary practice as to feminism, it is because I wish to point at the dangers of not acknowledging the connections between the two. (These problems—that "truths" can only be shored up by strategic exclusions, by declaring opposition where there is complicity, by denying the possibility of randomness, by proclaiming a provisional origin or point of departure as ground—are the substance of deconstructive concerns. The price of the insight into the tropological nature of a truth-claim is the blindness of truth-telling.)[2]

My historical caveat is, in sum, that feminism within the social relations and institutions of the metropolis has something like a relationship with the fight for individualism in the upwardly class-mobile bourgeois cultural politics of Europe in the nineteenth century. Thus, even as we feminist critics discover the troping error of the masculist truth-claim to universality or academic objectivity, we perform the lie of constituting a truth of global sisterhood where the mesmerizing model remains male and female sparring partners of generalizable or universalizable sexuality who are the chief protagonists in that European contest. In order to claim sexual difference where it makes a difference, global sisterhood must receive this articulation even if the sisters in question are Asian, African, or Arab.[3]

I will attempt to consolidate my general points by way of readings of three masculist texts: *Le cygne* by Baudelaire, "William the Conqueror" by Kipling, and a discussion paper laid before a secret meeting of the Court of Directors of the East India Company. The first two—a lyric of justly celebrated subtlety and a "popular" narrative of imperialist sentiments—can both be made to offer us a mirror of our performance of certain imperialist ideological structures even as we deconstruct the tropological error of masculism. The third, mere minutes of a meeting, shows the affinity between those structures and some of racism's crude presuppositions.

――――――▼――――――

Baudelaire's stunning poem begins "Andromaque, je pense à vous" (Andromache, I think of you). The poet transforms the "truth" of the memory of a cityscape to the allegorical troping of literary history and a metaphor for his consuming melancholy. The woman in the case, Queen Andromache, is no more than the poet's object, not only brought forth into textual existence by the magisterial "I think of you," not only celebrated as Homer's good heroine beside the erring Helen, not only used to establish the classic continuity of the brotherhood of European poetry—celebrating women from Homer through Virgil, Racine, and now Baudelaire—but utilized thus by way of the careful invocation of a woman mourning a husband. As if this were not enough, the boldly obvious pun in the title (in French *cygne* sounds like both *sign* and *swan*) gives her the status of sign rather than subject from the very start. Yet this emptying out—by phonocentric convention a sign means something other than itself, whereas a person is self-proximate, even self-identical—is accompanied by the usual gestures of hyperbolic admiration. By the time the "real" swan appears, its figuration as sign is not secure precisely because the word *cygne* happens, properly or literally, to mean *swan*. It is as if, by being the sign of the poet's prowess, Queen Andromache is more of a swan than the swan itself. It now begins to seem possible that, in the world of Baudelaire's poem, sign-status is not necessarily less fortunate than person-status, or indeed that in *Le cygne*, personhood might not be operated by the laws of everyday phonocentrism—the privileging of voice-consciousness over any system of mere signs.[4] Yet, as I have argued elsewhere, at whatever remove from phonocentrism we throw the dice, and however phonocentrism is critiqued, the ontic differential between the poet-operating-as-controlling-subject and the woman-manipulated-as-sign will not disappear.[5]

Once this is granted, we are free to notice the power of Andromache within the syntactic and metaphoric logic of the poem. The memory of the real city (given in the simple declarative of reportage) is put under the spell of the mirror image of the mythic Andromache (metonymically represented by her griefs) in the false river of her own tears (a quadruple representation) by the force of the word *jadis* (once), which is repeated strategically. It appears in line 2—"Ce petit fleuve / Pauvre et triste miroir ou *jadis* resplendit / L'immense majesté de vos douleurs de veuve" (That narrow stream, / poor and sad mirror that *once* resplended with / the immense majesty of your widow's grief [emphasis mine])[6]—and again in line 13—"La s'éta-lait *jadis* une ménagerie" (a menagerie *once* sprawled just there [emphasis mine]). If Andromache is forever present in every reading of the poem by the poet's magisterial act of thought, the real swan, as it is introduced after the spellbinding *jadis*, is controlled by the absolute past, stronger than the preterite in English: "je vis" (I saw [l. 14]).

Thus Andromache is the condition of the emergence of the image of the swan. But she is also its effect, for when the poet most specifies her by her kinship inscriptions, she is compared metonymically to the swan in the words *vil bétail* (vile cattle), a term with connotations of breeding-cattle which would relate interestingly in making Andromache the condition and effect of the fertilization of Baudelaire's memory as well.

Unlike the description of the predicament of the Woman as Queen in the Great Tradition, that of the poet's predicament is not made to shuttle rhetorically between the status of condition and effect. Lines 29 through 33—"Paris change . . . image m'opprime" (Paris is changing . . . an image oppresses me)—stand on their own. In fact we cannot be sure what image oppresses the poet; he keeps this secret. The delicate paratactic gesture of the colon with which the next movement opens—"Je pense à mon grand cygne" (I think of my grand swan [l. 34])—certainly draws the reader into thinking that the image is that of the swan. But is it not possible that this obsessed, oppressed, and melancholic speaker should turn to a dear memory to escape from the oppression of an image? Certainly a T. S. Eliot would claim affinity with Baudelaire on the issue of an "escape from personality" into "a medium . . . in which impressions and experiences combine in peculiar and unexpected ways."[7] Since parataxis, even more than the rhetorical question, will allow this indeterminacy, it seems fair to expect the deliberate syntactic logic of the poem to harbor it.

The point I am making, then, is that whatever the spectacular manipulative mechanics of Andromache as fertilizer might be, in *Le cygne* the poet-speaker retains a syntactically impregnable house and a rhetorically enigmatic "subjectivity."

At the end of the poem, the "à" (of) of "penser à" (think of) seems to change function and become a dedicatory "to" toward a crowd of lonely people until the text seems to disappear in the vague inconsequence of "bien d'aûtres encore" (and many others). Although Andromache does not appear, her singular control (as a memory-sign framed by the poet's apostrophe) over the production of the poem is reasserted by force of contrast. She remains the only "thou" in the poem. But she is also caught in the second person of the only apostrophe which is not quite one: "I *think* of you." The poet's self-deconstruction is made possible by the metaphor of the powerful woman.

——————▼——————

This is the outline of a reading that shows that not only the power but even the self-undermining of the man may be operated by the troping of the woman. I considered it an important moment in my education when I learned to read the homoerotic Great Tradition in this way.[8] I thought it a not insignificant supplement to theorizing about feminine subjectivity and retrieving women as object of investigation, two more justifiably important activities within feminist literary criticism in the United States. The price of learning such a tropological deconstruction of masculism, however, was the performance of a blindness to the other woman in the text.

Introducing the list of nameless people at the end of the poem, there stands a nameless woman moving her feet in the mud, who is distinguished by nothing but color, a derisive name for her ethnicity: "Je pense à la négresse" (I think of the negress [l. 42]).[9] Here the object of thought is clearly in the third person. Indeed, this blurred figure with her fixed and haggard eye is almost "naturalized" or "de-personified." (By contrast, the "natural" swan, looking up as, per Ovid, only man does, may be seen as "personified.") The negress is an image not of semiosis, but what de Man has called "the stutter, the *piétinement*" (her only named action in the poem) "of aimless enumeration."[10] The swan is gifted with speech. "Eau, quand donc pleuvras-tu? Quand tonneras-tu, foudre?" (O water, when will you rain down? O lightning, when will you rage?) the poet had heard him say (ll. 23–24). This woman is mute. Andromache begins the poem and usurps the first half of the second section, which Baudelaire brings to an end by addressing her again by name and specifying her, through intricate echoes of Virgil, as Hector's widow and Helenus's wife. Her geography is not only implicit in her history. In a metaphoric gender-switch, the *false* river Simois created by her tears had, to begin with, fertilized his memory of the intricate cartography of the changeful city of Paris, itself implausibly shadowed by the name of Homer's hero: "Ce Simois menteur qui par vos pleurs grandit, / A fécondé soudain ma mémoire fertile" (That lying Simois that grew from your tears, / Has suddenly enriched my fertile memory [ll. 4–5]). Against all this labyrinthine specificity and exchange between male and female is juxtaposed the immense vagueness of the negress's geography, etched in no more than three words: "la superbe Afrique" (superb Africa [l. 44]).

Indeed, if Andromache is the over-specified condition of emergence of the title-image (the swan), the only possible function of the negress would be to mark the indeterminate moment when specificity is dissolved at poem's end.

In the longer work of which this essay is a part, I have developed the idea of reading by interception of the text as it flies from implied sender to implied receiver, by animating the perspective of the "native informant," roughly as follows.

The clearing of a subject-position in order to speak or write is unavoidable. One way to reckon with this bind is an interminable preoccupation with the (autobiographical) self. If we are interested in a third-worldist criticism, however, we might want to acknowledge that access to autobiography, for whole groups of people, has only been possible through the dominant mediation of an investigator or field-worker. The "autobiographies" of such people have not entered the post-Enlightenment European "subjective" tradition of autobiography. They have gone, rather, to provide "objective evidence" for the "sciences" of anthropology and ethnolinguistics. "Oral history," coming of age in the sixties, tried to efface or at least minimize the role of the investigator. Much third-worldist feminist work has taken on this task of the effacement of the investigator in works typically entitled _____Women Speak. This brief account reveals the various alibis that the dominant subject-position gives itself as it constructs the subordinate as other. The curious "objectified" subject-position of this other is what, following the language of anthropology and linguistics, I call the position of the "native informant." In order to produce a critique of imperialism, I suggest the invention of a reading-subject's perspective that would occupy or cathect the representative space or blank presupposed by the dominant text. The space will remain specific to the dominant text which presupposes it, and yet, since this is not a space of the critic's autobiography as a marginal, it must be foregrounded as a historically representative space. We cannot avoid constituting the other by way of consolidating the self. This method will at least make the problems visible and the efforts at hedging the problems provisionally accessible to the reader.

Such a reading is, strictly speaking, inappropriate to the text. Yet deconstructive approaches have suggested for the last two decades that every reading is an upheaval para-sitical to the text.[11] Here, I use the resources of deconstruction "in the service of reading" to develop a strategy rather than a theory of reading that might be a critique of imperialism.

▼

If to develop such a perspective we look at the naming of the negress as negress, we uncover a curious tale. She might of course "be" Jeanne Duval, Baudelaire's famous Eurafrican mistress. But there is another, textual clue to her name as well. Lines 41–44 of *Le cygne* use two lines from another poem by Baudelaire titled "A une malabaraise"[12] ("To a Malabar Woman"): "L'oeil pensif, et suivant, dans nos sales brouillards, / Des cocotiers absents les fantomes épars" (Eyes pensive, pursuing, in our dirty fogs, / The vanished ghosts of absent palm trees [ll. 27–28]). The "original" of the negress in *Le cygne* is a textual palimpsest of the "original" of the agonist of "A une malabaraise," one of two women Baudelaire encountered in Mauritius and the island of Réunion, respectively. Who are these "malabarians"?

Malabar is the name of the southernmost stretch of the southwest coast of India. The islands of Mauritius and Réunion, terrains of military colonial exchange between France and Britain, have a sizeable population of Indian origin as a result of the British import of Indian indentured labor. These people are not necessarily, not even largely, from India's Malabar Coast. Their naming is like "American Indian" or "turkey-cock," a product of hegemonic false cartography. At the time of Baudelaire's writing, the French colonists treated these unfortunate people so harshly that the British imperial authorities finally prohibited further emigration of laborers from India (1882). It is this vague woman—encountered on either one of the two colonial possessions and misnamed by white convention—whom Baudelaire shifts and misplaces, for the poem's exigency, on an imagined native place as generalized as "Africa."

Under the principles of New Criticism, it is not permitted to introduce such "extraneous" considerations into a reading of the poem. Some deconstructive readings allow us to see the writing of a life (auto-bio-graphy) as a text imbricated in the production of literature or the discourse of the human sciences.[13] I am using that permission to suggest here that whereas Baudelaire, inscribing himself as poet within the tradition of European poetry, is meticulous about the specificity of that tradition, the inscription of himself as an admirer of negresses can only be deciphered by guesswork outside of the boundaries of the poem. It is seemingly irrelevant to the poem's proper functioning. And it is mired in a conventionally sanctioned carelessness about identities. I am suggesting further that if we recognize the lineaments of domination in the first case and ignore the foreclosure of the second, we are, in part, Baudelaire's accomplices.

Indeed, there are at least three ways of ignoring the inscription of that "negress": first by asserting, as did a woman student of mine from the United States, that perhaps Baudelaire meant to focus on her predicament as being exiled without history and geography (Lisa Jardine has correctly described this as "recovering some concealed radical message from ostensibly reactionary writing");[14] secondly, by bringing in precisely the details about Duval or the elusive "malabaraise" without attending to the way the negress is displayed in the poem; and thirdly—and this troubles me most—by suggesting as Edward Ahearn has done, that the negress is somehow Baudelaire's dark double.[15] These readings, as they deconstruct an error, themselves perform a lie.

▼

There is an element of chance in these three texts being put together in one essay. I discovered the scandal in Baudelaire's poem because I wanted to teach some Baudelaire (because Walter Benjamin had written on him) in a course combining theory and history in practical criticism; one could not bypass reactions to the age of revolution. The story by Kipling I discovered in a volume loaned by a white but politically correct South African friend in response to a desperate need for bedtime reading; there was a certain historical irony in *The Penguin Book of English Short Stories* passing between a South African and an Indian as a text to lull her into sleep. The East India Company minutes I found at the India Office Library in London while "looking for something else." What was striking to me was that in such a random trio of texts I should find the double standard that troubles me under the auspices of feminist literary criticism in my workplace.

▼

Writing in the 1890s, Kipling is attempting to create a species of New Woman in his short story "William the Conqueror"; and, in the attempt, he reveals most of the shortcomings of a benevolent masculism.[16] William is the name of the female protagonist. By implying archly that her conquest of the heart of the male protagonist is to be compared to the Norman Conquest of England, is Kipling producing a proleptic parody of "the personal is political"? We cannot know. If, however, in pondering this trivial question we overlook the fact that, under cover of the romance, the conquest of India is being effaced and reinscribed as a historically appropriate event rather than anything that could in fact be called a "conquest," we are once again applying the double standard.

Kipling's New Woman is distinctly unbeautiful. "Her face was white as bone, and in the centre of her forehead was a big silvery scar the size of a shilling—the mark of a Delhi sore."[17] She does the most unfeminine thing of travelling by dreadful train across horrid India in the company of men to tend the poor bestial Indians in the throes of the Madras famine of 1876–78. I think Kipling is ironic (again, somewhat archly, but that is his tone) about the traffic in British girls in the colonies. In recompense, to treat "William" differently, he makes her almost a man. She "look[s] more like a boy than ever" (*WC*, 229), and her brother admits that "'she's as clever as a man, confound her'" (*WC*, 235). In the end, however, Kipling shows that a woman's a woman for all that, and she conquers, as women will, through love. "Life with men who had a great deal of work to do, and very little time to do it in, had taught her the wisdom of effacing as well as of fending for herself" (*WC*, 236). And she nurtures sentiments appropriate to a true "man's woman": "[to make fun of a girl]'s different. . . . She was only a girl, and she hadn't done anything except walk like a quail, and she *does*. But it isn't fair to make fun of a man" (*WC*, 257).

Kipling does not write about sexual difference subtly. I will point at one more detail to indicate the kind of function it performs in his text. In the interest of creating a "different" kind of romance, Kipling gives to his hero some soft and "feminine" qualities: the protagonists come together in love when he teaches her how to milk goats to feed starving Indian babies. But this possible effeminacy is forestalled by a proper objective correlative from classical pastoral with Biblical overtones: "One waiting at the tent door beheld, with new eyes, a young man, beautiful as Paris, a god in a halo of golden dust, walking slowly at the head of his flocks, while at his knee ran small naked Cupids" (*WC*, 249). Before we dismiss this as Victorian kitsch—some critics find the passage admirable—we should note that this is the story's icon for imperialism *in loco parentis*.[18] That is made painfully clear a few pages later. "She dreamed for the twentieth time of the god in the golden dust, and woke refreshed to feed loathsome black children" (*WC*, 261) ironically illustrates "Kipling's attitude to children, with its special tenderness and understanding . . .").[19] At any rate, love flourishes and, at the end of the story, at the noble festival of Christmas, "drawing closer to Scott . . . it was William who wiped her eyes," even as some men of the Club sang "Glad tidings of great joy I bring / To you and all mankind" (*WC*, 274). It is one of the cliches of imperialism that the settlement of the colonies is part of these glad tidings.

There is a lot of self-conscious "local color" in the story. At first glance, then, it might seem as if the complaint about Baudelaire, that

he denies the negress her proper and specific space, cannot be enter-
tained concerning "William." And it is of course correct that Kipling
is a chronicler of "Indian life." Let us therefore pause a moment on
Kipling's technique of specifying India.[20]

"Is it officially declared yet?" are the first words of the text.
Narrative logic throws a good deal of weight on the answer to this
question. Indeed, the first movement of narrative energy in William
the Conqueror seems to be a demonstration of how an affirmative
answer to this question might be shaped. Slowly the reader comes to
sense that the "it" in question is the precise descriptive substantive—
famine—and that the affirmative answer to the initial question is in
the language of benevolent imperialism—"the operation of the Famine Code" (*WC*, 223): the exasperated yet heroic British tending the
incompetent, unreasonable, and childish south Indians. The pano-
ramic heterogeneity of the people and landscape of southern India is
offered in declaration of and apposition to the monolithic rubric:
famine.

The narrative purpose of "famine"—the container of the specificity of south India—is instrumental. When it has served to promote
love between the two human (that is, British) actors, the rubric is
dissolved, the declaration undone: "And so Love ran about the
camp unrebuked in broad daylight, while men picked up the pieces
and put them neatly away of the Famine in the Eight Districts"
(*WC*, 204).

The action moves back to northwest India, where it began.
Here is an account of that move:

> The large open names of the home towns were good to listen
> to. Umballa, Ludhiana, Phillour, Jullundur, they rang like mar-
> riage-bells in her ears, and William felt deeply and truly sorry
> for all strangers and outsiders—visitors, tourists, and those
> fresh-caught for the service of the country. (*WC*, 273)

These sonorous place-names are in Panjab. We have left Madras
behind as we have left "famine" behind. The mention of "home"
and "outside" is not a specification of India at all, but rather the
disappearance of India, if the place is defined as the habitation of
Indians. The description of William and Scott's "homecoming" to
the north leaves the distinct impression that the north is more
British—India has receded here. This is how the roll of names I
quote above is introduced:

The South of Pagodas and palm-trees, the over-populated Hindu South, was done with. Here was the land she knew, and before her lay the good life she understood, among folk of her own caste and mind. They were picking them up at almost every station now—men and women coming in for the Christmas Week, with racquets, with fox-terriers and saddles. . . . Scott would stroll up to William's window, and murmur: "Good enough, isn't it?" and William would answer with sighs of pure delight: "Good enough, indeed." (*WC*, 272)

Thus the incantation of the names, far from being a composition of place, is precisely that combination of effacement-of-specificity *and* appropriation that one might call violation. It starts early on in a benign way, as we encounter the hero putting on evening clothes: "Scott moved leisurely to his room, and changed into *the evening-dress of the season and the country*; spotless white linen from head to foot, with a broad silk cummerbund" (*WC*, 225; italics mine). "The dress of the season and country" sutures nature and culture and inscribes nature appropriately. Thus "home" and "outside" become terms of a distinction between the old and the new British in India. The words *Punjabi* and *Madrassi* are consistently used for the British who "serve" in those parts of India. The word *native*, which is supposed to mean "autochthonous," is paradoxically reinscribed as an unindividuated parahumanity that cannot aspire to a proper habitation.

Kipling uses many Hindusthani words in his text—pidgin Hindusthani, barbaric to the native speaker, devoid of syntactic connections, always infelicitous, almost always incorrect. The narrative practice sanctions this usage and establishes it as "correct," without, of course, any translation. This is British pidgin, originating in a decision that Hindusthani is a language of servants not worth mastering "correctly"; this is the version of the language that is established textually as "correct." By contrast, the Hindusthani speech of the Indian servants is painstakingly translated into archaic and awkward English. The servants' occasional forays into English are mocked in phonetic transcription. Let us call this ensemble of moves—in effect a mark of perceiving a language as subordinate—translation-as-violation. And let us contrast this to a high European moment in the discussion of translation as such.

Benjamin wrote as follows on the topic of translation from classical Greek into German: "Instead of making itself similar to the meaning . . . the translation must rather, lovingly and in detail, in its own language, form itself according to the manner of meaning in the original, to make both recognizable as broken parts of the greater language." This passage quite logically assumes that the language one translates from is structurally the language of authority rather than subordination. Commenting on this passage de Man writes: "The faithful translation, which is always literal, how can it also be free? It can only be free if it reveals the instability of the original, and if it reveals the instability as the linguistic tension between trope and meaning. Pure language is perhaps more present in the translation than in the original, but in the mode of trope."[21]

The distant model of this magisterial discourse on translation is the European Renaissance, when a tremendous activity of translation from texts of classical antiquity helped shape hegemonic Europe's image of itself. (The fact that German cultural self-representation in the eighteenth and nineteenth centuries was one of nonparticipation in the Renaissance gives the specifically German speculations on the problem of translation a particular poignancy.) When, however, the violence of imperialism straddles a subject-language, translation can become a species of violation. Freedom-introping arguments from the European Renaissance do not apply to the translation-as-violation in Kipling's text.

I have been arguing that the tropological deconstruction of masculism does not exempt us from performing the lie of imperialism. The last time I taught "William the Conqueror," I included David Arnold's recent essay on the Madras famine as required reading. (Some of the documentation provided in the essay puts the noble-whites-helping-incompetent-blacks scenario into question.)[22] The class was taken up by the analysis of the taming-of-the-tomboy routine between the two white protagonists. Toward the end of the hour I deflected the discussion to a moment in Arnold's essay, which quotes a Tamil sexual-role-reversal doggerel sung by peasant women to make the drought end: "A wonder has taken place, O Lord! / The male is grinding millet and the female is ploughing fields. / Is not your heart moved with pity, O God! / The widow Brahman is ploughing the field."[23] In order to think of this folk-ritual as potentially efficacious and evocative of chaos in an ordered universe, the women must, of course, have taken seriously a patriarchal division of sexual labor. What little time was left in the class was taken up with a young woman's insistence that the peasant women must have been singing the doggerel ironically. In the total ignorance of history and subject-constitution, this insistence on a post-Romantic concept of irony no doubt sprang from the imposition of her own historical and voluntarist constitution within the second wave of U.S. academic feminism as a "universal" model of the "natural" reactions of the female psyche.[24] This too is an example of translation-as-violation.

The structure of translation-as-violation describes certain tendencies within third-worldist literary pedagogy more directly. It is of course part of my general argument that, unless third-worldist feminist criticism develops a vigilance against such tendencies, it cannot help but participate in them: for example, our own mania for "Third World literature" anthologies, when the teacher or critic often has no sense of the original languages or of the subject-constitution of the social and gendered agents in question (and therefore the student cannot sense this as a loss), participates more in the logic of translation-as-violation than in the ideal of translation as freedom-in-troping. What is at play there is a phenomenon that can be called "sanctioned ignorance."

▼

Let us look briefly at the document from the East India Company. (Although a commercial company, between the end of the eighteenth and the middle of the nineteenth centuries, the East India Company governed its possessions in India. We are therefore reading about the employment of Indians in their own government.) The language here is so explicit that not much analytical effort is required. Let me tabulate the points I would emphasize. This document reflects an attempt in the interests of efficiency, to revise racial discrimination based on chromatism, the visible difference in skin color. (Chromatism seems to me to have something like a hold on the official philosophy of U.S. antiracist feminism. When it is not "Third World women," the catchphrase is "women of color." This leads to absurdities. Japanese women, for instance, have to be redefined as "Third World." Hispanics must be seen as "women of color." And postcolonial female subjects [women of the indigenous elite of Asia, Africa, Arabia], obvious examples of the production of Ariel—if Prospero is the imperial master—are invited to masquerade as Caliban in the margins.)[25]

The standards being applied in the document being used to legitimate racial discrimination show that both the native male and the native female are clearly inferior to the European female. Indeed, as in "William the Conqueror" and the classroom reaction to it, sexual difference comes into play only in the white arena. The concept of legitimacy in the union of the sexes only comes into being with the introduction of the European. And, even as Caliban is defined out, it is only the produced Ariel who is allowed into the arena; the final requirement for the acceptable half-caste is a "European liberal education."

Here, then, are extracts from the document itself:

> The chairman laid before (a Secret Court [of] the Directors of the Hon'ble Company Held on 6th March, 1822) a Paper signed by Himself and the Deputy Chairman submitting several suggestions in view to an exposition and practical illustration of the Standing Order of 1791 which provides "That no person the son of a Native Indian shall be appointed to employment in the Civil, Military, or Marine Service of the Company."[26]

Here are the passages on chromatism and the acceptability of the European female:

> It may be *fairly* deduced, that the *complexion* of those Persons was in view of the Court a serious objection to their admission. . . . The next object of consideration is the offspring of a connection between a European and a half-caste; and *it appears a matter of indifference whether the European blood be on the Male or the Female side.* The Candidates for admission to the Company's service, who have been of this class of persons, have since 1791 been subjected to the examination of one of the Committees of the Direction; and if they have exhibited signs of Native origin in their colour or otherwise, have been accepted or rejected by the Committee according to the degree in which their hue appeared objectionable or unobjectionable. These rejections . . . have produced some anomalies. One Brother has been accepted, another rejected. Europeans whose parents were both European, have been on the brink of Rejection for their dark complexion. . . . Discrepancies have arisen from the different views entertained by the Committee. (Italics mine.)

In the interest of the efficient management of these anomalies and absurdities, the following criteria are offered. Here we will encounter native intercourse implicitly placed outside of legitimacy as such, and the clinching requirement of a "European liberal education":

> It is submitted that the Sons of aboriginal Natives of India and of the Countries to the Eastward of Native Portugese Indians,

of Native West Indians, and of Africans of either sex, who are
the Offspring of a connection of such Natives with Europeans,
be invariably held ineligible. . . . That the Descendants from
aboriginal Native Indians in the second and succeeding generations shall be held eligible . . . on production of certain Certifi-
cates . . . that the grandfather or grandmother of the Candidate
. . . was bona fide an European . . . that the father or mother
of the Candidate was bona fide an European. A Certificate of
Marriage of the father and mother of the candidate. The Bap-
tismal Certificate of the Candidate. A certificate from the Master
or Masters of some reputable seminary or seminaries in the
United Kingdom of Great Britain and Ireland that the Candidate has had the benefit of a liberal Education under his or her
tuition for a period of six years. . . . The inconveniences which
might arise from the indiscriminate or unconditional admission
into the Company's service of the Descendants of aboriginal
native Indians in the second or succeeding generations will be
obviated . . . by the stipulated qualification of *legitimate birth*
and liberal European education. (Italics mine.)

To repeat, this distasteful document describes the efficient
articulation of the right of access to a white world administering the
black. Because I think that this point cannot be too strongly made, I
have put it forth as Exhibit C in my argument that much so-called
cross-cultural disciplinary practice—even when "feminist"—reproduces and forecloses colonialist structures: sanctioned ignorance and
a refusal of subject-status and thus "human"-ness; therefore, an
unexamined chromatism is not only no solution, but belongs to the
repertory of colonialist axiomatics. On the face of it, the document
seems infinitely more brutal and malevolent than anything that might
happen in the house of feminist criticism. But mere benevolence will
not remove the possibility that the *structural* effect of limited access
to the norm can be shared by two such disparate phenomena.

When versions of my general argument are presented to academic women's resource groups and the like, sympathy seems instan-
taneous. Yet, because of the presence of the double standard, the
difference in the quality or level of generosity of discourse and allocation that engage the first and the third worlds remains striking.
This discrepancy is also to be observed within curricular planning. In
the distribution of resources, feminist literary criticism celebrates the
heroines of the First World in a singular and individualist manner,
while treating the collective presence of women elsewhere in a plural-
ized and inchoate fashion. These tendencies are not covered over by

our campus battles for affirmative action on behalf of "women of color." Such battles should, of course, be fought with full participation. But these are ad hoc antisexist activities that should be distinguished from a specifically "feminist" enterprise. In the absence of persistent vigilance, there is no guarantee that an upwardly mobile woman of color in the U.S. academy would not participate in the structure I have outlined—at least to the extent of conflating the problems of ethnic domination in the United States with the problem of exploitation across the international division of labor (just as many in Britain tend to confuse it with problems of immigration law).[27] It may be painful to reckon that this, too, is a case of the certified half-caste's limited access to the norm. It is almost as if the problem of racism within feminism can qualify as such only when resident or aspiring to be resident in the First World.

Indeed, those of us who ask for these standards are becoming marginalized or tokenized within mainstream feminism. We are deeply interested in the tropological deconstruction of masculist universalism. But when questions of the inscription of feminine subject-effects arise, we do not want to be caught within the institutional performance of the imperialist lie. We know the "correction" of a performative deconstruction is to point at another troping and thus to another errant performance—that the critique must be persistent. We want the chance of an entry into the vertiginous process. And this can perhaps begin to happen if, in terms of disciplinary standards, you grant the thoroughly stratified larger theater of the Third World—the stage of so-called decolonization—equal rights of historical, geographical, and linguistic specificity as well as theoretical sophistication.

Notes

1. For a handy definition of essentialism, see Barry Hindess and Paul Q. Hirst, *Pre-capitalist Modes of Production* (London: Routledge, 1975), 9; for a discussion of essentialism in the feminist context, see Toril Moi, *Sexual/Textual Politics: Feminist Literary Theory* (New York: Methuen, 1985), 154 et passim. For a brief critique, see Spivak, "Criticism, Feminism, and the Institution," *Thesis Eleven* 10/11 (1984–85).

2. The references to these concerns are to be found pervasively in Paul de Man's later and Jacques Derrida's earlier works. For specific references, see de Man, *Allegories of Reading: Figural Language in Rousseau, Nietzsche, Rilke, and Proust* (New Haven: Yale University Press, 1979), 205, 208–9, 236, and 253; and Derrida, "Limited inc: abc," *Glyph* 2 (1977). For a practical reconsideration, see Spivak, "Sex and History in *The Prelude* (1805), Books Nine to Thirteen," in *In Other Worlds: Essays in Cultural Politics* (New York: Methuen, 1987), 46–47.

3. Because the Latin American countries have had a more direct and long-standing relationship with U. S. imperialism, the relationship and demands are more informed and specific even when oppressive.

4. For the dubious value of the truth of personhood in Baudelaire, see Paul de Man, *Blindness and Insight: Essays in the Rhetoric of Contemporary Criticism*, 2d. ed. (Minneapolis: University of Minnesota Press, 1983), 35; and *The Rhetoric of Romanticism* (New York: Columbia University Press, 1984), 243.

5. See Spivak, "Displacement and the Discourse of Woman," in *Displacement: Derrida and After,* ed. Mark Krupnick (Bloomington: Indiana University Press, 1983), 184–86.

6. Charles Baudelaire, *Baudelaire*, trans. Francis Scarpe (Baltimore: Penguin, 1961), 209. I have modified the translation when necessary and indicated line numbers in the text.

7. T. S. Eliot, "Tradition and the Individual Talent," in *The Sacred Wood: Essays on Poetry and Criticism*, 7th ed. (London: Methuen, 1967), 58 and 56, respectively.

8. For a more extensive account of this, see Spivak, "Finding Feminist Readings: Dante–Yeats," in *In Other Worlds*.

9. I will consider later the question of Jeanne Duval, Baudelaire's Eurafrican mistress. Here let me say that I am concerned with the deployment of the figure of the negress in the text. Of Duval, Baudelaire had written in his suicide note at age twenty-four: "[she] is the only woman I have ever loved—she has nothing" (Baudelaire, *Correspondence générale,* ed. Jacques Crépet [Paris: Louis Conrad, 1947], 1: 72; translation mine). Even if one were to read the poem as no more than a direct biographical transcript, one might wonder at the historical irony that produces such a hierarchized presentation of the only beloved woman.

10. De Man, *Romanticism*, 254.

11. I have discussed this at greater length in "Revolutions That As Yet Have No Model: Derrida's Limited Inc.," *Diacritics* 10, no. 4 (Winter 1980): 29–49.

12. Baudelaire, *Les Fleurs du mal*, ed. Antoine Adam (Paris: Garnier, 1961), 382.

13. For the most spectacular examples of this, see Derrida's treatment of Hegel in *Glas* (Paris: Galilée, 1974) and of Freud in *La Carte postale* (Paris: Flammarion, 1981).

14. Lisa Jardine, "'Girl Talk' (for Boys on the Left), or Marginalising Feminist Critical Praxis," *Oxford Literary Review* 8, nos. 1–2 (1986): 208–17.

15. Edward Ahearn, "Black Woman, White Poet: Exile and Exploitation in Baudelaire's Jeanne Duval Poems," *FR* 51 (1976). Andrew Bush, in a brilliant essay titled "'Le cygne' or 'El cisne': The History of a Misreading" (*Comparative Literature Studies* 17, no. 4 [December 1980]), completely reduces the asymmetrical deployment of the two women through a perfunctory continuist approach which disregards the rhetorical texture of the poem. Bush can thus speak of "the condition of exile, suffered variously by Andromache, the negress, the abandoned sailors, and the poet himself, all of whom are represented in the central images of the swan" (419). He traces the male line of Baudelaire's poetic brotherhood, adding Proust and Ruben Darío to the stars I have already mentioned. He emends "the opening words of 'Le cygne,' to . . . '*Andromaque* [Racine's play], je pense à vous!'" (422). Via Harold Bloom's notion of "the anxiety of influence," Bush goes on to a consideration of Baudelaire's oedipal problems: "An only child to a dead father and a mother, who, by remarriage, betrays the son, as he believes, Baudelaire would have us read Virgil, where he, a belated and corrupted Astyanax, is rewriting Racine" (423). Edward W. Kaplan ("Baudelaire's Portrait of the Poet as Widow: Three Poëmes en Prose and 'Le Cygne," *Symposium* 34, no. 3 [Fall 1980]) takes the male desire to appropriate the womb and the feminine in general as fulfilled in the declaration. Here too the rhetorical texture of the poem is ignored. "Baudelaire identifies here with bereaved women . . . as widow he is the exile," and finally, "[he] imitates the mother and creates" (245 and 246).

16. "It was a story about 'a new sort of woman,' wrote Carrie [Kipling's wife], and 'she turned out stunningly'. . . . She is presented in the round, as no earlier of Kipling's heroines had been" (Charles Carrington, *Rudyard Kipling: His Life and Work* [London: Macmillan, 1955], 223 and 224). But even such a temperate "feminist" gesture has been quickly misunderstood. The protagonist has been described as "a hard-riding young lady with a preference for men of action" (Stephen Lucius Gwynn, "The Madness of Mr. Kipling," in *Kipling: The Critical Heritage*, ed. Roger Lancelot Green [London: Routledge, 1971], 213).

17. Rudyard Kipling, *The Writings in Prose and Verse* (New York: Scribner's, 1913), 13:227. Hereafter cited in text as *WC*.

18. For favorable assessments of this passage, see *Kipling*, ed. Green, 213; and Carrington, *Rudyard Kipling*, 224.

19. Kingsley Amis, *Rudyard Kipling and His World* (New York: Scribners, 1975), 25.

20. I am not considering the vexed question of Kipling's "imperialism" here. I am looking rather at the fact that sexual difference becomes relevant in this text only in terms of the colonizer. It is, however, worth pointing at a poignant piece of evidence of the effects of imperialism. Almost all the Western critics I have read, many of them (such as T. S. Eliot, George Orwell, Lionel Trilling, Randall Jarrell) conveniently collected in *Kipling*, ed. Green, and in *Kipling and the Critics*, ed. Eliot L. Gilbert (New York: New York University Press, 1965), speak of the formative impact of Kipling's stories and novels upon their boyhood. Compare the following remark by a Bengali writer to that collective testimony: "I read Kipling's *Jungle Book* first at the age of ten in an East Bengal village, but never read anything else by him for fear of being hurt by his racial arrogance" (Nirad C. Chaudhuri, "The Wolf without a Pack," *TLS*, October 6, 1978: 1121). The above is a memory; it is followed in Chaudhuri's piece by a judgment, reflecting so-called decolonization and the disavowal of the economic, with which I cannot agree.

21. Both the Benjamin and the de Man passages are to be found in de Man, "'Conclusions': Walter Benjamin's 'The Task of the Translator'," in *The Resistance to Theory* (Minneapolis: University of Minnesota Press, 1986), 91–92.

22. David Arnold, "Famine in Peasant Consciousness and Peasant Action: Madras 1876–78," in *Subaltern Studies: Writings on South Asian History and Society*, ed. Ranajit Guha (Delhi: Oxford University Press, 1984). In this context, the representative assertion by Orwell, that Kipling's account of "nineteenth century Anglo-India" is "the best . . . picture we have" ("Rudyard Kipling," in *Kipling and the Critics*, ed. Gilbert, 82), must be understood to mean the best account of typical British self-representations of what India was about.

23. Arnold, "Famine," 73.

24. For considerations of a (sexed) subject-constitution outside of the discourse of psychoanalysis and counterpsychoanalysis, see Spivak, "Can the Subaltern Speak? Considerations of Widow-Sacrifice," *Wedge* nos. 7/8 (Winter/Spring 1985).

25. This distinction is taken from Roberto Fernandez Retamár, "Caliban: Notes Towards a Discussion of Culture in Our America," trans. Lynn Garafola et al., *Massachusetts Review* 15 (Winter/Spring 1979).

26. "L/P & S/1/2 Minutes of the Secret Court of Directors 1784–1858."

27. A text that puts us on guard against such conflations in the British context by frequently taking the geopolitical context into account is *Worlds Apart: Women under Immigration and Nationality Law*, ed. Jacqueline Bhabha et al. (London: Pluto Press, 1985).

Teletheory:
A Mystory

Gregory Ulmer

This whole book now is going to be a detective story of how to write.
—Gertrude Stein

The Future of Theory

What will have been beyond after postapplied grammatology? Thinking about the future of theory, now and then. And by chiasmus, inevitably, the theory of the future (futurology being for postcriticism what history was for classical criticism, or synchrony for modernism). But at the speed of thought now—mock something-or-other—it becomes necessary to ask what will have been next, in order to allow time for thought: tense, without anxiety. Hasn't this always been the temporality of the essay, whose narrator is his own John the Baptist? Still, a sapping perspective, a bird's-eye view in which one's work will no longer have been as influential or significant as it is not yet likely to become.

Let me think about something else, then and now. Not futurology, not history, not herstory (the most interesting possibility). I turn instead to *mystory:* the mystory of the future, of history and herstory; the *enigme* of my own next (to keep the French spelling in order to identify the specific dimension of theory in question. Roland Barthes taught us the usefulness of nomination and neologism for providing a glimpse of processes otherwise too fleeting, too elusive, too insignificant to be noticed—like dust settling, or cobwebs in the late afternoon, the level of reality to which Duchamp attended in his notebooks). A mystory is not prediction, description, prescription, or proscription, but self-exhortation, and in this respect it rejoins the

339

history of the essay as apostrophe. The mystorical derives from those parts of writers' journals in which unexecuted projects are described, as in this example from Barthes:

> An *Encyclopedia of Food* (dietetics, history, economy, geography, and above all, *symbolics*). A *Life of Illustrious Men* (read a lot of biographies and collect certain features, biographemes, as was done for Sade and Fourier). A *Compilation of Visual Stereotypes* ("Saw a North African in dark clothes, *Le Monde* under his arm, paying court to a blond girl sitting in a café"). *The Book/Life* (take some classic book and relate everything in life to it for a year). *Incidents* (mini-texts, one-liners, haiku, notations, puns, everything that falls, like a leaf). (Barthes, 1977, 150)

Such projects are assignments given to the future as a class and teach us something about the close relationship between theory and pedagogy. For Barthes, "it is not a question of recovering a pre-meaning, an origin of the world, of life, of facts, anterior to meaning, but rather to imagine a post-meaning: one must traverse, as though the length of an initiatic way, the whole of meaning, in order to be able to extenuate it, to exempt it" (87). Isn't this extenuation the temporality of teaching? In the classroom it is never a question, really, of what I mean, but this post-meaning: meaning not as denotation but as detonation, time bomb. Pragmatics, the effect of the communication on the receiver, is the linguistics of pedagogy. Once teachers were content to console themselves with the rare postcard from a former student—"thanks"—but now, in the moment of reader response and pragmatics, teachers begin to calculate the time of understanding, of *nachträglichkeit* (experienced as *déjà vu*). They mine the student heads, mined mind. The exploding drummers in *Spinal Tap* are an image of understanding.

Another image. A teacher works with time the way the pointillist, Georges Seurat, worked with color: an encyclopedia entry states that "this involved breaking down the colors present in nature into their constituent hues, transferring these to the canvas in their pure or primary state, as tiny brush strokes or dots, and leaving to the spectator's retina the task of re-constituting the hues as an optical mixture," to preserve the colors of nature in all their actuality and vividness. The method was based on the science of perception. Teachers work with cognition similarly, and their courses may be designed to be reconstituted in the minds of the students from a certain distance in time, just as, in order to get the proper effect of a pointillist painting, one must stand back a certain distance from the canvas. We need to know something about memory and the decay of information in the mind in order to work with post-meanings.

Derrida has investigated the peculiar temporality of theory, its already-not-yet structure, which, liberated from the metaphysics of teleology, may tell us something about the functioning of post-meanings. To understand the operation of theory we must remember, Derrida advises, that (for example) Freud, "the first and thus the only one to have undertaken, if not defined, self-analysis, did not himself know what it was" (Derrida, 1978, 121). The question Derrida poses with respect to Freud's example—the founding question of mystory—is: "how can an auto-biographical writing, in the abyss of an unterminated self-analysis, give *its* birth to a world institution?" (121).

I want to take note of two aspects of this question. First, part of Freud's lesson for the genre of theory concerns the time of understanding for the writer myself. Theory, that is, is written with the apostrophe of self-address typical of the essay method. A theoretical essay is not scholarship, obviously, not the communication of a prior sense, but the discovery of a direction in the process of writing. And it is also an assertion of comprehension that has much in common with the manifesto. Consider Derrida's assessment of the status of *Beyond the Pleasure Principle:*

> Psychoanalytic theory exists. The first words imply an affirmation to that effect: "In psychoanalytic theory, we admit . . ." etc. We are not obliged to believe it exists, yet we must be sure that Freud means that it exists and that things happen in it. This statement is not a performative; it claims to ascertain and take note, but it takes note of a note whose speaker is also its producer. He is supposed to have been its producer, and those whom he associates with the movement of this production all accepted the contract which institutes him as producer. Thus when Freud puts forward a statement implying that psychoanalytic theory exists, he is in no respect in the situation of a theoretician in the field of another science, an epistemologist, or a historian of science. He takes note of a title of which the contract implies that it is his by right. He makes a contract with himself, he writes to himself, as if someone were informing himself by registered letter (on duty-stamped paper) about the attested existence of a theoretical history which he himself had launched. (Derrida, 1978a, 86)

Here we have the temporality—the postal relay—of the *envoi:* Freud sends off a mystory and it comes back to him, to his name and credit, a science, or at least an institutionalized knowledge, a discursive formation. Discovery confirmed, repeated, legitimized.

So part of the theoretical process involves reception, in which one writer's question becomes another writer's premise. But the mystorical aspect intervenes on the side of discovery, with the problematic of the subject of knowledge. Derrida first raised this question in the context of Husserl's study of the origin of geometry, having to do with the problem of origins, of the foundation of a science on the ground of pre-science. The present of any idea is always pre-sent (*envoi*):

> Husserl repeatedly and obstinately returns to a question which is at bottom the following: how can the subjective egological evidence of sense become objective and intersubjective? How can it give rise to an ideal and true object, with all the characteristics that we know it to have: omnitemporal validity, universal normativity, intelligibility for "*everyone*," uprootedness out of all "*here and now*" factuality, and so forth? . . . How can subjectivity go out of itself in order to encounter or constitute the object? (Derrida, 1978b, 63).

In asking how a unique, individual subject discovers, invents, or otherwise gives rise to a system of knowledge, Derrida is posing the question of dissemination—the life of ideas in society, the relationship between invention and verification.

Derrida's extensive pursuit of this question is the basis for his interest in psychoanalysis, which he takes to be a potential model for a new notion of knowledge (that it might model a new order of reasoning in the way that geometry served as a model for classical science)—at least with regards to outlining the place of the idiosyncratic individual in a generalizable discourse formation. Freud is a good candidate for the study of invention (and for the exposure of the extent to which originality is part of the topos of *inventio*, the commonplaces of rhetoric), not only because he is close to us historically, but because of the nature of the knowledge he formulated. Freud's texts model a post-structuralist *inventio* in which theory formation is autobiographical, "but in a completely different way from what was believed before," in a way that will "force us to reconsider the whole topography of the *autos*, the self" (Derrida, 1978, 135).

In Freud's text, against the old model of "objective" science, "a 'domain' opens up in which the 'inscription' of a subject in his text is also the necessary condition for the pertinence and performance of a text, for its 'worth' beyond what is called empirical subjectivity. . . . The notion of truth value is utterly incapable of assessing this performance" (135). *Beyond the Pleasure Principle* manifests an inmixing of autobiographical and theoretical speculations, then, most notably the anecdote which Freud recited at the time of writing his text, recalling his stay with his daughter, Sophie, and watching his grandson play a game with a bobbin on a string—the famous *fort/da* game. That Freud's consideration of the Death Drive could be read as a kind of mourning, due to the untimely deaths of the daughter and grandson, is not the autobiographical element that interests Derrida. In place of an existentialist "abyss," Derrida explores the structure, so important to experimental fiction, of the *mise en abyme:*

> In every detail we can see the superposition of the subsequent description of the *fort/da* with the description of the speculative game, itself so assiduous and so repetitive, of the grandfather in writing *Beyond the Pleasure Principle*. It's not, strictly speaking, a matter of superposition, nor of parallelism, nor of analogy, nor of coincidence. The necessity that links the two descriptions is of a different sort: we shall not find it easy to give a name to it, but it is clearly the main thing at stake for me in the sifting, interested reading that I am repeating here. . . . The description of Ernst's game can also be read as an autobiography of Freud; not merely an auto-biography entrusting his life to his own more or less testamentary writing but a more or less living description of his own writing, of his way of writing *Beyond the Pleasure Principle* in particular. (Derrida, 1978, 119).

How is theory made by one who does not know? That is the question of mystory, the mystory of future theory, whose enigme is that somehow a particular anecdote can function as a general concept. Mystory shows how doxa and episteme are inscribed in one another.

In Nietzsche's *Ecce Homo*, Derrida finds another version of this structure that clarifies the status of the *auto* in this mystorical auto-bio-thanato-hetero-graphic writing scene:

> This account that buries the dead and saves the saved as immortal is not *auto*-biographical because the signatory narrates

his life, and the return of his past life as life and not as death; but rather because he tells *himself* the story of his life, he is the narration's first if not only consignee. Within the text. And since the "I" of this account only constitutes itself through the credit of the eternal return, the "I" does not exist, does not sign prior to the account qua eternal return. (Derrida, 1982, 25)

The *auto* of anecdotal invention merges with the *envoi* of the apostrophe, in mystory. We are admonished not to mistake Nietzsche for another, not to confuse the once living, now dead person with the text signed "Nietzsche," or "Freud." The anecdote inscribed in a theoretical text has a different status. It is told not for its informational interest, not in reference to a prior life, but as part of a "speculative" structure—the *mise en abyme*—a double take in which the narrative development of the event has formal, conceptual, explanatory consequences (it is the movement of the bobbin, away and back, that organizes Freud's formulation of the pleasure principle).

My question then is, Could tell-a-theory, the theoretical anecdote, be the mode best suited to televising theory? This question must be broken down into a series of problems, only a fraction of which can be elaborated in this essay. I predict, therefore, a series of essays forthcoming, dealing with the following matters (some of which will be touched on now): how to write an essay, rather than a treatise; how to generate a theory out of a personal anecdote; how to represent a concept by means of an anecdote; a refutation of the preceding procedures. The mystorical approach to the future of theory is to talk about what I plan to do next, which is somehow to do it before it gets done.

A Promising Essay

I am narrating an account of trying to figure out how to do something, how to make a certain kind of text. Specifically, I want to televise theory. Here is the introduction to a recent (unfunded) grant proposal, stating the problem that interests me:

> Wayne Booth, in his recent presidential address to the Modern Language Association, stated the problem that I wish to consider. "When we fail to test out scholarship by making its most important results accessible to nonspecialists, we also lose our capacity to address and thus recreate in each generation, the

literate public who can understand its stake in what we do.
. . . Our critical and scholarly jargons grow more recondite by
the day. While there's nothing inherently wrong in specialized
vocabulary for special subjects, there is something inherently
pathetic in a profession that cannot explain its work to the
public at least as well as the more articulate scientists manage
to explain theirs" (*PMLA* 98 [May 1983]). Booth identifies
what I take to be one of the major contemporary social and
cultural issues challenging our profession. The failure of the
humanities disciplines to communicate with the public may be
due in part to the fact that what separates specialized humanists
from laymen is not only our conceptual apparatus and the
discourses in which it is expressed, but the very medium in
which we work—the printed word. Our culture has experienced
a communications revolution. During the Renaissance, humanists led the educational reforms associated with the printing
press. Humanists today are similarly responsible for developing
the educational potential of the new technologies of writing.
Following the lessons of our Renaissance counterparts, this responsibility is twofold. The first is to translate into the "vulgate"
(television's audiovisual language now, rather than the national
languages) the principal works of the disciplines of knowledge.
The Annenberg Foundation recognized this need when it
granted $150 million to the Corporation for Public Broadcast-
ing "to create an innovative program of college courses for
Americans in their homes." These programs are supposed to be
more than "on-air blackboard lectures." The problem is that
our technology is more developed than are our theories of how
"to write" with our new instruments. Which poses the second
responsibility—the need to develop video essays worthy of the
name, to devise a new genre that will serve educators in the
electronic era as well as did the literary essay in the Gutenberg
era. The originality of my study will be its contention that
contemporary critical theory is not part of the problem, but is
the solution to the difficulties of popularization, in that it teaches
specialists how to do intellectual work in the new media. (And
so forth.)

Later in the proposal I promise to design a prototype for a new
educational program that will introduce lay adults to the languages
of the specialized disciplines, just as "Sesame Street" introduces pre-
schoolers to ordinary language.

The present essay is a speculation on the making of this prototype. I imagine, in fact, that this essay (any essay?) may be read in

several temporalities. At one level, keeping in mind my project to design a video writing capable of doing intellectual work—everything from research to popularization—based on post-structuralist theory and postmodernist art, this essay may be read as an attempt to define the "force" of "theory" as a hybrid genre. As Culler notes, "theory" is a genre because of the way its works function:

> These works exceed the disciplinary framework within which they would normally be evaluated and which would help to identify their solid contributions to knowledge. To put it another way, what distinguishes the members of this genre is their ability to function not as demonstrations within the parameters of a discipline but as redescriptions that challenge disciplinary boundaries. The works we allude to as "theory" are those that have had the power to make strange the familiar and to make readers conceive of their own thinking, behavior, and institutions in new ways. Though they may rely on familiar techniques of demonstration and argument, their force comes—and this is what places them in the genre I am identifying—not from the accepted procedures of a particular discipline but from the persuasive novelty of their redescriptions. (Culler, 9)

A close examination of the positioning of anecdotes in theoretical texts, especially the imitation in theory of the narrative structure of anecdotes, might be a clue to the power theory has to reorganize thought—to last within memory and hence to provide that around which ideas cohere.

At another level, everything discussed now is by way of anticipating one aspect of making a video essay: the problem of narration, narrative, of showing and telling theory. The value of this level is principally for me, although it may have pedagogical applications, How should I communicate with students in a theoretical way, in the "audio-visual" medium of classroom instruction? How may I teach theoretically—with the force of theory—rather than teach about theory? In short, these questions take into account that teaching theory is a practice, that theory and practice are never separable in pedagogy. Mystory approaches theory from the side of discovery, from the side of not yet knowing what it is, rather than from the side of verification, telling about it afterwards. And from this perspective, everyday life begins to function epistemically. I am promising a demonstration of mystory—next season.

But first, patiently hear a few preliminaries. In talking about plans for writing in video, it is also possible to show something about the essay mode (which, like narrative, is not specific to any one medium). The essay is to scholarship what drawings (preliminary sketches) are to finished paintings, to borrow Wittgenstein's analogy —crucial to the stylistic tradition upon which mystory may trade:

> After several unsuccessful attempts to weld my results together into a whole, I realized that I should never succeed. . . . My thoughts were soon crippled if I tried to force them on in any single direction against their natural inclination. —And this was, of course, connected with the very nature of the investigation. For this compels us to travel over a wide field of thought criss-cross in every direction. —The philosophical remarks in this book are, as it were, a number of sketches of landscapes which were made in the course of these long and involved journeyings. The same or almost the same points were always being approached afresh from different directions, and new sketches made. Very many of these were badly drawn or uncharacteristic, marked by all the defects of a weak draughtsman. And when they were rejected a number of tolerable ones were left, which now had to be arranged and sometimes cut down, so that if you looked at them you could get a picture of the landscape. Thus this book is really only an album. (Wittgenstein, 1968, ix)

Perhaps it is more important to observe that the sketching is being done on a walk through a field, and that such walks are an ancient topos for memory and for rhetorical invention. Moreover, this wandering, strolling walk, ever since Montaigne compared his mode of thought to such promenades, has become equally the topos for the modern essay form (Haas, 47). That a quantity of instances in which the experience of theoretical method is compared with traveling a road now occur to me suggests something about concept formation as aesthetic pattern. There is an aesthetic pleasure in bringing together various examples, and a conceptual result: informational enrichment as the examples coalesce into a model. "Thinking is perhaps, after all," Heidegger remarked, "an unavoidable path, which refuses to be a path of salvation and brings no new wisdom. The path is at most a field path, a path across fields, which does not just speak of renunciation but already has renounced, namely, renounced the claim to a binding doctrine and a valid cultural achievement or a deed of the spirit. Everything depends on the step back, fraught with error" (Heidegger, 1975, 185).

Then we recall that in *On the Way to Language* thinking as a walk in the country is contrasted explicitly with scientific method; against the directions of science, we are to follow language, to let it be, to say its own nature. To listen to language as itself an event is essential to the psychoanalytic episteme. Lacan noted a knot in the conjugations of *suivre* (to follow) and *être* (to be)—both conjugated in the first-person singular as *je suis* (I follow/I am). This knot becomes entangled in another one, the plurality of *sens*—"sense," "meaning," and "direction." In reading Lacan's version of thought as travel, we can understand why Derrida, in his own allegorical journey (the "Envois" section of *La carte postale*), suggested that to do a history of theory we would first need a history of roads:

> The highway is a particularly apt example of what I mean when I speak of the function of the signifier in as much as it polarizes, catches, groups a bundle of significations. . . . The signifier is polarizing. The signifier creates the field of significations. . . . Take a map of the superhighways of communication, and observe how is traced from south to north the route that crosses the country to link one river basin to another, one plain to another, to cross over bridges, organizing itself. You will notice that this map best expresses, in its relation of man to the earth, the role of the signifier. Let us now be like that person who marvelled that the water routes passed precisely through the towns. . . . What happens when we lack a highway, and we are forced, in order to go from one point to another, to put together one to another little byways, a more or less divided mode of clusters of significations. To go from one point to another, we would have a choice among different elements of the network. (Lacan, 328–29)

Lacan is speaking of the way the signifier organizes the unconscious, in the context of explaining the delirium of the schizophrenic President Schreber. The interest for teletheory is not the "idea" in each case, but the image, the pattern joining Wittgenstein, Heidegger, Lacan, Derrida (and a host of others) in a common model for the operations of thought and writing as wandering in a landscape, following a path, a road, and perhaps recording the journey or the landscape as one goes.

Narrative Explanation

To approach knowledge from the side of not knowing what it is, from the side of the one who is learning, not from that of the one who already knows, is to do mystory. What is the experience of knowing, of coming to or arriving at an understanding—characterized as following a path crisscrossing a field—if not a narrative experience, the experience of following a narrative? Narrativity as knowledge has a processual character: "the reader's attitude is a teleologically guided form of attention, always enlivened by the promise of additional insights. Following a story is very much a temporal process, not a logic sequitur" (Holdheim, 238–39). To the extent that a journey through a landscape is an adequate metaphor for theoretical method, the classic structure of narrative acts or functions—departure, interdiction, rendezvous—constitutes an allegory of comprehension.

Hayden White has noted the unity of narrative and explanation at this universal level of high generalization: "far from being a problem, narrative might well be considered a solution to a problem of general human concern, namely, the problem of how to translate *knowing* into *telling*" (White, 1). To support his point, he adds a footnote on etymology: "The words 'narrative,' 'narration,' 'to narrate,' and so on derive via the Latin *gnarus* ('knowing,' 'acquainted with,' 'expert,' 'skillful,' and so forth) and *narro* ('relate,' 'tell') from the Sanskrit root *gnâ* ('know')." In more specific terms, we can say that the two codes describing the forward movement of narrative—action and enigma (from Barthes)—have an equivalent in argument—demonstration and question. As Bill Nichols observes, in an excellent application of narrative theory to the language of film, narrative pleasure derives from the "simulation" of an explanation: "Things change. Yet the end refers us to the beginning. The middle gives us an account of this change. But it is more than simply a chronicle. Narratives are also a way of accounting *for* change. That is, they are a form of explanation and the great bulk of explanation takes place in the middle of a narrative" (Nichols, 76).

Nichols follows Kuhn in suggesting that historical narratives differ from science, "which explains deductively, by recourse to general laws or principles." Both historical and scientific explanations function by means of pattern recognition, but "if history is explanatory, that is not because its narratives are covered by general laws. Rather it is because the reader who says, 'now I know what happened,' is simultaneously saying, 'Now it makes sense; now I understand; what was for me previously a mere list of acts has fallen into a recognizable pattern'" (76–77). But Kurt Hübner, following A. C. Danto's formalization of historical science, sees little difference between narrative and deductive explanations. "Narration can be said to take the following basic form: 1) x is F at time t; 2) H happens to x at time t2; 3) x is G at time t3. Hence no. 2, the middle part of the narration, explains how the transition from no. 1 to no. 3 took place. The general law is indeed missing in this explanation, but it is indicated; it can be distilled, so to speak, from the explanation 'An F to which H happens changes to G' " (Hübner, 181). Holdheim perhaps strikes a compromise between these views when he notes that the hermeneutic circle unifies the aesthetic and cognitive aspects of narrative. He cites W. B. Gallie:

> "the logical texture, the ground of intelligibility, of stories matches exactly with that of everyday life." In fact it appears (though indirectly) from his discussion that even scientific prediction is really a sharpened, an absolutized version of normal presentiment and foresight; that existential contingency, similarly, has been transformed into a temporary obstacle to knowledge; that scientific verification itself is a methodological contraction of experiential processes; that the *sequitur* of causality is a somewhat Procrustean formalization of following in time. Scientific logic is firmly grounded in a *Lebenswelt* that it methodically rearranges for its own purposes, which are not those of narrative understanding. (Holdheim, 241)

That narratives may function as explanations, cognitively, or that explanations may produce the aesthetic pleasure of stories, provides a point of departure for the more specific question about the function of anecdotes in theory. But I delay that consideration in order to take note of one further preliminary issue. There is another way that theory and narrative converge: besides both being characterized as "following" (a path), both are organized around sight (for my purposes, at any rate, in dealing with film narrative). The Greek roots of "idea" and "theory," as Heidegger reminded us, are sight terms, a derivation that is still evident in the use of the expression "I see" to mean "I understand." Film (video = see) obviously addresses and organizes an act of seeing, literalizing, in a sense, the potential of the impulse that first led to the formulation of thought in terms of sight:

> We, late born, are no longer in a position to appreciate the significance of Plato's daring to use the word *eidos* for that which in everything and in each particular thing endures as present. For *eidos*, in the common speech, meant the outward

aspect [*Ansicht*] that a visible thing offers to the physical eye. Plato exacts of this word, however, something utterly extraordinary: that it name what precisely is not and never will be perceivable with physical eyes. (Heidegger, 1977, 20)

In principle, then, film should be fully capable of theoretical writing. Indeed, we could suppose that film is the technological realization or literalization of the ancient notion of contemplation, just as the airplane is the technological realization of the ancient dream of flight. (In this vein, in-flight movies would be a popularization of shamanistic trances.) The ratio of the sensible to the intelligible, mediated through the sense of sight, is a philosopheme of Western metaphysics at least since Plato, then—"logocentrism," in Derrida's terms.

The feminist critique of film narrative reveals the patriarchal ideology inherent in the philosopheme of theory as seeing. It is possible that narrative, like the gaze, is male. Teresa de Lauretis credits Barthes with noting the connection relating language, narrative, and the Oedipus, such that narrative movement is directed by masculine desire. De Lauretis, citing Barthes, writes: "The pleasure of the text is an Oedipal pleasure (to denude, to know, to learn the origin and the end), if it is true that every narrative (every unveiling of the truth) is a staging of the (absent, hidden, or hypostasized) father—which would explain the solidarity of narrative forms, of family structures, and of prohibitions of nudity" (de Lauretis, 107–8). Laura Mulvey, who observed a certain sadism in this narrative drive, provides a description of male pleasure in narrative cinema, based on a tension between a mode of representation of woman in film and conventions surrounding the diegesis (the imaginary space and time essential to filmic realism):

> Each is associated with a look: that of the spectator in direct scopophilic contact with the female form displayed for his enjoyment (connoting male fantasy) and that of the spectator fascinated with the image of his like set in an illusion of natural space, and through him gaining control and possession of the woman within the diegesis. . . . By means of identification with him, through participation in his power, the spectator can indirectly possess her too. (Mulvey, 421)

The implications of this matrix joining narrative, sight, and theory for mystory are numerous and complex. For now I would just emphasize one point already suggested in Barthes's remarks—that in phallogocentrism "truth is a woman." In sorting out what Nietzsche meant by this phrase, Derrida remarks that it has to do with the temporary convergence, in the history of science, of "idea" and "woman," as movements: in the era following Plato,

> the philosopher is no longer the truth. Severed from himself, he has been severed from truth. Whether he himself has been exiled, or whether it is because he has permitted the idea's exile, he can now only follow in its trace. At this moment history begins. Now the stories start. Distance—woman—averts truth—the philosopher. She bestows the idea. And the idea withdraws, becomes transcendent, inaccessible, seductive. It beckons from afar. Its veils float in the distance. The dream of death begins. It is woman. (Derrida, 1979, 87 and 89)

The question posed by feminism to film narrative concerns how the female spectator is positioned in a patriarchal ideology—how a female viewer comprehends narratives structured according to male desire. Posed in this way, it seems possible that there might be another way to tell stories, or that it might be possible to represent reality without narrative. What is at stake in this possibility may be best appreciated in this joining of truth and narrative—"truth" as a concept, delimited within an ideology. For the notion of truth in question has a history, we are told; it arose as a cosmology during the seventh to fifth centuries B.C. and has been variously termed "idealism," "monologism," and "logocentrism." Here is Paul Feyerabend's description of this "world view":

> Situations which made sense when tied to a particular type of cognition now become isolated, unreasonable, apparently inconsistent with other situations: we have a "chaos of appearances." The "chaos" is a direct consequence of the simplification of language that goes with the belief in a True World. Moreover, all the manifold abilities of the observers are now directed towards this True World, they are adapted to a *uniform* aim, shaped for *one particular* purpose, they become more similar to each other which means that man becomes impoverished together with his language. He becomes impoverished at precisely the moment he discovers an autonomous "I" and proceeds to what some have been pleased to call a "more advanced notion of God." . . . the distinction between appearance (first impression, mere opinion) and reality (true knowledge) spreads everywhere. Even the task of the *artist* now consists in arranging shapes in such a manner that the

underlying essence can be grasped with ease. (Feyerabend, 262)

Feyerabend's point is that style and epistemology are inscribed one within the other, imply one another. Whatever the gender situation might be, is it the case that everyone is positioned similarly with respect to the cosmology of a civilization? What is our situation now? We are changing our cosmology. Our notion of truth is undergoing change. How is this story to be told? Feminism suggests that the conventions of narrative realism must be abandoned and narrative pleasure denied, or at least this possibility is a matter of debate within feminism. "Disproving the epistemological claims of a particular medium or artistic practice is a different thing from analyzing its ideological effects in a particular conjuncture," Christine Gledhill remarks, and continues:

> Thus, I would argue that *Camera Obscura's* rejection of early women's filmmaking is both right and wrong: "We feel that most of these filmmakers fell into the trap of trying to employ an essentially male-oriented bourgeois notion of film—the notion of film as a window on the world, and have simply chosen to shoot out of other windows than did most filmmakers before the women's movement." It is not clear that "shooting out of other windows" could not be a very illuminating and subversive activity. (Gledhill, 28)

This question is crucial to mystory, with its interest in the anecdote—a quotidian form—as theory, in that the rejection of realist narrative is due in part to the possibility that "everyday life and its struggles can only be experienced in ideological terms; knowledge about the causes and nature of these struggles is produced only by theoretical practice" (26).

Feyerabend poses the feminist question on the level of epistemology and scientific method: how to satisfy the theoretical desire in an era in which intelligibility exceeds the range of reason? Pointing out that our very observational reports, our factual statements, "either *contain* theoretical assumptions or *assert* them by the manner in which they are used," Feyerabend wonders how to examine the presuppositions upon which our relation to the world is based. "The first step in our criticism of familiar concepts and procedures, the first step in our criticism of 'facts,' must therefore be an attempt to break the circle. We must invent a new conceptual system that suspends, or clashes with the most carefully established observational results"

(Feyerabend, 32). Derrida makes a similar point: "Are we dealing here with a circle or an abyss? The circle would consist in seeking to account for reason by reason, to render reason to the principle of reason, in appealing to the principle in order to make it speak of itself at the very point where, according to Heidegger, the principle of reason says nothing about reason itself. The abyss, the hole, the *Abgrund*, the empty 'gorge' would be the impossibility for a principle of grounding to ground itself" (Derrida, 1983, 9). Derrida is concerned here with the foundation of the modern university, "suspended above a most peculiar void." He has hinted at the way to think through this question, by shifting the "abyss" to the *"mise en abyme"* and the refunctioned *auto* (the vehicle for a theoretical road).

How to think in this situation? How to represent this thinking to ourselves? It is interesting to note how often modern theorists suggest the model of language learning for theoretical invention. Wittgenstein's *Philosophical Investigations* and his central strategy—the language games—are based on learning language from the child's point of view from the side of discovery, and hence are mystorical:

> Fundamental conceptual change presupposes new world views and new languages capable of expressing them. . . . by incorporation into a language of the future, which means *that one must learn to argue with unexplained terms and to use sentences for which no clear rules of usage are as yet available.* Just as a child who starts using words without yet understanding them, who adds more and more uncomprehended linguistic fragments to his playful activity, discovers the sense-giving principle only *after* he has been active in this way for a long time—in the same way the inventor of a new world view (and the philosopher of science who tries to understand his procedure) must be able to talk nonsense until the amount of nonsense created by him and his friends is big enough to give sense to all its parts. (Feyerabend, 256–57)

Since change is the issue, narrative should still be the best mode of representation for the new outlook. The analogy is especially suited to my project, attempting to learn a new language for inventing a video essay. The essential lesson in Feyerabend is that to be able to produce or to grasp new perceptual and conceptual relations, new styles of representation are needed; critical discussion alone is not sufficient for such changes. In short, a relationship to knowledge that would keep itself open to the future cannot rest exclusively on criticism, verification, and/or falsification, but must pursue irrelevant activities, play, and creativity. We have had sufficient calls for alternatives to interpretation, formal method, and the other traditional activities of our disciplines. What is needed now is some thought devoted to what the alternatives themselves might be. Feyerabend has at least named them.

Several points might be worth noting while we are still trying to clarify the conditions and terms with which future theory may work. First, with respect to language learning, current definitions of the ideological effect of film—the positioning of the subject that occurs in the "passage" of the film into comprehension—are formulated using Lacan's concepts of the Imaginary and the Symbolic, which are notions defining the developmental psychology of the entry into language. To view a film with pleasure, at a certain level, is to replay the negotiation of the Oedipal stage—"the symbolic realm involves a displacement away from this imaginary fix, a de-centering of the ego's place as the center of the self, to relationships, not of possession but of exchange" (Nichols, 32). Hence, Feyerabend's analogy for conceptual change has direct applicability to style in filmmaking and viewing.

Second, with respect to the stylistic experiments required for future theory, we may look to the history of narrative for some possible directions. The novel, of course, was a composite genre, made up of a variety of more basic, "simple" forms. Contemporary experimental fiction, it is said, represents the breakup or dissolution of the novel into its constituent simple forms, with each such form (temporarily) developing autonomously, or entering into new combinations. The essay, similarly, is a composite genre, synthesizing in a more or less didactic mode such simple forms as dialogue, speech, diary, aphorism, biography, and the like (Haas, 35). The anecdote is a simple form important to both the novel and the essay, and in the dissolution of the traditional or conventional organizing genres of the past, we may expect that this simple form is capable of new effects in a refunctioned essay. Just what this essay could be like is the mystory.

Theory Diegesis

How to film theory? There is the possibility that simply to enjoy a conventional narrative film, in the present ideological circumstances, is to experience a simulation of logocentric truth. Socrates, in any case, taught that falling in love put us on the way to understanding the Good. I said in my grant proposal that humanists today have a twofold responsibility—to translate existing theory into the vulgate of television, and to devise a new video essay capable of doing the cognitive work of future theory. Let me make at least a modest gesture towards figuring out how to accomplish some part of the first task, in a time in which love is changing just as much as is truth. A prelusive question, now. Is an essay by Heidegger or Wittgenstein, for example, filmable at all?

I finally understood why I enjoy reading Heidegger when I began to think about his texts in terms of the pleasure of narrative (as defined here by Nichols):

> Narrative dangles a lure before us; it promises to unfold in time, yet not run down or dissipate; to take form, to in-form. Desire—the desire to recognize a return, a closure, to enjoy pleasure as the subject-who-knows when we recognize the repetition/transformation of the beginning in the ending— snares us in these unraveling coils of events loosely called the story. Delay teases and tantalizes, like foreplay, with its promise of things to come. . . . If we take the lure, we yield to the tale. It carries us, transports us into a fictional world (the diegesis) where the desire invoked will be satisfied. Pleasure is not wholly deferred. Various puzzles, little enigmas are continually posed, deferred, and resolved; partially resolved; repressed or forgotten, replaced by new enigmas. Narrative plays upon a retrospective or retroactive principle in which the partiality of the moment is suspended only to be engaged by a later influx of supplemental significance. (Nichols, 74–75)

Two aspects of this discussion of narrative pleasure should be stressed: the concepts of enigma and of diegesis as they function in a theoretical essay. Before treating the specifically anecdotal dimension of theory, we should observe the operations of narrative as such in theory.

Barthes identified the motor codes of narrative, the means by which a narrative moves forward, as the codes of action and enigma. In his mastery of these devices, Heidegger is the Hitchcock of the essay. I want to indicate briefly with one example—"The Thing"— how Heidegger uses these narrative codes (saving for another time an *S/Z*–like reading of *Being and Time*), as well as how he constructs the diegesis. The "diegesis" is the imaginary or fictional space and time implied by the narrative. In classical narrative, as Nichols explains, the diegesis is unfragmented, closed, illusionistic; affords the pleasure of recognition (familiarity) and allows identification (of ourselves as subjects); and takes on thematic resonance through the use of symbols (signifiers already charged with meaning) and markers (items of daily life with fewer connotations), directed, Barthes would say, by the cultural and semic codes (Nichols, 85).

Part of the interest of "The Thing" is that it concerns Being in a world transformed by technology which has abolished all distance and shrunk space and time: "the peak of this abolition of every possibility of remoteness is reached by television, which will soon pervade and dominate the whole machinery of communications" (Heidegger, 1975, 165). He is right, which marks the imperative for learning television. "The Thing" announces itself from the beginning as a "monster thriller" (even if I had not associated it with Howard Hawks's *The Thing*), with a disaster warning due to our failure to relate properly with things, with the material world: "Man stares at what the explosion of the atom bomb could bring with it. He does not see that the atom bomb and its explosion are the mere final emission of what has long since taken place, has already happened. . . . What is this helpless anxiety still waiting for, if the terrible has already happened?" (166). Here is the already-not-yet temporality of theory again, joined with the raising of an enigma, delaying the resolution of this paradox. "The aesthetic gratification narrative affords helps attenuate the force of real contradictions; it also helps identify them. The power of this invocation of desire can be readily yoked to a reinforcement of the *status quo*, but it can also be harnessed to the possibilities of change" (Nichols, 103).

Having shown us the atom bomb, one of those symbols that "thickens the narrative," Heidegger turns to the level of detail—the close-up—to pose the more specific question, "What is a thing? Man has so far given no more thought to the thing as a thing than he has to nearness. The jug is a thing. What is a jug?" Now the story of the jug will be told, and in the telling a diegesis is established, a fictional situation in which a scene involving this jug is played out. Through a series of delays and partial answers, a kind of documentary of the jug unfolds—a potter who forms the clay into a vessel, the jug itself, the void of the empty jug, then filled with wine, to be poured out onto the ground finally. And with each shot, a voice-over narration that entertains and rejects a variety of possible definitions of the jug as "thing." The "thing," it turns out, in its essence, has never been represented. "What, then, is the thing as thing, that its essential nature has never yet been able to appear?" (Heidegger, 1975, 171).

With this enigma and its promise of solution I am completely hooked (lured into this sequence with the hope of seeing a completely other monster).

The partial solution to this enigma follows almost immediately; we are shown at once that it is not a question of the thing as such, but the function it fulfills as part of a human action or event that is the clue to the mystery. The dramatic action of the essay is suspended in mid-article with a freeze-frame on the pouring of a libation. "But the gift of the outpouring is what makes the jug a jug. In the jugness of the jug, sky and earth dwell. . . . The outpouring is the libation poured out for the immortal gods. . . . In the gift of the outpouring earth and sky, divinities and mortals dwell together all at once" (172–73). I realize that in the action of pouring (a mini-drama selected out of the activities of an entire civilization) we have been shown a *symbolic* gesture, that this nonsensical wasting of the wine is the clue to understanding the invisible, spiritual dimension of human culture, that this is Heidegger's solution to the problem of *eidos*, suggesting the intelligible by means of the sensible. The narrative diegesis extends only this far, but the essay continues, the enigmas multiply.

The libation was the act of a mortal who imagines immortals. Death, the most dramatic of events, is evoked. "The mortals are human beings. They are called mortals because they can die. To die means to be capable of death as death. Only man dies. The animal perishes. It has death neither ahead of itself nor behind it" (178). But this death is not a murder any detective can solve. Something happens to the narrative at this point: the promise to resolve the enigma is withdrawn and I am provoked instead with a riddle. "The world's worlding cannot be explained by anything else nor can it be fathomed through anything else; this impossibility does not lie in the inability of our human thinking to explain and fathom in this way. Rather, the inexplicable and unfathomable character of the world's worlding lies in this, that causes and ground remain unsuitable for the world's worlding. As soon as human cognition here calls for an explanation, it fails to transcend the world's nature, and falls short of it" (180). We are admonished to "step back from the thinking that merely represents—that is, explains—to the thinking that responds and recalls" (181). The step back replaces the truth of correspondence (representation) with a truth of co-respondence.

What has happened? I have been lured into an ersatz narrative, promised the pleasure of explanation, and frustrated instead with a riddle and its commentary (similar to the effect in *What is called thinking?* when we are led to expect a definition, but find instead a pun, encouraging us to imagine a thinking that is called, a calling, called into thought). The narrative enigma exceeds the action, thus turning the reader into the actant venturing on that path within language, out of a visible into an abstract diegesis. Now the enigma concerns the etymology of *thing* as a word (not as a jug). We are being weaned from narrative and from explanation at once, while being shown another way to think. The jug, we now learn, was chosen for discussion out of all possible things because one of the meanings (etymology) of the word *thing* is "gathering": the act of libation poured from a jug *gathers* the fourfold into one. Thinking, I gather from this image, may be a manner of assemblage, collecting. Heidegger is beginning to help us listen to language and respond to it with our own speech. "Thinking in this way, we are called by the thing as the thing. In the strict sense of the German word *bedingt*, we are the be-thinged, the conditioned ones" (181). A discovery. The text is no longer moving forward following narrative codes, but poetic ones—in this case the motivation is a homophonic relationship between *bedingt* and the imperative *denkt!* of *denken* (to think), similar to the *nearness* of *thing* and *think* in English. So this is the nearness we had not yet begun to think, or at least the nearness of *thing* to *think represents* what had been left unthought, or that which makes available for thought another way to write.

Let me try to summarize at least part of the lesson for teletheory in this reading, in this context. The model for performing theoretical explanation (in video, but also in the classroom) is narrative. In the comparison of explanation to narrative thus far, most attention has been given to the syntagmatic dimension of narrative tracing the process of change, especially as it involves the code of enigmas, also termed the "hermeneutic" code, and the "code of truth" (Barthes). But, as Barthes established in *S/Z*, narrative also includes three paradigmatic (nontemporal) codes—semic, cultural, and symbolic:

> The readerly text is a *tonal* text (for which habit creates a reading process just as conditioned as our hearing: one might say there is a *reading eye* as there is a tonal ear, so that to unlearn the readerly would be the same as to unlearn the tonal), and its tonal unity is basically dependent on two sequential codes: the revelation of truth and the coordination of the actions represented: there is the same constraint in the gradual order of melody and in the equally gradual order of the narrative sequence. Now, *it is precisely this constraint which*

> *reduces the plural of the classic text.* . . . The classic text,
> therefore, is actually tabular (and not linear), but its tabularity
> is vectorized, it follows a logico-temporal order. It is a multiva-
> lent but incompletely reversible system. What blocks its reversi-
> bility is just what limits the plural nature of the classic text.
> These blocks have names: on the one hand, truth; on the other,
> empiricism: against—or between—them, the modern text
> comes into being. (Barthes, 1974, 30)

The modern text—the writerly, rather than the readerly text—undoes
the code of truth, yet it may still function as a model for explanation.
"Who," Feyerabend asked, "has the fortitude, or even the insight, to
declare that 'truth' might be unimportant, and perhaps even undesirable?" (Feyerabend, 171). This question makes more sense when
we understand "truth" in Barthes's terms.

The crucial question for teletheory is whether and in what way
a writerly, experimental fiction may function as a model for an alternative mode of explanation. Holdheim, committed to hermeneutics
and to a realist notion of history, rejects this option, whereas White
promotes it. Feminism so far has offered the best argument for following White, in this regard, exploring the possibilities of herstory: a
new notion of history, as E. Ann Kaplan explains, that fuses a "subjective" history (history as personal memory) with the history of the
larger society; one that asks questions rather than offering answers:

> It is clear from *Dora* [the film] at least that the filmmakers are
> developing close links between history and fictional narrative—
> that they do not differentiate the two. Thus, the traditional
> (male) idea of history as a search for the past, for what is
> missing, is connected to the traditional notion of narrative as
> starting with a lack and involving the search for the hidden
> secret, usually linked to women's sexuality. A new kind of story-
> telling will therefore lead to a new kind of feminist history. . . .
> Taken as a whole, the entire structure of *Dora* abandons the
> linear/logical mode and reflects the new kind of fiction and
> history the filmmakers consider necessary. Like *Argument*,
> *Dora* is constructed in a manner closer to music or poetry than
> to prose narrative. Rhythm is an essential component in both
> films. (Kaplan, 152–53)

Theory films are already being made, in other words, and this is the
most important development in the current of theory and criticism
today. But these films are herstorical, not mystorical, the latter being
the thing I am trying to think.

Heidegger's "The Thing" is itself herstorical in its explanatory structure. Gledhill suggests, citing *Camera Obscura*'s attempt to reconcile antirealist cinema with the needs of a diversified women's movement, the possibility of a *mise en scène* presented without action and enigma: " 'What we felt we needed was not a person to identify with but situations in which we could imagine ourselves, within a structure of distanciation which insures room for critical analysis' " (Gledhill, 27). Now the production of such situations may be accomplished by means of the paradigmatic codes alone, which might be a way to focus on the particular dilemma of the female position in a patriarchal episteme. "The connotation 'non-male' or 'substitute phallus' required by patriarchal ideology is imposd through a system of iconic rather than fictional or narrative codes, so that women are realized filmically as 'to-be-looked-at' images rather than in speech or action. . . . 'in a way which places her role in the film as iconic rather than diegetic' " (32–33). Similarly, in a reevaluation of the usefulness of Pasolini, de Lauretis proposes "that the question of imaging—the articulation of meaning to image, language, and sound, and the viewer's subjective engagement in that process—must be reformulated in terms that are themselves to be elaborated, recast, or posed anew" (de Lauretis, 46–47).

Heidegger writes theory in a way that suggests a model for how to film theory in a feminist way. He begins with a minimal narrative, producing a diegetic effect that the essay then plays against and between, as Barthes proposed a writerly text should do. The diegesis furnishes a setting or *situation* with things or objects which operate at two levels—as things whose connotations must be read, and as words whose associations must be developed (both actions requiring an active reader). The "I am/I follow" (*je suis*) of the diegesis is replaced by an activity that may be named with a neologism: *be-think*. The jug-wine scene, for example, implies an allegory of meaning, representing an ancient metaphor for linguistic "form/content"—the container and the contained. The meaning (once was) in the text the way the wine is in the jug. But what does the scene tell us if not that "the step back" requires us to make a libation of meaning—for to empty the words, to pour out the meaning, is a wasteful gesture (non-sense)—before we may gather what *is* up. In any case, Barthes refunctions Balzac's narrative when he finds that the code of action and the symbolic code coincide, occupy the same level (the paradigmatic repeated in the syntagmatic—Jakobson's definition of poetry) in the castrato/castration problematic. The lesson:

read the diegesis in terms of the symbolic code, if you would film theory.

The Pensive Essay

Leaving a number of notes sounded in the preceding section unanswered, let me review one more example of a composition that bethinks, that is, one in which style functions as knowledge:

> Once it has been realized that close empirical fit is no virtue and that it must be relaxed in times of change, then style, elegance of expression, simplicity of presentation, tension of plot and narrative, and seductiveness of content become important features of our knowledge. They give life to what is said and help us to overcome the resistance of the observational material. They *create* and maintain interest in a theory that has been partly removed from the observational plane and would be inferior to its rivals when judged by the customary standards. (Feyerabend, 157)

Again, my point of departure is to attempt to identify the pleasure I derive from reading this essay—Wittgenstein's *Brown Book*—the way it instills in me the desire to know, the primary goal of teletheory. This example serves to illustrate a narrative operating principally in the paradigmatic codes. Barthes, of course, gives us the best description of how such essays work:

> Different from the "concept" and from the "notion," which are purely ideal, the *intellectual object* is created by a kind of leverage upon the signifier. . . . It is a good thing, he thought, that out of consideration for the reader, there should pass through the essay's discourse, from time to time, a sensual object (as in Werther, where suddenly there appeared a dish of green peas cooked in butter and a peeled orange separated into sections). A double advantage: sumptuous appearance of a materiality and a distortion, a sudden gap wedged into the intellectual murmur. . . . (Thus, sometimes, in Japanese haiku, the line of written words suddenly opens and there is the drawing of Mount Fuji or of a sardine which delicately appears in place of the abandoned word.) (Barthes, 1977, 135)

If Heidegger is the master of the theoretical enigma, Wittgenstein is the master of the theoretical *semé*. Barthes's definition of how this code functions hints at the musical rhythm to which herstory appeals:

The seme is "cited"; we would like to give this word its tauro-machian meaning: the *citar* is the stamp of the heel, the torero's arched stance which summons the bull to the banderilleros. Similarly, one cites the signified to make it come forth, while avoiding it in the discourse. This fleeting citation, this surreptitious and discontinuous way of stating themes, this alternating of flux and outburst, create together the *allure* of the connotation; the semes appear to float freely, to form a galaxy of trifling data in which we read no order of importance: the narrative technique is impressionistic: it breaks up the signifier into particles of verbal matter which make sense only by coalescing. (Barthes, 1974, 22)

The filmic analogy applies particularly well to Wittgenstein's text, which, with its numbered fragments consisting of scenes and descriptions of material or concrete examples, already presents an effect of editing, of montage. That he should favor the paradigmatic over the syntagmatic codes is a corollary of his belief that it is possible to show more than one can tell. His fragments function in the manner of shot sequences, given continuity (at the level of argument) by a pattern of repetitions and matches that "gather" significance through juxtaposition and arrangement rather than through direct commentary.

The first number of the *Brown Book* is a scene: "Imagine this language—Its function is the communication between a builder A and his man B" (Wittgenstein, 1965, 77). The scene concerns the enigma, "what is knowing?" A shouts, "Now I can go on." "What was it that happened when suddenly he saw how to go on?" (112). With the accumulation of such scenes, a diegesis begins to form; I accept the lure of examples and begin to identify an imaginary space and time of a particular situation. As an analogy for the reading process, for example, a Pianola is introduced into the scene, playing a roll of music, and I begin to think as much, if not more, about this instrument and its connotations as about the argument it purports to illustrate. "The mechanism which immediately suggests itself when we wish to show what in such a case we should call 'being guided by the signs' is a mechanism of the type of a pianola. Here, in the working of the pianola we have a clear case of certain actions, those of the hammers of the piano, being guided by the pattern of the holes in the pianola roll" (118). Part of this effect is due to the insistence on the example, the extension of the analogy at length, the writer's almost forgetting about the tenor to work through the details of the thing: the formula for allegory. But the argument itself reinforces this effect: "We could say that the notches and teeth forming a key bit are not comparable to the words making up a sentence but to the letters making up a word" (119). I want at first to know (desire, pleasure) what the word is. Then I realize that the example is itself the word, that the example itself directly conveys a meaning which I must name (connotation). At the same time, I am being taught how to read this text, its method of providing sensible things representing intelligible ideas. The concept is accessible through a modeling of quotidian situations and objects; it is not a hidden, private, psychological event.

How are we to read the models?

> It was not the function of our examples to show us the essence of "deriving," "reading," and so forth through a veil of inessential features; the examples were not descriptions of an outside letting us guess at an inside which for some reason or other could not be shown in its nakedness. We are tempted to think that our examples are indirect means for producing a certain image or idea in a person's mind,—that they *hint* at something which they cannot show. . . . Our method is *purely descriptive;* the descriptions we give are not hints of explanations. (125)

So, if we are not dealing with explanations, neither are we following a conventional narrative. How to describe (show) a concept (for example, the concept of familiarity)? In the same way that one might describe a thing:

> I gave the circumstances of recognizing the man as a means to the end of describing the precise situation of the recognition. One might object to this way of describing the *experience*, saying that it brought in irrelevant things, and in fact wasn't a description of the feeling at all. In saying this one takes as the prototype of a description, say, the description of a table, which tells you the exact shape, dimensions, the material which it is made of, and its color. Such a description one might say pieces the table together. There is on the other hand a different kind of description of a table, such as you might find in a novel, e.g., "It was a small rickety table decorated in Moorish style, the sort that is used for smoker's requisites." Such a description might be called an indirect one; but if the purpose of it is to bring a vivid image of the table before your mind in a flash, it might serve this purpose incomparably better than a detailed "direct" description. . . . These considerations should warn you not to think that there is one real and direct description of, say, the

feeling of recognition as opposed to the "indirect" one which I have given. (181)

Wittgenstein is willing to use novelistic descriptions to produce his semes, then, giving us a picture whose connotation may be read off the surface (as a sign), a language of things: "This example showed us one of the family of cases in which this word is used. And the explanation of the use of this word, as that of the use of the word 'reading,' or 'being guided by symbols,' essentially consists in describing a selection of examples exhibiting characteristic features, some examples showing these features in exaggeration, others showing transitions, certain series of examples showing the trailing off of such features" (125). He is showing us how items may be gathered into sets on the basis of similarity or resemblance; in short, how we form the categories by which we comprehend the world.

To appreciate the value of Wittgenstein's method we need to be clear about what is at stake in his narrative. First, his insight is that cognition is an *emotional* experience, a feeling of *familiarity*. To be more precise, the *Brown Book* describes something that, as Heidegger might say, has never yet come into appearance, whose very nature is not to appear: ideology. Narrative pleasure is one way to locate the pleasure-in-recognition central to the maintenance and persistence of ideological positioning. Nichols, in fact, focuses his study on just this phenomenon, the click of recognition by which meaning arises and boundaries are organized: "Instead of seeing the activity of our own perception and the construction of an image's meaning, we see through our perceptual habit and the image's construction to an already meaningful world (without, in this case, 'seeing through' the deception that is involved, the actual production or fabrication of meaning)" (Nichols, 38). He cites Althusser in support of the ideological operation of recognition: "It is indeed a peculiarity of ideology that it imposes obviousnesses as obviousnesses, which we cannot *fail to recognize* and before which we have the inevitable and natural reaction of crying out: 'That's obvious! That's right! That's true!' " (39).

The importance of the *Brown Book*, for teletheory, is that it makes visible the goes-without-saying dynamic of pleasure-in-recognition ("Now I can go on," in Wittgenstein's phrase). Not only that, but it shows us how to teach this elusive illusion upon which is based the *mis-recognition* "that traps us within an imaginary realm of identity and opposition governed by desire to be what we are not and to possess what cannot be 'had' " (Nichols, 42). We may observe how Wittgenstein accomplishes this demonstration in his central example, which happens to produce a diegetic effect: "Imagine that someone wished to give you an idea of the facial characteristics of a certain family, the So and so's, he would do it by showing you a set of family portraits and by drawing your attention to certain characteristic features, which, e.g., would enable you to see how certain influences gradually changed the features, in what characteristic ways the members of the family aged, what features appeared more strongly as they did so" (Wittgenstein, 1965, 125). In the diegesis, I find him thinking about his own family, growing old.

There being an analogy at work, we are not meant to forget about the abstract problem—concept formation, *gathering* particulars into a set: "We see that a vast net of family likenesses connects the cases in which the expressions of possibility, 'can,' 'to be able to,' etc. are used. Certain characteristic features, we may say, appear in these cases in different combinations" (Wittgenstein, 1965, 117). The difficulty is to communicate (represent) what the items in a set have in common: "Suppose I had explained to someone the word 'red' by having pointed to various red objects and given the ostensive explanation. . . . If he has really got hold of what is in common between all the objects I have shown him, he will be in the position to follow my order. But what is it that is in common to these objects?" (130).

Family resemblance. The experience of understanding is the same as (resembles) the feeling of familiarity one has in recognizing the faces of family members in the family photo album. An explanation, thus, consists of noting similarities. And the fundamental similarity established by the end of the *Brown Book* is that between recognizing the expression on a face and understanding expression in words (sensible-intelligible): "I am impressed by the reading of a sentence, and I say the sentence has shown me something, that I have noticed something in it" (Wittgenstein, 1965, 178). There follows a discussion of which "expression" best conveys the experience of "meaning": " 'Look at the line of these eyebrows' or 'The *dark* eyes and the *pale* face!', these expressions would draw attention to certain features. . . . 'The whole face expresses bewilderment' " (179). As Barthes said, "the pensive (in faces, in texts) is the signifier of the inexpressible, not of the unexpressed. . . . At its discreet urging, we want to ask the classic text: *What are you thinking about?* but the text, wilier than all those who try to escape by answering: *about nothing*, does not reply, giving meaning its last closure: suspension" (Barthes, 1974, 216–17).

Despite this illusion of allusion, of something more left unsaid (promising further explanation), a narrative, Barthes insists, only explains itself. Similarly, Wittgenstein wants to discourage us from looking for this "more." And to make his point, he turns to music: "It has sometimes been said that what music conveys to us are feelings of joyfulness, melancholy, triumph, etc. . . . To such an account we are tempted to reply 'Music conveys to us *itself*!' " (178). Like Heidegger, he wants to divert us from the pleasures of enigma organizing narrative and explanation: "The question itself keeps the mind pressing against a blank wall, thereby preventing it from ever finding the outlet. To show a man how to get out you have first of all to free him from the misleading influence of the question" (169).

At the same time that he has been arguing against the narrative impression, however, Wittgenstein has been building a diegesis to show us its effects, and how easily we become lured into its imaginary world. His theory of language is carried, finally, within an anecdotal scene. Whose dark eyes and pale face is it that we have been shown (whose photograph in the album)? Just as it was Freud's own grandson who played the *fort/da* game, so is this album Wittgenstein's own. The music he used to refute the reality effect is charged with what Barthes might call a "third" meaning that gathers in the Pianola playing a roll. The music functions within the semic code, whose connotations are disseminated throughout the text. We may ask, in this theory of expression, what is being expressed? Can a theory express an emotion? It can if cognition itself is emotional (in its ideological power). And this emotional dimension of comprehension is precisely what is in need of exposure, such that to tell us about cognition without making us at the same time experience it emotionally would be to give a false account.

"The pleasure of recognition, among other things," Nichols observes, "may provide at least one point of entry in an attempt to explain the aesthetic experience, a line of thought pursued quite often in traditional aesthetics, which will be replaced here by a greater emphasis upon the ideological implications of aesthetic experience" (Nichols, 41). When he shows us the analogy between "understanding a sentence" and "understanding a musical theme," Wittgenstein contributes to this investigation to which Nichols devotes his book. Wittgenstein withholds until the very last moment the crucial scene of the diegesis, which, following the feedback loop of narrative, gathers the semes into a situation:

> But isn't there also a peculiar feeling of pastness characteristic of images as memory images? . . . I will examine one particular case, that of a feeling which I shall roughly describe by saying it is the feeling of "long, long ago." These words and the tone in which they are said are a gesture of pastness. But I will specify the experience which I mean still further by saying that it is that corresponding to a certain tune (Davids Bündler Tänze—"Wie aus weiter Ferne"). I'm imagining this tune played with the right expression and thus recorded, say, for a gramophone. Then this is the most elaborate and exact expression of a feeling of pastness which I can imagine. (Wittgenstein, 1965, 184)

I confess that this fragment, really the one anecdote in the whole of the *Brown Book*, is the point of departure of my essay. I believe that it has the same importance for Wittgenstein's philosophy as the *fort/da* anecdote has for Freud's metapsychology. One of the motives for writing this piece was simply to understand why this scene gives me such enormous pleasure; and having come to the end of this essay, I am ready now to begin an account of mystory, the study of the anecdote in theory. But since that project must obviously be delayed, I will instead elaborate a bit on the significance of "Wie aus weiter Ferne." It reminds me, for one thing, of the way Barthes's *A Lover's Discourse* gathered itself around the scene of the lover seated in a cafe reading Goethe's *Sorrows of Young Werther* while waiting in vain for a phone call from his beloved. Or Barthes's *Camera Lucida*, organized around the enigma of his mother's photograph, withheld from our gaze, so that we would be forced to think of the image of our own mother. I imagine, being now in the snare of the diegesis, Wittgenstein discovering the explanatory power of "family resemblances" while paging through his family photo album, coming across a particular photo of his mother (dark eyes and pale face) or his beloved, and listening to "Wie aus weiter Ferne" on a gramophone. Far from detracting from the philosophical or cognitive effectiveness of his study, this image renders it memorable (for me, unforgettable). Thus are joined the particular and the general, the sensible and the intelligible.

Did Wittgenstein mean to communicate this emotion of nostalgia, perhaps of melancholy, by means of an extended analytical discussion, one of whose leitmotifs is "music"? Indeed, since

Wittgenstein tells us that the prototype for "the will" is "a muscular effort"—"But does our volition, as it were, play on a keyboard of muscles, choosing which one it was going to use next?" (153)—we may suppose that he has struggled mightily to resist the emotion that he at last expresses. The text, in any case, concludes with a statement about reception: "If I speak of communicating a feeling to someone else, mustn't I in order to understand what I say know what I shall call the criterion of having succeeded in communicating? We are inclined to say that when we communicate a feeling to someone, something which we can never know happens at the other end" (185). Then, to confound the separation of science and poetry, he adds one last analogy: "This is closely analogous to saying that we can never know when in Fizeau's experiment the ray of light reaches the mirror."

To Be Continued

Nichols notes that narrative, documentary, and experimental modes of filmmaking are not entirely distinct, but share certain structuring principles. The explanatory effect of a documentary, thus, may be described in terms of diegesis, especially if it uses a mode of indirect address. But the diegesis in exposition (as distinct from narrative)

> is no longer a spatio-temporal universe plausibly maintained in its autonomy, but rather a conceptual universe. . . . This removes diegesis from its close association, in Metz's writings for example, with the image track and the projection of an illusionistic universe; it makes diegesis a notion more closely linked with the sound track, primarily with speech and the logical universe of its ordering. In other words, exposition does not require the fabrication of an imaginary spatio-temporal universe so much as the fabrication of an imaginary rhetorical universe where demonstration, apparent or real, takes place. (Nichols, 183–84)

What I learned from reading Heidegger and Wittgenstein with this point in mind is that theoretical texts *do* create a diegesis in the narrative sense—the imaginary spatiotemporal world—but the world thus created functions in the text as part of the rhetorical demonstration. This fact of a rhetorical diegesis at work in theoretical texts is a major insight for teletheory, for it is precisely this diegesis that makes such texts filmable. I happily accept all the problems that accompany this possibility—the entire debate surrounding narrative realism in general must be brought to bear on the style in which theory is filmed. In any case, Heidegger and Wittgenstein, as we have seen, both were critical of the diegetic, narrative effects they created. Nonetheless, now I have the feeling of knowing how to go on, how to tell a theory, and that the force of theory is in the diegesis.

Works Cited

Barthes, Roland. 1974. *S/Z.* Translated by Richard Miller. New York: Hill and Wang.

——. 1977. *Roland Barthes.* Translated by Richard Howard. New York: Hill and Wang.

Culler, Jonathan. 1982. *On Deconstruction.* Ithaca: Cornell University Press.

Derrida, Jacques. 1978. "Coming into One's Own," in *Psychoanalysis and the Question of the Text.* Edited by Geoffrey H. Hartman. Baltimore: Johns Hopkins University Press.

——. 1978a. "Speculations—on Freud." *The Oxford Literary Review* 3.

——. 1978b. *Edmund Husserl's "Origin of Geometry": An Introduction.* Translated by John P. Leavey, Jr. Stony Brook: Nicolas Hays.

——. 1979. *Spurs: Nietzsche's Styles.* Translated by Barbara Harlow. Chicago: University of Chicago Press.

——. 1982. *L'oreille de l'autre: otobiographies, transferts, traductions. Textes et débats avec Jacques Derrida.* Montreal: VLB Editeur.

——. 1983. "The Principle of Reason: The University in the Eyes of Its Pupils." *Diacritics* 13.

Feyerabend, Paul. 1975. *Against Method: Outline of an Anarchist Theory of Knowledge.* London: Verso, NLB.

Gledhill, Christine. 1984. "Developments in Feminist Film Criticism," in *Re-vision: Essays in Feminist Film Criticism.* Edited by Mary Ann Doane, et al. Frederick, Md.: University Publications of America.

Haas, Gerhard. 1969. *Essay.* Stuttgart: Metzlersche.

Heidegger, Martin. 1975. *Poetry, Language, Thought.* Translated by Albert Hofstadter. New York: Harper.

——. 1977. *The Question Concerning Technology.* Translated by William Lovitt. New York: Harper.

Holdheim, W. Wolfgang. 1984. *The Hermeneutic Mode: Essays on Time in Literature and Literary Theory.* Ithaca: Cornell University Press.

Hübner, Kurt. 1983. *Critique of Scientific Reason*. Translated by Paul R. Dixon, Jr., and Hollis M. Dixon. Chicago: University of Chicago Press.

Kaplan, E. Ann. 1983. *Women and Film: Both Sides of the Camera*. New York: Methuen.

Lacan, Jacques. 1981. *Le Seminaire, Livre III: Les Psychoses. 1955–1956*. Paris: Editions du Seuil.

de Lauretis, Teresa. 1984. *Alice Doesn't: Feminism, Semiotics, Cinema*. Bloomington: Indiana University Press.

Mulvey, Laura. 1977. "Visual Pleasure and Narrative Cinema," in *Women and the Cinema: A Critical Anthology*. Edited by Karyn Kay and Gerald Peary. New York: Dutton.

Nichols, Bill. 1981. *Ideology and the Image: Social Representation in the Cinema and Other Media*. Bloomington: Indiana University Press.

White, Hayden. 1980. "The Value of Narrativity in the Representation of Reality," in *On Narrative*. Edited by W. J. T. Mitchell. Chicago: University of Chicago Press.

Wittgenstein, Ludwig. 1965. *The Blue and Brown Books*. New York: Harper.

————. 1968. *Philosophical Investigations*. Translated by G. E. M. Anscombe. Oxford: Oxford University Press.